THRESHOLDS OF WESTERN CULTURE

TEXTURES – PHILOSOPHY/LITERATURE/CULTURE SERIES

Series editor: Hugh J. Silverman, Stony Brook University, Stony Brook, New York, USA

An interdisciplinary series, *Textures* addresses questions of cultural meaning, difference, and experience.

Extreme Beauty: Aesthetics, Politics, Death
Edited by James E. Swearingen and Joanne Cutting-Gray

Thresholds of Western Culture: Identity, Postcoloniality, Transnationalism
Edited by John Burt Foster Jr. and Wayne J. Froman

Panorama: Philosophies of the Visible
Edited by Wilhelm S. Wurzer

Between Philosophy and Poetry: Writing, Rhythm, History
Edited by Massimo Verdicchio and Robert Burch

THRESHOLDS OF WESTERN CULTURE

IDENTITY, POSTCOLONIALITY, TRANSNATIONALISM

EDITED BY
JOHN BURT FOSTER JR. AND
WAYNE JEFFREY FROMAN

Continuum

The Tower Building, 11 York Road, London, SE1 7NX
370 Lexington Avenue, New York, NY 10017–6503

First published 2002

British Library Cataloguing-in-Publication Data
A catalogue record for this book is available from the British Library.

ISBN 0–8264–5999–4 (hardback)
0–8264–6001–1 (paperback)

Library of Congress Cataloging-in-Publication Data
Thresholds of western culture : identity, postcoloniality, transnationalism / edited by John Burt Foster, Jr. and Wayne Jeffrey Froman.
p. cm.—(Textures)
Includes bibliographical references and index.
ISBN 0–8264–5999–4—ISBN 0–8264–6001–1 (pbk)
1. Civilization, Western—History—20th century. I. Foster, John Burt, 1945–
II. Froman, Wayne Jeffrey, 1945– III. Textures (New York, N.Y.)

CB245 .T533 2002
909.82—dc21

2002074054

Typeset by Refinecatch Limited, Bungay, Suffolk
Printed and bound in Great Britain by
Biddles Limited, Guildford & King's Lynn

CONTENTS

ILLUSTRATIONS

GENERAL INTRODUCTION

THRESHOLDS OF WESTERN CULTURE

John Burt Foster Jr. and Wayne J. Froman

In common parlance, "the West" means an advanced society, either in Western Europe or of Western European heritage, and with democratic institutions, a dynamic and prosperous economy, and technological expertise. Modernity would be a synonym, except that this category is geographically more diffuse and culturally more varied – witness Japan, to take an obvious example. "Western culture," however, for observers with a historical sense and a critical bent, can be quite problematic. Especially after the academic and political debates over culture in the 1990s (the so-called "culture wars"), this phrase can seem slippery and vague at one extreme, overly prescriptive at another, and perhaps even irrelevant to realities outside the world of higher learning. On this last point, the editors of this volume can speak from personal experience. We teach at a university which enrolls students from many dozens of ethnic and language groups all over the world, and which commendably requires a course in non-Western culture. Yet the excluded term regularly mystifies students whose immediate life-world offers no clear sense of what Western culture might be.

At a brutally simplistic level, of course, "Western culture" has often simply meant race, in a Manichean world decreed to be split between whites and non-whites. Even when culture is rightly held to consist of something more inward, to be a complex texture of values, beliefs, behavior patterns, and their many modes of expression, the dangers of oversimplification still persist. For if "Western culture" presumes to single out a distinct, monolithic, and authoritative tradition from among the major geocultural groupings of humankind, that label falsifies a history full of tensions and divisions on the one hand and deeply marked by cross-cultural contact on the other. The tensions are immediately obvious to anyone who visits the Roman Colosseum with a lively sense of both Greco-Latin and Judeo-Christian traditions. Each of these major components of the Western heritage, moreover, is itself a hyphenated term that often has been broken down into opposing entities, not to mention the critique to which they have been subjected, more recently, from feminist, postcolonial, or multicultural perspectives. Nor is the role of significant intercultural contact any less striking than the multiple strands within the culture, for if most Westerners write with the Roman alphabet, most of them speak an Indo-European language, and do figures with Arabic numerals.

But, to pose a question that is equally complicated despite its surface simplicity, what does even the "West" in Western culture mean? Under scrutiny this geographical badge of identity turns out to be as elusive as its close relative, the East Pole that foils discovery in *Winnie the Pooh*. Not really a specific place despite a core identification with Western Europe, it is, instead, a mobile vector – and one that over time has undergone major, even dizzying gyrations. In contrast to the recent, more pejorative synonym "Eurocentric," it can attest to a destabilizing and centrifugal pressure within the culture itself, in its guise as the linguistic trace of a past sense of distance from an acknowledged center or reference point. Thus westernness has variously implied being placed at one remote edge of the Eurasian landmass (when that edge led nowhere on a world believed to be flat), within the imperilled half of a Roman Empire splitting apart, or at a far remove from a Holy Land taken over by Muslims, before spinning round after Columbus to become a transatlantic urge, a "Westward, ho!" that could turn its back on previous centers. In a similar reversal of perspective, the twentieth-century "West" could mean concerted opposition to the "Central Powers" of World War I, or Cold-War resistance to an Iron Curtain that left no center, only a line between Eastern and Western Europe.

Yet at other times, emulating an idealized classical Greece that had supposedly rejected Egypt and Africa to the south (as well as Persia and Asia to the east), the "West" could see itself as "northern." The Mediterranean could continue to serve as a vital benchmark when culture flourished to its immediate north in Renaissance Italy, Golden Age Spain, or neoclassical France, but the frame of reference pivoted to once-remote northern seas when initiative passed to the Netherlands, England, or Germany. In the nineteenth century, however, when the "West" splintered into polycentric multiplicity as the result of nationalism, but also moved hesitantly eastward into Russia and migrated west to a steadily less isolated United States, the name lost almost all sense of direction. Finally, after circling the globe every which way in the heyday of imperialism, it assumed a more modest North Atlantic identity by combining to form NATO.

To be sure, neither historical mobility nor a complex texture of traditions is unique to the West as a broad and persistent cultural entity. One thinks, for example, of the shifting capitals of the different Muslim empires, or of the importance of Taoist/Confucian/Buddhist syncretism for Chinese religion, mentioned by Eugene Eoyang in the final chapter of this volume. Still, it is a strong belief in the crucial role of cultural mobility and interchange for the West, disconcerting though these forces might be for sloganizers or for believers in hard-and-fast definitions, that has motivated this collection of essays. In *Thresholds of Western Culture* fourteen scholars from North America, Western and Eastern Europe, Africa, and Asia have come together to examine some key contemporary features of this dynamic process of continuous cultural transformation. They focus on telling, varied, and often dramatic examples of three issues that have increasingly combined over the past century to contest received Western attitudes toward cultural identity: the issue of identity itself, and the closely related topics of postcoloniality and transnationalism. To be more specific, it is well-known that around 1900 the West reached the height of its direct political control over the rest of the globe; despite important ambiguities and exceptions, it was able to project a corresponding sense of identity, one that radiated sovereign self-assurance and an aura of unchallenged mastery. The result was a system of rival geocultural configurations (the "Great Powers" and their "Empires") that had become fragmented within Europe to the point of denying a common Western identity, and that were imperially expansive elsewhere. Today, under somewhat different political and economic arrangements, most notably the emergence of a potentially transnational European Union, these attitudes still persist to some degree. But they now compete with possibilities of another kind. These new options, which are based on more tentative, interactive notions of identity, allow for greater receptivity to cross-cultural exchange, not just within a Eurocentric West, but within an emerging postcolonial and globally transnational world. However, since a full realization of these possibilities remains problematic, and since specific instances seem to lurch between fragile success and utter catastrophe – post-apartheid South Africa versus the former Yugoslavia, to use examples treated in this volume – it would be better to think simply of potential or incipient change. Like any evolving culture, the West faces thresholds that might or might not be crossed.

The ability to cross a cultural threshold assumes that one's connection with a given past can involve something richer and more creative than the unbending absorption of a heritage, can be reconceived as requiring a dynamic process of revision and transformation. This is an insight that even T. S. Eliot could endorse in "Tradition and the Individual Talent," and that Adrienne Rich reiterated in a more radical key when she called for feminist "re-vision."[1] But this kind of process does not simply take place *within* some culture; it can also be cross-cultural. In that case the rigidities of polarized opposition between rivals will yield to an issue-by-issue awareness of possible connection or at least of complementarity across former boundaries. Consider, for example, the "both/and" logics mentioned in Eoyang's essay, or, in a more conflicted setting, the attitude of cultural counterpoint recommended by Edward Said.[2] A cultural threshold, in short, has much the same ambiguity as the anthropological concept of liminality. In an original exclusionary sense, this term harks back to rigid barriers on the model of the *limes*, the old Roman wall that at various places in northern Europe protected the empire from aliens beyond the pale, aliens who ironically would later become members of the West. In a dynamic sense, however, as Mihai Spariosu indicates in extending Victor Turner's seminal concept,[3] liminality refers to a wide range of limit situations, all of which act to test cultural values, and which, though they may end by reaffirming those values, may also deepen or rework them by opening them to reappraisal, the need for new sanctions, or even outright rejection.

A suitable emblem for this cultural ambiguity would be a web – not the techno-utopian World Wide Web of cyberspace, however, but a spider-web. At once a glistening network of delicate interconnection and a deadly trap for unwary, hopelessly entangled insects, this image spotlights a major shift in attitude since Matthew Arnold quoted Jonathan Swift in the course of giving a heightened, almost religious allure to the word "culture." Swift's and Arnold's favored emblem, we recall, was not the spider but the bee, with its capacity to furnish "sweetness and light."[4] Following a century, however, whose nadir in the 1940s confirmed Walter Benjamin's insight into culture's affinities with barbarism,[5] it is only too clear that invocations of culture speak with a double tongue. If they can promise visions of harmony and deepened understanding, they can also provide alibis for hatred and injustice.

The chapters in this volume, in treating issues that can fall on either side of this equivocal set of possibilities, aim to enlarge, enrich, and usefully complicate our understanding of debates over the current situation and prospects of Western culture. The editors have selected a variety of approaches at the intersection of philosophy, literary study, and the arts that will demonstrate the fruitfulness of this kind of interdisciplinary inquiry. Conceptual analysis, thoughtful generalization, and the critical examination of first principles mingle productively and provocatively with theoretically informed criticism, rhetorical self-consciousness, and the exposition of strategically placed literary, musical, and visual works. The book ranges from pointed interrogations of classical literature and music at times of major crisis to a culturally illuminating genealogy of narrative perspective and the account of a symptomatic art-hoax. It also includes reappraisals of recent thinkers like Lyotard and Žižek; extends methods and insights identified with Derrida, Foucault, and Gadamer; and weighs the reactions against theory in contemporary novelists like Coetzee and Ozick. It analyzes as well the nature of cross-cultural contact at such varied locations as modernizing Japan, late apartheid South Africa, and communist Romania, and draws on fields ranging from Holocaust studies to semiotics, or from anthropology to international relations. In thus conjoining theoretical reflection with the critical study of literary and artistic expression, both the Continuum series "Textures – philosophy/literature/culture" and the International Association for Philosophy and Literature (the original sponsor of these essays) mean to illustrate and encourage their stimulating interaction.

* * *

The editors have organized this book's fourteen chapters into five interrelated parts, each of which addresses a major topic involving contemporary Western culture as it grapples with the issue of identity itself or with specific postcolonial and transnational aspects of that issue. Each part, in turn, consists of two to four essays that explore these topics from different but mutually illuminating angles. Since each of these parts begins with a brief introduction to its topic and how it will be developed in the chapters that follow, detailed commentary on the individual contributions will not be needed here. But a broad overview of how the parts relate to each other should help orient the reader and give further insight into this book's basic purposes.

Parts One and Two offer complementary discussions on how issues of identity have developed in the West, beginning in the first part with two essays on the twentieth-century reconfiguration of orthodox accounts of subjectivity. Emphasis falls on the broader resonances, in literature and anthropological thought, of what was initially a reasoned philosophical project on the part of Descartes, elements of which came down from classical antiquity. Robert Strozier, in the first chapter, follows how representative novelists over three centuries handled narrative point of view in ways that undermined the Cartesian identification of subjectivity with an inner self-knowledge that provided a basis for both morality and science. This literary development anticipated the well-known poststructuralist proclamation of the "death of the subject," which reflects back, critically if also indirectly, on Western attitudes of sovereign self-sufficiency. The second chapter, by Anthony John Harding, goes on to suggest the need to qualify this doctrine in one key area, that of insufficient attention to "personhood." This category, which derives from a different current of thinking about individuality, embodies an anthropologist's sensitivity to the distinctiveness of others, rather than egotistical self-assertion or the episemological priority of the subject. Along with its importance in fostering cross-cultural understanding, it is also an essential bulwark against human rights abuses, here discussed in the context of the 1940s.

These abuses evoke the shadow cast on twentieth-century Western history by the Fascist decades, whose ruthless intensification of turn-of-the-century nationalism and imperialism ended by giving a decisive new impetus, within the West itself, to transnationalism and postcoloniality. The impact of this uncrossed threshold is the subject of Part Two, which re-evaluates the vexed issue of Fascism in Western high culture, focusing on tragic drama and the classic symphony, but also considering Fascism's traumatic after-effects as expressed in Holocaust writings. As the agonies associated with Mussolini and Hitler recede into the past, neither blanket indictments of the West's most honored artistic traditions nor flat denials of all complicity in the name of artistic autonomy seem satisfactory. Fascism was not the whole of the Western tradition, but it did grow up *inside* the West, with all the complexities that confronting such a history imposes on the culture critic. In particular, a pointed sense of this ambiguity makes it difficult to accept the sweeping, even triumphant and overweening claims that have sometimes been made for Western culture as an instrument of moral guidance. After all, as Gaetano Salvemini has reported from direct observation, the members of early Fascist squadrons tended to be educated "custodians of civilization"; and George Steiner has noted the jarring fact that the administrators of the death camps included readers of Goethe and performers of Bach.[6]

Attention shifts in Part Three from developments within Europe to a major frontier in the projection of Western culture abroad, that southern frontier that gave rise to what Paul Gilroy has interpreted as "a counterculture of modernity."[7] I refer to the modern European arrogation of absolute supremacy in Africa and over Africans. This part studies two episodes from the ongoing reappraisal and attempted transcendence of this legacy, episodes in which there is an especially complex interplay among colonial residues, postcolonial initiatives, and intricate blendings of Western and indigenous elements. One episode involves Sierra Leone, before that country's present state of crisis when a movement of cultural renewal, reacting against the first generation of leaders after independence, reached back to the *Amistad* incident to create a new national self-image. The other involves South Africa, when dissident writers responded to the apartheid government's State of Emergency in the 1980s, and is discussed both by a South African and by an outside observer. In both cases inherited habits of thought and feeling bent, twisted, and snapped under the pressure of new recognitions and possibilities. The long-term result of these events remains to be seen. But it is already clear that they offer striking examples of the threshold situations in which cultural differences can be negotiated, reworked, and set into new perspectives. People can variously break with established attitudes, test and redefine their underlying principles, rededicate themselves to poorly remembered events and aspirations, or seek to initiate new traditions.

The fourth part, on Eastern Europe after communism, considers another outer border of the West, this time to the east rather than the south – or, to recall Cold War jargon, a border with the "second" rather than the "third" world. Some situations in the deeper past might even suggest that this area has functioned as a counterpart to colonial Africa in providing an arena for Western power and prestige. Thus the word "slave" derives from the medieval traffic in Slavic peoples that preceded the triangle trade across the Atlantic, while more recently the 1911 Agadir crisis suggested that World War I could have begun as a quarrel over Morocco and the Cameroons rather than Bosnia and Serbia. To name these borders in plain English – the color line and the Iron Curtain – is to realize how deeply they marked Western identity in the twentieth century.

Unlike postcolonial Africa, however, which has tended to seek an often elusive freedom from Western domination, Eastern Europe has related to the West on terms that have been more intimate, even tangled. Unwilling subservience to powers in the east, like Ottoman Turks, tsarist Russians, or most recently the Soviets, has led to a situation of two-sided marginality, or what one observer has called "inbetween peripherality."[8] The result, at the recent post-communist moment of liberation from the east, can be an intense identification with the West, to the point where the very label "Eastern Europe" is often rejected. But at least at first, Western reactions to this possible disappearance of an eastern boundary have been ambiguous. Bosnia, treated here in two complementary essays, was the most disturbing example, not just because the European Union's failure to act decisively hinted at a discreditable revival of an old southeast to northwest axis of value, but also because ethnic cleansing so pointedly recalled the West's sorry past when faced with Fascism. On the other hand, there does exist the possibility, discussed by Marcel Cornis-Pope and to some extent performed by Nikita Nankov, that outside the former Yugoslavia the Eastern European experience of multiple and intertwined ethnicities could lead to productive forms of transnational interaction. These experiences might then serve as models for the rest of the world, even for the West, despite the harsh reputation of "Balkanization."

Compared to the "narcissism of petty differences" that has set neighbors against each other who seem virtually identical to outsiders, the cultural separation between Western Europe and China or Japan has often seemed very broad.

The shift in subject matter in Part Five, from Eastern Europe to what Western observers have often called the "Far East," justifies a corresponding shift on our part from "West" to "Far West," not only to ensure a reciprocity of perspective, but also to highlight the relative historical independence of these two cultural spheres. This dearth of direct cultural contact gives a special importance to the thresholds presented here, one involving a Westerner's encounter with Japan around 1900, the other comparing major Far Eastern traditions with corresponding attitudes from the West's own Far West, today's United States. Analyzing the modes of cultural interpretation in the book that initiated the notorious Madame Butterfly stereotype, Rolf Goebel finds ample evidence of then-current Western commonplaces. But he also discerns brief flashes of greater awareness, of the ability for even a blinkered observer to experience a broadening of conceptual horizons that allowed him to see more of the foreign culture, to observe what he saw more accurately, and to go beyond mere dismissiveness in evaluating that culture. Eugene Eoyang contrasts long-standing tendencies in the Far East and Far West in the areas of logic, law, religion, and sport, thus underscoring the significance of those longer temporal perspectives that are so often missing from pragmatic "here-and-now" treatments of cross-cultural contact. Even more important, as Eoyang exposes his readers to a wide array of cultural variables, including ones that question basic Western assumptions about the nature of differences and the role of conflict, he artfully plays out the process of entering a cultural threshold. In a suitable final note for this book, accordingly, Eoyang hints at the rewards of transnational cultural encounter on a global scale, suggesting that despite the historical and spatial separation between Far East and Far West, the resulting cultural tensions are far from insuperable – indeed, could be liberating.

Examining situations on several of the West's defining borders, *Thresholds of Western Culture* begins with issues associated with the ongoing reconfiguration of Cartesian identity, then examines interrelated sites in Fascist Europe, in postcolonial Africa, in Eastern Europe after communism, and at the cusp between typical Western cultures and those of East Asia. Along the way, naturally, the book addresses many other topics besides culture's equivocal role over the past century. Some of these issues – such as the role of religion in marking cultural difference, the place of subjectivity, the question of cultural memory and its effacement by trauma, or the shadows cast by unacknowledged complicities and unmet commitments – will be noted when the occasion arises in the introductions to each part. Other issues of this kind will necessarily be left to the insight of curious and motivated readers, not least because these essays got their start at a conference marked by many crossing paths of insight, discussion, and debate. Above all, however, if this book can advance the ongoing work of putting the West in fuller and better touch with the world, it will have fulfilled the best hopes of its editors.

* * *

This volume grew out of the twentieth annual conference of the International Association for Philosophy and Literature (the IAPL) on the topic "Dramas of Culture," which was co-ordinated by the two editors and held at George Mason

University. The essays published here began as conference papers, and were enlarged and reworked by the authors before submission to the editors, who then suggested further revisions in light of the topics to be addressed. The overall structure of the book had begun to take shape during the many discussions and decisions that went into planning the conference, but only became explicit in the course of evaluating the completed essays, writing the introductions, and responding to readers. As befits an interdisciplinary project, all major decisions about organization and content involved careful consultation between the editors, one in continental philosophy and the other in comparative literature.

The editors wish to thank Frederick A. Rossini, then provost of George Mason University, who guaranteed the funding to support a large international conference; David Potter, then Dean of the College of Arts and Sciences, was also helpful in important ways. The Department of English, chaired by Rosemary Jann and Barbara Melosh, and the Department of Philosophy and Religious Studies, chaired by Wayne Froman, also provided support, as did the Ph.D. Program in Cultural Studies, first with Mark Jacobs as director and then with Deborah Kaplan as acting director. Thanks are due as well to IAPL Executive Board members Dalia Judovitz, Massimo Verdicchio, and Wilhelm Wurzer for helping to organize the conference; later on IAPL members Stephen Barker, Thomas Flynn, and Steve Martinot generously shared their experiences as editors. Session organizers Richard Brons, Marcel Cornis-Pope, Martin Donougho, Eugene Eoyang, Thomas Flynn (again), Carla Peterson, and Merle Williams also contributed by defining special topics for the conference, evaluating and commissioning papers, and providing the original venue for many of the essays. Hugh J. Silverman, the Executive Director of the IAPL, not only sponsored the paper by Herman Rapaport, but also offered indispensable advice and support at every stage, especially in the critical weeks before the conference and later in helping see this volume through to publication.

John Foster's work as lead editor for this volume was facilitated by the New College of Florida Humanities Division, chaired by Stephen Miles, which generously granted me the privileges of Research Scholar while on sabbatical. The Jane Bancroft Cook Library at the college was also helpful in many ways, not least by providing a convenient study. In the final stages, after my return to George Mason, I received valuable aid from my graduate research assistant, Yelizaveta Renfro. Neither this book nor the conference from which it originated could have been nearly as ambitious without the support, thoughtful advice, and much-tried patience of my wife Andrea Dimino, or the high spirits and artistic temperament of my daughter, Sophia.

PART ONE

THE CRISIS OF MODERN SUBJECTIVITY

INTRODUCTION

Wayne J. Froman and John Burt Foster Jr.

The essays in Part One prepare for this book's later discussions of Western culture by exploring ambiguities that surround modernity and the issue of subjectivity. Modernity here means the intellectual and historical innovations that occurred within the West since about 1600, as well as similar developments elsewhere. When contrasted with postmodernity, the term has also figured prominently in debates about recent changes in Western identity, which perhaps have a far-reaching significance. Discussions of modernity thus tend to emphasize two historical boundaries: an inaugural moment and a moment of closure or, more dramatically, of crisis. Like many others, Robert Strozier identifies the first boundary with Descartes and the rise of modern science. For French anthropologist Marcel Mauss, Anthony John Harding reminds us in his essay, the endpoint came in the late thirties and early forties – not in the sixties, as in many accounts. Though both essays consider the emergence of postmodernism beyond the regime of modernity, they do so only tentatively. They do agree, however, on the inadequacies of certain modern forms of subjectivity and on the vital importance of a post-subjectivist (if not unambiguously postmodern) sociality.

Both essays thus trace itineraries that move back and forth across the line between modern and postmodern identities. In the first chapter, Strozier addresses the relation of the experiential and the epistemic in the formation of modern subjectivity and connects them with problems of narrativity in both Descartes and Western fiction, bringing home difficulties inherent in modern subjectivity. Strozier tracks these difficulties to the threshold of postmodern analysis, where he shows how they persist in different forms. In the second chapter, Harding shows the detrimental juridical, political, and ethical implications of a postmodern, poststructuralist critique of subjectivity, due to a failure to distinguish between subject and self, on the one hand, and personhood, on the other. Harding proposes to sustain Mauss's category of "person," though in a way that would grant some priority to sociality, dispense with the cultural privilege associated with the Western sense of personhood, and extend the range of that personhood to fit better with the known variations. In effect, he advocates a fuller awareness for the modern fusion of person, subject, and self while taking issue with the postmodern tendency to eliminate personhood in the course of critiquing subjectivity and the sense of self.

Drawing on Foucault's analyses of the relation to self, the sense of interiority, and the knowledge based on that interiority, as well as on his hints about how to develop these analyses in the modern period, Strozier first considers Descartes' understanding of the connection between the interiority of a relation to self and knowledge. He also observes how, in Kant, any persistent tension between the experiential and the epistemic drops out. A significant middle position emerges with the Earl of Shaftsbury, who locates identity in feeling or affectivity, held to be largely social in nature. Strozier then follows the link between the experiential and the epistemic in narrative fiction from the eighteenth to the twentieth centuries. Passing from Fielding by way of Dickens to Conrad and Kate Chopin, he shows the opening of a discrepancy between the two elements, whose presumed compatibility comes apart when the epistemic, in effect, absorbs the experiential.

The analysis ends with a debate between Roy Pascal and Ann Banfield in the 1970s and 1980s that responded to this breakdown and centered on free indirect discourse, a form of narrative perspective perfected by Flaubert. The debate, though predicated on modern categories of analysis, takes us to the threshold of the postmodern, poststructuralist critique of subjectivity. Strozier ends with the thought-provoking suggestion that, with this displacement from identity understood as interiority to an older sense of identity as relational with respect to gender, race, and ethnicity, there has in fact been no definitive break with the modern dynamic of identity. The question then arises whether the emergence of relational identity is discursive in a Foucauldian sense, or whether, instead, it is based on feeling.

This essay's emphasis on how experiential interiority relates to the epistemic context of knowledge recalls Kant's *Critique of Judgment*. Further, the role of experience in Strozier's dynamic of identity brings to mind, behind the Foucauldian historical analysis, Heidegger's analysis of "experience" in Hegel's development of Kant's transcendental philosophy in the *Phenomenology of Spirit*,[1] where both full self-knowledge and the presumed fulfillment of history in the modern age are at issue. Both Kant's point of departure in an analysis of "taste," and Hegel's understanding of the intermediate role of culture, as well as the excessive promotion of culture for culture's sake,[2] bring out the complexity behind the ambiguities associated with the emphasis on culture in current scholarship.

In the second chapter, Harding looks back at Mauss's lecture on different categories of the mind, and argues for retaining his emphasis on personhood, especially given poststructuralist tendencies to neglect the major differences marking "person" off from both "subject" and "self." By way of Mauss, we return to Kant's analysis of subject and self, and so to issues at the heart of Strozier's essay. Here Kant is praised insofar as he prepared for the emergence of personhood as a distinct category, once Fichte added a fuller sense of selfhood to this mix of ideas. Even though the conflation of "self" and "subject" at this point lays the basis for the poststructuralist threat, what Mauss appreciated in this development of post-Enlightenment thought was its fuller recognition of "personhood," including a genealogy going back to ancient Roman custom, Stoicism, and Christianity, but now divested of those cultural and metaphysical claims.

The fragility of personhood, and its resulting vulnerability to poststructuralist campaigns, may be attributed, at least in part, to the uneasy association between the experiential relation to self and the epistemic subject of knowledge, already described by Strozier. Mauss's essay dates, moreover, from 1938, when "the forces that threatened the category of the person were real indeed." Harding also identifies the problem with Mauss's assumption that personhood is a great achievement of Western culture deserving universal extension. As a less ethnocentric alternative, Harding proposes accentuating the social character of "personhood," thereby allowing for non-Western options. This recourse to sociality chimes with Strozier's interest in the similar bearing of affectivity in Shaftesbury. Harding thus suggests a viable alternative to current notions of identity as discursive altogether, in a sense often associated with Foucault, although Harding himself is careful to note a continuity between Mauss and Foucault.

Giving some priority to a sociality without ethnocentrism might offer an antidote to the risks and ambiguities that go with appeals to cultural identity. Not only has this kind of appeal been manipulated to serve the exclusive interests of a cultural elite; it can also produce an almost unlimited growth of concentrated political power. However, even as these chapters probe ambiguities in Western conceptions of identity, Harding has introduced the question of non-Western dimensions to the category of personhood. Alongside Mauss's reaction to the Fascist decades, which anticipates the topic of the next set of essays, Harding thus directs attention to postcolonial issues that will come to the fore in Part Three.

1

INTERIORITY, IDENTITY, KNOWLEDGE

UNRAVELING THE CARTESIAN COGITO

Robert Strozier

My subject is the modern age in a broad sense, from the seventeenth century, the period in which Foucault says the deployment of sexuality began to displace and reorient the deployment of alliance, down into the twentieth century. Foucault is referring here to changing notions of identity: in the earlier period, identity was constituted in terms of relationship (e.g., family, patronage) and in the later age in terms of the interior self. My concern is historical: another narrative of ourselves and our "historical ontology." Without attempting to construct a comprehensive new view of this era, I do intend to make some uncharacteristic connections among familiar notions of modernity as well as among familiar texts. A footnote to Foucault, one focusing on the nature of knowledge.

Foucault's histories of sexuality provide an immediate context: both the narrative of the emergence of the deployment of sexuality since the seventeenth century (in *The History of Sexuality, I*) and his later concern with self-relation and the ascesis by which the self produces itself as a moral agent (in the two later volumes on sexuality, *The Use of Pleasure* and *The Care of the Self*). The deployment of sexuality entails the production of human interiority and the tendency to construct that interiority as individual identity; this interiority is the locus of our sexuality or desire, or, more generically, "feeling," as Foucault sometimes puts it. Since Foucault only investigates self-relation from the fourth century, BCE, through the first few centuries of the common era, more needs to be said about the historical form of self-relation in the modern period.

The immediate point of departure is some comments of Foucault's in a 1983 interview, that Descartes "succeeded in substituting a subject as founder of practices of knowledge . . . for a subject constituted through practices of the self."[1] Descartes broke the traditional link between a prior ascesis and the access to truth. "After Descartes [Foucault says], we have a nonascetic subject of knowledge" (*FR*, p. 372). Simply put, "I can be immoral and know the truth." This characterization seems to call for a revision.

Perhaps it would make more sense to consider Descartes as having adapted a historically prior model of ascesis in order to produce a new kind of subject, a subject produced in accordance with specific historical contingencies. The new, epistemological ascesis seems to Descartes to be incorporated with an ethical ascesis; in other words, one cannot be immoral and yet a knower of truth, not without conscious choice. What Descartes argues here is in itself an inversion: self-knowledge and objective knowledge become necessarily prior to one's construction of oneself as a moral agent. The twentieth century is another matter: Tom Lehrer's song about Werner von Braun and rocketry makes the point: I just send them up; where they come down is not my business. Descartes' new ascesis is based on a new form of self-relation: the self's relation to its own interiority – an interiority which is in fact produced by the self-relation. Foucault says as much about the effect of the technique of confession by the beginning of the seventeenth century. And from Descartes on that interiority is increasingly recognized as constituting human identity, universal at first and then increasingly individual. The new ascesis allowed Descartes to produce two distinct but related forms of knowledge, experience and objective truth. The particular kind of experience noted here is self-experience and self-knowledge: the subject's relation to truth must detour through its own self-reflexive inquiry, that is, into itself as an object of knowledge; if I can know myself, my essence, then I come to the recognition of my identity as a subject of knowledge and its foundation. This ascesis also produces the new space of the secular, that is, once the self recognizes itself as an object of knowledge. Knowledge of the material world, of ethics or manners, even theology, then become separated forms of knowledge consequent to the constitution of the subject of knowledge. The secular becomes the incorporative principle subsequent to self-knowledge rather than arising in opposition to religious (and ethical) knowledge.

This chapter has several sections: first, a more detailed analysis of Descartes' new form of self-relation and the production of knowledges; next, the representation of interiority in a typical eighteenth-century novel, *Joseph Andrews*, and a nineteenth-century one, *Great Expectations*, with a focus on the status and relation of the two forms of knowledge – which is the ultimate focus of the chapter; finally, the problematics of interiority and the relation of self-experience to knowledge in two turn-of-the-century works of fiction, *Heart of Darkness* and *The Awakening*, and in a prominent disagreement in twentieth-century critical treatment of free indirect discourse, between Roy Pascal and Ann Banfield. The narrative here: after roughly two and a half centuries of compatibility, the two forms of knowledge begin to undergo a discontinuous split. The crisis is often represented (as here) in literature in the twentieth century as the failure of objective knowledge, although the triumph of individual experience is often pyrrhic. There are complementary traditions as well: a continued assumption of the compatibility of the two knowledges in the sciences, attempts at reconciliation or distributions such as the separation of the domains of science and poetry, and so on. But one of the emerging issues is the discontinuity.

INTERIORITY AND THE FOUNDATION OF KNOWLEDGE

In Part I of *Discourse on the Method* . . . Descartes sets the stage for his self-inquiry by setting up a clear opposition between exterior and interior in relation to the subject: Descartes undertakes academic training and travel and then rejects both letters and his observation of behavior and belief in different cultures because they provide little more than a chaos of opinions, attitudes, and activities that obscures the singular path to truth. In opposition to this influx of irreconcilable notions, he resolves "to undertake studies within myself."

Foucault's notion of the increasing production of interiority as identity seems to have its origin here with Descartes' strategy of foundationalizing introspection. This is a constant theme of the late Foucault; for example, in a 1978 lecture on the conjunction of law and psychiatry he shows that in a contemporary legal case a typical demand was made of the defendant to confess, to offer a self-revelation "of what one is," which if not given would hinder the administration of punishment.[2]

This inwardness is not, however, unique in the history of thought: in the early Hellenistic period, a similar interiorizing takes place, notably in Epicurus, Aristippus and the Cyrenaics, the Skeptics, and especially the Stoics. In Epicurus and the Stoics, for example, interiority takes a potentially "skeptical" form in that the relation between consciousness and exteriority is the first issue that must be addressed by philosophy. Accordingly canonic or the criterion (i.e., the measure or standard of knowledge) is the first part of philosophy. The historian Diogenes Laertius says the following about the canonic of the Stoics:

> The Stoics resolved to place the questions of appearances and of sensation first, since the criteria for the existence of external reality are the kinds of appearances [i.e., what occurs within consciousness]. . . .[3]

For the Stoics the *kataleptiké phantasia* is the criterion of the relation of truth existing between external and internal reality; that is, the striking and detailed image in consciousness is the sign of external existence. The traditional metaphor of the Stoics is of the seal impressed into wax.[4] The evidence of truth is clearly internal, but the more important point is that a cognitive relation between self and world has to be established as a first step in philosophy. It might be called an epistemological ascesis, or the working out of how self is placed within world by a self-inquiry into one's interiority – the constitution of oneself as a subject of knowledge. The canonic of Epicurus has not survived except for brief notes at the beginning of one of the Letters reproduced by Diogenes Laertius. After he has established the link between interiority and the external world, Epicurus argues that knowledge of physics and meteorology allows the individual to form itself as a moral subject. Specifically, this means that the individual is able to create an interior state of *ataraxia* or undisturbedness: that is, self-management. Descartes will be seen to repeat some of these Hellenistic inclinations.

Petrarch in the fourteenth century also exhibits notable interiorizing tendencies. Yet by the sixteenth and early seventeen centuries in Europe there is little concern for a prior epistemology evident in intellectual texts, that is, no concern with interiority as an a priori problematic or with the necessity of a self-reflexive link with one's own interiority. Bacon's ascesis is not one at all, but an organum or instrument. Descartes' notion of self-relation has in fact become a sign of modernity, particularly in terms of its emphasis on self-inquiry into interiority.

On the other hand, Descartes' notion of "our natural light" provided to humans by God through the functioning of the intelligible mind seems linked to Reformation texts of the prior century (although this natural light appears as a conclusion for Descartes, not an initial assumption); and from Foucault's occasional references to the Christian confession of the flesh, we can note profound similarities between Descartes' method and Christian self-decipherment: that is, the self seeks to know its own deepest desires and their provenance, with the goal of self-renunciation and purification under the aegis of divine law. But it is Descartes' adaptation of this ascetic process which is in focus here.

To return to Descartes' interiorizing process: after his disappointment concerning the truth of the opinions fed into him or acquired in transit, Descartes finds himself detained by the weather in "a stove-heated room, where I was completely free to converse with myself about my own thoughts."[5] This room, according to Baillet, was in a village near Ulm, and the sequestration occurred on November 10 1619. This is not merely a localization, but an important step in the process of interiorization. Isolation from the exterior world is the key: "finding no conversation to divert me and fortunately having no cares or passions to trouble me" (*PWD*, p. 116). "Conversation" refers to the outer world of opinion. In a letter to Elizabeth, the Princess Palatine, with whom he corresponded frequently in later life, Descartes describes the passions as thoughts or cerebral impressions aroused (i.e., passive) by external sensations and internal ones – the latter deriving from the body.[6] Descartes' contingent isolation and his good health are thus the primary step in self-interrogation: he is able to free himself of whole ranges of what might be roughly called "incoming stimuli" – an instance of partial self-neutralization or purification, so to speak. This first step opens up self-inquiry by allowing him to focus on the active part of his interiority: soul, reason, and will.

In the ensuing process of self-constitution, the relation to self is positioned as a continuing self-decipherment which produces a progressively limited and essentialized interiority as the object of knowledge. It should be noted, as deconstructive critics have pointed out, that the constitution of the self as a subject of knowledge is *already* assumed in the self-reflexive splitting of the subject, the existence of a self as potential knower of its own interior identity. Self-knowledge already implies a subject of knowledge.

The most familiar part of the *Discourse*, Part IV, completes the process of self-inquiry and self-constitution: complete doubt, and then, in doubt, the self-reflexive discovery of the essential interior self: that it exists and that it is a certain kind of substance – thinking being – "by which I am what I am" (*PWD*, p. 127) or which is my identity. A self-discernment. The *cogito* might be paraphrased as follows: I, the subject of knowledge, external and objective, observe my more inner self or process of consciousness to be one of thinking (doubt is a kind of thought). Therefore I (exterior) conclude that I (interior to the prior "I") exist, since thinking cannot occur apart from being (see below). The fact that this conclusion is also a form of thought and that therefore an even more exterior "I" might be necessary in order to insure that this thinking is identical in form with "doubt-thinking" and also that an integral subject exists – ad infinitum – all this doesn't seem to bother Descartes.

What we see in this argument is that the subject of knowledge is produced simultaneously with self-reflection, that is, when becoming the object of self-inquiry and self-knowledge necessitates the existence of the self as objectifier or knower. The self-knower produces the self as knowledge, proving by a kind of circularity that its position as objective knower is justified. Stated more in Descartes' terms: self-knowledge is the first knowledge according to the logic of the ascesis: it is the production, the instance, and the proof that the self can act validly as a subject of other knowledges.

The individual which constructs itself as a moral subject in Foucault's latest writings entails the assumption that the individual exists prior to its self-construction, as with Descartes. This should not be taken as a humanist assumption on the part of Foucault, as a return of the subject. It is an assumption of the cultures he studies, the starting point for his "historical ontology" of what has usually been conceived as a constant human nature. Descartes produces the subject of knowledge by means of an ethical process in which the subject is already entailed, but the point is that this subject of knowledge is fundamental to our own, modern "historical ontology" as well, not as a transcendent truth of human nature.

There are numerous further details of Descartes' self-inquiry: for example, having educed one true proposition, the *cogito* itself, his realization that "I see clearly that in order to think it is necessary to exist" (*PWD*, p. 127) leads to a rule about the relation between clear conceptions and evident truth (it is necessary to remember that this is a transcendental inquiry, not an empirical one).

But the important point is that self-inquiry, self-analysis, self-experience, and self-knowledge of one's constituent interiority are necessary to found the possibility of knowledge in the subject; it consequently serves as "the true method of attaining the knowledge of everything within my mental capabilities" (*PWD*, p. 119). Thus, as he shortly after brings the self-inquiry to completion, Descartes moves on to knowledge of nature and the exterior world in general. This reverses the Hellenistic orientation, which uses knowledge to establish moral self-maintenance. But Descartes eventually goes on to talk about the relation of knowledge to moral agency.

There are two kinds of knowledge at issue here: first, the ascesis or self-relation that produces self-knowledge through a process of self-experience of one's interiority. This is perforce individual knowledge. In Descartes this individuality of self-knowledge is only a part of the process, the institution of the subject of objective knowledge, that is, of the second kind. In fact, Descartes poses himself as a singular individual who undergoes a private ascesis, one which should not serve as a model for others (*PWD*, pp. 112, 118, *passim*), whilst at the same time positioning himself within the "normal," as a subject of reason or the "good sense" that "is naturally equal in all . . ." (*PWD*, p. 111).

The epistemological ascesis insures the coincidence of rationality with human identity, and hence universality.

The individual, by knowing itself and thereby producing itself as a subject of knowledge, opens the possibility of scientific or objective knowledge. This knowledge by definition transcends the individual subject: it is knowledge which is compatible with self-knowledge and arises from it, but it is different in kind. But the two kinds redouble each other. Rationality is produced by an inquiry into the inner, essential self considered as an object of knowledge; hence it is objective knowledge. With "the invention of man" which begins in the seventeenth century and intensifies in the nineteenth, scientific knowledge becomes increasingly self-reflexive, producing the human sciences of medicine, psychoanalysis and so on. Modern thought has been described as the attempt to think "the unthought" of its thinking and so to excavate or to produce the truth of human nature.[7] Foucault's image of this objective self-reflexive knowledge in *The Birth of the Clinic* is the autopsy: humans penetrating into deeper and deeper levels of human interiority – that is, into themselves.

What happens to the purely ethical ascesis in Descartes, the a priori necessity of constituting oneself as the moral subject of one's actions? I have argued that Descartes adapted that ascesis toward the end of producing a subject of knowledge; but it also remains an ethical ascesis. The turn that philosophy takes along with Descartes forces an epistemological problematic: do we know? if so, how and what do we know? what are the limits of knowledge? and primarily for Descartes, what is it that knows? In his "stove-heated room" Descartes intends to reject all opinions and replace them with truths produced by the application of "the standards of reason," beginning with the ascesis. Only then does the question of what is traditionally thought of as moral activity occur. As one critic puts it, "[T]he privileged position of a morality was increasingly identified with rational knowledge and the subject who was in a position to know it."[8]

By means of the truths which replace opinions, Descartes argues, "I would succeed in conducting my life much better" (*PWD*, p. 117). Virtue thus becomes the resultant of rational knowledge: reason, which produces "a true knowledge of good," is the prior foundation of action (*PLD*, p. 166). Descartes, in other words, allows for the production of the self as a moral agent only after the production of the self in relation to knowledge. Another example: in the *Discourse* Descartes recognizes that he must find some place to dwell while he applies himself to the destruction of all opinions and also while "[re-]building is in progress." He decides to constitute himself as a moral subject temporarily, basing his behavior on "the laws and customs of my country" along with the opinions of the "most sensible" members of his culture (*PWD*, p. 122). Even in the absence of certain knowledge, the best opinion must serve as the foundation for constituting the self as a moral agent.

Thus moral behavior becomes part of objective knowledge, in the sense that it necessarily follows from both the Cartesian ascesis and consequent knowledge of the world; then the individual can calculate the potential good of any intended action. The autopsy, mentioned above as the medical form of objective yet self-reflexive knowledge is, like moral knowledge, distinct from the primary Cartesian ascesis and posterior to it. The prior ascesis, which produces interiority by representing it to the self, persists, but tends in the future to become detached from scientific inquiry and to constitute a different and even opposed kind of knowledge. In the many forms which it takes in our modern knowledge-society it most often comes to constitute unique individual experience and identity.

To pursue this eventual conflict of knowledges, we must jump far ahead, filling in only a few blank spaces. For example, Kant in his first *Critique* dispenses with the ascesis. The focus is human interiority or more precisely the already given subject of knowledge in terms of its faculties of cognition, their operation, and the limits on the human knowledge consequently produced. Kant's approach is transcendental – that is, the inquiry into human cognition is prior to empirical experience – and certainly individual self-inquiry and experience have no place here. David Hoy argues that for Kant "Genuine self-knowledge is in a sense impossible, since the self that we make appear to ourselves as an object of knowledge will never be identical to the self that is constructing that object" (*FMP*, p. 16); hence the ascesis is irrelevant and is replaced only by transcendental apperception. In terms of "the invention of man," however, Kant's *Critique* is scientifically self-reflexive, an objective human perspective on human nature.

The Earl of Shaftesbury at the beginning of the eighteenth century seems poised between Descartes and Kant in terms of the necessity of the prior ascesis. Shaftesbury, whose thought apparently derives from the Cambridge Platonists (roughly contemporary with Descartes), continues the emphasis on interiority but also produces a form of interior identity different from Descartes and the rationalists. This is an important shift as it applies to the novel, as will be clear shortly. This shift in interior identity also facilitates the split between objective knowledge and experience.

Shaftesbury considers the argument of Descartes' self-inquiry logically suspect, although he is willing to accept self-existence as evident. Thus it is peculiar that at times he seems to reproduce the Cartesian ascesis, arguing that individuals must turn their eyes toward their own interiority or "take the inward way" as a first step, even to the point of doubting the existence of the external world. The self-reflexive process is necessary to found the self as a subject of knowledge, which is ultimately the result of an inquiry into the nature of the affections. Then humans are able "to trust [their] own eyes and take for real the whole creation."[9]

Yet in the *Inquiry Concerning Virtue* . . . Shaftesbury takes up a position much like that which Kant will take up later: human identity is constructed as an unreflective natural inclination motivated by the affections (*CMM*, vol. 1, p. 243), which are, incidentally, largely social. And this is the usual *métier* of Shaftesbury: the objective inquiry of the scientific knower into human identity, one which is also self-reflexive in the objective sense. But Shaftesbury is significant because of his fixing of human identity in the feelings instead of reason; however universalized his approach, he produces an ethical substance that will become central to individual identity in the following two centuries.

INTERIORITY AND SELF-KNOWLEDGE

Literary texts of the period reflect these essentially modern concerns with self-reflexivity, interiority, and the relation of the two forms of knowledge. This may be particularly true of the novel, which has been traditionally assumed to be coincident with modern or bourgeois society. Fictional texts are usually taken as exemplifications, but ultimately they are as productive of interiority as modern philosophical texts. They only differ in one respect: they call attention to narrative structure or, what is the same thing, the positionality of the subject of knowledge and the structure of knowing. This question is as relevant to philosophical texts – as has been made clear – because they are in one sense narrative fictions. Witness the effect of the splitting of the subject in Descartes' *Discourse*, in which the later subject, beyond the narrative, recounts the process of his own constitution of himself as a subject of knowledge – that is, from the perspective of the subject of knowledge. But for the purposes here, so-called literary texts are the most interesting.

Shaftesbury leads us to Henry Fielding, who represents one tradition of the eighteenth-century novel. In *Joseph Andrews*, for example, feeling – benevolence, good will or, in opposition, self-love – constitutes the moral identity of the characters. The older form of identity, by means of alliance or relation, to class, family, nation, religion, gender, etc., but in Fielding predominantly to the human community, is partially refounded on individual interiority, specifically feeling or the social affections. The primary characters in *Joseph Andrews* act unreflectingly on their feelings of benevolence; an interiority constituted by self-reflection and self-experience of one's feelings is notably absent from the text. Interiority or the affections are necessitated but not represented, with the exception of Lady Booby. This raises the question of narrative structure.

Joseph Andrews is a third-person narration, which foregrounds the position of the objective or scientific knower. The subject of knowledge is outside, detached, able to render an objective, rational judgment. This structure seems relatively uncomplicated in the novel, except that it elides our usual separation between author and narrator – in order to form a rhetoric of truth – and collapses the expected distance between author-narrator and reader, who is directly addressed at strategic points and is the recipient of a complete chapter. By this means the same affective relations are produced between reader and characters as obtain among the characters.

The author-narrator is also related by benevolent feeling to his characters. This is expressed in displaced fashion in Parson Adams' panegyric on Homer's "pathetic" writing: "The images [of Andromache] are so extremely tender . . . that I am convinced that the poet had the worthiest and best heart imaginable."[10] Fielding, in an epic of his own devising, would expect to duplicate that affective relation, and that relation is clear in his treatment of Adams, Joseph, and Fanny throughout. On returning to Lady Booby's parish, Adams is produced as one who "exprest a satisfaction in his face which nothing but benevolence made happy by its objects [i.e., the parishioners] could infuse." Along with Joseph and Fanny, "no three persons could be more kindly received, as, indeed, none ever more deserved to be universally beloved" (*JA*, p. 236). The author-narrator's as well as the characters' self-experience of relation is marked here, though neither is directly represented except as outward manifestation.

Fielding has it both ways: the author-narrator is objective and affective as well: he is the outside subject of knowledge of the truth of the characters and the person joined by good will to these other "real" persons of the story. And he "knows" these characters by means of his affective relation to them: scientific knowledge is effected by and founded on the self-experience of affective bonds. The two forms of knowledge are inherently compatible – so much so that knowledge of human nature comprehends and encloses interiority without any necessity for representation of it.

In the nineteenth century the representation of interiority in fiction becomes an important issue. The development of free indirect discourse is a case in point, in Jane Austen, Flaubert, Zola, and others. Free indirect discourse is a style in which the narrator's discourse represents the thought of the character more or less directly.[11] Charles Dickens's *Great Expectations* manifests a similar concern about the representation of interiority. Incidentally, Dickens's novel is in some senses a reprise of *Joseph Andrews*, so a few of the same questions may be addressed to it. The structure of the representation of interiority in *Great Expectations* is different from that in Flaubert and other examples of free indirect discourse: it is a first-person narration. This kind of narrative is structurally self-reflexive, entailing as it does a double narration. The older, mature Pip stands at the end of the narration, virtually outside it as an objective observer, and stages or frames the immediate inner experience of the younger Pip. The novel centers on a series of these moments of interiority – especially moments of self-reflection and self-decipherment, often misguided, within the structural frame of self-reflection.

The lesson of *Great Expectations* is the same as that of *Joseph Andrews*: a matter of benevolence or love that binds humans (although in the former, interestingly enough, it is no longer the human community but a very restricted group of relatives and friends). Now, however, it is a lesson to be learned by experience – by event and a process of self-reflection that eventually produces self-knowledge. *Great Expectations* is a typical *Bildungsroman*, a narrative of inner growth and maturation. The events which propel Pip toward self-knowledge are devastating at first, but eventually he transforms himself by producing deeper and more hidden feelings – ones present in the first self-representation of the thought of the frightened young Pip in his encounter with the escaped convict.[12] The process is thus one of self-recognition.

The end of the novel brings the narrative separation of the two Pips toward closure, allowing for the smooth emergence of individual experience into objective knowledge. As with Descartes, whose *Discourse* is also a first-person narrative, self-reflexivity in the form of self-examination and self-knowledge is the structure of the ascesis or method by which the individual constitutes itself as a moral subject at the same time it qualifies itself as a subject of knowledge. This subject of knowledge, that is, the objective observer of human nature set apart from daily human intercourse yet bound affectively to it, is produced by self-experience. In the original ending of the novel this is the position of the older Pip. The two kinds of knowledge are compatible and necessary to each other, one growing out of the other. That is guaranteed by the narrative structure: the two Pips are the same character.

The representation of interiority becomes important in the nineteenth century, but it is often tinged with irony and a certain embarrassment. In *Great Expectations* self-reflection is indistinguishable from self-absorption and self-love. This is one reason why self-reflexivity and the representation of interiority are not factors in Fielding's novel except for the characters motivated by self-love. In Dickens, a century later, it is necessary to represent interiority in order to constitute individual identity, but even as it occurs it must be transcended. As Pip matures in the final third of the novel he necessarily becomes a subject of action and much less a self-reflective subject of thought. Something of the same occurs in other nineteenth-century novels; in *Madame Bovary*, for example, the representation of interiority cannot be separated from irony. In the twentieth century or in "late" modernity, however, the self-absorbed constitution of one's identity is central and rarely completely ironic.

INTERIORITY AND THE SUBJECTIVIZATION OF KNOWLEDGE

The nineteenth century was witness to an increased concern with the representation of interiority, self-experience and self-knowledge, and the individualizing effects of such a concern. The emergence of the production of inwardness within discursivity seems increasingly to unsettle the relation of knowledge and experience so that by the end of the century self-experience comes to contest and even oppose objective knowledge. This is doubtless related to a contradiction which arose within the Enlightenment project. One function was to articulate reason's powers in knowledge-politics. Foucault says there emerged a confused opposition between a rationalization-prone society and individual liberty that it was the task of philosophy since Kant to adjudicate (*FPPC*, pp. 58–9). The contradiction lies in the fact that Enlightenment self-reflexivity also produced the individual subject.

Literature, in its nineteenth-century form of concern with the interiority and particularity of individual characters in the novel, seems to have entered the lists along with philosophy. This might be read as a "genealogical moment," for Foucault argues in *Power/Knowledge* that genealogy "entertains the claims to attention of local, discontinuous, disqualified, illegitimate knowledges against the claims of a unitary body of theory which would filter, hierarchise and order them in the name of some true knowledge and some arbitrary idea of what constitutes a science and its objects."[13] Interiority has been subjected to knowledge throughout the nineteenth century, so the genealogical moment referred to here seems to be one of closure or refusal, since the alternative to incorporation into objective knowledge is not readily available. Hence the denial in the two novels to be discussed that interiority can emerge into the appropriation by knowledge. This, in turn, can be said to found one of the traditions of the twentieth-century modern: the artist-hero, self-absorbed and self-constituted as elitist other, self-defined as different from the vulgar: T. S. Eliot in any of the longer poems or the conversation of Stephen Dedalus in Joyce's *Portrait of the Artist* with the dean of studies at his school, in which the latter consistently misunderstands the more intellectual Stephen and in which Stephen's narrated thoughts are consistently condescending: "Stephen saw the silent soul of a jesuit look out at him from the pale loveless eyes. Like Ignatius he was lame but in his eyes burned no spark of Ignatius' enthusiasm."[14] The subject becomes the other of discourse.

The conflict of the two kinds of knowledge is apparent in Joseph Conrad's *Heart of Darkness* (1899). The story is structured by two first-person narratives, one enclosing the other, the unnamed narrator telling the story of Marlow telling a story of his relation to Kurtz. The remarkable thing about *Heart of Darkness* is that in each instance the outside, objective observer – in contrast to the mature, older Pip – does not know and even cannot know. The subject of knowledge is in crisis. To put it another way: at the center of the inner narration is Kurtz and his self-experience – what Marlow the narrator characterizes as self-gratification or the gratification of "monstrous . . . passions." That Marlow characterizes this interiority of Kurtz is an important issue, and we will return to it shortly.

Marlow begins his journey up river as a rather cynical and detached observer of the greedy ineptitude of the "pilgrims" at the outer and central stations, who represent the more banal aspects of European exploitation of Africa: he stands above and overhears the manager and his uncle at one point as they relish the thought of Kurtz's demise.[15] As Marlow moves closer to Kurtz he becomes less detached; in other words his own self-experience becomes a factor. The image of the binoculars, by which Marlow, standing safely on the boat at the inner station dock, is thrust immediately into the center of the compound and confronted with the inward-facing heads on stakes (*HD*, pp. 132–3), serves as a sign of that. Marlow is affected by the wilderness and by Kurtz; while the latter goes completely over the edge, Marlow is somehow restrained; he merely looks over the edge at Kurtz, lying at the bottom, immersed in darkness.

Consider, however, the outer level of the narration. The unnamed narrator is a member of a group of men of the sea who listen to Marlow's story; this narrator reports not only the story but Marlow's frequent breaks from it in order to address the listeners directly. His statements to them are all of a piece: you are all enmeshed in civilization; you are urban and cosseted, made safe by a policeman on every corner. The listening group forms a community of knowers, the recipients of communicable cultural knowledge. Cultural knowledge is in fact structurally the same as scientific knowledge – depending on how specific the institution is which presides over the production of knowledge. Discursivity and communicability are the signs of objective knowledge. Marlow says again and again that they, his listeners, subjects of knowledge, can never understand his experience in the heart of darkness: "You can't understand. How could you . . ." (*HD*, p. 122). Yet he is at the same time attempting to make his and Kurtz's self-experience discursive: he constructs by the fact of his narration the possibility of objective knowledge detached from but produced by self-experience.

This latter claim focuses attention on the economy of knowledge and experience in the inner narrative: if Marlow's group, idling away time on a boat anchored in the estuary of the Thames within sight of the center of a great civilization, can know Marlow's experience half a world away, in "darkest Africa," then Marlow can know Kurtz's interiority: "The thing was to know what he belonged to, how many powers of darkness claimed him for their own" (*HD*, p. 121). This is of course to place Kurtz within the categories of knowledge-constitution. Yet everyone who has read *Heart of Darkness* knows what the central enigma is, what might be called the absent center: what is missing is Kurtz's interiority, his own first-person narration. And this puts Marlow's knowledge in doubt. The heart of darkness is not dark because it contains "unspeakable rites" (*HD*, p. 123) or "forgotten and brutal instincts, gratified and monstrous passions" (*HD*, p. 143) or "abominable satisfactions" (*HD*, p. 149), but because it cannot be known, except as self-experience. When Marlow characterizes Kurtz in terms of the "Hollow[ness] at [his] core" (*HD*, p. 133) or "the barren darkness of his heart" (*HD*, p. 146) he is admitting to the discontinuity between experience and knowledge. "His was an impenetrable darkness," says Marlow of Kurtz (*HD*, p. 147).

Kurtz is always an enigma to Marlow, despite the fact that his narrative emphasizes the contagion that speads from Kurtz to himself, and his insistence on the similarity of their experiences. Marlow's binocular metaphor virtually claims that he enters Kurtz's consciousness. Marlow does indeed know *about* Kurtz: the reports of "the unspeakable rites . . . offered up to him" were "reluctantly gathered" from hearsay. He knows Kurtz through the form of a series of oppositions, that is, within language and discourse. Kurtz is fixed within a structure defined by: light/darkness, civilized/primitive, reason/passion (or restraint and its absence), the licit/illicit (e.g., "this alone had beguiled his unlawful soul beyond the bounds of permitted aspirations" [*HD*, p. 143]), etc. At the moment of experience, however, language fails; witness the eloquence of Kurtz's report to the International Society for the Suppression of Savage Customs. Marlow says: "It was eloquent, vibrating with eloquence. . . ." He quotes "noble words" from the report: "we can exert a power for good [on the natives] practically unbounded" (*HD*, p. 123).

Kurtz's impenetrable darkness can be characterized thus: simply put, detached from European civilization, Kurtz turns inward self-reflexively, and this takes the form of self-experience – "his soul . . . had looked within itself . . . had gone mad" (*HD*, p. 144) – Marlow labels it the monstrous self-gratification of every desire. But of course non-critical self-experience is by definition self-gratification.

This characterization remains along the lines of Marlow's insights as an observer and a discourser precisely because self-experience is seen as discontinuous with discourse and knowledge. Descartes argues that self-reflexive knowledge of one's interiority is the foundation of knowledge, but for Conrad there is a fundamental differentiation. On board, going down the river, with Kurtz "as good as dead," Marlow has a kind of negative epiphany about a supposed epiphany of Kurtz: "And for a moment it seemed to me as if I also were buried in a vast grave full of unspeakable secrets. I felt an intolerable weight oppressing my breast . . . [in] the darkness of an impenetrable night" (*HD*, p. 139). There is a claim to sympathy and connection here: "I also," Marlow says, experienced what Kurtz did. But "secrets"? hidden from whom, if not Marlow?

Secrets, the impenetrable, that which cannot be known. "Unspeakable": that is, if known, never to be contained in discourse: but of course discourse is knowledge. Thus the site where Marlow wishes most strongly to claim intimacy with Kurtz is compromised by counter argument.

At other points Marlow distinguishes clearly between his own self-experience and Kurtz's. The moment of Kurtz's self-recognition – i.e., his rational or civilized self-reflection on his self-experience once he is descending out of the wilderness and is near death – all of this is put by Marlow in the form of a question because he is only the observer, unable to penetrate Kurtz's interiority: was this "the supreme moment of complete knowledge?" (*HD*, p. 147). Here the discontinuity seems to be emphasized. The distinction is even clearer at another strategic point in the narrative where Marlow seems intent on marking the difference between his knowledge and Kurtz's experience: "he had made that last stride, he had stepped over the edge, while I had been permitted to draw back my hesitating foot. And perhaps in this is the whole difference; perhaps all the wisdom, and all the truth, and all sincerity are just compressed into that inappreciable moment of time in which we step over the threshold of the invisible" (*HD*, p. 149). Marlow admittedly speculates, because Kurtz's interiority is not accessible to him. It should be noted that this is the moment of total self-experience for Kurtz – this stepping over – and not his moment of critical self-recognition, which comes later. At the moment of stepping over, he clearly has no objective knowledge, even of his own interiority.

There are other issues: even if Kurtz's experience becomes accessible as Marlow's self-experience, it is still unspeakable to anyone else; Marlow's first-person narration is also end-loaded: his immediate inner experience in the heart of darkness seems remote; seen through the wrong end of the telescope, it is attenuated and obscured at the moment of telling by the framing of philosophic and scientific language and by objectification; and finally the outer narrator, who sits on the boat anchored in the Thames with Marlow and others and tells the story of Marlow telling his story of the Congo: his description of the difficulty of Marlow's stories with their surrounding luminosity – "to him the meaning of an episode was not inside like a kernel but outside, enveloping the tale which brought it out only as a glow brings out a haze" (*HD*, p. 68) – that is, allowing for understanding only in terms of an intuition of the self-experience of the other, not its articulation; this narrator only learns from Marlow's story that "the heart of an immense darkness" is "out there," proving the incommensurability of knowledge and experience.

Marlow's first-person narrative promise of access to interiority is thoroughly ironic. The third-person-narrative structure of *The Awakening*, published the same year as *Heart of Darkness*, would suggest a similar access by different means – that is, by free indirect discourse and other techniques available to it. Both novels are about self-experience or, what is the same thing, self-realization, the actualization of one's inner potential. Since interest in Chopin's novel is thus focused on the emotional changes Edna Pontellier undergoes throughout, it would seem natural to represent that interiority completely. Peculiarly enough, this is a promise not quite fulfilled, and this makes the two novels companion pieces.

In *The Awakening* objective knowledge takes the form of cultural knowledge, although the scope is more curtailed and specific and gender oriented: Edna Pontellier becomes part of a New Orleans Creole subculture, which is represented as different from, for example, Accadian or Cajun culture. The knowledge of this culture is embedded in a set of attitudes and social roles and duties. Edna Pontellier's interiority is posed against this social truth in the novel. But the same opposition appears in the relation of the narrative perspective to Edna's self-experience. This perspective mediates Edna's self-experience and strictly frames its representation. It is objective without being quite the voice of the culture. For example, when Edna finally learns to swim, she is likened by the narrative to a child first learning to walk, "boldly and with overconfidence"; further:

> A feeling of exultation overtook her, as if some power of significant import had been given her to control the working of her body and soul. She grew daring and reckless, overestimating her strength. She wanted to swim far out. . . .[16]

This is clearly Edna's self-experience; but it appears by way of a thoroughly mediated access: the objective, cautious, even ironic narrative perspective. And it is not merely the irony: typically, the narrative merely summarizes and thereby controls Edna's burgeoning self-experience. The short chapter 28, after Edna sleeps with Arobin, provides another illustration.

Why limit access to the interiority of the only character who matters in this novel, and the only one who undergoes any sort of significant inner transformation? There is no doubt that Edna's self-experience is central here: she emerges from the cocoon of rather indifferent social propriety to undergo the experience of a succession of her emotions and her desires – and their gratification as often as not. It is the experience of her inner self, of all her emotional potential as an individual. This is staged in one instance, during her sleepy Sunday afternoon at Madame Antoine's, when she luxuriates in examining and feeling the round firm sensuousness of her body (*A*, p. 48). Her new identity is the product of this intense self-experience; it in fact is that self-experience.

The objectifying, summarizing narrative that frames and distances Edna's interiority could be said at the same time to obscure it from prying eyes, to allow it to remain Edna's interiority. Edna herself tends to be private, self-circumscribed, and isolative. She moves to her own home to be alone; she realizes that males constitute, like signs, a chain of substitutions, and that eventually all of them will fade from memory:

> There was no human being whom she wanted near her except Robert; and she even realized that the day would come when he, too, and the thought of him would melt out of her existence, leaving her alone. (*A*, p. 151)

Toward the end of the novel, when she has just undergone the devastating experience of witnessing childbirth, and when Dr. Mandelet offers to allow her to pour out her confused feelings to him, she makes a signal refusal. She is her inner experience, however disturbed at the moment, and she deliberately chooses to cloister it: once communicated, it is no longer inner or individual; it is no longer her unique identity if shared. In a similar way the narrative perspective, by its very objectivity, seems to grant Edna the space of her own interiority; even the irony about Edna's transformation can be seen as a technique of non-penetration, a way of remaining outside and detached.

This provides a new perspective on Edna's suicide. The confusion which comes from witnessing childbirth is based on her desire for freedom and her visceral knowledge of her connection to her children, which she defers but must eventually face: she says to Mandelet, "I want to be let alone. Nobody has any right – except children, perhaps – and even then, it seems to me . . ." and trails off. Then: "I shouldn't want to trample upon the little lives. Oh! I don't know what I'm saying . . ." (*A*, p. 147).

Edna's interiority, even in its severely mediated form, disappears shortly after and is not represented again until the next day when she stands poised on the beach at Grand Isle. Her thoughts – partly interior monologue – are reported by the narration as what has occurred the previous night. In these thoughts her children are still her "antagonists," the unbreakable link that binds her to the social world. "But she knew a way to elude them" (*A*, p. 151). Then the narrator brackets Edna between the sea and the sensuous self-experience of her nakedness, her memory of her loosening attachments, that is, her interiority and its separateness. Edna's final narrative act is to swim directly out into the Gulf; suicide, yes, but it is fundamentally an act of "eluding" the narrative perspective; she simply swims out of it, refusing in a final act to allow her interiority to be compromised.

There is an irony here. In order to preserve her interiority intact, Edna herself opens it up to the outside – the sea, the meadow, and the unlimited. This is precisely in the terms of the narrative perspective, for which these are the outward signs of Edna's innerness. In one sense, then, she remains contained by knowledge. Nonetheless, Edna does escape this control. She simultaneously moves in mind into memory, barricading her interiority, and moves outward, beyond the grasp of the narrative – with the apparent compliance of the narrative perspective.

As in *Heart of Darkness*, in *The Awakening* the narrative of interiority faces the problematic of its own production. The representation of interiority by whatever technique disrupts the interior/exterior opposition. Objective knowledge is always knowledge-power, the production of truth under the auspices and control of the institution. Objective knowledge, persuading itself of its own distance from power, ends by opening up avenues along which power penetrates – simultaneously (*FPPC*, pp. 43, 106). The truth of interiority produced or represented, that is, as the object of knowledge, is no longer interior and protected. That is the dilemma that Edna faces, and problematically escapes. In *Heart of Darkness* the claims of knowledge to comprehend inner experience are always seen to fall short.

In both novels, in contrast to the earlier examples, the narratability of interiority is called into question, as well as language and discourse themselves, by which knowledge is produced. The fundamental disjunction of knowledge and self-experience is represented in the later novels by the testing of limits and attempts to broach the discontinuity. This suggests that these texts assume the disjunction from the outset, test it, make forays into understanding interiority, and end by affirming the intractability of the difference. Interiority is then confirmed by its absence from discourse, although it took a century of producing that interiority to make such a conclusion an arguable one.

Conrad and Chopin could thus be considered as a reaction against the instrumentality of reason or scientific and political rationality in the human sciences, the resistance to the penetration of knowledge-power. But what is interesting at this point are their resources for this reaction: against *the* history of reason they have recourse only to its other, irrationality, madness, and egocentrism. And they throw up a barrier to penetration by setting off a separate and unknowable truth of the individual interior self; yet by doing this they, like Freud, set up another realm that holds out the promise of yielding its secrets to objective knowledge. They unwittingly do the work of knowledge.

These texts also seem to introduce the twentieth-century modern: the artist as alien, who produces him/herself by self-inquiry, self-experience, self-knowledge, and the consequent self-constitution as a unique interiority discontinuous from the social. The goal of Descartes' self-inquiry and self-knowledge is only temporarily asocial. His ultimate end is normalization and the creation of the foundation for objective knowledge. Late modernism is thus seen to turn its back on its origin, and on rationality.

There remains the paradox, noted above, that interiority exists only by being represented in discourse and thus becoming part of institutional knowledge. In the twentieth century there are prominent attempts to limit narrative control such as stream-of-consciousness narration, the intensified use of indirect discourse, dreams, surreality, which all propose the attenuation of objective knowledge. I. A. Richards and others approach the problem by distinguishing the two discourses of science and poetry, exterior and interior truth; but Richards also constructs interiority as a form of psychological intelligibility in his *Principles of Literary Criticism*.[17]

Not all the first half of the twentieth century is of a piece. Fiction often continues to integrate narrative knowledge with the self-experience of the characters, as in Thomas Mann's *Death in Venice*. Aschenbach's "degeneration" from detached and objective observer into his own interiority is yet objectively observed and precisely recorded by the narration. And in the thirties and forties a shift occurs which alters the problematic of interiority. Interiority doesn't disappear, but becomes textualized. This is the era of language and discourse, of the intentional fallacy and then of structuralism. Up until structuralism interiority was assumed to be expressed or manifested by the text. It was not a long step toward saying that only the text existed, that writing or discourse produced interiority and the subject and its identity as well; this was said by the sixties.

NARRATIVE PRODUCTION OF INTERIORITY

The critical discourse of the seventies and early eighties concerning free indirect discourse shows how the same conflict of knowledge and experience appears as well at the theoretical level. A particular difference within the more traditional part of this criticism demonstrates how the problematic of interiority persists in the textual era alongside poststructural notions of originary absence and the demise of the subject. Free indirect discourse was a literary response to the increased attention paid to interiority in the nineteenth century in disciplines from religion to medicine to philosophy, and this literary inclination continued into the twentieth century along with techniques such as stream-of-consciousness. Roy Pascal's *The Dual Voice* (1977) is concerned primarily with the earlier century.[18] The title is indicative: Pascal argues the traditional continuity of objective knowledge and inner experience within the structure of free indirect discourse. There is no representation without a representer: the narrative perspective or "voice" seamlessly transforms the characters' interiority into discourse; the narrative perspective is the embodiment of the formal and textualizing impulse. We must remember that Pascal operates under the aegis of fictional realism, that is, under the assumption that the origin of the representation of interiority is an actual if hypothetical consciousness, which is brought into discourse.

Against Pascal's traditional reading the linguist Ann Banfield poses a forceful alternative argument in *Unspeakable Sentences* (1982).[19] These are the sentences of narration and represented speech and thought, the latter her name for free indirect discourse. These sentences are in effect unspoken by the (previously supposed) narrator or agency of narration. Banfield in fact denies the existence of a narrative agency within the text, putting into doubt the textual era's normal distinction of author and narrator. Banfield thus produces what appears in most of her book as a direct, unframed representation of interiority arising as the inner self-expression of the self-experience of a character. There is immediate access to this interiority, although the self-representation is linguistic, that is, represented. This would indeed be the triumph of interiority, its rupture of the external frame of objectivity, notwithstanding the continued irony of its exterior representation.

Yet Banfield makes ultimate reference to the author if not the narrator. She argues that in literate societies, such as nineteenth-century France and England had become – that is, societies in which writing becomes central – free indirect discourse found its development. Writing allows for the deferral of the speaker/author and the present or "now" of the act of writing; in other words these are left outside the text. Objective knowledge is now external to the text. The text self-circumscribes its own interiority. Within the text are representations of the interiority of the characters situated by constative (fictional) narrative sentences (e.g., "The war ended."). According to Banfield the frame of objective knowledge has disappeared from the text insofar as it knows interiority; but of course it has only been displaced.

Pascal and Banfield represent the classic argument about the relation or difference between objective and scientific knowledge – the external perspective – and the interiority of self-experience and self-knowledge. One, in a direct line from Descartes, but without benefit of an ascesis, asserts both the duality and the coincidence of the two forms of knowledge. The other asserts the priority of the self-production of interiority, but not without a certain sleight of hand. Both views are traditional from a nineties' perspective: Banfield's deferral is not poststructural; for her the author remains the origin of signification.

There is no attempt here to extend this analysis into the poststructural era, but the death of the subject is familiar, as well as the later claim that such news was greatly exaggerated. The former suggests at least the beginning of the end of the era in which interiority is identity. "The postmodern paradigm is not profundity but complexity" of the surface or text (*FMP*, p. 28). Is it a coincidence, then, that a new impetus was given to the premodern deployment of alliance or relational identity, now based on gender, race, and ethnicity in the same decade that God died and Derrida and Foucault appeared on the scene? The question that needs to be asked is whether this new identity is discursive or whether it is founded on interiority – how it *feels* to be a woman or African-American. The poststructural conclusion that subjectivity is discursively produced or that we have moved to a new era of historical ontology seems on the one hand to have prevailed, yet on the other seems continually challenged by what is sometimes called the uncompleted project of modernity.[20]

2

SUBJECT, SELF, PERSON

MARCEL MAUSS AND THE LIMITS OF POSTSTRUCTURALIST CRITIQUE

Anthony John Harding

During the early phase of poststructuralist enquiry, reconsideration of the concept or category of the person was largely overshadowed by the primary need to critique and dismantle the dominant concepts of the unitary subject and the individualistic self. Now, with increasing attention being paid to questions of agency, right, and ethics in a poststructuralist context, the concept of the person is making a return to the debate. Though closely associated with "self" since the early nineteenth century, the term "person" has escaped most of the destructive effects of the poststructuralist critique of "subject" and "self." Perhaps this is because through its etymology the word "person" seems to acknowledge, as "subject" and "self" do not, the preexistence of relationality and the social context, not only to human interaction but to any individual's self-concept. The ancient perception that a human being is always already in some role with respect to others, and can be defined only against the background of relationality, takes on a new persuasiveness when language is understood as instrumental in structuring the subject-position of the individual ("*le sujet de l'énonciation*" in Benveniste's well-known phrase), and as logically prior to the "subject."

We can now more clearly recognize that the category of the person, which until recently has been understood as intimately connected with the idea of "self" and through "self" with the increasingly problematic Western notion of consciousness, must be more carefully distinguished from, and perhaps saved from, these notions historically associated with it. That the category of the person remains foundational for the conceptualization of human rights seems to be generally agreed. Organizations committed to the defense of human rights will often criticize governments for failing to treat their subjects as persons. In some slightly less politically charged but still vital areas of human interaction (education, law, community development, social work, "race relations," sexual relations), treating others *as persons* is frequently put forward as the first principle, or at least as one of the first principles, of ethical and even of legally-sanctioned behavior. Yet work needs to be done to re-articulate this ethical, humanitarian, and jurisprudential consensus with a new theoretical understanding of the person. In particular, much feminist, poststructuralist, and postcolonialist theory questions the way that the term *person* has become too closely identified with the Western philosophical tradition focusing on the autonomous, rational, self-determining individual. Thus the term is treated as suspect in much contemporary theory, while retaining its crucial role in the discourse of law, social administration, and education theory.

The object of this paper is to argue that, while the concept of the person should be preserved, for the reasons suggested above, it needs to be reformulated on the basis of relationality, rather than solipsistic individualism. Further, my paper will suggest that the category of the person must connote not only the right to (physical, individual) survival but the need and the right to be in relationship to the extent and in the manner that physical health, psychology, and socialization allow.

The French philosopher Francis Jacques observes that "the concept of the person is emerging as dominant in present-day philosophical enquiry," and he proceeds carefully to differentiate his own project – which is to make the relational condition, instead of the Cartesian "I think," constitutive of the personal self – from the effort to rehabilitate or reconstruct the selfhood in the sense of the "classical ego," which, he avers, "can no longer be allowed to take over the central transcendental role."[1] The term "person" also appears frequently in the work of the feminist theorist Diana Tietjens Meyers, who develops an approach to moral identity based on "empathic thought," a concept derived partly from Nancy Chodorow and Jessica Benjamin but with added emphasis on the need for "dissident speech" to make empathy more wide-ranging, less bounded by a person's immediate social group. Meyers places much emphasis on the "interpersonal," explaining that "the aim of broad empathy is to achieve an understanding of another's psychic constitution and the ways in which the various components of that constitution interrelated."[2] As a means of focusing the value-term "empathy" for practical moral reflection in actual situations, Meyers proposes the question "Do you want to be the sort of person who would do that?" (*SS*, p. 128). The concept of "being a person" in relation to others, and able to imagine how others might feel about one's actions, thus becomes basic to Meyers's model of empathy.

As is evident from these examples, reconsideration of the category of the person is of necessity an interdisciplinary project. Even Francis Jacques, whose enquiry at least starts as a strictly philosophical one, draws on the work of linguists, psychologists, anthropologists, theologians, and novelists, as well as other philosophers. The very richness of these intersecting fields can make synthesis difficult, however.

The first interdisciplinary attempt to describe the category of the person and sketch a genealogy for it was Marcel Mauss's 1938 lecture "A category of the human mind: the notion of person; the notion of self." This lecture was Mauss's last work to be made public. Delivered in French as the 1938 Huxley Memorial

Lecture for the Royal Anthropological Institute of Great Britain and Ireland, it was published the same year in the *Journal of the Royal Anthropological Institute* under the title "Une Catégorie de l'Esprit Humain: La Notion de Personne, Celle de 'Moi,'" and reprinted in Mauss's *Sociologie et anthropologie* (Paris: Presses Universitaires de France, 1950).[3] Its first appearance in English was in 1979, when a translation by Ben Brewster was included in Mauss's *Sociology and Psychology* (London: Routledge and Kegan Paul, 1979). The lecture remains widely influential. Its implications have been assessed and critiqued by sociologists, anthropologists, and philosophers, and it is cited in studies of the growth of the "modern self" and the "history of subjectivity."[4]

However, its pioneering interdisciplinarity, and the rapidity with which it outlines the historical development of the category, have left a number of important issues unresolved. Principally, although the title of the lecture suggests that the two categories, "person" and "self," are one and the same, what Mauss actually shows is that this is not true for every society or at all stages of development. He also implies that in European societies at any rate the full fusion of the two categories did not take place until the end of the eighteenth century. I wish to re-examine Mauss's lecture here not in order to "deconstruct" it but as a means of clarifying and advancing the current renewal of interest in the category of the person, and in particular to show more precisely why there is a need to keep "person," "self," and "subject" distinct. It is important to recognize the boldness of the lecture, and the significance of its appearance at a crucial juncture in European history, but it is also essential, I think, to move beyond the developmental and teleological assumptions that cause most of the difficulties modern readers have with the lecture. First, then, I wish to outline some problems raised by the concept of the person put forward in the lecture; second, I will describe what seem to me some shortcomings in the solutions offered by Mauss's critics; and third, I will propose, not a solution of my own, but some ways in which I think discussion might move forward.

Beginning from the fairly sweeping assertion that "there has never existed a human being who has not been aware not only of his body, but also at the same time of his individuality, both spiritual and physical," Mauss's lecture first surveys some of the most ancient "forms assumed by the notion of 'self' (*moi*)" (*CP*, p. 3). The Pueblo and the Kwakiutl of North America, and the Arunta, Loritja, and Kakadu of Australia, are brought forward as examples of the way in which "individuality" is understood in tribal society, where, even though each member does "act out, each insofar as it concerns him, the prefigured totality of the life of the clan," nevertheless the clan is seen to be made up of individuals: not exactly "persons" as Europeans understand the term, but "'characters' (*personnages*)" (*CP*, p. 5). Such characters, in tribal societies, are not so much a right to be claimed as an honor that is bestowed in some form of public drama or ritual. Traces of this public, dramatized process in which the "character" is passed on from one generation to the next remain even in the Senate of ancient Rome. After brief digressions into the Hindu concepts of *aham* and *Ahamkâra* ("I," "creation of the 'I'"), and the Chinese concept of the *ming* ("name"), Mauss returns to what can now emerge as a narrative of development. The Romans, he says, "established the notion of 'person' (*personne*)," the social and legal entity, as the birthright of every free individual. In Roman law and custom, the *persona* is "synonymous with the true value of the individual," something from which only slaves are excluded (*CP*, p. 17). Then Stoicism and Christianity gave this social and legal concept metaphysical weight and authority. Christian thinkers developed the theologically-based idea of the *persona* as rational, individual substance, *substantia rationalis individua*. In the past three hundred years, European philosophers – most notably and definitively Kant and Fichte – "[made] of this rational, individual substance what it is today, a consciousness and a category" (*CP*, p. 20). "Kant," Mauss summarizes, "had already made of the individual consciousness, the sacred character of the human person, the condition for Practical Reason. It was Fichte who made of it as well the category of the 'self' (*moi*), the condition of consciousness and of science, of Pure Reason" (*CP*, p. 22). Yet far from being established as an immutable law of the moral world it remains "imprecise, delicate and fragile," still very much in need of further elaboration (*CP*, p. 1).

Even this very short account of what is already a highly condensed narrative will have brought to light some features that most contemporary theorists would find troubling. First, there is the conflict – noted by almost all Mauss's commentators – between the sociologist's recognition that "categories of the mind" are not universal to all human beings, but differ at different times and in different societies (a finding which Mauss shared with Durkheim), and the European intellectual's sense that, while the category of the person "is formulated only for us, among us" (meaning European intellectuals), it is also an incomparably valuable cultural "possession" which is threatened in a very real and immediate way by powerful, perhaps irresistible forces. It is as if the enterprise of historicizing the notion of person, showing how "the human mind" evolved and perfected it, becomes possible and necessary only at the eleventh hour, when it is in danger of disappearing for ever.

In 1938 the forces that threatened the category of the person were real indeed. The Durkheimian view that social life, the life of the collective, underlay all moral concepts, individual choice and agency virtually disappearing into the matrix of a society's needs and provisions, was dealt a terminal blow by the advent of Nazism. "Nuremberg," said Léon Brunschvig, "is religion according to Durkheim, society adoring itself."[5] When Mauss said of the category of person "With us the idea could disappear" (*CP*, p. 22), he was not indulging in an intellectual's Spenglerian pessimism, nor was he being carelessly Eurocentric. He was alluding to the possibility, which must have seemed very close to realization in 1938, that the Third Reich would subjugate the Western world and crush the fragile concept of person, and the rights and liberties that had come to be associated with it, out of existence.

The contemporary critic, however, has to register as well the fact that what Mauss offers in his lecture has the form of a narrative, and that it is by implication, if not in intention, a "totalizing" narrative. That is, it clearly proposes that the Kantian category of the person – as distinct from the "subject" and the self (Mauss's "moi"), even though Fichte brought self and person together, instigating the modern tendency to regard them as identical – is something which was always implicit in other, earlier concepts of selfhood, including those held by the Pueblo, the Kwakiutl, the Arunta, and so on. It took a European level of cultural and, particularly, philosophical development, the lecture suggests, to bring this category to full birth. "Slowly" (Mauss says) "does it succeed in expressing itself, through time, through societies, their contacts and metamorphoses . . ." (*CP*, p. 23). There is, in formulations like these, more than a hint of the Hegelian heritage of Mauss's analysis, a tradition which (down to Renouvier and Durkheim) sees the free, self-determining citizen of the modern Western democratic state as the highest point of development humankind has yet reached. In *Les formes élementaires de la vie religieuse* Durkheim did attempt to demystify the *process* by which logical categories developed in one culture might become philosophically and culturally "autonomous" and so acquire universality (*CCP*, p. 54). But most contemporary readers would be uncomfortable with the implication clearly present in both Durkheim's and Mauss's accounts: that this particular "category of the human mind," the category of the person, achieved its highest point of refinement in Europe in the nineteenth and twentieth centuries, and should therefore be embraced in this form by non-Europeans as self-evidently the best that the human race has yet managed to think on the topic.

The complaint of Eurocentrism is not the only objection that can be raised, however. Though Mauss describes Kant as "a feeble philosopher but a well-informed psychologist and theologian" (*CP*, p. 22), Kant's *Critiques* emerge in this account as crucial to the full flowering of the concept of person. Mauss's narrative culminates with the question that Kant left unresolved, "whether the 'self' (*moi*), *das Ich*, is a category," and Fichte's answer, "that every act of consciousness was an act of the 'self'" (*CP*, p. 22). This moment in the philosophy of the post-Enlightenment period, when Kant's disguised Pietism met Fichte's enthusiastic avowal of the all-powerful ego, drew self and person together and so defined, for European thought at any rate, what was implicit in the developing concept of the person: that the sacred human person, "the condition for Practical Reason," was one and the same with the category of the self, and that this self was in principle present in every act of consciousness. At this historical moment, it became apparent that "Each of us has our 'self' (*moi*), an echo of the Declaration of the Rights of Man, which had predated both Kant and Fichte" – in other words, each of us has both personhood, the focus of all our moral relations, and selfhood, a unitary, "inward" self, the agent of "every act of consciousness" (*CP*, p. 22). For Mauss, that is, the ethical concept of the autonomous individual, and of the individual as rational will, is the basis of Kant's and Fichte's construction of the self, in its moral relations. Kant made it possible to detach the autonomous self from metaphysical concepts like "soul" and "conscience" by putting in their place the idea of will as practical rationality. This separation of the ethical realm from the metaphysical is achieved by arguing that the autonomous individual can be the basis of an ethic. As a recent commentator on Kant summarizes this principle, the rational will "has merely never to act in such a way that its modes of action are self-contradictory." So, Kant proposes, it is because categorical obligations undeniably exist that we must conclude we are free agents; and "only autonomy as self-legislation yields for Kant an intelligible account of that freedom."[6] In Kant, so to speak, autonomous individuality is there for regulative purposes, to *make* the I a person – that is, to enable the construction of a rational ethic without the aid of a metaphysic. In Fichte, autonomous individuality itself takes on a constitutive, even metaphysical quality. The "self," conceived in a way that escapes Kant's careful delimiting of what things can and what cannot be objects of knowledge, is made the agent in every act of consciousness.

What Mauss's analysis evidently bypasses is the rigorous and damaging philosophical analysis that the notion of autonomous selfhood, as first posited by Kant and developed by Fichte, has undergone since the early nineteenth century. The main direction of this critique is well summarized by Werner Hamacher. Hamacher points out that for many post-Kantian thinkers the idea of the autonomous self is compromised by the following circumstances:

> [that] the individual must remain inaccessible to a finite faculty of representation, that its particularity cannot be grasped using general linguistic conventions, and that, because it is itself finite, even it does not possess the means to express itself in its totality as individual. In expressing itself as individual, it neither expresses itself as a whole nor expresses itself wholly: the whole has become, for knowledge and for language, a merely finite, temporally as well as structurally limited generality.[7]

The result of such critiques, in poststructuralist theory, is that the self is no longer considered a unitary entity in its own right, whether knowable or not, but "an ideological construct articulated in the language available to the individual at a particular historical moment."[8] To the extent that Mauss's description of the "category of the person" is tied to Kantian concepts of the category, and a post-Kantian understanding of the possibility of constructing the autonomous individual, it too is vulnerable to critique by the disciplines which have had most to say about the illusoriness of the autonomous self: psychoanalysis, linguistics, structuralism, sociology, and recent philosophy. (Nussbaum cites most particularly, in this connection, Lacan, Foucault, and Althusser.)

To some commentators, this critique itself amounts to an attack on personhood and free agency comparable to (if not actually cognate with) the totalitarianism Mauss was warning against. David Bromwich, fighting a rearguard action against what he sees as the dehumanizing and politically debilitating effect of deconstructionist rhetoric, states that "An implication of most deconstructionist criticism is that an end of self-deception requires an end of the self."[9] And the skepticism about self, he charges, inevitably contaminates the social-political category of the person. Bromwich is well aware that "self," "person," "subject," and "agency" are different things. He takes some time to critique Foucault's use of Nietzsche, for instance, by pointing out that the genealogies of humanist values with which Nietzsche subverted humanism stop short of denying or disproving the self (*CI*, p. 278). Nevertheless, he says that for the poststructuralist critic "Talking about persons . . . is prohibited in advance by the exclusion that Foucault and Derrida alike enforce against comparable entities," such as character and self (*CI*, p. 276). This Foucauldian aversion to allowing any degree of personal agency into the social equation is traced by Bromwich to French Marxism, which needed, he says, "a vocabulary which incorporated persons only as the bearers of structures" as a "plausible, Western constituent of an apology for the historical necessity of Stalinism" (*CI*, p. 279). In other words, to defend the indefensible (a totalitarian system which crushed personal freedom), French Marxists redefined the person out of existence, making it merely a "bearer of structures," not an entity with its own coherence, autonomy, and privileges, let alone a consciousness. Foucault followed this example of bad faith by "prohibit[ing] in advance" all analysis of the role of persons in history.

The problem with this argument is that in order to defend the category of the person – this category of thought which, if Mauss is even partly right, took many centuries to develop – Bromwich needs to see it as autonomous, as perfected and for-all-time, having reached its *telos*. Thus, he would have to refute or discredit the sociological, anthropological, and historicist traditions which, long before Foucault, had studied the various ways in which the individual was understood in different historical periods. By implication, too, it seems Bromwich wants to minimize the role of those social structures and collectively developed concepts which themselves eventually produced the very category of person he clearly regards as precious. Reading Bromwich in the context of Mauss it begins to seem as if the very process of historicizing the category of the person, of tracing the social and ideological matrix in which it took its present Western conceptual form, is believed to have destroyed its authority once and for all, even though other relatively late-developing human institutions which have been similarly historicized (democracy, international law, even marriage) have continued to evolve, without signs of terminal damage. In some anti-poststructuralist writing about the person, it is implied that once we know too much about the history of a given practice or concept, that practice or concept is doomed (as if in fact every genealogy were a Nietzschean, destructive genealogy). In this vein Anya Taylor suggests a parallel between the efforts of Kant, Jacobi, Schelling, and Coleridge and the work of moralists and philosophers of our own time who, she says, "are trying to rescue the person for similar reasons, but now not so much from nature as from history, class, ideology, and . . . language."[10] Thus by seeming to authorize the historicist analysis of the category of the person, Mauss, who praises Kant and whose aim was certainly not to destroy the category but on the contrary to reaffirm and protect its value, would seem to be guilty of siding with the barbarians, Hume, Nietzsche, and Foucault. The "rescue operations," Taylor admits, "may in fact have captured only for a brief moment an idea of individual value which flourished under certain historical circumstances" (*CPD*, p. 374). This was Mauss's fear; but it is far from clear that having now been historicized the category of the person must actually disappear.

It is perfectly possible to read Foucault's work on the historical changes that led to modern Western "practices of the self" as a furthering of Mauss's aims in "A category of the human mind: the notion of person; the notion of self." Foucault fills in his predecessor's outline of the intertwined but (in principle) distinct and separable concepts of person and self. Discussing the project on the "care of the self" that he embarked on after completing the first two parts of his *History of Sexuality*, Foucault writes that this new enquiry began as an investigation, not into "the evolution of sexual behavior" as such, but rather into a primary element of the concern with the self: the obligation to confront and tell the truth about oneself, especially with regard to sexual conduct. "How had the subject been compelled to decipher himself in regard to what was forbidden?"[11] This enquiry led Foucault to research the concern with self that was apparent in Greek and Roman ethical philosophers of the period from the second century B.C.E. to the end of the second century of the common era: principally such philosophers as Musonius, Soranus, Seneca, Plutarch, Epictetus, and Marcus Aurelius. These are the authors of whom Mauss said that it was in their work that the public and juridical meaning of "persona" became linked with the ethical dimension, the "sense of being conscious, independent, autonomous, free, and responsible" (*CP*, p. 18).

Foucault agrees with Mauss in finding that in Greek and Roman ethical thought of this period the precepts that had to do with "mastery over oneself" (*TOS*, p. 35), and the practices that these authors counselled, did not set forth the cultivation of one's self as an end in its own right but rather as an aspect of what one owed to others: ultimately, to the polis or state; and (increasingly, during the first two centuries of the common era) to a more universal notion of the appropriate behavior for a responsible, rational being.

> Around the care of the self, there developed an entire activity of speaking and writing in which the work of oneself on oneself and communication with others were linked together.
>
> Here we touch on one of the most important aspects of this activity devoted to oneself: it constituted, not an exercise in solitude, but a true social practice.[12]

Thus in both the late Stoic writer Epictetus and in Plutarch (who is considered a Platonist, not a Stoic, and who opposed some of the Stoics' teachings), the "modelling of political work" took place through the "modality of a rational being," through laws to be exercised on the basis of the individual's "retreat within himself," not through laws about how those possessing high social status should best govern others. However, the end of one's concern with the self remained the improvement of one's relations with others. In other words, these thinkers of late antiquity made "the ethical work of the self on the self" the foundation of good social and political conduct (*CS*, p. 91).

Similarly, Foucault finds that marriage, the social institution that played the largest role in private life, though at first in this period sanctioned by the polis and viewed primarily as a pragmatic measure to ensure the proper upbringing of future citizens, was more and more defined in terms of a bond between two individuals that had its own inherent rightness and value (*CS*, p. 148). Like the practices and regimens by which the individual's own physical and moral health were to be maintained, marriage developed from being seen as something that was primarily good for the polis to being seen as something that "refers more and more to universal principles of nature or reason, which everyone must observe in the same way, whatever their social status" (*CS*, p. 67).

Historically, then, this particular concept of the "self" as independent, autonomous, and responsible, including the arts of introspection, of seeking "the truth concerning what one is" (*CS*, p. 68), evolved out of the need to be *in proper relation with others* – at first in order to govern others well, to be a good ruler, or leader, or head of household; but later, and increasingly, in order to act appropriately in all one's social relations, whatever one's social status. The early Christian writers took over many of the arguments and precepts of the Greek and Roman thinkers in this regard, even though the ultimate aim in Christian teaching was more the preparation of the soul for eternity than the regulation and improvement of one's conduct toward others in the community.

The critical stance adopted by Foucault toward both humanist and Christian ethics has prompted a neo-humanist reaction, as we have seen, raising alarm that the concepts of self, personal agency, and even human rights may be endangered if this version of their historical development is adopted. I would argue, to the contrary, that where *The Care of the Self* goes beyond Mauss is precisely in the way it shows the danger of arguing that the category of the person reached ultimate perfection (its *telos*) at one historical juncture, such as the nineteenth century, the point where the category of the person fused with the post-Kantian category of the self. As Foucault pointed out in an interview given in 1982:

> Through these different practices . . . a certain idea or model of humanity was developed, and now this idea of man has become normative, self-evident, and is supposed to be universal. Humanism may not be universal but may be quite relative to a certain situation. . . . This does not mean that we have to get rid of what we call human rights or freedom, but we can't say that freedom or human rights has to be limited at certain frontiers.[13]

In the discourse of human rights, then, protection of the person cannot be made contingent on the continued association of the category of the person with a particular definition of the category of the self, no matter how valuable we might otherwise consider the latter to be.

Certainly, in Anglo-American literary studies, both Mauss and Foucault are often cited by scholars and theorists interested either in demystifying authorship or in the related endeavor of showing how certain "technologies of the self," such as journal-keeping, conversion narratives, confessions, autobiography, and travel writing, contributed to the development of a new understanding of subjectivity in the seventeenth, eighteenth, and early nineteenth centuries.[14] These studies, however, position themselves at the point where text (as material object), textuality (use of a text at a given historical juncture), and subject (individual consciousness at a moment of time) intersect. They are not dealing primarily with the category of the person as such, nor yet with the category of the "self," though their findings may well be relevant to the history of these concepts, since Western ideas of the self and the person were evidently shaped, and helped towards their modern realizations, by the kind of inwardness that such practices as journal-keeping produced.

Admittedly, theorists who wish to historicize the subject sometimes seem to threaten, by a kind of contamination, the stability of the concept of person, since in Western thought the person has been for so long associated with consciousness and self-consciousness. Studies such as Nussbaum's *The Autobiographical Subject*, which illuminates the development of this link from the early modern period up to the nineteenth century, have no doubt influenced such observations as Barry N. Olshen's: "The ancient and modern problem of personal identity has emerged in the postmodern age as a problem of textuality."[15] Olshen, like Bromwich and Taylor, distrusts the linguistic turn of much recent theory, lamenting that in poststructuralism "the self has too often become a mere representation, a textual signifier that is part of the unstable processes of signification" (*SPS*, p. 8). Yet he also admits the need for a three-way distinction such as that Francis Jacques makes, between "subject," "self," and "person."

Post-Kantian writers, from Coleridge and Thoreau to Virginia Woolf, tried to fuse self and subject into one, and even to blur the distinction between subject, or (conscious) mind, and persona.[16] Now that this practice has been to a large extent demystified, and the (textual) subject can no longer be simply identified with either the consciousness of the writer or her or his whole "identity," we may be in a better position to proceed forward from Mauss's defense of the category of the person, which is not necessarily to be identified with either "subject" or "self."

Despite the fears of Bromwich, Taylor, and other commentators, it seems clear that the universality of the category of the person as Mauss formulated it cannot be maintained. Postcolonial and poststructural criticism has made it necessary to ask, whenever history is appealed to in explanation, "whose history? history produced by whom and to serve what ends?" Poststructuralism rejects altogether the concept of the world-historical narrative, and not only permits but builds on "the right of formerly un- or mis-represented human groups to speak for and represent themselves in domains defined, politically and intellectually, as normally excluding them, usurping their signifying and representing functions, overriding their historical reality."[17] In discussion of the category of the person, non-Europeans constitute such an under-represented and mis-represented human group. For reasons such as these, the authority claimed for categories or forms of thought in modern philosophy is often a "contingent authority," that is, not a priori but qualified by the particular circumstances of the individual agent (*CCP*, p. 70). Further, the idea of the selfhood or *moi* – for Mauss, the matrix out of which the category of the person eventually emerged *as* a "category of the human mind" – has been decoupled from the teleology, the quasi-Hegelian developmental narrative which still haunts Mauss's account.

Mauss's later interpreters have tried to reground the category of the person on something less "Eurocentric" and less subject to ideological critique. Collins recommends as the basis for a renewed concept of person a version of the idea that biology necessitates one image of the individual, namely, the body, and socialization another – "that part of consciousness which is both moral or conscience . . . and . . . conceptual awareness" (*CCP*, p. 62). A given historical account of the category can then be seen as "an example of the way in which the general form of human experience described in the *homo duplex* view is given particular content" (*CCP*, p. 65). "Person," then, means a human being possessing both body and that "part of consciousness" which derives its moral nature and conceptual awareness from socialization: a neutral model which different kinds of socialization fill in differently. But Martin Hollis, dissenting from such a close association between the category of person and the processes of socialization, argues that "social forms can never shape human beings completely, because social forms owe their own shape to the fact that human beings are social agents with ideas about social forms." He warns that "social identity is not to be confused with social placement."[18] There has to be at least some breathing-room, an opening in the social structure, through which dissent and social change can make an appearance.

Hollis is surely right to try to preserve the idea of agency in the way he does. The experiences of totalitarianism and colonialism teach that, if the category of the person has any value at all, it is as an attempt to recognize somewhere the absolute wrongness of systematically destroying human beings in order to advance this or that model of society or this or that program for the perfection of someone else's historical narrative. The attempt to give this principle a measure of international recognition and suasive force is surely reflected in such documents as the United Nations' "Universal Declaration of Human Rights" (1948) Articles 3 and 6, and the related "International Covenant on Civil and Political Rights" (1976), Articles 2, 10, 14, 26. These articles use the term "person" in precisely this sense, as the concept fundamental to a minimum provision for recognizing and protecting human rights.

Yet even Hollis's careful defense of the concept of human agency still ends up having to appeal to a historical schema: the Maussian argument that human beings "have slowly been learning to express what has all along underlain their universal sense of self," which is, of course, something like Mauss's "category of the person," or the "idea of identity as what is expressed in relations with others" (*MM*, p. 232). The danger here is not so much that this schema is historical, but that it universalizes, invokes the kind of history that tends to make European thought once again the bringer of higher wisdom to the rest of the world. It makes it seem that European analysis and social evolution finally explain to the people of the "Third World" what was implicit all along in what they were thinking (*OR*, pp. 22–3). This presumption that Mauss did at least demonstrate the superiority of the European concept of personhood is obviously to be avoided if future discussion of the category of the person is to escape the imputation that it is a disguised kind of imperialism, and if it is to have global and not merely European or Euro-American relevance.

The worldwide renaissance of Indigenous cultures and the idea of tribal survivance (a term I borrow from Gerald Vizenor)[19] show that there are other ways of being and conceiving of a "person" than the largely atomistic, individualistic, and rational model derived from the Europe of the Enlightenment and nineteenth century. This is not to pretend that every society in the world can live in a cultural bubble protected from global influence. Many poststructuralists, and many of those who stress the community dimension in concepts of the person, reject European definitions of the person as inadequate (too atomistic and individualistic). Basing the concept of the person on the category of the relation, as Francis Jacques proposes, that is, reversing the usual order of reasoning about personal identity in the mainstream Western tradition, is a positive step, since relationality is obviously a category that really does correspond to something that every human being experiences in one form or another. One of Jacques' key points, in fact, is that too much emphasis has been placed on the dyad, I/Thou or self/other, and that a *three*-way relationship, I/Thou/He-She, is logically and linguistically present in the communicational act (*DS*, p. 41). This approach has the evident advantage of making language theory, and our sense of all the relations that are founded on language, less narcissistic and more inclusive. But clearly, other perceptions of the need to be in relationship and ways of being in relationship have to be admitted as having significance for the category of the person. Personhood, that is, must connote not only the right to (physical, individual) survival – the "predicament" of the human being – but the need and the right to be in relationship to the extent and in the manner that physical health, psychology, and socialization allow. This would include as persons the lone eccentric, the drifter and the recluse, as well as the dimension of community, sect, or tribal survivance where such is the pattern of the individual's life. It would have to extend, evidently, to the criminal and the sociopath: the concept of the person cannot be restricted just to those who fit easily into a society's image of itself, and indeed it rarely needs to be invoked except where some kind of social deviance is in question. Much can be learned from the feminists' advocacy of empathy, but the category of the person remains a necessary protection wherever empathy breaks down.

It would be wrong, too, to suggest that Indigenous ways of thinking about the person will be found to constitute one single, identifiable alternative to some uniform and hegemonic European way. The diversity of value systems, kinship patterns, childrearing practices, and psychosocial development, even among the Indigenous peoples of North America, is such that there is nothing to be gained by positing a uniform First Nations or Native American "concept of the person." This is implied in Mauss's own work and confirmed by the work of more recent scholars, both Indigenous and non-Indigenous.[20] The history of contact between Native Americans and Europeans also complicates the search for an originary or authentic Indigenous concept of the person (*AA*, p. 106). To take just two instances: Hallowell finds among the Ojibway of Lac du Flambeau, in Northern Wisconsin, a tradition of "self-reliance through direct supernatural aid," and writes of the "so-called 'social atomism'" of Ojibwa culture which has been breaking down under the influence of acculturation to "western" values (*AA*, p. 112). By contrast, Kathryn T. Molohon has found many features indicating very strong *kinship* values (as opposed both to individualistic and to community-oriented ones) among the Cree of Northern Ontario: "kinship is still the primary focus of identity and social organization."[21]

For reasons such as these, if future discussion of the category of the person is to avoid multiculturalist blandness, it must continue to be given fuller content, through the full admission of the histories of the subaltern and silenced. Edward Said has shown how the project in which he played a key role, the critique of "Orientalism," really involves "a plurality of audiences and constituencies . . . a plurality of terrains, multiple experiences and different constituencies, each with its admitted (as opposed to denied) interest, political desiderata, disciplinary goals" (*OR*, p. 25). The category of the person, as Mauss saw, can continue to exert authority only as a historicized entity and therefore only in a contingent manner. It needs to be not less historicized, but more fully historicized, and not according to a single, "Western" perspective but so as to represent the "plurality of audiences and constituencies."

PART TWO

SHADOWS OF FASCISM AND WESTERN CULTURE

INTRODUCTION

John Burt Foster Jr.

In charting the reorientation of subjectivity away from the all-knowing Cartesian subject, with its possible implications for a chauvinistic cultural politics, while emphasizing personhood as a bulwark against enforced homogeneity, Part One already drew some attention to the threat that Fascism posed for Western societies. Part Two will consider this issue in more detail, by revisiting the controversial topic of what the Fascist decades from the early 1920s to 1945 implied about the health of Western culture. Each essay in this part will treat this period from a different temporal perspective, moving from anticipation, to contemporaneity, and then to aftermath.

Within the academic study of philosophy and literature, the Heidegger and de Man cases of the 1980s probably meant the most in reviving interest about the impact of the Fascist past, though continued uneasiness about the Holocaust, as described below by James Berger, had more influence among the public. Before then, however, discussion of Fascism as symptomatic of a major crisis in the Western cultural heritage (rather than in its political or economic system) had long been dormant, after a phase of violent, and often highly partisan accusation during the thirties and forties. Art and thought, it was widely felt, existed on a higher plane than politics; and this attitude forestalled questions about the commitments of leading intellectuals before and during World War II. This prior reticence helps explain the widespread shock at the revelations about Heidegger and de Man.

Western culture as discussed by our three essayists has two meanings. In a narrower sense, it refers to "high culture," to those elite forms of artistic expression with special prestige in such institutions as universities, theatres, museums, or symphony orchestras – sites of "cultural capital," in Bourdieu's phrase. In this sense Mary Ann Witt's essay on Gabriele D'Annunzio's tragedy *Fedra* and Herman Rapaport's reflections on modern music anticipate Lars Engle's exploration, in Part Three, of how some Western classics fared in two novels written during the South African State of Emergency. But if Engle stresses how the deeper meanings of a true classic can be enhanced by such a test, Witt and Rapaport inquire into the ambivalences that Fascism revealed in the inherited monuments. They do not go so far, however, as to insist on collaboration or complicity. They are interested instead in what can metaphorically be called "shadows" of Fascism: the disquieting analogies or parallels that evoke this period in Western history, yet cannot be called the thing itself.

In pursuing this question, Witt and Rapaport take approaches which recall that of Thomas Mann in *Doctor Faustus* (1947). This novel, written with advice from Adorno, narrates the career of a German composer from 1900 to 1945, but contrary to many critics Mann does not simply equate the artist-hero with an infusion of the Nazi outlook into high culture. Rather, he asks readers to weigh the problematic meaning of the variable and uncertain relationship between his hero's music and the events around him.

A shadow suggests more than uncertainty, however; it can also mean an advance warning, as in "foreshadowing." This kind of premonitory significance informs Witt's essay on D'Annunzio's involvement with tragic drama in the decade before the Italian war over Libya in 1912, which was a key moment in the prehistory of Fascism. Noting the pendulum swings from political accusation to aesthetic neutrality in Italian scholarship on D'Annunzio, Witt develops Zeev Sternhell's thesis that a volatile "cultural Fascism" arose a generation before the political movement. As a result, disquieting analogies abound between high culture and politics without the "smoking gun" of a direct causal link. Most disturbing of all, even beyond the vexed issue of D'Annunzio's personal ties with Mussolini, is the role of tragic drama itself in this period before Fascism. Along with the epic, it has been the supreme classical genre; yet, in contrast to the reaffirmation of Shakespearean tragedy that Engle will find in Nadine Gordimer, Witt shows the tragic hero to be a possible model for the charismatic fascist leader.

In this particular case, however, there are significant counter-currents, beginning with D'Annunzio's fascination for a tragic *heroine* and his transsexual cult of feminine virility, both of which contradict the fascist cult for "real manhood." D'Annunzio's version of the Phaedra myth also stresses tensions between Thebes and Crete as polities, the one Apollinian and masculinist, the other Dionysian and mindful of the "Great Mother." And if Theseus suggests total commitment to imperial adventure, Hippolytus may embody doubts about Italy's readiness for such a role. Neither ambivalence, Witt concludes, fits easily with viewing the play as propaganda for Mussolini's dreams of Roman imperial revival and Italian grandeur.

Shadows in a literal sense are traces of nearby objects; and in this spirit of contemporaneity, Rapaport compares two famous conductors of Beethoven's *Fifth Symphony*, both closely linked with the fascist decades. Arturo Toscanini left Mussolini's Italy for the United States; while Wilhelm Furtwängler stayed in Germany despite his contempt for the Nazis and numbered Hitler among his admirers. In commenting on the uncertain, even paradoxical political bearings of their Beethoven performances, Rapaport grounds his remarks in a project of Derrida's, which interprets the situation of European culture through the metaphoric lens of the "heading." This translation of the French word *cap* (or "headland") can refer to the head, thus suggesting the intellect and culture; to a title or other summary label used to master a complex phenomenon; or (in Valéry's famous metaphor) to Europe itself as a peninsula of Asia. It can also evoke the need to steer a course when sailing near a cape, and in this context "heading" means a sense of direction or orientation. What strikes Rapaport in

Derrida's analysis is his emphasis on the simultaneous presence of several different directions or possibilities in European culture which, pushed to their limits, can come back together or "reunify," even with seeming oppositions.

This logic is obviously relevant to the latent fascism-in-democracy and democracy-in-fascism that Rapaport senses in the conductors' renditions of Beethoven; and it extends as well to the larger issue of "modern music." Despite its promise as a transnational European art (and music would seem better suited to such a role than literature), "modern music" in fact was often connected with national projects – with Fascism, of course, the supremely radical version of the latter. Thus Schönberg's vision of serial music as a new international style could coexist with his disciple Webern's enthusiasm for Hitler, in an incisive restatement of the ambiguous correlation of opposites in *Doctor Faustus*.

Alongside high culture artifacts like tragic drama or symphonic music, Western culture in these essays also covers something much larger, the basic narrative of Western history. Here is where Berger's analysis of Holocaust writings becomes relevant, for he ultimately treats this catastrophe with an eye to cultural meanings beyond its immediate contexts in Jewish, German, or even European history. When Berger closes by evoking the "still open wounds the Shoah has left on Western culture," his use of the Hebrew word for the Nazi "final solution" opens up a wider vista that includes the long, troubled history of Jewish life in the West – a counter-history indeed for Westerners to ponder.

The "shadows" of Fascism take on still another meaning in this essay, for in his concern with how people can even process an event like the Holocaust, much less reflect on its implications for the West, Berger focuses on traumatic aftermaths. Yet alongside the fixation on the past in Holocaust writing, which Berger interprets psychoanalytically as a compulsion to return and repeat, he also identifies a growing tendency to lose touch with that very past. This tendency can be analyzed as a Derridean process of dissemination; but rather than taking the Holocaust as the never-to-be-recovered origin, Berger assigns that role to the disappearance of direct witnesses, which started attracting attention in the late 1970s. Reviewing a wide range of mainly American writings since that date, he finds an uneasy theoretical synthesis of rhetoric, theology, and psychoanalysis (focusing in turn on the sublime, the sacred, and the traumatic), combined with a need to attach historically irrelevant material to Holocaust-related fictions. Yet none of this activity can compensate for the irremediable and steadily increasing belatedness of the writers.

For Berger, Cynthia Ozick's 1987 novel *The Messiah of Stockholm* has been the best attempt to diagnose this situation, but is itself another symptom. Ozick has been scornful both of thinkers who assign too much religious meaning to the Holocaust (and thus she can seem to be "writing back" to the theorists) and of fellow writers who exploit it in their fiction. This scorn clearly informs her novel, above all in its emphasis on both a false Messiah and a forged manuscript. Yet Berger's analysis of how the word "wild" acts as a linguistic shuttle point among sublime, sacred, and traumatic layers of meaning also shows that this book edges over into the same disseminating network as other Holocaust writings. Despite Ozick's forceful criticisms, therefore, she cannot avoid the consequences of living in the aftermath of the Holocaust. For Berger, however, the true aftermath to this culminating disaster of the Fascist decades did not begin with discovery of the camps in 1945. It began much later, with a dawning awareness in the late 1970s that the witnesses to those atrocious events would soon be gone.

3

AESTHETIC FASCISM AND MODERN TRAGEDY

D'ANNUNZIO'S *FEDRA*

Mary Ann Frese Witt

Any attempt to define Fascism seems notoriously doomed to failure. Its ideology was so protean – or so vacuous – that it incorporated the most divergent political, economic, cultural, and aesthetic tendencies, not to mention its various national incarnations. Indeed one inherent characteristic of Fascism seems to be its tendency to fuse and bind apparent opposites (one need only think of the origin of the word and the image of the *fasces*). Yet this heterogeneity does not mean that it is impossible to discern certain underlying characteristics – what Umberto Eco has called "Ur-fascism"[1] and Roger Griffin "Generic Fascism." Griffin offers "palingenetic ultranationalism" as an all-purpose definition of Fascism – a term that exemplifies in its two words the characteristic fusion of opposites. Stressing the decadence and degeneration of the present, fascist ideology attempts to create at once a nostalgic, organic nationalist myth of the past and a future-oriented myth of regeneration and rebirth – the latter a Nietzschean project postulating the apppearance of "a 'new man' embodying the qualities of the redeemed nation."[2] The fusion of mythical past with utopian future, a characteristic also emphasized by Eco, tends to shun the present, historical time, and becoming, for a sense of timelessness, or circular/mythical time.

Such a broad definition is of course not all-inclusive but does reveal a certain core of the movement and significantly points to its deep *cultural*, rather than merely political appeal. On one level, it could be argued that Fascism was not a political movement in the usual sense of the term at all. Mussolini confided to Emil Ludwig that "Everything depends on dominating the mass like an artist," and that his ambition was to make a dramatic masterpiece of his own life,[3] while he reserved the term "politician" for democrats or socialists. Fascism's presentation of itself as an art – and particularly a theatrical sort of art – helps to explain its appeal to artists, writers, and intellectuals. Italian Fascism, especially in its early stages, had an investment in "high" literary and artistic culture as well as in popular culture, and sometimes in their fusion.

The argument that Fascism existed as a culture *before* it became political, that is around the turn of the century, has been made most recently by Zeev Sternhell. Sternhell differentiates Italian and French Fascism from German Nazism, finding that the former two have common origins in *fin de siècle* trends that began in France but were shared in Italy through the notion of a common "Latin" bond. The matrix of this early fascist culture was a complex of pro-imperialist, aestheticist, reactionary, irrationalist, and syndicalist-revolutionary thinking. More specifically, in Sternhell's view, Fascism stemmed from a fusion of the apparently clashing doctrines of the reactionary nationalism of thinkers such as Charles Maurras and the revolutionary syndicalism led by Georges Sorel. What these two poles had in common was a revulsion against the enlightenment and nineteenth-century "bourgeois" values already decried by Nietzsche: universalism, individualism, progress, natural rights, equality, parliamentary democracy, and the like.

The relationship between this early Fascism and *fin de siècle* aestheticism is one that has been often mentioned but little developed. Walter Benjamin provocatively stated that the fascist aesthetization of politics is "the consummation of *l'art pour l'art*."[4] Does this mean that a political phenomenon can somehow evolve from a literary and artistic movement whose credo is based on the separation between art and "reality"? Benjamin seems to suggest that aestheticism and Fascism share formal, rather than ideological qualities in that the fascist manipulation of crowds, like the Art Work, is constructed so as to valorize spectacle and prohibit intersubjective communication.[5] Thus the concept of "aura" can apply to the mystical authority of the Leader as well as to the perfection of artistic form.

A work on aesthetics that would have a profound impact on early fascist cultural discourse was Nietzsche's *Birth of Tragedy*. The passage below from Edouard Berth, disciple of Sorel, reader of Nietzsche, and author of *Les Méfaits des intellectuels* (1914) is exemplary. Berth sees the rapprochement of the ideas of Maurras and Sorel (for Sternhell, the fusion that produced Fascism) as ushering in a new era. Wrapping his insight in the language of *The Birth of Tragedy*, he suggests that the new era will recuperate past greatness while obliterating what he defines elsewhere in the book as present "decadence."

> From the fraternal alliance of Dionysus and Apollo emerged the immortal Greek tragedy . . . Similarly, L'Action française – which with Maurras, is a new incarnation of the Apollonian spirit – through its collaboration with syndicalism – which, with Sorel, represents the Dionysian spirit – will be able to give birth to a new grand siècle, one of those historical achievements which afterward for a long time leave the world dazzled and fascinated.[6]

Berth further explains that syndicalist violence "calls for order, as the sublime calls for the beautiful; Apollo must complete the work of Dionysus."[7] Thus political discourse is aestheticized – or is aesthetic discourse politicized? In Berth's conflation of the two, it is sometimes difficult to know of which order he is speaking. The mythical and the heroic are necessary elements of Sorel's general strike, and the renaissance of tragedy Berth calls for will serve as a remedy against social as well as artistic decadence. Berth's aspiration is not for a new political system but for a transcendence of politics in culture. The language of Sorel and Maurras themselves, like the language of fascist theorists to come, reflects the same irrationalist desire for an aesthetic transcendence which will relegate the "political" to the sphere of inferior, rationalistic parliamentary democracies. Thus Sorel cultivates violence, energy, heroism, sacrifice, and "poetry" in the sphere of social action. Maurras, the traditionalist, appeals to a sense of classical "grandeur." Berth envisions the transcendant fusion of these two aesthetic approaches to politics through Nietzsche's understanding of tragedy.

The title of an earlier work by Mario Morasso, *L'Imperialismo artistico* (1903), is representative of the fusion of aesthetic with nationalist and imperialist discourse in Italy. Morasso sees a great age of imperialistic expansion dawning. As the Western powers prepare to conquer inferior peoples, democracy will be transformed into nationalism. The art of the coming era will move beyond both symbolism and the democratic, everyday, and inferior realism epitomized by Zola to return to a "grandiose realism" celebrating nature, the hero, the race, and the nation.[8] It is *tragedy* that will be the primary art form of the superior civilization to come. If classical tragedy represented the "magnificent duel between the hero . . . and fate" made possible by an aristocratic society (*IA*, p. 170), modern tragedy will have to create its own form of the classical agon by drawing on the energies of mass society for the invention of a hero who will cut through the "imbecilities" and false egalitarianism of parliamentary democracy with the will to combat fate in the form of imperial domination. The author most promising for the creation of the new tragedy is, for Morasso, Gabriele D'Annunzio, who had by then written only one play (*La Città morta*, *The Dead City*, 1896) in the new genre. If Italy, still under the weak parliamentary government of Giolitti, has not yet produced the strong leader capable of inspiring true tragic grandeur, Morasso is optimistic that a heroic and imperialistic society is in the process of being formed, and that D'Annunzio, along with others to come, will be its tragic poet.

If there is one figure who, in both his career and his literary production, typifies the fusion of aesthetics and politics at the turn of the century, it is indeed Gabriele D'Annunzio. Elected to parliament as "il deputato della bellezza" (the deputy of beauty) in 1897, the most famous act of the poet-politician was his walk from the extreme right of the chamber to the extreme left, a gesture explained by his earlier Nietzschean declaration, "I am beyond the *right* and the *left*, as beyond good and evil."[9] In a 1902 interview he would declare, "Art and politics have never been disassociated in my thought."[10] As important as theatrics were to his political life, it seems hardly coincidental that he composed his first "modern tragedy" shortly before his election. Determined to write tragedy for Italy and for the modern age after his reading of *The Birth of Tragedy*, D'Annunzio was also the first to introduce Nietzsche into Italian political and aesthetic discourse.

The first document in which D'Annunzio discusses his ideas on modern tragedy is an article entitled "La Rinascità della tragedia" ("The Rebirth of

Tragedy"), August, 1897. Enthused about the revival of outdoor theaters such as the Roman theater in Orange (in southern France), D'Annunzio explains that one of the major objectives of the modern tragic poet is to communicate to the crowd "the virile and heroic dreams which suddenly transfigure life." The new tragedy, in its recuperation of Dionysian "religious" energies for modernity, will become "a rite or a message." The function of the actor is to "incarnate on the stage the word of a Revealer" who will speak to a multitude "mute as if in a temple."[11]

The multitude enchanted by the Poet-Revealer suggests clear parallels with later crowds, enchanted into submission by the spectacle of the political orator. The ideal of a fusion of religious, political, dramatic, and poetic discourse through the rebirth of outdoor theater and modern tragedy is further developed by D'Annunzio in his novel *Il Fuoco* (*The Flame of Life*), begun in 1894 and published in 1899. In Venice, the hero Stelio Effrena, in his dual role as political orator and dramatic poet, hopes to "aestheticize" the crowd in both piazza and theater by transforming the decadent city into a site of a renascent nationalism while creating for Italy a modern tragedy equal to that of Wagner, though with more emphasis on the value of the Word. A major theme in the novel is that of "possession," whether of a "Dionysian woman" by the hero, a theatrical audience by the poet, or a crowd by the orator. D'Annunzio's own modern tragedies will all center to some extent on this fusion of political, aesthetic, and sexual possession.

Any suggestion of a link between D'Annunzio and Fascism today is bound to raise some strenuous objections, especially in Italy. In the early eighties, D'Annunzio criticism entered into a phase of re-evaluation which is still in full force. If critics of the postwar period tended to dismiss the "national bard" as a bombastic fascist whose language, along with his politics, were a disgrace to Italy, the D'Annunzian revisionists have brought out the considerable political and personal differences between il Commandante and il Duce, while rethinking the original and important contributions of the writer to European – not only Italian – poetry, theater, and fiction.[12] A representative article is that of Giovanni Antonucci, entitled "Political Language in the Theater of Gabriele D'Annunzio," but written to prove that there is no such thing and that D'Annunzio's theater is one of poetry, not politics; of myths, not ideology.[13] What is missing in this argument is any consideration that "poetry" and "politics" might not be mutually exclusive categories, or that aesthetics and ideology could be bound. Roughly speaking, there seems to be a tendency to swing the pendulum from a view of D'Annunzio as a bad writer and a fascist to D'Annunzio as a good or even great writer and (therefore?) a non- or even anti-fascist. While the eminent historian of Fascism, Renzo de Felice, has convincingly outlined the political differences between D'Annunzio and Mussolini, he concedes that il Duce inherited from the poet-politician a certain political *style*. Thus D'Annunzio anticipated the fascist approach to mass politics with rituals such as the speech from the balcony, the call and response dialogue, the mystical fusion of leader with crowd, the Roman salute, and the ritual cry – in other words a politics of *spectacle*.[14]

If we are to accept the argument that aesthetics were an integral part of fascist culture from its early beginnings, the question of style cannot be dismissed as merely superficial. We have seen that D'Annunzio's writings on modern tragedy, based on his reading of Nietzsche, intertwine aesthetic and political discourses somewhat in the manner of a theorist such as Edouard Berth. D'Annunzio's connection with the turn-of-the-century cultural movement that was to blossom as Fascism was indeed aesthetic, but this is exactly what makes him such an important bridge figure. His rewriting of the Phaedra myth into modern tragedy, incorporating the notions of "possession" discussed above, may be considered an example of what I will call his aesthetic Fascism.

Written in an archaic and precious language with heavy use of predecessors (Euripides, Seneca, Racine, and Swinburne) along with archeological references, particularly to recent excavations in Crete, and under the influence of Nietzsche, D'Annunzio's reworking of the classical myth in *Fedra* (1908) is in one sense an exquisite humanistic-scholastic exercise in intertextuality. Drawing on his recent travel to "the mythic motherland," Greece, along with his reading of *The Birth of Tragedy*, D'Annunzio self-consciously sought to create a "primitive," Cretan Phaedra modelled on her mother Pasiphae who, consumed with love for the Cretan bull, conceived the minotaur: a chaotic, "Dionysian" natural force. He had another interest in the myth as well. In a 1909 interview, he explained that his tragedy was also about Phaedra's father, "Minos, the first lord of the Mediterranean, the first of the Thalassocrats, the ancient founder of marine imperialism."[15] Written just after *La Nave* (*The Ship*), a play that can be considered D'Annunzio's hymn to Italian marine imperialism, and shortly before the Italian invasion of Libya in 1912, D'Annunzio's tragedy was conceived in a cultural climate afire with imperialistic fervor and the desire to possess the Mediterranean, *mare nostrum*.

Fedra is dedicated to D'Annunzio's mistress of the moment, Nathalie de Gouloubeff, whom he calls, significantly, "Thalassia." Like her predecessors, "Thalassia" serves the poet-creator as a Dionysian woman, or an erotic muse. The metaphor D'Annunzio used to describe her role in a December 1908 letter develops, however, a new variation. He writes (in French) of his decision to treat the myth of Phaedra thus: "I jumped on my prey with the speed of great predatory birds. Truly, I *possessed* Phaedra in the shade of the myrtle tree pierced by her gold pin. After Euripides, after Seneca, after Racine, I dare to produce a new Phaedra. You have given me the power to fertilize the worn-out womb."[16] The beloved-as-muse appears here as the bestower of power in the accomplishment of a kind of literary rape! The origins of the tragedy are thus formulated in terms of possession and a conflation of sexual-aesthetic-imperialistic possession will function in it significantly. *Fedra* is indeed a mythic drama in the D'Annunzian sense in that it transcends both linear time and history, transporting dramatic action to an agon of ritual and frenzy where events seem to emerge from the depths of time rather than actually to take place. The refuge in myth and poetry suggests not only a revolt against the linearity of bourgeois drama in the attempt to "re-fertilize the womb of ancient tragedy," but concurrently a flight from liberal-parliamentary "Italietta" – what the nationalists called the "little Italy" of Giolitti – into the emerging metahistorical vision of heroic-imperialist Italy.[17]

The epigraph to all three acts – *O thanate paien* (O healing death) – suggests the motivating force of the drama. Fedra's first words, after hearing the false rumor of Theseus's death, are "O Thanatos, light is in your eyes!" (*F*, p. 50). She seems at first to belong to the chorus of mourning women, but her strangeness manifests itself almost immediately. Whereas the other women uphold the laws of Athens and of the Olympic gods, the "Titaness" or "Minoan," as she is repeatedly called, exists without and beyond the rule of both Athens and Mount Olympus. Her being is dominated by the gods' curse as visited on her mother, rendered in a powerful image as she tells another woman, ". . . nor do you, fraught with horror, hear bellowing within you the monster brother" (*F*, p. 56).

The curse of Aphrodite becomes in D'Annunzio's version the source not only of Fedra's downfall but also of her "titanic" and "Dionysian" strength to revolt and defy. Fedra finds a model for herself in the tale of Evadne, the wife of Capaneus, the hero who defied the gods during the war against Thebes. For Fedra, Evadne's self-immolation on her husband's funeral pyre signifies a "titanic" triumph, a renunciation of service to the Olympian gods (*F*, p. 72) in a fusion of revolt, erotic desire, and healing death in the "beautiful flame" of the sacrificial act. This fusion will function importantly in the tragedy.

One of D'Annunzio's additions to the Phaedra myth is the character of a beautiful Theban slave named Ipponoe, a gift from the spoils of war for Hippolytus. Fedra's decision to sacrifice the virgin to Hecate is usually seen as a manifestation of her extreme jealousy, which of course it is, but it is more complex. Struck by a vision of Aphrodite, Fedra seizes her long hair pin (the one we heard about in Gabriele's letter to Nathalie), and "drunk with sacrilege" pierces leaf by leaf the myrtle tree sacred to the goddess. Frenzied both with the horror of the family curse and with pride as a Titan defying an Olympian, she is now prepared for the sacrifice. But the language with which she addresses her victim resembles more that of a lover than of a rival. "You are hidden in a thousand folds, like a flower closed with a thousand petals . . . Open yourself. Do not tremble. I will be gentle to you. . . . You are beautiful" (*F*, p. 87). In the language of the stage directions, the moment of sacrifice resembles a rape. "Under the cruel and devouring glare, the virgin grows stiff with terror . . . Burning with mad desire . . . is the daughter of Pasiphae" (*F*, p. 96).

This scene of the sacrifice of Ipponoe by Fedra becomes a veritable maelstrom of transexuality. Ipponoe's name foreshadows that of Hippolytus, Phaedra's stepson and the object of her uncontrollable lust in the tragedy from Euripides onward, as well as the horses with which he is traditionally associated. Suggesting some sort of masculine identity, Ipponoe describes herself as a young Spartan athlete. The pin with which Fedra pierces the tree of Aphrodite and (rapes?) kills the young girl might be seen as a manifestation of the "virile vulva" – a synecdoche for the masculinized female hero identified in D'Annunzio's political rhetoric by Barbara Spackman.[18] The term "virile vulva" actually comes from a novel by Carlo Emilio Gadda satirizing Fascism's tendency to carry virilization to the extreme; Spackman however applies it to D'Annunzio, who uses such terms as "heroic womb" for the Italian mother.

Fedra's scene with Ipponoe is in some ways a dress rehearsal for her scene with Hippolytus. The latter repeats the movement from eroticized sweetness to the frenzy of desired possession. Departing from her traditionally more reticent character, this Fedra violently declares the passion that consumes her, causing Hippolytus to see in her a panther preparing to leap on its prey (*F*, p. 159). In conformity with tradition, she begs Hippolytus to stab her, asking however not for *his* sword but for the sword of his mother, the Amazon Antiope. She then seems to assume for herself the role of the sacrificed virgin as she attributes *her* previous role as lover/rapist to Hippolytus: "Be gentle . . . Then pierce me with all your strength, treat me like prey" (*F*, p. 161). We have here not only the stereotypical lustful woman begging for male violence but also a complex intertextual weaving of a mythology of rape, possession, power, and trans-sexuality. Fedra's desire to be loved/killed by Hippolytus fuses with her desire to be avenged on Theseus, who raped her as a young girl. This desire for vengeance also represents solidarity with the Amazons who stormed the "masculine towers of Athens" (*F*, p. 167). While desiring Hippolytus as lover and son, she also desires the maternal phallus, the virile vulva, Antiope's sword.

From the point of view of Hippolytus and Theseus, the act of rape as the affirmation of virility is clearly fused with acts of imperial conquest. Unlike the chaste adolescent of antiquity, D'Annunzio's Hippolytus envisages his access to manhood as an identification with the father-as-rapist through a father-son expedition to abduct the young Helen of Troy – a re-enactment, in this play of eternal returns, of Theseus's abduction of the young Fedra. The expedition will at the same time initiate Hippolytus into conquest and power over the sea, thus fusing imperial with sexual possession. Attempting to dissuade him from this route to manhood, Fedra offers him the ships of Crete: like her father, the founder of maritime imperialism, Hippolytus can thus become a "Thalassocrat" (*F*, p. 130). Fedra's stepson rejects her offers of power as he rejects her desire, responding that he will accompany his father on an "enterprise of men" (*F*, p. 131). To accept Fedra would connote for him the subversion of paternal Athens and regression into the maternal labyrinth of Crete.

Within the context of this web of mythical rapes, Fedra's revenge – her accusation to Theseus that Hippolytus attempted to rape her – is tinged with more irony than in the classical and subsequent versions. The Hippolytus that she portrays to his father – "drunk with desire to rape" (*F*, p. 183) – is the very Hippolytus that Theseus would initiate into manhood in Troy. Preparing, like her model Evadne, to die next to the body of her beloved, Fedra avenges herself on her rapist husband and becomes the possessor of the Amazon's sword. Her triumph resides also in the subversion of the laws of Athens (also called the law of Cronus, the seemingly incontrovertible law of linear time). "My name is ineffable, like the name of one who subverts ancient laws to impose her own arcane law" (*F*, p. 205), she says.[19]

What are we to make of this tangle of eros, thanatos, and sacrifice; rape, imperial desire, eternal return, and subversion of time and law? It would be a facile distortion to label D'Annunzio as macho-rapist-imperialist or indeed to identify the rapist-imperialist Theseus as the hero of the play, which he clearly is not. The "Dionysian" figure, the force to be reckoned with here, is Fedra – "unforgettable Fedra" as she is called in the closing line of each act. The domain of the feminine – Crete, the primitive land of the "Great Mother," the labyrinth, and unconscious, unbridled lust – is indeed in D'Annunzio's view "unforgettable"; that is, we "forget" that domain at our peril if we rely solely on Apollonian-Athenian masculine linearity, law, and obedience to the gods. The desirability of subverting abstract, rationalistic laws for the creation of new laws was also a commonplace of the irrationalist rhetoric of the early twentieth century, as it continued to be in later fascist ideology.

Although the Dionysian figure of Fedra undoubtedly dominates the stage, as well as the text, the tragic hero is in a sense Hippolytus. One way of reading his tragedy is as a society's failure to realize in its young hero an ideal, transcendent fusion of Apollo and Dionysus, modernity and myth, traditional and arcane/irrational law, clarity and desire, the realms of the father and of the mother. Hippolytus's tragedy might also be read as the tragedy of a nation not yet ready to accomplish the feats of heroic imperialism envisaged by a Mario Morasso. If Theseus's raping and plundering suggest modern "virile" imperialistic warfare, the legendary Minoan "thalassocrats" might be associated with mother Italy's deep-rooted claim to *mare nostrum*. Here too it is a fusion of maternal and paternal, as well as of mythical past and dynamic future that is envisaged, and lost. Hippolytus "forgets" at his peril what his stepmother offers.

There is another sense in which Fedra is "unforgettable" and in which she is "possessed." This has to do with a character that I have not yet mentioned but whose role is crucial to the binding and fusing operations in the play: that is the messenger turned bard, Eurito (another D'Annunzian invention). It is he who recounts the death of Hippolytus to Theseus, serving Fedra's revenge. If the Minoan queen is unforgettable, it is because Eurito will, as they both acknowledge, give her "an eternal robe" through his poetry. He is the poet, too, of the eternal return: "What was, woman, will return," are his words to Fedra. Her sacrifice acquires power and meaning only through the poet's iteration. D'Annunzio, it would seem, has "possessed" his Fedra by inscribing himself into the figure of the bard. The poet alone has the capacity to transform primitive energies into the forms and words with which to inflame and possess the masses. Just as Nathalie's erotic energy gave Gabriele the power to "fertilize the worn out womb," so Fedra's triumphant sacrifice to Aphrodite becomes an "eternal return" (as opposed to a linear narrative) through the bard's transposition of it into language.

Part of D'Annunzio's disillusion with the actual fascist regime in Italy seems to stem from the fact that it failed to incorporate into its ideology and ritual his own emphasis on "Dionysian," feminine, and even transsexual erotics, tending instead toward a simplistic *maschilismo* or exaltation of virility. Nor can it be argued that the complexities of D'Annunzio's dramatic style had anything to do with a later simple-minded fascist theater of propaganda. Yet not only did D'Annunzio's modern tragedies and other plays enjoy revivals to great acclaim throughout the regime; "il vate" – the national bard – was touted as "the soul of fascism." While these sorts of epithets undoubtedly distorted D'Annunzio's later political position, his contribution to early twentieth-century "aesthetic fascism" is a real one. In *Fedra* we can already perceive something of an aesthetic rendering of the definitions of Fascism outlined at the beginning of this essay.

Just as fascist ideology, as in the *fasces*, fuses and binds organic myths of the past with regenerative myths of the future, so D'Annunzio recuperates the Phaedra myth for an imperialist vision. As in the culture of Fascism, D'Annunzio's modern tragedy, exemplified by *Fedra*, retreats from the present, or the historical time of realist drama, for a representation of mythical timelessness, or eternal return. D'Annunzio's binding and fusing techniques effect a transcendence, in aesthetic terms, of binary poles such as male and female, classical and modern, archaic and historical, Apollonian and Dionysian. The enchanting discourse of the poet like that of the orator, as Stelio discovers in *Il Fuoco*, and as D'Annunzio himself and later Mussolini will put into practice, mystically binds the creator of the Word to the crowd, whether in the theater or the piazza.

The final objective of "possession" in *Fedra*, although it is portrayed primarily in its erotic form, is the possession of the crowd through the Word – also a kind of erotic possession. The locus of power in D'Annunzio's modern tragedy lies finally with none of the mythological characters but with the Poet whose verses will render Phaedra "unforgettable" and in whom D'Annunzio inscribes himself. When *Fedra* was revived in an outdoor production amidst the ruins of the Roman forum in October of 1922, on the eve of the march on Rome, one reviewer spoke of the "perfect fusion between stage and audience that seemed to transform the spectacle into a rite, a celebration."[20] The performance must have achieved something of the same mesmerizing effect on the crowd as the march: the creation of that "aura" that Benjamin saw as common to Art and fascist politics. In this respect, at least, *il vate* preceded *il duce*.

4

OF MUSICAL HEADINGS

TOSCANINI'S AND FURTWÄNGLER'S *FIFTH SYMPHONIES*, 1939–54

Herman Rapaport

Since the late 1980s, Derrida has written books that are torsos or fragments of studies that he could have written had he world enough and time. *De l'esprit*, for example, reads like an abridged text with a number of missing sections, some already written and published elsewhere, and some that may be supplied in the future. Focusing on Heidegger's deployment and non-deployment of the term *Geist* in his philosophical writings, *De l'esprit*'s footnote apparatus suggests numerous junctures at which Derrida already has or will branch off into closely related and lengthy analyses. Indeed, these supplementary sections have the status of Derrida's "faux bond" or "no show" in *Glas* and appear to have been suppressed, as if there were a limit or governor that was restricting the amount of text that Derrida is permitted to deliver (cf. the logic of the limit in "Limited Inc."). There are numerous connections, for example, with Derrida's previous book, *Psyché*, that seem to be purposely held back; an interlocution with Helvétius's book, *De l'esprit* (1764) that can only be suggested before being broken off; a sidelong glance at Husserl's "Philosophy and the Crisis of European Humanity" whose development has to be severely truncated; a lengthy examination of Heidegger's writings on Hölderlin that fails to take place; a very suggestive examination of Nazism that is only sketched out in the barest outlines; the leaving to one side of arguments made elsewhere on *Geschlecht* that are of central importance to Derrida's project; and so on. What becomes evident in Derrida's subsequent thinking about the Paul de Man affair, is that, to some extent, it also brings something to bear on *De l'esprit*, namely, the dynamics of what it means for a thinker who collaborated with Nazism to be at war or in conflict with himself. In Heidegger that has been declared in terms of his struggle with Spirit, a crucial struggle whose relevance only Derrida has perceived with immense acuity and sensitivity.[1]

Some years after *De l'esprit*'s publication, Derrida again supplies what seem to be some missing pages from *De l'esprit* in the form of an amplified discussion of Paul Valéry's interwar writings on European culture and spirit, writings Derrida mentions in a lengthy footnote to chapter seven of *De l'esprit*. *L'autre cap* is the title that Derrida gave to this installment of his *esprit* project. And it could be read as a text that hinges two headings, a fascist one alluded to in *De l'esprit* and a communist one that pertains to Marx in the book Derrida entitled *Spectres de Marx*. As it turns out, I'm less interested right now in the specificity of Derrida's particular political headings than in the point, which I made in my book, *Heidegger and Derrida*, that Derrida is often headed in opposite directions at once.[2] In the English translation of *L'autre cap*, Pascale Anne Brault and Michael Nass decided to translate the title as "The Other Heading." It may be a felicitous equivalent for the very reason that it isn't as loaded a phrase as Derrida's, something that helps us focus on the question of what it means to not only head in a particular direction but to allow oneself to come under a heading of some sort.[3]

Since my topic is music, what concerns me in particular are the headings of what we might call classical music in our own century. This is a complex issue because it concerns not only musical styles but their interrelation with questions of national, ethnic, and cultural identity that are mediated by historical events. Of course, to begin talking about this in its broader terms, one would have to consider the history of modern music within the politics of nationhood during the earlier part of our century, say, in terms of Igor Stravinsky's anthropological interests that motivated the composition of *Le sacre du printemps*, Béla Bartok's ethnographic observations that led to the composition of works like the *Two Rhapsodies for Violin and Orchestra*, or the vernacular and national imagination that informs Charles Ives' *Symphony of Holidays*. In all these compositions one notices that a number of different headings or directions are taken at once and that they are by no means all *avant garde*. Theodor Adorno puts this rather succinctly when he says that music is a universal language without being an Esperanto. That is, despite all its universalist pretensions, modern music is still nationalist in scope since its development occurred within national boundaries. Indeed, what typifies the organization of such music is that its national characteristics are precisely realized *as* universalism.[4] To this discussion belongs the question of how contemporary music has tried to speak to society as if it were in a meaningful dialogue with public values and attitudes within and across national boundaries.

It is no secret, of course, that the general public reception of modern music has been quite hostile from the outset and that by the 1950s contemporary composers affiliated with groups like the Darmstadt School were extremely marginalized. A major question that has dogged contemporary composers of all sorts is whether music has been headed in the wrong direction. It's a question that entirely shaped the early reception of Stravinsky and that caused many major composers to despair of the idea that they might ever be seriously listened to. Public apprehension during the late 1950s of rock and roll as well as the so-called death of jazz that followed from the "free jazz" movement of the mid 1960s are significant parallels in that, once again, the fate of musical art forms is countersigned by public doubt concerning the question of headings.

To provide just a bit of recent evidence that this is still quite a significant issue, I quote from a recent interview with minimalist composer, John Adams. Question: "*Do you think Western contemporary art music has gone off the rails?*" Adams replies: "No, I don't think it has gone off the rails. I think that, starting with Schoenberg, it was an experiment basically in atomization of the elements to see if music could be organized by other principles than it had been since recorded history began." However, Adams continues by contradicting himself. "I don't see that these organizational principles developed by Schoenberg, Cage, and Babbitt are really the beginning of a huge new millennium in music. I see them more as a specialized, individual thing. There's a very interesting book by an American theorist, Fred Leodol, called *Toward a Generative Grammar of Tonal Music*. That had a lot of influence on me."[5] Adams goes on to argue that Leodol is right in suggesting that a tonal grammar is natural and intuitive for the human psyche, whereas atonal grammar is counter-intuitive and alien to human apperception. Whereas Adams takes pains to relativize the various languages of music, "what's fundamentally important is that composers write the music that means something to themselves," he is really saying something quite different, namely, that music did go off on a tangent when it turned to serialism and that even the most simple musical language of Tonic, Subdominant, and Dominant chords is a much needed correction to the experiments of the Vienna and Darmstadt Schools. Although I can't go into this at any length, let me just interject that the word "experimental" raises a red flag, since it is a term near and dear to very conservative and even right wing critics who had once used the word experimental as a means for keeping atonal music in the quarantine of a laboratory or controlled space – in short, out of the concert hall and therefore away from the public sphere.

John Adams would probably feel comfortable with that. In response to a question concerning how he relates to European art music, he replies:

> I'm not very interested in Western art music right now. I don't listen to any contemporary music. I find it unbelievably boring, though that doesn't mean I feel that what other composers are doing is not important. It just doesn't interest me. What I listen to almost all the time now is music from other cultures. I'm very interested in Arabic, African, and Indian music and lots of different musics from the Americas. I've always been that way. I grew up in a family where there was lots of music in the house, recorded music, performed music, chamber music . . . The nice thing about the family was that there was never a distinction made between what was important music and what wasn't important music – it was just music. After years of college and sophistication, I'm trying to rediscover that sense of innocence I had as a child where, as long as something had an intensity of feeling and a thoroughness of execution, it didn't matter where it was from or for whom it was written. (*NV*, pp. 8–9)

Leaving aside the attempt to appear politically correct in an age when bashing high culture is everyone's pastime, Adams implicitly raises the issue of what Derrida in *L'autre cap* calls reunification, the attempt to transcend nationality in the names of internationalism, cosmopolitanism, and globalization. In a text I downloaded from the Internet's Derrida Web Site – entitled "Of the Humanities and the Philosophical Discipline (1994)" – Derrida argues that Eurocentrism and anti-colonialism are both symptoms of a colonial and missionary culture.[6] That is, Eurocentrism and anti-colonialism are two headings under which what is called the "right to philosophy" comes to pass. Apparently, the right to philosophy is a license to philosophize whose authority is grounded in a notion of responsibility that draws from the unifying dialectic of the contrary headings, Eurocentrism/anti-colonialism. Elsewhere in this lecture addressed to UNESCO – Derrida views UNESCO as a site of globalization with its own tradition of philosophical aspirations, among them, the responsibility and hence right to philosophize – we are told that Eurocentrism and anti-colonialism are to be thought of as two "hegemonic references" whose constitutions or rights are always already intra-European. To compress a bit, Derrida is of the opinion that the headings, Eurocentric/anti-colonial, are not thinkable within a dialectical or oppositional relationship but, rather, within a non-finite distribution or field of idiomatic displacements and conjunctions – reductively put, a disseminative rhetoric – that can't be regulated, any longer, by terms such as identity, law, ecology, subjectivity, or the international. Yet, in embarking on a very different sort of heading, Derrida also specifies that one cannot dissociate the right-to-philosophy from a cosmopolitical point of view in which the motif or philosopheme of a "democracy to come" is inscribed. It's here that *L'autre cap*'s thinking on reunification has been extended somewhat, though already in *L'autre cap* it is apparent that Derrida is asking questions about how Europe is composed as a cosmopolitical space that is always capable of thinking its other at the limit of an infinite questioning that a priori has appeared to have exhausted itself in the name of a democracy to come.

To recall John Adams's remarks, one might say in this context that various idioms of twentieth-century music have been eager to think their other at the limit of an infinite theoretical questioning that appears to have exhausted itself in the name of a democracy to come. Of course, Adams's reluctance to listen to Western art music while dwelling on "musics from the Americas" is hardly a rupture with Eurocentricism. It's hardly an other heading, because his return to innocence and the bosom of a family in which no distinction was made between important and unimportant music is, clearly, a symptom of what Derrida calls a "democracy to come," a horizon of reunification under which what we could call the "right to make art" is re-legitimized.

Of course, Arnold Schoenberg, whose atonal compositions have met with such resistance throughout the twentieth century, was actually operating under a similar assumption, namely, that serialism could triumph as a new international style that would transcend national and ethnic boundaries. Obviously, Schoenberg's identity as a Jew discouraged him from promoting some of the national and ethnic agendas whose religious foundations were rooted in Catholicism. In fact, the tension between Stravinsky and Schoenberg is concentrated in a fundamental rift over nationalism/internationalism, Stravinsky being for Schoenberg a poseur (Schoenberg nicknamed him Igor Modernsky) who superficially manipulates musical styles in a pseudo-modern fashion for the sake of upholding conservative nationalist (Russian, French, American) and religious (Catholic) social orders by means of going back to some artistic arche that has no real social relevance to the bourgeoisie. This is Adorno's complaint, as well, in his *Philosophy of Modern Music* where Stravinsky is attacked for writing works like *Les Noces* in which the marriage rite of a pre-industrial society is statically organized according to a progress of harmonic suspensions that refuse development and condemn the singers and dancers to represent a world without psychological or individual meaning – all under the auspices of achieving an authenticity of human existence lost in the modern era.[7] In contrast, Schoenberg's *Erwartung* would be exemplary of a work that sets Freudian psychology to music in order to restore a lonely subjectivity to musical representations of madness that is not socially recoverable as ritual or parable.

Although Schoenberg's *Moses und Aron*, *Survivor of Warsaw*, and *Hebrew Psalms* are exemplary of a Jewish response to the cultural headings and constitutedness of Europe, these, like his musical practices, exceed the limit of European thinking about its own identity or heading. This, of course, is what made Schoenberg attractive after 1945 to young composers in Germany who had repudiated Nazism, though, interestingly enough, like Stravinsky himself, they worshipped at the altar of Anton Webern who, it now turns out, was a very enthusiastic supporter of Hitler and even of ethnic cleansing in Europe, something he reveals in letters during the early years of the war. Here, of course, one is tempted to think about how at the limit of European musical thought, Schoenberg's other heading wasn't as *other* as one might imagine. That is, the other or Jewish heading was already being politically contradicted or divided up by his most important student, Webern, whose letters to Schoenberg during the Nazi period contained in their return address the words Gross-Deutschland.

* * *

Adams' interview, to return to it a last time, raises the inevitable question that was raised many times during the 1940s of whether one had to depart from Europe in order to direct Europe back to itself in a responsible way, something that brings me to another complex of relations that is, in fact, of major interest: the headings of two conductors, Arturo Toscanini and Wilhelm Furtwängler.

Recall that in the thirties and forties Arturo Toscanini and Wilhelm Furtwängler were trying to steer a course for Europe. And therein lies a tale, because both Toscanini and Furtwängler were conducting their orchestras under very different headings that were not only geographical, but aesthetic and political as well. Two conductors, two headings, two careers, two allegiances. As we'll see somewhat later, it's the story of two reunifications, ever the same, ever different. According to a certain Derridean logic one has to ask how divergent the headings of these two conductors really were. For example, what kind of beach-head was Beethoven for Toscanini? Was it an American beach-head, assaulted by Toscanini with the NBC Orchestra, or was it really a European one? To compress, wasn't the Beethoven of Toscanini always a Beethoven of what we might call *l'autre cap*? the *other* heading? – that "other" heading always being the heading other than the one we are led to think it is.

Analogously think of Furtwängler who is, clearly, the more problematic. Let's ask of him, too, where his Beethoven was headed? or under whose or what heading it took place? This is a nasty question because, as we know, at some point the heading or *cap*(ital) for this Beethoven goes under the name of not only Berlin, but, even more specifically, the Nazi high command, and, even more specifically than that, of the Führer whose personal interest in and liking for Furtwängler's performances insured that Furtwängler could exist in the very nation whose government he unabashedly despised even to the point of saying in public at one concert in Vienna, his hand pointing to the Nazi flags draped around the hall, that until those rags are removed there will be no music. Under what insignia or heading was Furtwängler's Beethoven taking place that evening? What course for Germany was Furtwängler setting when he decided to remain in Germany but not play his Beethoven to Hitler's tune, a refusal that only made Hitler adore Furtwängler's music all the more? Was Hitler, too, under the sway of what Derrida calls *l'autre cap*? Of an other heading for Germany than the one for which Hitler had set course? Is this thinkable, never mind possible?

Derrida reminds us that in French "cap" refers to an aim or end. "It here assigns to navigation the pole, the end, the telos of an oriented, calculated, deliberate, voluntary, ordered movement: ordered most often by the *man* in charge. Not by a woman, for in general, and especially in wartime, it is a man who decides on the heading, from the advanced point that he himself is, the prow, at the head of the ship or plane that he pilots." There are those others, however, who would pilot us in a different direction than that of the captain who is in the director's role. Not only would there be a heading of the other, Derrida says, but the other of the heading – "a relation of identity with the other that no longer obeys the form, the sign, or the logic of the heading, nor even of the anti-heading – of beheading, of decapitation."[8] Is it to this heading that Furtwängler was headed? Did he even take elements of the Nazi high command with him? which is to say, to the "other" of their heading, or to the place or direction where they were precisely not headed? Was it for this that Furtwängler stayed in Germany, refused the other heading of people like Toscanini . . . for the sake of a gamble? to steer Europe clear of a cataclysmic shipwreck? The remarks of Furtwängler and of his defenders after the war, Yehudi Menuhin among them, suggested as much.[9]

Again, let's compress. Essentially what's on my mind are the idioms through which both Toscanini and Furtwängler enter into a logic of the other heading. My exhibits for discussing this are four performances of Beethoven's *Fifth Symphony*. The first is conducted by Toscanini in 1939 with the NBC Symphony Orchestra, the second is conducted by Furtwängler in 1943 in Berlin at a gala concert where high-ranking Nazi officials were present, the third is conducted by Toscanini in 1951 with the NBC orchestra and the fourth is conducted by Furtwängler in 1954 with the Vienna Symphony.[10] None of these performances would matter if they hadn't been fateful for performance practices in the second half of our century, or, for what we have come to know as the proper idioms for representing Beethoven in a cosmo-political context.

First let's talk about Toscanini. There must have been a reason why he allowed his music to become associated with a sound studio acoustic that was about as dead as sound can get. The only answer I can imagine is that this necessarily belonged to a kind of truth in art mentality whereby Toscanini wanted to demystify music by stripping away what people like John Adams now call its "sound envelope." To ears unaccustomed to these recordings, Beethoven sounds like he's being played by an unusually gifted high school orchestra in the local band room. This gives Toscanini's Beethoven an extremely perfunctory quality, something that is intensified by the rapidity of some of the tempos. The speed and dryness of these performances also has the effect of making Beethoven sound more like Verdi or Rossini than Beethoven. What clinches that association for me is the fact that Toscanini's recorded performances stress the operatic idiom of the tutti that suggests a strongly unified choral tone indicative of what, in the Derrida context, I'd call the "democracy to come."[11] In addition, if you listen closely to the 1951 recording, it's clear that Toscanini stood Beethoven down from an epic scope to something more like an intimate conversational or essayistic interplay that gives the *Fifth Symphony* a rhetorical rather than a rhapsodic sensibility. Toscanini not only strips the notes of their sound envelopes, but he forces the phrases to behave like sentences or propositions that, as in Puccini, are cast into a dialogue.

The Furtwängler recordings head in a very different direction. I would say that especially in the 1943 recording one encounters not just an intoxicating rhapsodic performance that quickly takes control over the emotions, but a poetic understanding of the alterity of Beethoven's phrases, even to the point that they begin to suggest the major poetry of Friedrich Hölderlin, in that for Furtwängler it is the unfinished or fragmentary nature of Beethoven's phrases and their inability to fully come into dialogue with one another that pre-occupies the overall conception of how Beethoven is to be musically rendered. In the Furtwängler performances you could say that *Umnachtung* plays a certain role that it never could in the straightjacketed performances of Toscanini. That is, in distinction from Toscanini's attempts to rationalize and domesticate Beethoven for an American audience that is, a priori, positioned at an analytical distance from the music as a rhetorical ensemble of relationships, Furtwängler's Beethoven has all the disturbing and dark qualities we associate with Hölderlin and Trakl – not the least of which are their irrational and mercurial shifts of mood. There is also, in the 1943 performance, a prolongation of musical fermatas that have the effect of a total wringing out of emotion, as if one's psyche had undergone a profound catharsis whose aftereffect is a feeling of total submission to the work. Furtwängler's Beethoven is not an artistic work to which one listens at a distance, but a work that takes over one's consciousness by storm. Once one submits to this performance, I think it is hard to accept any other. Worse, I am afraid that submission to Furtwängler's performance amounts to some sort of conversion to Fascism in the sense that one has to accept the conditions of the work's performance as at least propitious. That, if I may be permitted the aside, is what is at issue in the admiration of Heidegger's philosophy as well. One has to take the bathwater with the baby.

Not surprisingly, distinguished Furtwängler fans like Henry Fogel are overtly open about the trepidation with which they encounter these wartime performances. Like many afficionados, Fogel, who manages the Chicago Symphony Orchestra, argues that it is the 1950s recordings by Furtwängler that are recommended for new listeners since their balance and good judgment are to be prized.[12] The earlier recordings are dangerous because they lay claim to one's soul. John Ardoin, who has written an exhaustive study of all of Furtwängler's recorded perfomances, suggests that at no time in his career had Furtwängler been as audacious and aggressive an interpreter of Beethoven as during the war years, something that had quite a bit to do with the mental state of the Berlin Symphony whose membership had been purged of all Jews.[13] Unquestionably, one has to be troubled by the fact that it is the Berlin performance of 1943 that is clearly superior to the rather prosaic Toscanini if not to Furtwängler's own performances on EMI after the war. Even if you conclude it is the fruit of evil, rarely has a performance been recorded that so profoundly reveals Beethoven's disturbed and titanic genius. What is entirely inimical is Furtwängler's correct intuition that in Beethoven there is no unifying tempo for any of the movements but that each of the phrases exists in a temporality unique to itself. In other words, there is no unified musical heading, but a non-finite proliferation of multiple temporal idioms that the conductor conducts as just so many hegemonic references. It's precisely in this acknowledgment of another temporality, never before disclosed in the history of musical conducting, that Furtwängler crosses the limit line of the mercurial or the merely mad for the sake of encountering what Derrida calls the right-to-philosophy, a heading other than the heading in which we thought we were being directed. It is in this new heading that Furtwängler anticipates an entelechy that is very reminiscent of Derrida's advent of democracy in that the particular is not at all simply submerged in the general. It is here, furthermore, that ironically the most tainted great musical performances in human history bear out Adorno's criteria for greatness in modern music: the refusal of the individual unit to meld into the general context while finding an inevitable niche there all the same.

In comparison, Toscanini, whose music is the fruit of good, appears to be much more confining and dictatorial. His music refuses the kind of atomization and alterity that would allow for a proliferation of hegemonic references. If Toscanini has a philosophy, it is one of regimenting and of ranking, a philosophy of bringing phrases and audiences in line with a work whose truth is the occurrence of a conversation or debate that could take place anywhere among anyone. It is in that regimentation of music as a kind of cultural and political "tutti" that the arrival of a democratic moment can be glimpsed. For Toscanini, however, this heading can only be reached if Beethoven is de-transcendentalized or cut down to size. The excesses of the particulars must never be allowed to escape the grasp of a generality or mediocrity that restricts and contains. For those of you who would like definitive proof of this tendency, listen to the long-withheld recording of Toscanini's 1949 performance of Gershwin's *An American in Paris* where any hint of swing has been carefully suppressed, a suppression that in the past has led to accusations of a decidedly unAmerican agenda on Toscanini's part. It would be here, no doubt, that the race question can once again be raised on the shore of another heading.

Although more elaboration is warranted, it is already not hard to see that the question of musical headings would be interesting to pursue from the standpoint of the right to make art in terms of a cosmo-political context. As a brief coda to this, I will end with a curiosity that relates to Toscanini. You may have already wondered if Toscanini was, indeed, quite as poor a philosopher as I have made him out to be. In fact, Toscanini shares a Heideggerian insight about art reminiscent of a famous sentence from "The Origin of the Work of Art." "Beethoven's quartets lie in the storerooms of the publishing house like potatoes in a cellar." That "all works have [a] thingly character" (of course, this is not all Heidegger has to say on the matter) was, very much, the philosophical heading under which Toscanini and his followers have been conducting music. What Toscanini hated, above all, was the metaphysical heading of music – the idea that the music is "something else over and above the thingly element."[14] Here we should be aware of the metaphysical/anti-metaphysical headings under which Furtwängler and Toscanini found themselves, something that would change their performances greatly in relation to how we would estimate them. When Heidegger tells us that "The art work is, to be sure, a thing that is made, but it says something other than the mere thing itself . . . The work makes public something other than itself; it manifests something other; it is an allegory" (*OWA*, p. 20), he is raising an issue that Toscanini wanted to demystify, the notion that the work must manifest itself as something *other* – that it manifest itself as having an *other heading* or course than the internal headings of the musical phrases. Provided we can imagine Toscanini playing a certain Heideggerian kind of Beethoven, a Beethoven as earthy as a dry sack of potatoes in the root-cellar, but by no means representative of one, we would then have to start asking questions about whether Toscanini and Furtwängler were actually headed in such different philosophical directions after all, since the hegemonic philosophical point of reference would be a slice of *German* philosophy that would bring the two conductors under somewhat of the same aesthetic heading.

Yet, hasn't an *Entgleisung* occurred? Hasn't something gone off the rails? Isn't Beethoven being headed in the wrong direction by the NBC Orchestra? Haven't we gotten our musical coordinates all wrong? Is this the sort of reunification we were bargaining for? Does it call the right to make music into question? Even if we're still in the bosom of Eurocentrism, does this divisibility and overlapping of musical headings not point towards a deconstruction of a Eurocentric horizon – perhaps even the Eurocentric itself – that would exceed the unifying determinations of, say, the dialectical stability of Eurocentric versus the post-colonial? Judging from current performance practices, the division or différance of merely an other, German heading has not even been entirely worked through yet, given that we have not yet taken into account a young violinist by the name of Anne Sophie Mutter. But that's another story under the heading of a ravishing beauty that will have to be taken up elsewhere.

5

HOLOCAUST TESTIMONY AND POST-HOLOCAUST FICTION

CYNTHIA OZICK'S *THE MESSIAH OF STOCKHOLM*

James Berger

My argument starts from the observation that the "boom" (roughly since the late 1970s) in Holocaust fiction, film, theory, and memorials has coincided with the aging and deaths of the generation of survivors whose testimonial accounts have provided so much of our knowledge and moral understanding of the Shoah. The enormous value we have placed on the testimonies of these witnesses has led to a crisis in Holocaust representation as these witnesses have disappeared. The proliferation of highly problematic novels and films about the Holocaust illustrates our contemporary condition in which the traumatic impact of the Shoah still is felt, but the event itself has been lost to personal memory and exists today only as a set of texts. Holocaust representations after the end of testimony try to figure ways in which one can bear witness to texts.

TESTIMONY AND THE HOLOCAUST

Testimony has always occupied a privileged place in Holocaust writing. Just after the war, the legal testimony of survivors helped to prosecute Nazi war criminals; indeed, the very fact of living voices emerging from the genocide indicated a resistance to, and a victory over, the murderers. Gradually, testimony took on an even deeper significance, seeming to provide the principal access to this most inaccessible event. The testimony of the survivor acquired several distinct but related forms of authority. It took on an epistemological authority, for the survivor saw, knew, and said what no one else could see and know. This authority based on first hand knowledge conferred an ethical authority, for the survivor's knowledge was a knowledge of the most radical transgression of moral boundaries. And this ethical authority easily blended into a spiritual authority as the Shoah came to be seen as an ultimate or limit case of modern evil. Finally, testimony acquired an aesthetic authority as well.

Even fictional representations of the Holocaust have seemed compelled to invoke the authority of the witness and often to assume the testimony's generic form.

The authority that underwrites these others is ontological. The eyewitness was *there*, was present at the event, went through the event. And we take from this ontological primacy of the witness an assumption of a transparency in his testimony. The survivor was present, and his testimony seems to make us present, and thereby gives back to us, the listeners and readers, something of the epistemological, ethical, and spiritual authority we had previously ascribed to the survivor.

This direct transmission of the presence and experience of the witness/survivor is complicated by the question of what exactly the survivor went through. What the survivor witnessed, or suffered – and the word "martyr" comes from the Greek word for witness – was the event of mass death. And yet, the survivor did not die. This fact may seem obvious and scarcely relevant – of course the survivor didn't die; otherwise he or she wouldn't be a survivor and would not be giving testimony. The observation that the survivor did not die in the genocide might even seem insidious, akin to the Holocaust denier Robert Faurisson's objection that no living person has seen the inside of a gas chamber.[1] But, since we are considering not the empirical question of whether the genocide took place, but rather the question of the witness's moral and spiritual authority, the issue of the survivor's status as living and not dead becomes important, for these forms of authority come from the proximity to the genocide. Survivors themselves have testified to this anxiety. As Primo Levi insists in *The Drowned and the Saved*,

> . . . we, the survivors, are not the true witnesses . . . those who saw the Gorgon have not returned to tell about it or have returned mute, but they are . . . the complete witnesses, the ones whose deposition would have a general significance.[2]

The only true witnesses, then, are the dead, and survivors attempt to speak *for* the dead. More crucial to a rhetoric of testimony, however, survivors attempt to speak *as* the dead. The survivor as living-dead, as returned from collective death, is the crucial trope of Elie Wiesel's testimonial novel *Night*. First, near the beginning of the novel, Moche the Beadle returns to Wiesel's village in order, as he says, "to tell you the story of my death." And as the novel ends, Wiesel, now himself a survivor, repeats this verbal gesture. Looking into a mirror for the first time since his deportation, Wiesel writes, "a corpse gazed back at me. The look in his eyes, as they stared into mine, has never left me."[3] It is, presumably, this "corpse," the one who has seen the "Gorgon," who composes the testimony published under Wiesel's name. Wiesel presents himself as indelibly marked by the genocide and transformed into a pure vessel of testimony; no longer possessing a life, only a voice. The authority of testimony rests on the supposition of a symbolic death, as the witness passes through the Holocaust and emerges as his own ghost. An important corollary of this supposition is that the testimony of the living-dead witness provides face-to-face, unmediated access to what we, in the post-Auschwitz world, figure as the most radical, inconceivable alterity.

Critical and theoretical considerations of Holocaust testimony have largely shared this sense of testimony's authority as direct transmission of the Shoah, as imprint of mass death and absolute alterity. Indeed, recent discussions of Holocaust testimony often resemble the theological accounts of testimony given by Paul Ricoeur and Emmanuel Levinas.[4] As in Levinas, testimony of the Shoah is the voice of the Other which cannot be thematized, which calls as an ethical imperative. And Holocaust testimony is seen, as Ricoeur describes testimony in general, as a witnessing of the absolute as it appears historically. Levinas and Ricoeur, of course, are writing about testimony to divinity, while commentaries on Holocaust testimony are concerned with the witnessing of an ultimate evil; and yet the terms are largely the same. Discussions of Holocaust testimony, often against their own intentions, slide toward theology. For Terrence Des Pres, Holocaust testimony transmits the experiences of those

> who return from the grave . . . pass through Hell. The concentration camps have done what art always does: they have brought us face to face with archetypes . . . they have given visible embodiment to man's spiritual universe . . .[5]

Lawrence Langer also emphasizes testimony's potential for providing face-to-face immediacy. He criticizes written memoirs as inevitably retaining the mediating devices of literary style and genre, then praises oral testimony as direct because non-literary and spontaneous. For Langer, oral testimony's discontinuities and incoherences represent "the quintessence of the experiences they record."[6] Listening to the oral testimony of a survivor, Langer writes, "we are present at the birth of a self made permanently provisional as a result of fragmentary excavations that never coalesce into a single, recognizable monument to the past" (*HT*, p. 161). Langer shows how even inadvertent shifts in verb tense bear witness to the survivor's living death. " 'Because I was sure I am dead now' " (*HT*, p. 190), he quotes one survivor. Testimony, then, for Langer is a direct, only barely mediated transmission of the experience of self-shattering into an analogously shattered language.

Robert Brinkley and Steven Youra use Charles Peirce's concept of the semiotic index to show how the Shoah can be transmitted directly into testimonial language. The index, in Peirce's semiology, is a direct trace or imprint of an event: lightning is the index of particular atmospheric conditions; a bullet hole is the index of the bullet's passage. Using Claude Lanzmann's *Shoah* as an example, Brinkley and Youra argue that verbal testimony can take on a similar indexical status. Witnessing, they argue, "works not by representing but by referring, not through interpretive substitution but by pointing out."[7] Thus the testimony as index has a referential force "that exists prior to any interpretive response" and its meaning is produced not by interpretation but "by the event that produced it" (*TS*, p. 121). The testimony, in effect, is the event. The witnesses do not "merely recall the past but participate in it again," and the film's audience "is made contiguous to the events" (*TS*, p. 122). Brinkley and Youra claim that *Shoah*'s status as indexical testimony is made possible by Lanzmann's rigorous empiricism, his refusal to place interpretation over fact. I would argue, however, that, like Wiesel, Des Pres, and Langer, their view of testimony as direct transmission of the inconceivable event is ultimately more theological than empirical. It is fitting that they end their essay with a reference to Emmanuel Levinas's account of an ethical obligation to the call of the other, a call which Levinas terms an "epiphany." The encounter with the other, as Levinas describes it, must be an encounter with the "face," which is to say, a direct encounter, unmediated by one's own conceptual framework. Testimony as index, for Brinkley and Youra, is the Levinasian voice of the other.

Dori Laub and Shoshana Felman criticize the sacralizing of the Holocaust and its witnesses, but they too reinstate a theological perspective within their psychoanalytic descriptions. Felman argues that Claude Lanzmann's *Shoah* "is the story of the liberation of testimony through its desacralization; the story of the decanonization of the Holocaust for the sake of its previously impossible historicization." The specificity of Lanzmann's questions, she writes, "resists, above all, any possible canonization of the experience of the Holocaust."[8] At the same time, however, Felman uses Levinasian terminology of the "other" and the "face." The paradoxical task of testimony is to speak

> *from inside the very language of the Other*: to speak from within the Other's tongue insofar precisely as the *tongue of the Other* is by definition the very tongue *we* do not speak, the tongue that, by its very nature and position, one by definition *does not understand*. To testify from inside Otherness is thus to bear witness from inside the living pathos of a tongue which nonetheless is bound to be heard as mere noise.
>
> (*TCW*, p. 231, Felman's emphasis)

This position "inside Otherness" is, once again, as for Wiesel and Levi, the position of the dead:

> [S]pokesmen for the dead, living voices of returning witnesses that have seen their own death – and the death of their own people – face to face, address us in the film both from inside life and from beyond the grave and carry on, with the aloneness of the testifying voice, the mission of singing from within the burning. (*TCW*, p. 280)

Summing up this essentially theological description of testimony, Felman refers to Lanzmann's description of *Shoah* as "an incarnation, a resurrection" (*TCW*, p. 214).

James Young has provided the most thorough critique of the epistemological and theological bases of testimony. Young presents a poststructuralist analysis of testimony that relies largely on Derrida's description of "dissemination"; the idea that any written text, once produced, can never return to its origin and thus cannot retain the authority that such a connection with its origin would imply. Testimony, Young argues, cannot constitute an exception.

> Once he withdraws from his words, the writer has in effect also withdrawn from the word's evidentiary authority, the only link it ever had to its object in the world. The writer's absence thus becomes the absence of authority for the word itself, making it nothing more than a signifier that gestures back toward the writer and his experiences, but that is now only a gesture, a fugitive report.[9]

Young rejects any sense of an indexical relation between event and testimony. The witness, Young writes, would like "to show somehow that [his] words are material fragments of experience" and that he is a "walking trace" of events, but this is an "impossible task" (*WRH*, p. 23).

Young's argument, however, takes a crucial turn away from a strict post-structuralist critique, and Young tries from another angle to complete this "impossible task" of linking word to event. The link between the experience of the Shoah and the survivor's testimony is lost irretrievably; and testimony's empirical status as evidence can never absolutely be maintained; therefore, for Young (following Hayden White), the testimonial text (like any historical narrative) is more a construction than an accurate representation of events. Nevertheless, in almost a Cartesian move, Young argues that testimony does at least give evidence of "the writing act itself," evidence that a particular person in a particular situation produced these words. The witness exists not because she experienced certain events, but because she bears witness. Thus, Young continues, "even if narrative cannot document events, or constitute perfect *fact*uality, it can document the *act*uality of writer and text" (*WRH*, p. 37, Young's emphasis).

Young's emphasis on the act of testimony is a move toward re-establishing its ontological authority. Testimony is still important because the writer was *there*, even if "there" may now be defined as the scene of writing or testifying rather than the scene of genocide. Young has thereby reversed one step of the process of textual dissemination, bringing the text back to at least an intermediate origin. But, by implication, he must take the next step as well. Although of some theoretical importance in resituating the "author" banished by post-structuralism, the witness's being "there" at the moment of composing testimony is only relevant to a discussion of the Holocaust if the witness was also "there" at the event itself. Young recognizes this need when he observes that the key difference between fiction and non-fiction representations of the Shoah "may not be between degrees of actual evidential authority, but between the ontological sources of this sense of authority" (*WRH*, p. 61). Finally, it would seem that the second part of Young's argument reverses the first part: the witness's original presence at the scene of genocide gives authority to his testimony even in the witness's absence.[10]

HOLOCAUST FICTION, TRAUMA, AND THE TESTIMONIAL TEXT

Given this massive, almost supernatural or prophetic authority of Holocaust testimony, what can we do now that the generation of witnesses is aging and dying? The reliance on testimony and witnessing that are no longer possible has, since the late 1970s, brought on a crisis in representation of the Shoah. There has been an enormous proliferation of Holocaust representations since this time, and this proliferation, both in sheer number and in variety of forms, is evidence of the cultural anxiety in the face of the loss of the link to the event provided by the witness. Some of these representations have the clear intention of preserving the testimonial link – the various video testimony projects; and, in a different way, the attempts to preserve memory in public memorials and monuments (as James Young describes in *The Texture of Memory*).[11]

In fiction and film, however, the products have been far more problematic. Few of the better known Holocaust novels and films since the late 1970s have not been highly controversial: *Sophie's Choice*, *Portage to San Cristobal of A.H.*, *The White Hotel*, *The Ghost Writer*, *Maus*, *Time's Arrow*, *Europa Europa*, and so on. Alvin Rosenfeld and Saul Friedländer, in particular, have condemned many of these works.[12] Their criticisms have largely centered on how such works blur the historical and ethical significance of the Shoah, and combine accounts of the Shoah with autobiographical, aesthetic, comic, and erotic intentions that are distracting and misleading. While sharing their concerns, I believe it is more useful to read these problematic works in relation to the anxiety over the growing impossibility of direct testimony.

These controversial contemporary novels and films attempt to represent not the events of the Shoah itself, but our contemporary relation to those events. And our relation is not to the events, but to the textual testimonies to the events. There is certainly no shortage of documentation of the Shoah – of historical records and of textual and video testimonies. Recent Holocaust representations, I would argue, are still bearing witness – and in these works, the primacy of testimony and witness is still acknowledged – but they are now bearing witness not to events, but to texts. And this is a historical moment when a Derridean account of "dissemination" becomes relevant. James Young described all written testimony in terms of dissemination, arguing for every text's immediate separation from its original significance. What has actually occurred in our culture, however, is that this strictly linguistic sense of dissemination did not take place. Survivors and their testimonies, as I have described, retained their privileged status. The process of dissemination only began with the disappearance of the witnesses, with the physical and biological separation of the texts from their authors. Only at this point were we left with nothing but text, with no necessary connection to event or to meaning. And at this point, in the late 1970s, the proliferation of forms of Holocaust representation began.

The more controversial fictional responses to the Shoah of the past twenty years have adopted two related strategies. The first has been an appropriation of a Holocaust narrative to personal or political concerns. In *Sophie's Choice*, for instance, the autobiographical protagonist and narrator links his exploration of the Holocaust to his personal struggles with his heritage in the racist south; the Holocaust becomes part of Stingo's *Bildungsroman*. George Steiner's *Portage to San Cristobal* shows this process of appropriation on a broader scale, as all the characters in that novel construct their own Hitlers, their own Shoah narratives, according to their various personalities, histories, and political stakes. The most distinctive, most controversial, and, to me, the most brilliant feature of *Portage* is that Steiner has not exempted himself, as author, from the process of appropriation. The Hitler who finally speaks at the end of the novel is a Steinerian Hitler who delivers a distorted version of Steiner's own interpretation of the Shoah.[13]

It is not an adequate response simply to condemn these narratives for *using* the Holocaust and incorporating it into other stories. Certainly, the phenomenon is troubling. To ensure a properly contextualized historical understanding of the Shoah itself, we must sever its narratives from extraneous contemporary concerns. What do Styron's problems as a southern writer or Steiner's as a European philosopher have to do with our understanding the Nazi genocide? Nevertheless, for a better understanding of our own history and culture in the wake of the Shoah, these accounts of appropriation are crucial. They show, above all, that the Shoah is the principal event that our culture lives *after*,[14] and they show specifically how the transmitted memories of the genocide inform our thoughts and actions forty and fifty years later – after all, or almost all, the victims, survivors, perpetrators, and bystanders are dead, and only their texts remain.

The second strategy seen in these controversial fictions is an emphasis on the fictional text's relation to a testimonial text. Even in many of the most bizarre and problematic recent fictions, the testimonial text remains central. Thus, Zuckerman's fantasies in *The Ghost Writer* emanate from his reading of Anne Frank's diaries. The extraordinary combinations of aesthetics, psychoanalysis, and eroticism in *The White Hotel* are both generated from and negated by a testimonial text inserted in the novel. In Emily Prager's *Eve's Tattoo*, the protagonist inscribes on herself that most indexical of Holocaust texts, the concentration camp tattoo. Both David Grossman's *See Under: Love* and Cynthia Ozick's *The Messiah of Stockholm* use the figure of Bruno Schulz as a murdered witness survived only by his symptomatic, obliquely testimonial stories. These emphases and inclusions of the testimonial text in contemporary fiction after the end of testimony accurately portray a more general condition. The ontological, epistemological, moral, and even aesthetic authority of witnessing remains after the possibility of witnessing is gone. The urge, the need, to testify to the events of the Shoah remain; but these events now exist not even in personal memory, but only through the encounter with texts, particularly the texts of testimony.[15]

I would argue, then, that the bizarre and problematic post-testimonial holocaust fictions we are discussing are themselves forms of testimony: they bear witness to the continuing impact of Holocaust testimony in the form that it now exists, as text. (The influence of video testimony can be seen in the endings of the films *Europa Europa* and *Schindler's List*, when the survivors who have been the subjects [played by actors] of these highly stylized narratives appear as themselves, in effect, to verify, validate, authorize the films that have used their stories.) These post-testimonial fictions show the opposing forces that tear writing away from its experiential and historical sources and simultaneously bring writing back to these sources.

Dissemination and appropriation are words for tendencies or forces that separate writing from events and authors, and that relocate writing in other contexts. They are tendencies toward proliferation, implying an infinite production of forms and perspectives. But these processes, as I have described, are only half the story. What then brings Holocaust writing consistently back to the testimonial text, which is to say, back to the closest possible approach to the event itself? Or, to put it differently, what motivates the repetition and return of the testimonial text into post-testimonial fiction?

The terms I have used – repetition and return – give the answer away: I am referring to trauma. I propose that the presence of the testimonial text in Holocaust representations that otherwise use the most varied, ingenious, and bizarre literary forms shows the insistent return of the traumatic historical presence of the Shoah. Recall that the witness, whether living or dead, speaks as a kind of ghost, as the one who passed through, or closest to, death; who carries death on him like a symptomatic mark and who relates his testimony in language we take, or wish, to be connected indexically to the experiences it describes. The ghost itself is as much a symptom of past wounds as it is a speaking emissary. Like the return of trauma, the ghost is propelled from one time into another; its presence is a sign of some traumatic disorder in the past, some crime that has not been witnessed or put right – and is therefore a sign also that the present still suffers from that traumatic disorder. Trauma is what returns, and it returns as symptom, which is itself a re-enactment of trauma. The existence of the symptom, like the presence of the ghost, is a sign that the trauma is still active, still has power to wound and disrupt.[16]

But how can the traumatic symptom appear as text? In the Lacanian view of trauma that informs most current thinking (at least among literary scholars), trauma is associated with the Real, and is outside and resistant to any symbolic expression. Trauma's initial effect is to disrupt understanding, language, identity – to rip apart the symbolic order, to efface memory. The traumatic event is always reconstructed in retrospect; when it occurs it is only a silent or screaming gap, wound, or void. Testimony, as Felman and Laub describe it, is at least in part an attempt to remember and tell the traumatic event and thereby work through it. But testimony is also partly the refusal to work through; it is a remembering of the trauma that seeks to eternize its traumatic impact. Recall Wiesel's powerful repetitions in *Night* of phrases beginning with "Never shall I forget . . ." which conclude, "Never shall I forget these things, even if I am condemned to live as long as God Himself. Never."[17] This litany is no working-through; it attempts to transmit trauma untransformed, in as close an approximation to the original wound as language can convey.[18]

Symptoms, as Freud described them, are somatic, and Freud contrasted the somatic symptom, the unconscious acting out, against the verbal, and therapeutic, remembering and working-through. But language, obviously, can act out as well, can compulsively repeat, can haunt future uses of language. Language, like the body or the psyche, can be wounded and can wound. A text can be traumatized and can transmit trauma. A text can disrupt the symbolic order in which it appears, and can force readers to restructure that order in light of the traumatic disruption.[19]

But is a traumatic return as a text that bears witness to trauma the same as the first-hand experience? Obviously not. To bear traumatic witness to a testimonial text is not the same as to have been there at the event. It is something, but it is not the same. It is all we have, and it is not enough. To read the testimony of the witness compels further testimony.[20] The contemporary writer is affected by the trauma transmitted through the testimonial text, but in his own place and manner. He is less traumatized than the original witness. It may be that literary ingenuity comes to substitute for the ghostly presence: literary ingenuity and the literal return of the ghostly text.

Such, at least, is the wish and the need of works like *The White Hotel*, *Maus*, *The Messiah of Stockholm*. And here lies the tension of Holocaust writing after the end of testimony. The act of writing is separated from the ontological authority of witnessing. The text that bears witness to text tends toward infinite proliferation at the same time as it is shattered, transfixed, and reordered by the trauma transmitted by the testimonial text. This textual trauma, moreover, retains some of the original traumatic unreadability. It remains, in Lacanian terms, linked to the Real; that is, it shatters the symbolic order, the forms of understanding, in which it appears. The traumatic real is incommensurable with narrative and representation, and therefore the traumatic text may be confused with some other discourse of the incommensurable – as a form of the sublime or of the sacred. These three discourses of the incommensurable – the traumatic, the sublime, and the sacred – tend to merge. A traumatic discourse may be represented in terms of the sublime (as a shattering aesthetic experience), and then interpreted as sacred. I believe this process underlies much recent theorizing about Holocaust testimony, as well as recent Holocaust fiction.[21]

FORGERIES AND FALSE MESSIAHS

Cynthia Ozick's 1987 novel *The Messiah of Stockholm*[22] shows brilliantly the problematic status of Holocaust testimony at a time when it can exist only as text. Testimony becomes the creation of texts in response to texts. And these new texts, these testimonies to testimonies, inevitably spin into countless directions, as the traumatic impact of the Holocaust merges with the private concerns of individuals, their own obsessions, their artistic ambitions. Ozick's protagonist, an orphaned Swede named Lars Andemening, invents an identity as the son of a Holocaust victim, the Polish-Jewish writer Bruno Schulz, and thus invests himself with the moral authority of the dead and with the genius of a seemingly prophetic writer. Lars's greatest obsession is with Schulz's *missing* text, entitled *The Messiah*, the novel his adopted "father" was working on when he was shot. If he could find this text, his identification – both moral and aesthetic – with his "father" would be complete. The missing text, precisely because of its absence, becomes more than a text: it is the experience itself, forever unavailable and yet continually appropriated. It is the book, I believe, that every post-testimonial Holocaust fiction in some way attempts to be. It is always entitled *The Messiah*, and if found – as it is, later in Ozick's novel – it is always a forgery.

Lars is obsessed with origins. Heidi Eklund, the bookseller who is the only person to whom Lars confides his secret identity as Bruno Schulz's "son," calls him "a priest of the original" (*MS*, p. 99). Lars learns to read Schulz in the original Polish, as if in this way he will make direct contact with what his "father" saw and knew. And although this transmission from the past is, and can only be, textual, Lars imagines a contact that would be direct and immediate. In his sleep, he sees through Schulz's "murdered eye," joining Schulz as witness. Lars wakes from this merging as from death. Ozick writes, "He had no dreams. Afterward his lids clicked open like a marionette's and he *saw*" (*MS*, p. 8). What Lars sees through Schulz's eye, however, is not the Shoah, not the murder of the Polish-Jewish writer by the SS, but rather the literary aftershocks of the Holocaust. On waking, he writes inspired book reviews of novels by Eastern European writers following in Schulz's difficult legacy.

Lars is caught in a contradiction. He desires a direct transmission from the Holocaust – direct in terms both of biology and of experience. And yet, even in his nocturnal experience of the eye, the transmission is textual. Lars's vision is a vision conveyed through his intimate, obsessive understanding of Schulz's fiction. Schulz's stories, of course, are not exactly testimony. And yet, like Kafka's fiction, in retrospect we interpret these stories as a prophetic witnessing to a world about to disintegrate into horror. Schulz, the author as Holocaust victim, becomes for Lars the ultimate source of authority. Schulz's text becomes sacred. Immersion in that text (and Ozick describes Lars's experience as he writes his visionary reviews as "a crisis of inundation," *MS*, p. 8) is a direct contact with the inconceivable alterity of the Shoah. Or rather, it is and it is not. For what Lars's experience with Schulz's text and Schulz's imagined eye inspires is a desire for the real and ultimate text that can transmit the reality of the Holocaust as no existing text can do. Lars wishes for a text that somehow would *be* the experience of witnessing, that would truly, directly, physically testify.

That text, the missing text, would give all the answers. If found, that text would be the messiah. Ozick's narrator and her characters continually use religious terms when referring to the purported manuscript of Schulz's lost novel. "There on the table lay the scattered Messiah . . . resurrected; redeemed" (*MS*, p. 104). When Adela (a young woman who astonishes Lars by claiming to be his sister, Bruno Schulz's daughter, and, as proof, actually produces what she says is the lost manuscript) shakes the bag that contains the supposed manuscript, they hear "the sound of fifty wings" (*MS*, p. 71). Heidi uses the language of origin, of essence, and of witnessing, calling the manuscript "the original. The thing itself. I saw it with my own eyes" (*MS*, p. 53).

Ozick, in her essays and interviews, has always been critical of all forms of idolatry, and especially the idolatry of literature. (And Lars is said to have "thrown himself on the altar of literature," *MS*, p. 7.) This manuscript of a messiah, so overloaded with redemptive imagery, seems clearly to be false, a forgery. Indeed, the plot that Ozick invents for the manuscript is about the destruction of idols. Her "Messiah" can be read as a cautionary tale against false messiahs and fetishized texts, especially those that claim to provide some communion with victims of the Shoah. As Ozick said in a 1993 interview, "if a {Holocaust] novel must be written, let it be written by a true witness."[23] There is no murdered eye we have access to, no messianic text to be discovered.

The Messiah of Stockholm as a whole, however, suggests more complicated relations between text and event. In Lars's relationship with Heidi Eklund, there is a recurring dispute. While Lars is obsessed with Schulz's textual legacy (and with his own status as Schulz's only true son and authentic reader), Heidi rejects what she calls his "ceremonial mystification" (*MS*, p. 33) and turns their conversations always back to the "catastrophe of fact" (*MS*, p. 32). As opposed to Lars's quotation from Schulz that "reality is thin as paper," Heidi counters, "what's real is real" (*MS*, p. 37), and "death's reliable" (*MS*, p. 42). Heidi claims not to like or understand Schulz's writing at all, describing it as full of "animism, sacrifice, mortification, repugnance! Everything abnormal, everything wild" (*MS*, p. 33). This last adjective, "wild," however, sets off resonances in the novel, for Schulz's murder was part of a larger massacre, labeled by the Gestapo the "wild action" (*MS*, p. 38).

Heidi wants to move away from text toward fact, but her language connects that fatal, wild, action to the incomprehensible, wild, text. Somehow, the wildness of violence and of immediacy – which resist textualization – enter the text, and this linkage based on the word "wild" becomes the central connection in the novel. Ozick emphasizes the link, or thread, between *fact* and *text*: "Whatever they touched on, Heidi rattled her links – everything belonged to the shooting. Everything was connected to the shooting." But a paragraph later, Lars complains, "You get me off the track. You make me lose the thread." Heidi replies, "The thread? The thread? What's this thread? What's this track?" And Lars answers, "My father's books. His sentences" (*MS*, p. 39). For Heidi, the significant connection is to Schulz's murder; for Lars, it is to Schulz's texts. For Ozick's novel, it is both. The text contains and transmits the wildness of the event. And, I will argue, the psychoanalytic term for the "wildness" is trauma.

This wildness, this trauma, however, is misapprehended by Lars, who feels it most acutely, as something sacred: "the *wilderness* of God" that he receives through his imagined father's eye (*MS*, p. 69, my emphasis). Ozick shows here, and later in her brilliant imagining of Schulz's missing *Messiah*, how the sublime, the divine, and the traumatic – those three versions of the inconceivable, the unrepresentable, and the shattering – can be conflated. The trauma of witnessing, now separate from the witness, receives an aesthetic representation that tries to recuperate and transmit its power, and the sublime representation is interpreted finally in theological, salvational terms.

The lost manuscript of *The Messiah*, miraculously revealed by Adela, confirms all these linkages between literary language and the "catastrophe of fact," and between the sublime, the divine, and the traumatic. It consists, Ozick writes, of

> intricately hedged byways of a language so incised, so *bleeding* – a touch could set off a hundred slicing blades – that it could catch a traveller

> anywhere along the way with this knife or that prong. Lars did not resist or hide; he let his flesh rip. Nothing detained him, nothing slowed him down. The terrible speed of his hunger, chewing through hook and blade, tongue and voice, of the true *Messiah*! (*MS*, p. 105, Ozick's emphasis)

The manuscript is a symptom – a physical manifestation of past injury – and is also itself a continuing trauma. It is both wounded and wounding, not only representing catastrophe but also transmitting it.

Within the manuscript, the figure of the messiah itself has qualities both of a somatic organism and a text. "It was as if a fundamental internal member had set out to live on its own in the great world – a spleen, say, or a pancreas, or a bowel, or a brain" (*MS*, p. 109). And yet, "more than anything else, the Messiah . . . resembled a book." It is, as Lars reads it, "the authentic Book, the holy original, however degraded and humiliated at present." The messiah's body is inscribed with "peculiar tattoos" which resemble cuneiform, and which compose an "unreadable text," "an unknown alphabet" (*MS*, p. 110). Lars had previously noted that the mixed-up pages of the manuscript could be read in any order, that they resembled "the mountain ranges growing out of the chasm of the world," and that in them he experienced "everything voluminously overlapping, everything simultaneous and multiform" (*MS*, p. 106). This would seem to be a description of an aesthetic sublime. Later, again like an experience of trauma, the manuscript wipes out the memory of itself, and yet Lars feels certain that the vision of the manuscript must have originated in the same murdered eye that inspired his literary texts (*MS*, p. 115).

The Messiah as Ozick presents it through Lars's perceptions is the ultimate and original text of the lost witness: a text that is more than a text, immediate and unreadable, presenting and transmitting its wounds as if from body to body; it is sublime, an aesthetic object with the overwhelming power of a force of nature; and it is sacred and redemptive – it is the Messiah. In showing Lars's response to the would-be messianic text of Bruno Schulz, Ozick shows our own contemporary response to the loss of the generation of witnesses. As the "originals" disappear, we feel increasingly the need to create the text – the missing text – that will place us at the Shoah, that will be the "eye" of the Holocaust and allow us also to witness with the witnesses. And thereby, Ozick suggests, we conflate catastrophe with redemption, with aesthetics as the means that allows this conflation.

Is then the text a forgery and a false messiah? Obviously it is the latter. The text itself makes that clear. The creaking, messianic, organic, textual contraption, having destroyed the idols of the town of Drohobycz (where Schulz lived, and the locale of all his stories), collapses and gives birth to a bird which completes the destruction. The text contains no redemption, only destruction. The messiah is by definition a false messiah. There is no other kind. And certainly no messiah has come from out of the Shoah.

But the question of the status of the manuscript as forgery is trickier. Lars quickly concludes that Dr. Eklund (Heidi's mysterious husband, possibly Adela's real father) composed the manuscript. But Dr. Eklund, Heidi, and

Adela, though admitted con artists, maintain to the end that the manuscript is authentic. "*I* could make that? I, I?" Dr. Eklund protests.

> A seraph made it! Idiocy – *I* could make that? Instinct's the maker! Transfiguration, is this your belief? Conspiracy gives birth to a masterwork? You had your look, you saw! You think what's born sublime can be connived at? How? How, without that dead man's genius? What is there to empower such an impersonation? . . . Do you think there is a magical eye that drops from heaven to inspire? Barbarian, where is there such an eye? (*MS*, pp. 127–8)

Lars himself, by this time, acknowledges that there is no eye, no direct transmission from the witness, from the dead to the living. And who *could* produce such a brilliant imitation of Bruno Schulz's fiction? The stolid Dr. Eklund would not seem a likely candidate. But Dr. Eklund's argument immediately breaks down, for we as readers know that the manuscript text *is* a forgery, an imitation. Cynthia Ozick, not Bruno Schulz, composed this astonishing apocalyptic fiction that seems, like Schulz's work, to speak prophetically from the borders of the Holocaust. So, even if there is no magical eye, there is nevertheless some form of transmission from the dead to the living.

And there is more to Dr. Eklund than we or Lars initially see. After Dr. Eklund's outburst at Lars, denying his authorship of the manuscript, Ozick suddenly redescribes Dr. Eklund so as to locate him entirely in the shifting site of trauma that moves between event and text, between the witness to event and the witness to text. First, she refers to his eyes: "His naked eyes spilled catastrophe." Then Ozick brings back the word that had previously stood at the boundary between event and text: "wild." Dr. Eklund's "big scraped face with its awful nostril-craters rambled on, a worn old landscape lost to any habitation. Wild, wild" (*MS*, p. 128).

The forger and his text seem to share the same terms and features that Ozick had identified with originality and authenticity. The forger's face, like the action in which Bruno Schulz was killed, and like Schulz's language, is "wild." His eyes, like the fantastic murdered eye, overflow with catastrophe. Neither Lars nor Dr. Eklund share the ontological privilege of witnessing the Shoah, yet both produce texts that transmit its trauma. And they do so by testifying to the text of the absent witness. Both Lars's fantasies and Dr. Eklund's forgery paradoxically bear true witness to Schulz's traumatic text. The "wildness," that is, the incomprehensible traumatic nature of Schulz's death and his language provokes a wild, traumatic response in Schulz's readers. The bleeding testimonial text continues to wound; and the texts it inspires bear the wound as they bear witness to it.

Ozick's novel is a warning against such forgeries, against a sanctification of the Holocaust and the urge to identify with Holocaust victims and survivors; against making the Holocaust the sole locus of meaning and the generator of lost "messiahs." But at the same time, *The Messiah of Stockholm*, like other problematic recent Holocaust fiction, shows that the continuing traumatic impact of the Holocaust on contemporary culture continues to demand responses. These responses will be partly symptoms – evidence of the scars and still open wounds the Shoah has left on Western culture – and partly the working through of these symptoms. They will be forgeries, false testimonies to events their authors never experienced: and they will be the most real and necessary responses we can make.

PART THREE

AFRICA AT THE PASSING OF WHITE SUPREMACY

INTRODUCTION

John Burt Foster Jr.

White supremacy, as a phrase for the Atlantic slave trade and New World slavery, European empire-building in Africa, and segregation and apartheid, is a term to trouble white readers. Do we feel defensiveness or shame at the deeds of ancestors, shock that an extremist slogan can cover an entire phase of Western history, or anxiety that such words might still be a rallying cry? Yet for all its harshness the phrase is definitely one for promoting self-consciousness about the West's position in the world.

Part Three considers a current, postcolonial inflection of these issues, by focusing on cultural change in Africa over a generation after direct colonial rule. To that end it brings together three case studies, all of sites where black and white have been intricately braided together, which proceed from different but overlapping points of view. Bearing in mind the complexity of these cases, and that labels refer to the material treated but not necessarily to the essayists' beliefs, we can say that they represent a diasporic, postcolonial, and posthumanist approach to the passing of white supremacy.

The *Amistad* incident, when Iyunolu Osagie wrote her essay, was not yet a Steven Spielberg movie. The material treated here, which as the illustrations suggest draws on visual spectacle on a very different scale, is African and diasporic, in a sense consistent with Paul Gilroy's idea of "the black Atlantic" as a cultural space. Not only does the original event take Sengbe Pieh and his companions from Sierra Leone to North America and back, but the reawakened memory involves similar transits. Thus the *Amistad*'s renown in Sierra Leone owes its fortunes to the teachings of an African American, and the nation's new leader visits the *Amistad* monument in New Haven, Connecticut. Moreover, even the history of Sierra Leone, founded by British foes of the slave trade and settled by returning New World blacks, involves similar intercontinental networks. From this angle the *Amistad*'s erratic course, toward Africa by day and toward the United States by night, though meant as a cynical deception, is itself an emblem for the process of diasporic identity into which it was later absorbed.

The history of popular awareness of the *Amistad* incident provides a litmus test for the ebbing of white supremacy. How could "the beautiful story," as Osagie puts it, of enslaved Africans freeing themselves from kidnappers and being vindicated by a United States court which their surviving captors expected would uphold *them*, how could this story be forgotten for so long? In tracing the ups and downs of cultural memory in Sierra Leone, the essay brings out colonial, neo-colonial, and indigenous factors that combined to discourage popular identification, all of them related to a climate of white supremacy. But it points especially to the depressing, not to say traumatic after-effects of slavery. In nineteenth-century Freetown, the vernacular term for returning liberated slaves did not highlight emancipation; these people were "recaptives," and in considering a time of "self-cynicism" Osagie states tersely: "*captivity is a way of life*." It took a movement of cultural revival several decades after independence for the story to emerge from a state of potential availability.

Only time will tell whether this revival can outlast the current troubles in Sierra Leone. Equally uncertain is the *Amistad*'s fate in the United States, where Spielberg's movie had only a limited success. In popular mythology the liberator-president is Abraham Lincoln, not the aged and irascible John Quincy Adams; and even Lincoln is no longer a vibrant, honored presence for many Americans, including the political party he brought to power. As for Sengbe Pieh, the *Amistad* leader, Osagie notes that the last time the American mass media trumpeted his name, as Cinque of the Symbionese Liberation Army, it was overshadowed by the saga of Patty Hearst.

With its history of diasporic regathering, Sierra Leone has been settled for a longer time by people who previously lived in the West than any other African nation except, ironically, South Africa. This country's fiction during the apartheid government's State of Emergency in the 1980s, in perhaps the last gasp of traditional white supremacy, is the subject of both Michiel Heyns's and Lars Engle's essays. In a polarized situation where culture fueled a life-or-death struggle, Heyns brings out the ambiguous, even mutually exclusive meanings of postcoloniality for the two sides. Partisans of apartheid might claim postcolonial identity because they had won independence from imperial authority. But for enemies and victims of the regime, the "post" could only refer to another turning point, either (as Heyns remarks) to the end of apartheid or (in other usages) to the start of colonial rule, whose oppressive practices intensified under the successor regime. Within Africa, at any rate, Heyns suggests that the apartheid state resembles the overweening first-generation black governments it fulminated against – only because they were black. The white bullies in Mrs. Curren's classes, in Coetzee's *Age of Iron*, are counterparts to "Josephine" Momoh, the bodyguard turned president of Sierra Leone in Osagie's essay.

By reading Coetzee's novel alongside those of two black authors, Mongane Serote and Lewis Nkosi, Heyns practices a South African culture criticism after white supremacy. In this context Western elite culture or Arnoldian "sweetness and light," as personified by Mrs. Curren, seems deeply flawed, both for being ineffectual and, more drastically, for offering an alibi to the apartheid "saviors of civilization." Yet Nkosi's novel, despite praise from postcolonial critics elsewhere, seems even more locked into the old order's Manichean dichotomies. It is Serote who, in accepting the need for struggle while showing its tragic costs, emerges as a herald of a possible new dispensation; from within a desperate age of iron, he looks past its limits, and hopes for birth. This wary opening toward futurity also marks Richard Kearney's words on commitments that "have *not yet* been fulfilled." Beyond the polarized hostilities of apartheid, Heyns envisions an ethics that, not just open to or tolerant of group differences, will even "identify with an Other it normally shuns." To the extent that Western culture, for all its past complicities with white supremacy, can join in this project (presumably by keeping unmet commitments), Mrs. Curren's verdict seems appropriate: "There is not only death inside me. There is life too."

Lars Engle also discusses *Age of Iron*; but by pairing it with a contemporaneous novel by another dissident white South African writer, Nadine Gordimer's *My Son's Story*, he places the crisis of white supremacy in South Africa in posthumanist perspective. This term, made famous by Barthes and Foucault, can become overly vague outside its French context; but here it means a critical attitude toward the bland sense of achieved perfection and universality often attached to traditions anchored in the Greek and Roman classics. Beyond its political importance, Engle contends, the State of Emergency also contributed to the perennial testing of the Western canon, a testing which necessarily involves human urgencies, even if it is distinct from mere humanistic serenity. Indeed, the word "canon" implies something more academic than what Engle has in mind: the imagined projection, in works written during the emergency, of major classics into the turmoil of people's lives. One parallel would be the chapter from *Survival in Auschwitz* where Primo Levi shares cherished fragments from Dante's *Inferno* with a fellow prisoner.

The Emergency was not yet Auschwitz, but in one sense it did put the classics to a sterner test: because apartheid so relentlessly split black from white, its claim to represent the whole of Western culture, seen as a "white world," was slightly more plausible than that of the Nazis, who spoke for Germany. In these circumstances, which raise some of the same questions as the essays in Part Two, on Fascism in European high culture, Engle asks if the great names of Western literature and music can live up to their reputation. And if so, what did Gordimer and Coetzee propose, not in programmatic statements but in the elliptical yet often more intellectually daring mode of fictively dramatized allusions? A multi-faceted analysis suggests that Gordimer envisions phoenix-like survival. Under the pressure of events, a real if somewhat hollow Shakespearean grandeur unfolds to reveal lived complexities of both love and love/hate. Gordimer's focus on mixed-race characters and situations also seems to convey a hope that these tragic urgencies will continue to resonate, if only as dissident truth-telling, in the emerging hybrid cultures of South Africa and elsewhere.

Coetzee, for Engle as for Heyns, is less certain about the future. Analyzing Mrs. Curren as a composite of several white dissidents, Engle brings out the odd irrelevance of her direct public appeal to a classic. Though Thucydides' account of the Peloponnesian War would seem to warn whites about *hubris*, she ignores that audience, perhaps as incorrigible; instead, she vainly tries to interest a wounded black activist in Thucydides' lessons against violence. Engle then confronts art with theory by examining the role of Bach's music in the novel alongside Coetzee's defense of the composer, in his essay "What is a Classic?" against the charge of cultural theorists that canons merely transmit vested social interests. As a critic Coetzee welcomes this essential sifting process, and notes Bach's power to outlive his chauvinistic German boosters. But as a novelist, Engle finds, he is more "partisan, ethical, and desperate," for in *Age of Iron* Bach makes a real difference for the dying protagonist and her marginal audience of one; talk of social interests seems meaningless here.

A vision of the future, however, belongs to Virgil in Coetzee's novel. His lines on Aeneas between Troy and Rome recall, like Coetzee's Bach between Germany and the English-speaking world, Western culture's mobility across battle lines and among peoples. But alluding to Virgil leaves two questions open. What new South Africa will emerge from the ashes of the old? And in that nation (and in others, beyond the lingering influence of white supremacy) will the humanist "matter of the West" live on transformed, just as the Homeric "matter of Troy" survived in Virgil's epic?

6

REVISITING THE *AMISTAD* REVOLT IN SIERRA LEONE

Iyunolu Osagie

INTRODUCTION

In the year 1807 the Sierra Leone Company, which had helped to found a small community of settlers in the area of Sierra Leone called Freetown, decided that Freetown had become too much of a burden for it to maintain.[1] What else could the Company do, faced with the barrage of problems from the settler community that constantly challenged the authority of the Company; from the Temne natives who saw both the Company and its settlers (the Nova Scotians, Maroons, and rescued slaves from other African countries) as a threat to their own existence; and from the French who had, at least once, attempted to claim Freetown as booty in one of its territorial skirmishes with the British? Overburdened indeed, the Company handed over to the British, and Freetown became a Crown Colony in 1808. From then until Sierra Leone became an independent nation in 1961, the colony was a proud jewel in the British crown because it stood out as a token of Britain's benevolence to Africa – a home for displaced Africans and for returning captives from the Americas.

Sierra Leone of the 1800s was a colony struggling to define itself. Even its borders were not clearly defined; it could hardly have been called "a nation," or for that matter "a people." Far from being a community melting pot, Sierra Leone was a place where the "recaptives" tended to identify with communities with which they shared deeper historical ties and a deeper historical consciousness. Thus, for example, the Maroons from the West Indies; the Black Nova Scotians, who were denied their dreams of social recognition in the British colony; and other "recaptives" fresh off the coastal areas of West Africa often lived in separate communities and erected complex social boundaries in their interaction with each other. Needless to say, the relationship of the liberated blacks to the natives of Sierra Leone was culturally strained. Settlers and natives were suspicious of each other. Out of this chaos of an imposed historical identity, Sierra Leoneans struggled to sketch themselves into the canvas of national identity.

It was against this historical backdrop that the *Amistad* captives, originally captured in and around Sierra Leone, returned to Sierra Leone in 1842. Their return was not marked by any fanfare. No welcoming party awaited them.

Indeed the return of the captives could not have been of any particular interest to the growing settler community of Freetown, for they all had some personal story of mishap; all recaptives were either captured into slavery (or their ancestors were) or were free Negroes in the Americas who decided that life in Africa would be preferable to the vicissitudes of white racism. The *Amistad* captives' story was just one more settler-story whose particular nuances disappeared into the public canvas of nation-building.

Why then, after one hundred and fifty years, has the story become a memorable event in Sierra Leone? What accounts for the lack of interest in years past? My genealogical project attempts to understand the years of silence and the story's mnemonic reappearance in the national consciousness of the Sierra Leonean people.

COLLECTIVE MEMORY

The literature on collective memory seems to suggest that a society's selection and ascription of significance to a historical event is not an arbitrary process. According to Barry Schwartz, Yael Zerubavel, and Bernice Barnett, in an essay on Masada,

> Memory of the past is preserved mainly by the chronicling of events and their sequence; however, the events selected for chronicling are not evaluated in the same way. To some of these events we remain indifferent; other events are commemorated – they are invested with an extraordinary significance and assigned a qualitatively distinct place in our conception of the past.[2]

Consequently, collective memory scholars pay much attention to the analysis of the commemorative processes of history. According to G. H. Mead in *The Philosophy of the Present* and Maurice Halbwachs in *On Collective Memory*, how a society understands its past is significant to how that society constructs its present values.[3] However, Mead and Halbwachs differ in their theoretical emphasis, as Schwartz points out: "While Halbwachs seeks to show how the present situation affects our perception of the past, Mead's aim is to understand the use of historical knowledge in interpreting the present" (*SZB*, p. 149). Nonetheless, both scholars believe that the past is, in the words of Barry Schwartz, "a social construction shaped by the concerns and needs of the present."[4]

Constructionist theorists like Halbwachs and Mead also agree that our mnemonic exercises in recovering history are not arbitrary and random but constructively employed to meaningful and useful ends: in other words, because the past helps us interpret our present day reality, we are careful to select material that will in fact serve the purpose of interpreting the present. Thus we learn that past events are commemorated "only when the contemporary society is motivated to define them as such" (*SZB*, p. 149). We should note further that for Mead the past always implies a present reality. It is only *from the standpoint of the present that we can recall the past*. The past exists because there is a present from which we exercise the images of the mind "backward." In the same vein, the future exists because we exercise our minds from the standpoint of the present "forward." Thus, David R. Maines, Noreen M. Sugrue, and Michael A. Katovich can summarize Mead's radical conception of time in this manner:

> The question of boundaries marking off the past, present, and future are fundamental for Mead, but he maintained that no matter how far we build out from the present, *the events that constitute the referents of the past and future always belong to the present*[5]. (emphasis added)

Since the present determines our conception of the past and future, it is safe to say that the past and future, like the present, are dynamic and given to change. Mead states that the past is "as hypothetical as the future" (*PP*, p. 12); the past is not "final and irrevocable" (*PP*, p. 95) as we so often believe; the past's structural meaning – and meaning is always in the present – is constructed on the basis of a given present. As Maines, Sugrue, and Katovich conclude, "For Mead, the existence of events is beyond doubt: the meaning of those events, however, is problematic" (*MSK*, p. 165). So whether the past is mythical or implied objective, its validity lies in the position it occupies in society's shared consciousness or collective memory. By implied objective past Mead means that a past action must have occurred for the present to be what it is. By extension, the *Amistad* events are believable because they happened *in fact* and they led to, and fit in with, the establishment of the Mende mission in Sierra Leone in the nineteenth century. The Mende mission was the result of the desire by American abolitionists both to continue the work of Christianizing the *Amistad* Africans and to establish a mission base in the Africans' homeland. The evidence of the Mende mission and its contribution to the nation are still very much in place today.

Yet the *Amistad* event of 1839–42 as an objective past registered little on the consciousness of the nation of Sierra Leone. Although the final stage of the incident played itself out in Sierra Leone, it left no visible marks on the collective memory of the nation. Why did the nation forget? More importantly, why does the nation now remember?

Interestingly, it is not as if this event has not been chronicled anywhere. In the United States, both before and after the American civil war, many books were written on the incident. The existence of these books, however, did not erase public ignorance of the *Amistad* event. Even the use of an *Amistad* symbol – Cingue – in a stirring national event in 1974 could not translate the *Amistad* incident into a familiar American story. Donald David DeFreeze, leader of the Symbionese Liberation Army (SLA) operating out of California as an anti-government guerrilla group in 1974, adopted the name of Cingue Mtume as the worthy title of a revolutionary fighter. Although DeFreeze had named himself after the *Amistad* leader, Cingue, his SLA code of freedom for the oppressed peoples of the world from capitalist tyranny was not borne out by the indiscriminate shootings and terrorist activities that he and other SLA members were carrying out. Thus, the SLA is better remembered for its abduction and initiation of Patty Campbell Hearst, the daughter of Randolph Hearst, the millionaire chairman of the Hearst Corporation which owned, among other media operations, the San Francisco *Examiner*, than for DeFreeze's identification with the *Amistad* revolt leader, Cingue. As a result, the 1974–76 SLA saga did not revisit the *Amistad* revolt appropriately. In fact, given the relative lack of attention to the *Amistad* connection by the media, we can assume that the SLA succeeded in discouraging American identification with the *Amistad* story.[6]

In Sierra Leone, American books on the *Amistad* story are available in university libraries; but the *Amistad* event has never been studied as part of the official history of Sierra Leone, and it has never been studied in the school system or translated into the folk traditions of the people. In other words, the *Amistad* incident is an event that Sierra Leoneans, before the 1980s, never identified with as part of their national history. I intend here to trace how the validity of this objective past has recently taken its place in the shared consciousness of the people of Sierra Leone.

AMISTAD REVOLT

The events of the *Amistad* story began in 1839 when a group of African slaves on board an American-built schooner named *Friendship* (*La Amistad* in Spanish) mutinied, killed the captain and the cook, and took charge of the ship. Little did they know at the time of their action's significance. Two Spaniards, Jose Ruiz and Pedro Montez, had chartered the schooner from the owner and captain of the *Amistad*, Ramon Ferrer, to transport their recently bought slaves. A Portuguese slave trader, Pedro Blanco, had purchased and transported some six hundred slaves on board a Portuguese slaver *Tecora* from a slave holding port south of Freetown, the capital of Sierra Leone, to a barracoon just outside Havana, Cuba. It was in one of Blanco's advertised sales that Montez bought three girls and one boy all under twelve years of age, and Jose Ruiz bought forty-nine men. On June 28, 1839, Ferrer, the captain of the *Amistad*, his half caste cook Celestino and African cabin boy Antonio, together with Ruiz, Montez, two other Spanish seamen, and the fifty-three Sierra Leonean slaves, sailed for a port near Puerto Príncipe, now called Camagüey, about three hundred miles east-south-east of Havana. Due to contrary winds, the journey took longer than expected and on the third night the slaves, led by Sengbe Pieh (known in America as Joseph Cingue), armed themselves with cane knives, fatally attacked the captain and the cook, and took charge of the ship. In the ensuing struggle, Montez was wounded by the Sierra Leonean slaves, the two other Spanish seamen escaped overboard on a small boat, and two of the slaves lost their lives. The charismatic leader of the revolt, Sengbe Pieh, then ordered that the ship sail east, towards the rising sun, in the direction of Africa.

Although the slaves all seemed to speak or understand Mende, the dominant language in South West Sierra Leone, they were from the interior parts of Sierra Leone and had no navigational skills. Consequently, they had to keep Ruiz and Montez alive so that they could navigate the ship. These two men had no intention of taking the slaves to Africa. During the day they headed east as commanded, and at night Montez sailed west and north by the stars, hoping to reach American shores. The schooner followed its erratic route for almost two months until it was captured on August 26 by Commander Gedney and his crew who were on board the *Washington* near Culloden Point, Long Island, New York. Gedney towed the *Amistad* to New London, Connecticut. The Africans were charged with murder and piracy and jailed in New Haven. When the case, taken up by the abolitionists, eventually reached the Supreme Court, the Africans won their freedom, and on November 27, 1841, they boarded the *Gentleman*, along with some American missionaries, for Freetown, Sierra Leone.[7]

The case caused plenty of tension among three major Western powers – Spain, England, and the United States. As Spain sought ways to influence the American government to repatriate the *Amistad* slaves to Havana for trial, she found herself testing the strength of her 1817 treaty agreement with England on the suppression of the African slave trade. England reminded the American government of its duty to free the Africans who were, according to its treaty agreement with Spain, free men, not slaves. The American government itself was on trial as President Van Buren, who on two occasions tried to influence the courts against the captives, was seemingly "tried" and found wanting by former President John Quincy Adams who defended the Africans and won. Scrutinizing the tyrannical attempts of the Van Buren government to influence the judicial system, Adams, widely known as a strong "Constitution Man," defended the Africans by linking their rights to the power of the American judicial system to interpret the Constitution without undue influence from any outside force. The eloquent Adams was quick to link the appropriateness of self-defense in the case of the *Amistad* captives with the affirmation of the same right, provided by the Constitution, for the American citizen. By portraying the victimization of the judicial system through the helplessness of the Africans, Adams won the sympathy of the Supreme Court Justices. As a result, Cuba and the Spanish world as a whole suffered a major diplomatic defeat as hopes for compensation and the return of the schooner, with its human cargo, were dashed.

Indeed, the outcome of the *Amistad* trial had far-reaching effects both in America and abroad. It was, for the American Antislavery movement, which had suffered numerous divisions in its ranks, a rallying point, a time of healing, and a refreshing new sense of direction. The publicity of the case exposed more Americans to the debate over slavery, and sympathy for the Antislavery agenda increased.

Although with the return of the captives to Africa, the immediate fascination and celebrity nature of the case disappeared from the American psyche, the historical impact of the *Amistad* incident continued to have its effect on both the United States and Sierra Leone. For example, the *Amistad* Committee, headed by Lewis Tappan, which had supported the Mende captives in America, saw its role strengthened; and its desire to see them embrace Christianity in their homeland expanded into a new organization called the American Missionary Association (founded in 1846). The AMA has been credited with establishing hundreds of schools and colleges for blacks during the reconstruction years. In this way, they helped lay the foundation for the Civil Rights Movement decades later.

Sierra Leonean historian Arthur Abraham notes that Sierra Leone, as a nation, has benefited, also, from the processes set in motion by the *Amistad* incident even though "the origins are mostly forgotten today."[8] Abraham further points out the "positive consequences" of American missionary work in Sierra Leone: churches and mission schools helped to "create an elite group that excelled not only in Sierra Leone but in the United States as well" (*AR*, p. 21). Members of this elite class would later press for independence from its colonial rulers – the British.

Ironically, both nations have paid little attention to the origins of these well-documented historical and cultural events. As Clifton Johnson points out in a contribution to David Driskell's *Amistad II: Afro-American Art*, it is mainly artists and writers in the United States who have kept the "drama of the *Amistad* incident" alive in the US imagination.[9] For Sierra Leoneans, unfortunately, ignorance of the grand events of the *Amistad* story largely robbed them of a victorious national identity. In recent years, however, the *Amistad* story has been birthed in the imagination of Sierra Leonean artists.

FORGETTING HISTORY . . .

My interest in the *Amistad* episode began when I read Charles Johnson's *Middle Passage* (1990), a novel that takes the *Amistad* incident as its point of departure. In reading through microfilms about the *Amistad* revolt, which impressed me as a truly revolutionary story, I was shocked to find out that the principal actors in the revolt were from Sierra Leone. I was not only born in Freetown, Sierra Leone, but also received my formal education there. In all my years in Freetown I never once heard this revolutionary story told; it was not a part of our school curriculum. Therefore my encounter with the *Amistad* case opened for me a window through which I could contemplate the past and the present. What did I, as a child of independence, know about our history, our ancestors, and their struggles to survive in a land ridden with slave-catchers long after the Atlantic slave trade was banned? What possible memories could be buried in the national psyche that needed to be exhumed for long lost markers of identity? How could an event of the *Amistad*'s magnitude escape memory?

I wish to suggest, in line with Mead's theory of the past, that up until 1992 the *Amistad* was only an inherited past, that is to say an implied objective past. I hasten to argue that the *Amistad*'s factual existence in the past does not necessarily make for an inherited memory. Although I agree with Mead's essay, "The Nature of the Past," that the *refusal to remember* does not mean that "the past is lost,"[10] Sierra Leoneans actually *forgot* the *Amistad* story. What, then, does it take to remember the collective past? Constructionist theorists of the past see tradition and commemorative rites as transmitted through a "guiding pattern" to "subsequent generations" (*SCCM*, p. 222). This transmission is important because, as Schwartz states, "Stable memories . . . creat[e] links between the living and the dead and promot[e] consensus over time" (*SCCM*, p. 222). The *Amistad* account entered history but not memory because the mnemonic structure of the oral tradition, which is the guiding pattern common to Sierra Leonean groups, was not in place in the *Amistad* story. Most of what we recall today about the *Amistad* is culled from written history about the events in the US. Even the events that followed in Sierra Leone were largely transmitted through the letters of missionaries to their home base in the US. Given that, even today, some 80 per cent of the Sierra Leonean population is illiterate, the existence of written chronicles could never translate history into memory. We should also remember that the *Amistad* captives returned not to freedom but to a land under colonial rule. Should the colonial masters have celebrated the colonized's momentary victory over the master class by declaring a national holiday, or the like? British colonial education characteristically discouraged all national histories and, by imperially instituting its own history, Colonial Britain instilled in Sierra Leoneans an attitude of self-cynicism.

This attitude of self-cynicism can be seen, perhaps more clearly, in the legendary resistance of Bai Bureh, a Temne chief, to the attempts of the British to impose a hut tax on Sierra Leonean natives. The Colonial administration in 1897 attempted to curtail the deteriorating relations between the different ethnic groups and clans by imposing a house or hut tax throughout the hinterland. Since the natives were to pay either in cash or in kind – mainly produce from the land – the District Commissioner hoped to stop the inter-ethnic raids incited by the continued demand for indigenous slave labor necessary for the cultivation of farmlands owned by chiefs. This seeming goodwill on the part of the Colonial government lacked good judgment, as A. B. C. Sibthorpe, a shrewd Sierra Leonean historian of the era, notes:

> That a people not accustomed to pay tax to their natural Kings, and without knowledge of it in their traditions, that such a people, their Chiefs and their Kings, would easily submit to taxation ought not to have been supposed. Common-sense should have dictated that they all would act 'as a bull unaccustomed to the yoke' [Jer. xxxi. 18].[11]

The Colonial power's naive arrogance agitated the citizens in the Protectorate on whom the levy had been imposed; this led to armed resistance in some districts. Historian Joe Alie notes that Bai Bureh, "a resilient general" and "military strategist," initiated a "successful guerrilla warfare" against the Colonial government.[12] His initial success incited other communities to resist the hut tax aggressively. Lives were lost on both sides of the struggle, but in the end, government forces maintained their pre-eminence. Although Bai Bureh gave himself up nine months later, he had evaded capture for months, and his name, to British ears, commanded a certain fear and respect. Though he became a State prisoner and was banished to the Gold Coast until 1905, it is on record that Her Majesty the Queen pleaded that Bai Bureh be treated humanely. He did return to Sierra Leone and was reinstated as Chief of Kasseh.

Sierra Leoneans now view Bai Bureh's ingenious resistance ambivalently. To their minds, Bai Bureh's legendary ability to make himself invincible in defiance of the British may have a victorious ring, but, being a practical people, Sierra Leoneans concede his mortality in his ultimate surrender to the

British. Often recalling the Bai Bureh story, Sierra Leoneans deal with both the ambiguity of victory and defeat, invincibility and mortality. Distancing themselves from both victory and defeat, from both the British conquerors and the conquered natives, Sierra Leoneans, in a spirit of cynicism almost unique to them, are adept at making themselves unruffled spectators, umpires at the game of life. Situating themselves as commentators who can mold any event to a manageable size, they whittle down the major events of the Bai Bureh story, as illustrated by this song handed down from generation to generation:

> Bai Bureh was a warrior
> He fought against the British,
> The British made him surrender,
> *I ala Koto Maimu*
> *"E Koto Maimu, E Koto Gbekitong,"*
> *I ala Koto Maimu.*[13]

The first two lines of the song are chanted as historical fact, untainted by any social commentary. The third line, in its very presentation, sharply deviates from this objective slant. It is no longer that Bai Bureh surrendered himself to the British, as the story officially goes, but that the British "made him" give himself up. By making Bai Bureh's active move to surrender a passive one, any residue of heroism that might have accompanied his decision to surrender himself is erased from the picture. Also, the song makes no reference to the fact that he was restored to his former position as chief. Consequently, in the fourth, fifth and sixth lines of the song, rendered in Temne, the public distances itself from the great warrior's then predictable fall through their decision to ridicule what they choose to define as his personal failure.[14] Sierra Leoneans are generally intolerant of failure, and they absorb Bai Bureh's failure – and by extension the nation's failure – with a well-rehearsed indifference to the idea of success. Besides, the settler communities, the Krio people, who were the elite in the nation, tended to identify with the colonialists more than they did the indigenous natives. This "psychopathology," as Frantz Fanon puts it in *Black Skins, White Masks*,[15] aptly describes the fault lines along which the very idea of nation has been forged. Thus for Sierra Leoneans, their collective memory as a nation easily translates into a collective amnesia, especially when what they remember highlights the present failures of the nation.

This ambivalent and unstable character of the national memory, as in the case of Bai Bureh, was certainly more marked fifty years earlier when Sengbe Pieh and the *Amistad* captives reached the shores of Sierra Leone. The victory which they had celebrated in America all but dissipated once they reached their native land. When the missionaries and the captives disembarked from the *Gentleman* in 1842, their plans to stay together and build a mission house around Mani, Sengbe Pieh's much talked-about village, evaporated with each passing day. Among the many problems facing the establishment of the Mende Mission, James Steele, one of the white missionaries, found the tropical climate inclement to his physical constitution; he became ill and had to return to America. Mr. and Mrs. Wilson, the African-American couple who had also volunteered for the Mende Mission, lost their missionary zeal. In fact, their marital conflict was such that they eventually parted ways. Then word came that Pieh's village had been razed, and his family killed. With the vision that would have kept them together no longer feasible, the liberated captives mostly scattered. Nonetheless, Sengbe Pieh did help the AMA with much needed contact, and the missionaries finally settled in Bonthe Sherbro. Pieh, however, was restless. Desouza George, in his play *The Broken Handcuff*, describes Pieh as a man who "could not quite gather the bits and pieces together again."[16] Pieh decided not to stay with the missionaries. He became a trader and then faded from historical significance.

From Pieh's tragic loss, we can surmise that his memorable loss of land and family symbolizes a loss of memory in the psyche of the nation. Having fought for his freedom in the United States, Pieh returned not to his wife and children who were, perhaps, captured into slavery, or killed, but to the reality of territorial wars instigated by the still thriving slave trade. Under the conditions of return to their native land, the *Amistad* group had little basis on which to hand down the beautiful story of victory in the US. With the ever-present danger of being recaptured into slavery, the issue of their survival remained unresolved. This reality, coupled with the fact that there was a power tussle between Pieh and Williams over who should lead the mission in Sierra Leone, slowly but surely chipped away at the profound nature of their victorious experiences in America. It should not be surprising to us, therefore, that Pieh and the other freed captives chose, in neglecting to perform the story's continuity through the oral tradition, to forget their own story. Liberated Africans, in general, seem to have handed down and established in the minds of Sierra Leoneans, not their sporadic victories of eluding capture, not even their achievement of freedom after capture, but their irreducible conviction that *captivity is a way of life*. The experience of Sengbe Pieh in his native land as well as the experiences of many Sierra Leoneans thereafter did not establish a basis for them to commemorate their past.

REMEMBERING HISTORY . . .

Why then is the Middle Passage experience of the *Amistad* captives receiving such attention in Sierra Leone today? During my visit to Sierra Leone in April of 1994, I examined the means through which diasporic memory of the *Amistad* event has been articulated in the Sierra Leone society. I discovered that through the active medium of cultural performance the event has taken on new-found significance, and the result is a cultural and historical unfolding of a new political awakening.

The inception of the African Studies Department in 1985 at Fourah Bay College, now the University of Sierra Leone, should be credited with the initial steps taken in disseminating knowledge about the *Amistad* incident. Although Fourah Bay College was founded in 1876 and was considered the Athens of learning in West Africa, it was not until a decade ago that the young, enthusiastic Humanities faculty at the University were able to achieve their dream of establishing an African Studies Institute. Ethno-musicologists, historians, anthropologists, and theater specialists are some of the core faculty in this department. Joseph Opala, an American anthropologist and a lecturer at Fourah Bay College from 1985 to 1991, was also a key player in the *Amistad* story in Freetown. His course titled "Art, Anthropology, and National Consciousness" was the Pandora's box in introducing students to the *Amistad* affair. In acquainting students with past historical figures of stature, Opala laid emphasis on the historical importance of the *Amistad* incident and the role Sengbe Pieh played. Perhaps Opala's success in getting through to his hearers was heightened not just by the fact that students were being exposed to this story for the first time but also, as Desouza George, a lecturer of theater arts in the African Studies Institute, points out, by the fact that Opala's lectures were, in themselves, "captivating and infectious."[17] Opala, it seemed, had learned the value of putting the oral tradition to work, the guiding pattern through which Sierra Leoneans are most influenced. Desouza George found inspiration for his play *The Broken Handcuff*, a play that honors the spirit of Sengbe Pieh, from one such lecture to the Fourah Bay College History students in 1989. Charlie Haffner, a student at the institute in 1986, also found inspiration for his play *Amistad Kata Kata* from this eye-opening encounter in one of Opala's lectures (see Figure 1).

Haffner's play would become the channel through which a majority of the Sierra Leone population gained access to Sengbe Pieh as hero. Haffner, founder of *The Freetong Players*, the first professional theater group in Freetown, and one of the most popular theater groups ever, told me of the effect Opala's lecture had on him. He said simply, "I wept when I heard [Sengbe Pieh's] story."

Figure 1: The Freetong Players in a street performance of the play, *Amistad Kata Kata or, A Story of Sengbe Pieh and the Amistad Revolt*, written by Charlie Haffner.

Observing Haffner's emotional response, Opala encouraged Haffner to write a play on Sengbe Pieh for his thesis project. The end result was the play *The Amistad Kata Kata or, A Story of Sengbe Pieh and the Amistad Revolt* which premiered at the British Council Hall in May 1988. Before Haffner's play, the general public knew nothing about the *Amistad* story. Acquainted with a history of defeat for so long, many doubted that such a victorious-sounding incident could ever have occurred. As Haffner said, "Sierra Leoneans denied that it ever happened. They felt that I made up the whole story as it was not possible, in their judgment, that any such accounts could exist that they knew nothing about."[18]

It is in response to the constant negative reflection of themselves that Desouza George, in *The Broken Handcuff*, comments on the dishonorable manner in which Sierra Leoneans treat their heroes, and in effect their own national identity:

> Ridicule. That is the usual epitaph we ascribe to the memory of our valiant sons of the soil. Those worthy sons we neglect as we bask in our chronic aura of nationalistic indifference and ignorance. (*BH*, p. 2)

Denied the opportunity to cast the *Amistad* story in a dismal light, Sierra Leoneans found Haffner's *Amistad Kata Kata* beautiful but of little use to them. It would take several modes of presentation, including formal theater, street drama, and improvisations performed in a variety of settings, to convince the populace that the story was not fiction but historical reality.

Nonetheless, the play, in no small measure, introduced the people to a new sense of national and historical awareness. With gratitude, the people embraced the Freetong Players as a theater of relevance, a theater for the people. The play in fact catapulted the Freetong Players to both national and international prominence. In 1992, through a grant from the National Black Arts Festival, Charlie Haffner and the Freetong Players toured New Haven, Connecticut, where the dialectics of freedom for the *Amistad* captives had been hotly debated a century earlier, and other northern and southeastern cities of the United States.

OBJECTIVE MEMORY

Although denial of the *Amistad* story was dispelled through constant education, the ingredients needed to make the story not just a known historical past but an "available past," a commemorative event belonging to the people of Sierra Leone, was still wanting. The *Amistad* plays by Charlie Haffner and Raymond Desouza George were certainly educational to Sierra Leonean audiences; even before these plays, the cultural icon of the *Amistad* had appeared on a 1985 stamp pointing people to their own forgotten history. Still, the *Amistad* story did not quite inscribe itself on the national psyche as usable in the present, as valid to their own experiences. Mead's theory of the symbolically reconstructed past emphasizes the use-value of past events as determinant of the kinds of historical past we recall for present use. What, then, was the present time in which this revelation was born?

In the 1980s, Joseph Momoh, the army chief-of-staff of Siaka Stevens's All People's Congress (APC) – the one-party government in power – succeeded Stevens as Head of State through an undemocratic process of "heir to the throne." Having known Momoh as Stevens's most trusted bodyguard, Sierra Leoneans received Momoh's conferred leadership in an indifferent and cynical manner. Their cynicism was articulated mainly in their re-christening of his name from Joseph to Josephine, a name they felt was more suited to his overfed, overly pampered, round figure. During Momoh's regime, cultural advocates like the American Joseph Opala requested that the APC government commission a publication on the neglected heroes of Sierra Leone, and the book finally emerged titled, *Sierra Leonean Heroes*. Since 1968, the All People's Congress had ruled Sierra Leone as its personal property and offered very little in terms of national esteem and integrity. Corrupt officials grew fat on bribes, while the people languished in poverty that worsened with each passing year. The historian John Cartwright points out that the chronic skepticism of the populace towards government started with the very first two Prime Ministers of Sierra Leone, Sir Milton Margai and his brother Albert Margai:

> . . . the effects of the Margais' style of politics had accustomed most people to thinking that politicians were out primarily for their own good, that professions of altruism were to be treated skeptically. Politics was a source of material payoffs, not of sacrifices.[19]

Sierra Leone has been plagued with unprofitable leadership since its independence in 1961, thus enhancing the anxieties of nationhood which have beset its very attempt to define itself as a place of "unity, freedom, justice."[20]

It is no wonder that even with the publication of *Sierra Leonean Heroes*, meant to promote the richness and diversity of Sierra Leonean cultures, the demoralizing lifestyle of the nation's leaders continued to feed the barren trope of cultural nationalism. It was not until the National Provisional Revolutionary Council (NPRC) overthrew the Momoh government in a military coup on April 29, 1992 that the work received an unprecedented acclaim in paintings of artists and youths who were in search of heroic symbols to match the enthusiasm with which they hailed the NPRC. Opala's recent work on street art, *Ecstatic Renovations*, gives a detailed analysis of this exciting cultural outburst. Opala writes of the series of almost incidental events that led to the establishment of Sengbe Pieh as national hero in *Ecstatic Renovations*:

> The April 29 coup occurred during a symposium at City Hall, named for the *Amistad* Revolt, and when young people took to the streets to celebrate [the coup], they found a ready-made symbol of their liberation in the form of a twenty-foot model of the ship *Amistad* on the City Hall steps. They paraded it through the streets, chanting praises to the soldiers and Sengbe Pieh. (*ER*, p. 10)[21]

This spontaneous iconographic moment made available to the revolution symbolized the dramatic directions being taken by the new regime; it was a regime sailing swiftly in the determined direction of hope, liberty, and justice.

This iconographic representation in the form of the *Amistad* ship became an imprint in the nation's unconscious. Lloyd Warner's *The Living and the Dead*, Michael Kammen's "Revolutionary Iconography in National Tradition," and Barry Schwartz's "Social Context of Commemoration" all draw our attention to the significant role iconography plays in the collective memory of a people. Schwartz's reference to the "pictorial" significance of representation reminds us that iconography is often the quiet, yet effective, way to commemorate dated events.[22] Far beyond official celebrations, iconographic representations such as paintings and busts continue the work of harmonizing national identification with the celebrated historic moment, thus making the historical past part of the present-day landscape. Indeed, the iconographic object is often imbued with mythical value. It is in this manner that the objective past of the *Amistad* narrative, implied in the cumulative events from 1985 to 1992, served as a gateway to the creation of an *Amistad* mythical past. This transition, which corresponds to Mead's distinction between the mythical past and the implied objective past (which I discussed earlier), can be recognized in the broader popularity which the *Amistad* story now enjoys in Sierra Leone.

MYTHIC MEMORY

Indeed, the NPRC government in Freetown was quick to realize that the cultural icons displayed by young enthusiasts were in fact doing the work of the revolution. Artists – painters, dramatists, and musicians – became the unofficial cheerleaders for the government. The birth of the NPRC was, as it were, the birth of a new cultural identity. The political revolution and the cultural awakening were so intertwined that each helped to fuel the other. Although, as Opala points out, the present NPRC government did not officially take over the unfolding cultural revolution, it acknowledged its impact on the political scene. Furthermore, through the cultural significance of the *Amistad* event to the United States, the NPRC regime received recognition in this country, thus affirming itself at home. Opala notes:

> by another coincidence, Captain Strasser [the leader of the new government] was in the United States for the unveiling of a statue of Sengbe Pieh, only five months after the coup, generating considerable publicity back home. Strasser was seeking treatment for wounds he suffered in the Rebel War, and, otherwise, would probably not have left the country so soon after taking power. (*ER*, p. 10)[23]

Such cultural events did indeed strengthen Strasser's political base, and the political revolution, in turn, made Sengbe Pieh, leader of the *Amistad* revolt, "the unofficial symbol of the [NPRC] revolution" (*ER*, p. 10).

To the youth of Freetown, the parallels between Pieh and Strasser were unmistakable: like Sengbe Pieh, Head of State Valentine Strasser was doing the unprecedented in Sierra Leone history. Like Sengbe Pieh who, with the singular

Figure 2: A 5,000 Leone bank note, the highest circulating denomination, with a picture of Sengbe Pieh imprinted on it.

force of a cane knife, resisted the established tradition of slavery, Strasser was defying a tradition of African nation regimes: corruption in high places. Like Sengbe Pieh who was believed to have been in his twenties, Captain Strasser took the helm of government as a mere youth in his twenties. Easily, Strasser's popularity rides on the back of the rediscovered hero, Sengbe Pieh, but more interestingly, Sengbe's ascendancy to national recognition and identification has rebounded to memory because of its present usefulness in the new political environment. It was not long before the NPRC government accepted artists' requests that Sengbe Pieh grace the nation's currency (see Figure 2). Sengbe Pieh's appearance on wall paintings around the city and in many neighborhoods has made the *Amistad* event a part of household vocabulary. Opala notes that this type of "patriotic art showcasing the nation's history and culture" is unprecedented in "a country with almost no tradition for patriotic imagery" (*ER*, p. 6).

The incident is now a collective memory celebrated, and revitalized, by the people because they are now able to see a reflection of part of themselves in the struggles of Sengbe Pieh and the other slaves. Collective memory in this sense, as Schwartz and others point out, "becomes a significant force in a dialectic of social change" (*SZB*, p. 160). The *Amistad* incident, to which the people now have access, was appropriated to express their present recognition of themselves as historical agents. It took the direct impact of the new political upheaval, the audio-visual advantages of the theater, and the iconography of wall paintings and sculptures in *an interpretive exchange with the people's social interests and concerns* to elevate Sengbe Pieh and the *Amistad* event to their present status as the symbol of a new national consciousness.

7

AN ETHICAL UNIVERSAL IN THE POSTCOLONIAL NOVEL

"A CERTAIN SIMPLE RESPECT"?

Michiel Heyns

One of the obstacles to achieving a peaceful settlement of the Inkhata–ANC conflict in South Africa has been the matter of the carrying of "cultural weapons" – according to Inkhata, the traditional prerogative of the Zulu man, according to their opponents a euphemism for the public wielding of weapons of war. We need not take sides in this conflict in order to recognize that the culture that is represented by such implements is a warlike one – indeed, that such a culture defines itself in opposition, even armed opposition, to other cultures. In such a South African context, the "right to bear arms" cherished by some in the United States as a constitutional right tends to become all too easily the bearing of arms against a fellow-citizen perceived as an alien. What John Burt Foster has called "cultural multiplicity," and which he locates in a "more intimately personal cultural site" becomes simplified and impoverished into mere oppositionality.[1]

This, clearly, is culture at some remove from, say, Matthew Arnold's definition of "the best that has been known and said in the world," that is, the sum of the spiritual-intellectual achievement of human society. A less normative modern definition is more attentive to the relativity of cultural values to their social context:

> . . . culture is the *information* which humans are *not* born with but which they need in order to interact with each other in social life. It must be learned during the long process of education, socialisation, maturing and growing old.[2]

For one example of what this might mean in practice we could consider an extract from Mongane Serote's novel, *To Every Birth Its Blood* (1981). The narrator, Tsi Molope, returns from a year in Lesotho to his home ground, Alexandra Township on the outskirts of Johannesburg:

> Coming back from Lesotho, I felt grateful for what Alexandra's streets had taught me. . . . a kind of animal agility, a kind of tiger alertness, cynicism, distrust, and a readiness to defend my life at all costs.[3]

This passage, read against the previous one, suggests that culture in the theoretical sense of "the *information* which humans . . . need in order to interact with each other in social life" may in practice be not too dissimilar from the skills needed to survive in the jungle – "a kind of animal agility, a kind of tiger alertness." From this perspective, the idea of a cultural weapon is not the contradiction in terms which Matthew Arnold might have deemed it. Indeed, Homi Bhabha has argued that "those who have suffered the sentence of history – subjugation, domination, diaspora, displacement" develop what he calls "cultures of survival,"[4] and in such an environment the dramas of culture will take place in a theater that is also a battleground – as Edward Said has maintained, culture as "a source of identity, and a rather combative one at that," is "a sort of theatre where various political and ideological causes engage one another. Far from being a placid realm of Apollonian gentility, culture can even be a battleground on which causes expose themselves to the light of day and contend with one another."[5]

Shifting his controlling metaphor from theater to battleground, Said implies that the drama of culture is no less prone to conflict than the theatrical kind. Accepting, then, that culture may itself be the site of conflict, what status do we ascribe to such products of a culture as are themselves usually loosely described as *cultural*? For, as Serote's novel enables us to see, if the ferocity of the fight for survival is superficially more apparent amongst "those who have suffered the sentence of history," then that sentence is passed and executed by the more privileged culture that needs or seeks to subjugate the other. More particularly, that cultural artefact that we call the novel may be seen not only as chronicler of the drama, but as participant – player and audience alike, or even, then, as cultural weapon.

Since the title of this paper promises a discussion of the postcolonial novel, I had better state on what understanding of *postcolonialism* I am proceeding. A usefully broad working definition is provided by Ashcroft *et al.* in their influential *The Empire Writes Back*:

> We use the term "post-colonial" . . . to cover all the culture affected by the imperial process from the moment of colonization to the present day. This is because there is a continuity of preoccupations throughout the historical process initiated by European imperial aggression. . . . What each of these literatures has in common beyond their special and distinctive regional characteristics is that they emerged in their present form out of the experience of colonization and asserted themselves by foregrounding the tension with the imperial power, and by emphasizing their differences from the assumptions of the imperial centre.[6]

Even as tolerant a definition as this, however, may not be able to consolidate what Annamaria Carusi has called "the uneasy hold of the post-colonial label on the South African context generally, and in a very specific way, on any form of its cultural production."[7] Identifying the center of "European imperial aggression," though apparently a basic enough operation, is here by no means straightforward. To many Afrikaners, for instance, colonial domination meant the English occupation of the Cape and Natal and the annexation of the Boer republics; the Nationalist victory in 1948 and the declaration of a Republic in 1961 would then to these people represent the liberation from colonization.[8] But those dates of course signal to the majority of South Africans the accession to power of a racist nationalism much more repressive than the colonial power had been, and the vast body of South African literature, and certainly black South African literature, since then has defined itself against that power.[9] Recognizing, then, that the term begs more questions than it answers, we may for the sake of convenience define *postcolonialism* purely technically as pertaining to a period following upon some decisive act of secession from a colonial power: in this instance, by the declaration of South Africa as a Republic in 1961. This rather bland – and yet by no means uncontroversial – definition makes possible an alignment of South African fiction with African postcolonial fiction in general, at any rate in terms of Anthony Appiah's model, as set out in his *In My Father's House*. He distinguishes a first celebratory nationalist stage of immediately postcolonial writing, followed by a second reassessing, some might say disillusioned,[10] stage:

> Far from being a celebration of the nation . . . the novels of the second, postcolonial, stage are novels of delegitimation: they reject not only the Western *Imperium* but also the nationalist project of the postcolonial national bourgeoisie. . . . Africa's postcolonial novelists, novelists anxious to escape neocolonialism, are no longer committed to the nation.[11]

With the advent of a new dispensation in South Africa, of course, a further postcolonial stage may yet follow the demise of the old regime; it's probably too early to predict what form this post-postcolonialism will take, although the early signs are that there is indeed something of a postcolonial *tristesse* setting in.[12] The novels I'm discussing, however, all emanate from the days of the Emergency,[13] and are all in their different ways novels of delegitimation, in Appiah's phrase. It is true, of course, that South African fiction was never much given to celebration of the nationalist project of Verwoerd's republic,[14] but from the 1960s onwards the ferocity of the state's suppression of dissent prompted a correspondingly fierce resistance amongst writers that may in this respect at least be comparable to Appiah's second phase of postcolonial writing, the process of delegitimation. "The basis for that project of delegitimation," he says, "cannot be the postmodernist one: rather, it is grounded in an appeal to an ethical universal. Indeed it is based, as intellectual responses to oppression in Africa largely are based, in an appeal to a certain simple respect for human suffering, a fundamental revolt against the endless misery of the last thirty years." As Appiah well knows,[15] to talk of an "ethical universal" is to court the strictures of those who see in such a universal only another form of Western arrogance, universalizing its own culturally conditioned norms; but it is part of his point that there is something patronizing in insisting that African art be judged somehow on "its own terms" in the belief "that the first and last mistake is to judge the Other on one's own terms" (*FH*, p. 224). He goes on to say that "Maybe, then, we can recover within postmodernism the postcolonial writers' humanism – the concern for human suffering, for the victims of the postcolonial state . . . while still rejecting the master-narratives of modernism" (*FH*, p. 250).

In questioning the applicability of this to South African writing I am not setting out to prove or disprove Appiah's contention; rather, I want to use his terms as a way of focusing the concerns of three rather different novels, to suggest some ways in which culture is not so much embodied as activated in fiction. Given that, as I have argued, the drama of cultures is, in a situation such as the South African one, essentially combative, can it be conducted in a humanist spirit of concern for suffering? Can the culture of survival afford an ethical universal?

* * *

This is, amongst others, the question J. M. Coetzee also poses in his novel *Age of Iron* (1990) through the choice of a protagonist who is steeped in Western humanism; Mrs. Curren, a retired Classics lecturer, quotes Thucydides at the young black revolutionary, the boy who calls himself John, who is lying in hospital after being concussed in an accident engineered by the police:

> "If you had been in my Thucydides class," I went on, "you might have learnt something about what can happen to our humanity in time of war. Our humanity, that we are born with, that we are born into."[16]

But the young man has learnt in a far more direct way than this "what can happen to our humanity in time of war." He has been brutalized in the name of a culture that counts Thucydides as one of its ornaments; for if Thucydides is as alien to the South African police as to the young revolutionary, he is, broadly speaking, part of that Western civilization that they would claim to be defending[17] – just as, to her chagrin, Mrs. Curren also is. In her furious diatribes to the police she is met by almost invariable kindness or at any rate protectiveness: she is part of the white elite they are paid to defend. Mrs. Curren's survival, ironically, matters to the South African police.

Mrs. Curren is an educated English-speaking white South African, out of sympathy with the white Afrikaans rulers of the country, sympathetic to the plight of the blacks but averse to the revolutionary methods of the Struggle. She would probably subscribe to some such definition of culture as Matthew Arnold's, and the concept of a culture of survival would be foreign to her, in both of its complementary manifestations of black radicalism and white repression. What Mrs. Curren sees without understanding is the clash between two cultures of survival. This is dramatized in her helpless horror at the devastation and carnage she sees in Guguletu where the young Bheki, the son of her domestic help, is killed. For all her faith in words, indeed perhaps because of her faith in words, she cannot pronounce on the atrocities she witnesses, and finds she has nothing to say when challenged to do so:

> "These are terrible sights," I repeated, faltering. "They are to be condemned. But I cannot denounce them in other people's words. I must find my own words, from myself. Otherwise it is not the truth. That is all I can say now."
>
> "This woman talks shit," said a man in the crowd. He looked around. "Shit," he said. No one contradicted him. Already some were drifting away.
>
> "Yes," I said, speaking directly to him – "you are right, what you say is true." (*AI*, pp. 98–9)

The only "truth" Mrs. Curren can find is that spoken by the man who calls her confession "shit": the last privilege of liberalism is acquiescing to its own irrelevance. And in facing the soldiers, whom Mr. Thabane, her escort, sardonically calls "your boys" (*AI*, p. 101), Mrs. Curren finds even less to say:

> I had hoped the words I needed would just come, but they did not. I held out my hands, palms upwards. I am bereft, my hands said, bereft of speech. I come to speak but I have nothing to say. (*AI*, p. 105)

Tired, cold, demoralized, she asks Mr. Thabane for directions to go home to white Cape Town:

> "Get on to the tar road, turn right, follow the signs," he said curtly.
>
> "Yes, but which signs?"
>
> "The signs to civilization." And he turned on his heel. (*AI*, p. 107)

Mrs. Curren would deny Mr. Thabane's implication that her concept of civilization is so constructed as to exclude anything that is antipathetic to its view of itself, but in fact in her repeated diatribes against the Afrikaner regime she is implicitly denying complicity in white South Africa's defense of its privileges: there is perhaps something self-exculpating in the fluency and vehemence with which she, now not bereft of speech, blames the age of iron on "The bullies in the last row of school-desks, raw-boned, lumpish boys, grown up now and promoted to rule the land. . . . a locust horde, a plague of black locusts infesting the country, munching without cease, devouring lives" (*AI*, p. 28).

By this interpretation, the rulers are in fact inhuman, which is always, for humans, a comforting perspective on evil. But Mrs. Curren cannot altogether suppress the suspicion that her own values are inadequate in the face of this evil, and it is this that turns the novel's gaze upon itself. Although Mrs. Curren is of course placed for us in a context larger than her own field of reference, her dilemma is also the novelist's, in that his novel, as much as her learning, is part of that culture that is defending itself so ferociously. If the novel as a whole would seem to encompass more than Mrs. Curren's judgments, it yet as novel, or as a particular kind of novel, privileges the rational, the articulate, the ordered, over the violent and destructive, and the ironic, the tentative, and the contingent over the single-minded, the pragmatic, and the absolute; and in this it shares its protagonist's predilection. Mrs. Curren dutifully tries to overcome her dislike of the young activist, but her description of him sees him as essentially other, almost a different species to what she calls "real people": "A simplified person, simplified in every way: swifter, nimbler, more tireless than real people, without doubts or scruples, without humor, ruthless, innocent" (*AI*, p. 78). Interestingly, she describes his limitations too, like those of the white rulers, in terms of his performance in school: "He knew and he did not listen, as he had never listened to any of his teachers, but had sat like a stone in the classroom, impervious to words, waiting for the bell to ring, biding his time" (*AI*, p. 80). But the boy is perhaps not so much "impervious to words" as indifferent to the words Mrs. Curren and his teachers have tried to get him to attend to. Mrs. Curren's impatience is the exasperation of a teacher faced with a recalcitrant pupil: convinced of the value of what she has to teach, she cannot understand why he doesn't want to learn.

Abdul JanMohamed has argued that "Genuine and thorough comprehension of Otherness is possible only if the self can somehow negate or at least severely bracket the values, assumptions, and ideology of his culture" (*EMA*, p. 65), which Mrs. Curren cannot do. And though the novel can make us aware of her limitations, it cannot take us beyond them, for instance into a comprehension of John's experience;[18] her narration remains centered on and limited to precisely "the values, assumptions, and ideology" of her culture. This is as she recognizes, the privilege and the price of storytelling:

> I tell you the story of this morning mindful that the story-teller, from her office, claims the place of right. . . . It is through my eyes that you see; the voice that speaks in your head is mine. Through me alone do you find yourself here on these desolate flats, smell the smoke in the air, see the bodies of the dead, hear the weeping, shiver in the rain. . . . To me your sympathies flow; your heart beats with mine. (*AI*, p. 103)

Mrs. Curren is nominally addressing her daughter, but it is the reader to whose sympathies she lays claim. She realizes, of course, that in the scene she is describing, the bodies of the dead, the weeping, there are grounds for sympathy relative to which her claim would seem to be insubstantial; but, as she says, "from her office" her plight claims priority, even as, and perhaps especially as, she deprecates our sympathy: "So I ask you: attend to the writing, not to me. If lies and pleas and excuses weave among the words, listen for them. Do not pass them over, do not forgive them easily" (*AI*, p. 104). But how to attend to the writing and not to the narrator? And how not to attend to the narrator but listen for her lies and pleas?

In Ovid's account of the age of iron, the era is characterized not so much by physical hardship as by moral degeneracy: "Last of all arose the age of hard iron: immediately . . ., in this period which took its name from a baser ore, all manner of crime broke out: modesty, truth and loyalty fled. . . . All proper affection lay vanquished and, last of the immortals, the maiden Justice left the blood-soaked earth."[19] In such an age, human suffering takes place in an ethical void which offers no purchase to Mrs. Curren's notions of humanity. In an article written in 1986, presumably while writing *Age of Iron*, Coetzee said, about the scene in Gordimer's *Burger's Daughter* in which Rosa Burger witnesses the flogging of a donkey by its drunken driver: "The spectacle comes from the inner reaches of Dante's hell, beyond the scope of morality. For morality is human, whereas the two figures locked to the cart belong to a damned, dehumanized world . . . a world of blind force and mute suffering, debased, beneath good and evil."[20] Clearly Coetzee's own novel is also an exploration of this world, with Mrs. Curren another such helpless spectator of the two figures locked to the cart. It is possible that the novel ultimately has more to say about the plight of the spectator than about "the two figures locked to the cart."

* * *

Serote's novel *To Every Birth Its Blood* (1981), no less than Coetzee's, is an attempt to say something in a world in which "No words were left. Everything seemed so futile. Energy. Strength. Care. Shit" (*TEBB*, p. 53).[21] But as the title indicates, the novel accepts bloodshed as a necessary part of transition, and in that acceptance adopts the perspective of a participant in the deadly struggle. The willingness to accept death is set against the African humanism that Tsi, the narrator, learnt in Lesotho:

> In Lesotho, with its emphasis on communities, gentleness, there was a circular movement: where the beginning is humility and the search is a desire to be humble, in the process of making a life. It taught me the value of human life. Perhaps it was that realisation that showed me something else: that when man allows his heart to rot, we are capable of beginning to feed on the worms that rise, weave, create all sorts of patterns as they emerge from the rot. (*TEBB*, pp. 71–2)

"The value of human life" is what Mrs. Curren sees as denied and betrayed by the South African regime and the revolutionary resistance alike. Serote's protagonist does not in fact deny that value; but in the image of a man's heart rotting he tries to explain how a culture of gentleness and concern can be supplanted by the culture of survival. His novel makes comprehensible the revolutionary age which he depicts as not so much a loss of humanity as a deliberate response to an inhuman regime. As such it forms a necessary complement to the liberal-humanist engagement with suffering in Coetzee's novel.

Homi Bhabha, discussing Richard Rorty's contention that "liberal society already contains the institutions for its own improvement" (*PC*, p. 458), quotes Rorty's view that the "consensual overlapping of 'final vocabularies' . . . allow[s] imaginative identification with the other so long as certain words – '*kindness, decency, dignity*' – are held in common." Against this, Bhabha argues that "we must force the dialogue to acknowledge postcolonial social and cultural theory that reveals the limits of liberalism in the postcolonial perspective." We have seen Coetzee testing "the limits of liberalism" through Mrs.

Curren, exactly as a trying of the "final vocabularies" in which Rorty places his faith. Serote does something similar in a discussion between Fix, the brother of the protagonist, now in detention, and Boykie, a militant colleague,

> He [Boykie] and Fix, almost every time they met, fought so viciously with their tongues: . . . he saying Fix was sharp but clumsy, Fix saying, "I was taught to love and respect and be polite. I cannot disregard that because whites are doing what they are doing. I have to find a way of using their gift."
>
> "Gift? Gift?" Boykie would say. "Shit like that you call gift?"
>
> . . . "You are calling your past shit," Fix would say.
>
> "My past has left me in shit, that is why!" Boykie would say. When I told him that Fix had been picked up, he said coolly: "That will teach him a lesson." After that, every time I wanted to talk to him about that, he would say; "Many black people are in jail. Fix is just one of them," and then go on to talk about something else. (*TEBB*, pp. 93–4)

Boykie, then, is driven by his rejection of the "gift" of the ability to "love and respect and be polite" also to feel or affect indifference to the fate of his friend Fix. His apparent callousness is on the one hand an angry recognition of the irony of Fix's fate, being locked up by the very people from whom, perhaps rather strangely, he believed he had received the gift of love and respect, and on the other a larger, more pragmatic view that individual suffering is relatively unimportant in the face of the communal plight. This latter implication is embodied also in the much-discussed feature of the novel's construction, the abrupt shift from a first-person narrator in Part One to the multiple focalizers in the second. There is some disagreement as to the exact implications of this shift,[22] but however we read it, the effect is to broaden the spectrum of presentation, as a central revolutionary vision dispersed amongst a variety of characters. There is a relativizing implication in the technique, which moves from character to character apparently indifferently; as the struggle is passed from person to person, the fragmented narration of Part Two reflects the radical refusal to privilege individual experience over communal action. The death of Oupa, the first narrator's nephew, is the most poignant incident in a novel that does not make much of poignancy; this is the moral Yao, one of the other activists, draws from his death in detention:

> You see, when we love we cannot forget, and this means that we know a lot about hatred. We cannot give birth to children like Oupa, and have them thrown out of windows or killed the way Oupa was killed. But that did happen, and we know it happened, and we loved Oupa – shit, now we know too much. (*TEBB*, p. 357)

We know too much, the implication seems to be, to forget or to forgive. Love is turned into hate, and suffering into action. The knowledge of suffering, then, may require a certain cultivated disregard of suffering, as a precondition of liberation, and necessitated by the ruthlessness of the enemy, that is the State.

Boykie explains to Tsi the nature of the "game" as, according to him, it is perceived by white South Africa:

> . . . understand the name of the game, it is called "them and us." No shit, the rules are fuck them up, kill, destroy, ride on their backs, rape their women, get hold of the men's balls, pull and tear; anyone disobeying this is unpatriotic, is against the traditional way of life in South Africa, and will be punished. . . . (*TEBB*, p. 96)

To Boykie, the white imagination has turned the survival of its "traditional way of life" into a priority necessitating the destruction or humiliation of the black, a battle to the death, in which there are only two sides. Tsi himself recognizes that he is doomed to be the Other of somebody else's paranoid imagination, in his sardonic job description of the elevator operator in the building where he works: "His job, as a white South African, was to remind me that I was a kaffir, and I had taken it upon myself to remind him he was a settler" (*TEBB*, p. 127).

This division of roles sounds like a crude version of what Abdul JanMohamed terms "the central feature of the colonial cognitive framework and colonialist literary representation: the manichean allegory – a field of diverse yet interchangeable oppositions between white and black, good and evil, superiority and inferiority, civilization and savagery, intelligence and emotion, rationality and sensuality, self and Other, subject and object" (*EMA*, p. 63). But whereas colonial fiction, according to JanMohamed, falls unconsciously into the Manichean opposition, Serote, in such passages as the above, deploys his stereotypes knowingly, as the necessary reductions of a polarization not of his making, but of the political dispensation that he's describing. And by and large the black–white distinction is not one that informs much of the novel: whites in this novel tend to be rather shadowy and ineffectual presences when they're not downright unpleasant.

* * *

By contrast, Lewis Nkosi's novel, *Mating Birds* (1987), works almost entirely in terms of a black–white opposition, in that it purports to be the memoirs of a black man awaiting execution for the rape of a white woman. The novel has been admiringly discussed in *The Empire Writes Back*,[23] and it has been stringently criticized by, amongst others, André Brink;[24] but what concerns me is not so much the admittedly numerous implausibilities and absurdities of the novel as Nkosi's re-enactment of what JanMohamed calls "the fetishization of the Other," which, according to him, "[i]n its extreme form . . . transmutes all specificity and difference into a magical essence" (*EMA*, p. 67). Here that fetishization is near-literal, in that the white woman becomes for the black protagonist an object of sexual obsession, as he spends his days on Durban beach staring at her lying just on the other side of the dividing line between black and white swimmers. Passages such as the following, in which the narrator happens to collide with the woman in a seaside shop, swathe the white woman in a torrid haze of prurience:

> Still damp from suntan oil and swimming, Veronica bumped into me with the force of a clumsy young elephant, her full breasts charging ahead of her. To this day I remember exactly the feeling, the prickly sensation of my skin as our bodies touched, caressed. I can hear the singing of blood in my veins at the feel of the silk garment she wore, the smooth texture of the skin in her naked arms.[25]

Nkosi's novel, paradoxically, harks back to the colonial text as described by JanMohamed, in that it perpetuates, from the other side of the line, as it were, "the manichean opposition between the putative superiority of the European and the supposed inferiority of the native" – satirically, of course, but even while the narrator is mocking the assumption of inferiority, he is enacting, through his slavish subjection to "the English girl," the fantasy of "the white woman." It is in fact difficult to escape the suspicion that the novel is intended for the delectation of just that white audience that it pretends to satirize in the depiction of the white visitors to the prison:

> What beefy, red-faced Afrikaner farmers from the *platteland* come down to the coast to see is a "Kaffir Boy" who had the temerity, the audacity to seize a "respectable" white woman in her bungalow and insert his horrible, oversized "black thing" into her – *Here my nadir*![26] The very thought of it is enough to bring tears to their eyes. (*MB*, p. 12)

The prurient dwelling upon the details of the narrator's obsession could be of interest only to some such audience fascinated by the lure of forbidden interracial attraction. Oddly, Nkosi's novel, casting "the white girl" as just such a "magical essence" as JanMohamed describes, emerges as a prototypical colonial text, Manichean allegory and all.[27] This precludes the kind of ethical engagement described by Richard Kearney:

> An ethical imagination responsive to the demands of the other . . . refuses to accept that the self is nothing but a heap of reified technique or commodified desire. It bids us tell and retell the story of ourselves not to shore up the illusion of self-sufficiency or repose complacently within the walls of our sealed-off subjectivity but out of fidelity to the other. . . . Ethics, in other words, presupposes the existence of a certain *narrative identity*: a self which remembers its commitments to the other (both in its personal and collective history) and recalls that these commitments have *not yet* been fulfilled.[28]

In this sense, I think both Coetzee's and Serote's novels, unlike Nkosi's, are works of the ethical imagination, but exactly in imagining Coetzee's "world beneath good and evil": not denying the existence of these basic ethical categories but basing their own narrative identities on resistance to, protest against their absence in the age of iron. Mrs. Curren, proclaiming "I want to rage against the men who have created these times" (*AI*, p. 117), may be, as she later realizes,[29] appropriating an absolution she is not entitled to, but she is pronouncing an ethical imperative as universal as Appiah's "simple respect for human suffering." That respect is a humane and honourable response to "the demands of the other"; but in the world beneath good and evil it may not be enough. In their different ways, both Coetzee and Serote record the limitations as well as the value of such respect; but their novels are more than records: as I have implied earlier, in their context they are political acts, intended to have certain political consequences. Serote's novel teaches us, as one of the lessons in a culture of survival, "that there was no such thing as freedom being asked for, that freedom must be fetched, must be won, must be fought for" (*TEBB*, p. 232). It is in contributing to that fight that his novel is also a cultural weapon.

Coetzee's novel faces that possibility more obliquely, partly through Mrs. Curren's sense that her values have been superseded by the priorities of a struggle in which she is not equipped either temperamentally or physically to participate:

> What I had not calculated on was that more might be called for than to be good. For there are plenty of good people in this country. We are two a penny, we good and nearly-good. What the times call for is quite different from goodness. The times call for heroism. A word that, as I speak it, sounds foreign to my lips. I doubt that I have ever used it before, even in a lecture. . . . I would have used the words *heroic status* instead, I think, in a lecture. The hero with his heroic status. The hero, that antique naked figure. (*AI*, pp. 165–6)

The ethical imagination here has to transcend the usual categories of good and evil, and identify with an Other it normally shuns. Here, too, there is a clash of cultures: the culture that locates heroism in an "antique naked figure," as against the culture of survival that produces the heroes of the Struggle. But if Coetzee's novel, as I have suggested, is a product of the former of these cultural modes, it reaches out to that which transcends the temporal: "I am trying to keep a soul alive in times not hospitable to the soul" (*AI*, p. 130). The novel itself becomes the instrument of that act, and the agent of a duty that is all the more urgent for its very perversity: "There is not only death inside me. There is life too. The death is strong, the life is weak. But my duty is to the life. I must keep it alive. I must" (*AI*, p. 145).

Coetzee does not shirk the sheer irrelevance of Mrs. Curren's ambition to the priorities of the Struggle: she fails to keep alive the young man to whom she speaks these words, for instance: he is shot like a dog – or a hero – in spite of her efforts to intercede on his behalf. But she carries on writing her letter, as Coetzee carries on writing his novel, in a sort of desperate desire to prove that there is something to carry on writing for. Like *To Every Birth Its Blood*, which finds words and purpose where "No words were left. Everything seemed so futile," *Age of Iron* becomes in itself an act of faith in the face of despair. Serote's activist position and Coetzee's questioning of that position concur in this, that they look forward, however tentatively, to the birth that follows the blood – if not as an ethical universal, then at least as a more hopeful manifestation of a culture of survival.

8

WESTERN CLASSICS IN THE SOUTH AFRICAN STATE OF EMERGENCY

GORDIMER'S *MY SON'S STORY* AND COETZEE'S *AGE OF IRON*

Lars Engle

My title refers to the formal State of Emergency of the mid- to late 1980s in South Africa, years marked by a general bleak acceptance that heightened violence and repression had become endemic in the country and that only worsening conflict was in sight. The light we now know to have been just around a sharp bend in the tunnel was visible to almost no one, certainly not to white anti-government intellectuals. Both J. M. Coetzee's *Age of Iron* and Nadine Gordimer's *My Son's Story* were written in the late 1980s and published in 1990. *Age of Iron* is entirely, and *My Son's Story* largely, set in the Emergency. Both novels – far too new to be thought of in any meaningful way as candidates for classic status themselves – confront directly, almost literally, questions about the utility and power of the Western literary tradition in this emergency: an emergency consisting, at base, of a confrontation between a white state power which claimed to be European in its core beliefs and an oppressed non-white majority which had encountered European traditions in the form of colonialism, racist capitalism, and white-owned technologies of oppressive power. Under such circumstances the Western literary tradition operates at a disadvantage, under cogent political accusation as an instrument of oppression, or as a sop offered by oppressors, or as a distracting irrelevance. Such a disadvantage might be emblematized by the final tableau in *My Son's Story*. Sonny, the mixed-race Shakespeare-loving ANC activist, speaks to mixed-race neighbors amid the smoking ruins of his house, which has been firebombed by angry white reactionaries. His son Will narrates:

> We can't be bombed out, he said, we're that bird, you know, it's called the phoenix, that always rises from the ashes . . .

> Flocks of papery cinders were drifting, floating about us – beds, clothing – his books?[1]

Sonny's "books" – which Will suddenly sees in ashes floating around his father – are above all his precious complete Shakespeare: a classic reduced to ashes, but possibly the Phoenix's self-renewing ashes, by the Emergency.

Age of Iron is hardly less direct, if somewhat less material, in bringing classics into the Emergency. Mrs. Curren, the narrator, seeks out the teenage comrade John, concussed after the police have knocked him off his bicycle in the war against the children, in a black ward of Groote Schuur Hospital in Cape Town. When she finds him she delivers a short, incongruous, heartfelt lecture which begins "If you had been in my Thucydides class . . . you might have learned something about what can happen to our humanity in time of war."[2] Not only does she bring this classic into the Emergency, she cites Thucydides on how humanity is lost when states of Emergency galvanize collective action.

While these books bring classic texts into the politics, violence, and horror of this grim period of South African history, both also reflect more generally on the contemporary role of writings which claim a lasting hold on those who find themselves in a line (however crooked or far-flung) of European thought, writings which have long enjoyed a privileged place in elite identity formation and now find that place less secure in South Africa and elsewhere. One sign of this insecurity is the general replacement of "the classic" by "the canonical" in academic discussion of great texts, a replacement intended to stress the set of interests and negotiations involved in picking some texts for special veneration in education. For both Coetzee and Gordimer, however, it is appropriate to write of "the classic" rather than "the canonical." Both stage confrontations between classic texts and disenfranchised people which largely bypass the agency of the school or university, and neither is concerned directly with the cultural politics of curricula. Sonny has been a teacher, but we never see him teaching. Mrs. Curren imagines what John would have learned in her Thucydides class, but has no memories or reflections about her experiences as a teacher, and encounters no former students who bear the imprint of what she taught and how she taught it. Both novels concern the direct use of classic texts in emergent political and personal crises.

It is an interesting question, too complex to be treated properly here, whether these novels frame, or are framed by, John Guillory's insistence that the school is the primary and for his purposes the only important site for discussion of literary canon formation and its relation to the reproduction of social institutions.[3] Both Gordimer and Coetzee, at any rate, show the South African emergency bringing classics out of the schools and into yet more labile political settings, and both promote reflection on what powers classics have outside the school. Where classics exercise powers within the self-understanding of protagonists, the powers may well be residues of formal education (though this is unmentioned in the novels). When classics are invoked in situations where they do not have such residual relations to schooling, they are being tested for survival when the apparatus that has upheld them is disabled.

Ancient explanations of the classic have them rising to or retaining prominence by virtue of time-tested excellence – a somewhat tautological account, but not thereby wrong. Recent explanations stress political and institutional factors in the selection of canonical works. In view of the non-institutional but intensely political treatment of the classics in *My Son's Story* and *Age of Iron*, it might help to offer a naturalizing metaphor for this doubleness. Suppose that a classic endures in culture in the complex way a landmark endures in a landscape: in a relation of slow frictive natural interchange, leading sometimes to diminished, sometimes enhanced prominence, and also as a marker to be variously named and sometimes abruptly renamed according to changing cultural and political purposes. If so, the classics in these two books are both alive in the culture that produces the protagonists in the slow mode of acculturation I would liken to ecology, and are also visible political markers by which protagonists orient themselves and measure others.

Given my topic, I originally expected to use Gordimer as a foil to Coetzee. I read *My Son's Story* when it came out, found it spoke to me less powerfully than some of Gordimer's earlier novels, and set it aside; *Age of Iron* fascinated me instantly. I expected a comparison of the treatment of the classic in the two books to favor Coetzee over Gordimer, or at least to reveal this as a more deeply integral concern of his than hers. But *My Son's Story* turns out to be considerably more subtle and interesting on this score than I thought on first reading.

In *My Son's Story* Shakespeare is quoted frequently throughout and supplies the novel's epigraph (from Sonnet 13: "You had a father, let your son say so"). Sonny, the father/son of the epigraph (his son, who makes himself custodian of his father's story, becomes thereby a kind of son/father), a young teacher in the colored high school in Benoni, an industrial city near Johannesburg, has formed himself and his family to some degree around Shakespeare:

> The boy was Will, diminutive of William. He was named for Shakespeare, whose works, in a cheap complete edition bound in fake leather, stood in the glassfronted bookcase in the small sitting room and were no mere ornamental pretension to culture. Sonny read and reread them with devotion; although the gilt lettering had been eaten away by fishmoth, and the volume he wanted had to be selected blindly, his hand always went straight to it. (*MSS*, p. 6)

Shakespeare names and gives meaning to the father–son relation, and hints that there will be some parallel between Sonny's relation to Shakespeare and Sonny's relation to Will. This hint gains force from the odd patterns of naming in the family: Sonny and his daughter Baby have names that sound like roles in a family romance. Moreover, the account of Sonny's hand going blindly but unerringly to a text that no longer has a visible title or author suggests the way a choice initially guided by Shakespeare's cultural prestige has become part of a form of life.

The narrative alternates between present first-person from Will's viewpoint as child, angry adolescent, and young adult, on one hand, and past third-person, often using Sonny as a center of consciousness, but sometimes Hannah

Plowman, Sonny's white lover, or a more general center like that of the state security forces, on the other. Shakespeare figures prominently in both strands of narrative, which mark Sonny's development toward radical political involvement through a series of Shakespeare references, as Sonny explores the consequences in apartheid South Africa of his shared discovery with his wife Aila that "for both of them the meaning of life seemed to be contained, if mysteriously, in leading useful lives" (*MSS*, p. 9). Sonny sees his teacherly responsibilities to his students "open out":

> He saw the need to bring together the schools and the community in which it performed an isolated function – education as a luxury, a privilege apart from the survival preoccupation of the parents. He bought books that kept him from Shakespeare. He read them over and over again in order to grasp and adapt the theory that recognized social education of the community, the parents and relatives and neighbours of the pupils as part of the school's function. (*MSS*, p. 9)

Gordimer thus establishes early on an opposition between Shakespeare and the language of politics that runs right through the novel. But she also documents from the start a kind of power in Shakespeare that inoculates Sonny and Aila against the appeal of hire-purchase gentility, "bedroom 'schemes' and lounge 'suites' named to bring to cramped and crumbling hovels the dimensions of palaces, 'Granada,' 'Versailles'" (*MSS*, p. 11).

> Sonny and his wife did not covet "Granada" or "Versailles": with an understanding of Shakespeare there comes a release from the gullibility that makes you prey to the great shopkeeper who runs the world, and who would sell you cheap to illusion. (*MSS*, p. 11)

And Shakespeare helps Sonny's start in politics (as do his man-of-the-people nickname and his dark skin):

> He . . . was only gratified that his years of reading – that individualistic, withdrawn preoccupation, as he was beginning to think of it – were being put directly to the use of the community in providing him with a vocabulary adequate to what needed to be said. Words came flying to his tongue from the roosts of his private pleasures. (*MSS*, p. 33)

Literature, a private luxury, aids the rhetoric of public engagement.

It is interesting that Shakespeare never figures in *My Son's Story* as an instrument of oppression. Gordimer does of course show alertness to the ways classic literature gets inscribed in authority structures. Horace's *Carpe Diem* stands over the entrance to the whites-only municipal library: Sonny reads Kafka and absorbs a "profoundly defeatist" way of allegorizing his social weakness (*MSS*, p. 17), but

> He knew better. There were the local law-makers, proconsuls, gauleiters

> in the town's council chamber under the photographs of past mayors and the motto CARPE DIEM. (*MSS*, p. 18)

Horace's phrase echoes through the novel, shadowing both the love affair that complicates Sonny's life and the political struggle to seize their day in which he and all the other characters are by the end engaged. But for the first half of the novel Gordimer treats Shakespeare and Shakespeare education implicitly as moral/aesthetic rather than political experiences. Sonny's passage into anti-government politics is neither fostered nor impeded by his love for Shakespeare. Literature rather appears for him, as he rises in the movement, as a mildly but not deeply regretted alternative. Imprisoned for the first time, Sonny reflects:

> He knew he was on his way to prison from his days back in the Coloured location . . . or if he didn't know it, he should have; he realized this as, instinctively taking up one form of political action after another, he understood that the mystery of the meaning of life he and Aila had vaguely known to be contained in leading useful lives was no mystery. For them, their kind, black like the others, there was only one meaning: the political struggle. (As he loved the magnificent choices of Shakespearean language, the crudely reductive terms of political concepts were an embarrassment to him, but he had to use them, like everybody else.)
> (*MSS*, pp. 47–8)

Up to this point in the novel Shakespeare functions as a marker of beautiful mental freedom – the "magnificent choices of Shakespearean language" – which nonetheless can pose no real threat to the necessity of the struggle, even if it points up the relative flatness of revolutionary rhetoric. When Will discovers Sonny's affair with Hannah, Sonny feels awkward in the same way about both kinds of speech:

> —It's the "cleansing of the graves" of the nine youngsters who were shot by the police last week outside Jubilee Hall. They were buried yesterday. The Street Committees have asked for some kind of oration. The kids were comrades.—
>
> As he said "oration" the boy came in, after all. In the glance of greeting he gave his son he felt a tic of embarrassment, as if he had been caught out quoting Shakespeare as he used to do to give the boy the freedom, at least, of great art. (*MSS*, p. 99)

Sonny's idea of Shakespeare as "freedom," "greatness," "choice" offers a rather thin incarnation of the familiar humanist idea that literature liberates and exalts us into an unlocalized space where we encounter general human nature and thus meet as free equals. This is not a currently fashionable notion, and it is not one that Gordimer embraces elsewhere. Sonny's view of Shakespeare, then, with its naivety and potential sentimentality, does not suggest that he's an especially perceptive reader – or, to put the matter more damagingly, it does not show Gordimer thinking very precisely about what it might mean to enter the struggle with a Shakespearean sensibility. Shakespeare appears as a general good that must temporarily be foregone for the struggle.

The novel's treatment of Shakespeare becomes more complex, however, as Sonny's political life leads him to a love-affair with Hannah, since the affair is shadowed by Shakespearean references. Sonny falls in love with Hannah when she visits him in prison. Unlike Sonny's wife Aila, Hannah can develop "a private, oblique language" to give information to Will past the prison guards who oversee their conversations: when a warden stops Sonny from answering a question about prison conditions, she says

> —Well, I suppose you find sermons in stones—. . .
>
> He grinned to receive this, another kind of message, she was almost certainly not aware of; elated to be able to recognize it.—And good in your kindness in coming to see me.— (*MSS*, pp. 49–50)

Hannah's tag from *As You Like It* – from Duke Senior's "Sweet are the used of adversity" speech – unlocks something for Sonny: "A stranger has no love-talk, but she was the one who unknowingly found the way to connect him with home" (*MSS*, p. 49). Hannah allows Sonny to unite his literary romanticism with his political commitment. Though Gordimer, perhaps surprisingly, quotes *Othello* only once late in the novel, it is clear that white Hannah loved black Sonny for the dangers he had passed, and he loved her that she did pity them.

It is what happens to Shakespeare and to the literary late in the novel that establishes the subtlety of Gordimer's treatment of the issue. Sonny's family has been, in predictably painful ways, transformed by the never-opened but widely-known secret of his double life. Aila, Baby, and Will all separately make their discoveries. Hannah is a smoker; her smell lingers on Sonny. Baby cuts her wrists, not fatally; Aila cuts her long beautiful hair; Will pointedly ignores both his father's political and his literary aspirations and reads commerce at university. Sonny finds him "such a disappointment" (*MSS*, p. 137), and Sonny's disappointment is clearly a victory for Sonny's son. Both Aila and Baby, without consulting Sonny, join Umkhonto we Sizwe, the armed resistance wing of the ANC. They thus opt for more direct, and even more dangerous, anti-government activity than Sonny's, and end up in exile in Lusaka. Moreover, Sonny's affair with Hannah – undisclosed to his comrades – also limits, he thinks, his advancement in the movement: he finds himself doubted, outmaneuvered, and ultimately demoted in the ANC executive because of his double life.

> So why not a triple life? If a man of his old and proven integrity could withhold information from the movement to which total dedication was due, loyalty was the letter of faith, he also might be vulnerable – open, like a wound – to disaffection.
>
> *Better to be vile than vile esteemed, when not to be receives reproach of being.*
>
> He hated to have coming up at him these tags from an old habit of

> pedantry; useless, useless to him. In a schoolteacher's safe small life, aphorisms summed up so pleasingly dangers that were never going to have to be lived. There is no elegance in the actuality – the distress of calumny and self-betrayal, difficult to disentangle. (*MSS*, p. 190, italics Gordimer's)

Here and elsewhere with increasing pressure as the novel closes, Shakespeare returns as the sign not of freedom but of ambivalence, not as a dreamy alternative to a life of action, or a beautiful vision of the rich cultural engagement a life of action might aim to provide future South Africans, but rather as a way of mapping the failures and limits of Sonny's life in politics. Sonny has insomnia: "If he could get to sleep; *But then begins a journey in my head, to work my mind*. The old consolation of fine words become a taunt" (*MSS*, p. 183, italics Gordimer's, from sonnet 27).

As Shakespeare appears refigured in this way, Will begins to emerge as author: "I've begun a project – call it that – that needs solitude" (*MSS*, p. 196). With Will's literary vocation, a new kind of literary reference enters the novel. Hannah tells Sonny, after lovemaking, that she has been offered an important UN job based in Addis Ababa.

> —I haven't even replied. . . . They've written again. By courier.—
> —Of course. They want you. Highly recommended.—
> —Lie down, I can't talk to your back . . . please.—
> He sank beside her. They were stretched out like two figures on a tomb commemorating a faithful life together. She took his hand. (*MSS*, p. 203)

Will has had little opportunity to view medieval sepulchral sculpture, but he seems to have been reading modern poetry. The description echoes and possibly derives from Philip Larkin's "An Arundel Tomb," especially the first two verses and the last:

> Side by side, their faces blurred,
> The earl and countess lie in stone,
> Their proper habits vaguely shown
> As jointed armour, stiffened pleat,
> And that faint hint of the absurd –
> The little dogs under their feet.
>
> Such plainness of the pre-baroque
> Hardly involves the eye, until
> It meets his left-hand gauntlet, still
> Clasped empty in the other; and
> One sees, with a sharp tender shock
> His hand withdrawn, holding her hand.
>
> . . . Only an attitude remains:
>
> Time has transfigured them into
> Untruth. The stone fidelity
> They hardly meant has come to be

Their final blazon, and to prove
Our almost-instinct almost true:
What will survive of us is love.[4]

A poem about how political meaning gives way to eros over time gets ironically invoked at the moment when Hannah's political career is about to end their love affair, to which Sonny has partially sacrificed both his own family and his own career, taking off his armor to hold her hand. Sonny now quotes *Othello* with a vengeance:

—I'll be able to come back sometimes.—Oh thou weed.
Oh thou weed: who art so lovely faire, and smell'st so sweet that the sense aches at thee, Would thou had'st never been born.
(*MSS*, p. 224, italics Gordimer's)

And Will takes up here more vaguely a Shakespearean motif from the sonnets (especially 60, "Like as the waves make toward the pebbled shore / So do our minutes hasten to their end") in describing Sonny's eroding connection with his own past:

He turned fifty-two. The day was not remarked in any way. His son did not remember the birthday . . .

A tide wearing away a coastline, little by little, falling into the ocean of time. (*MSS*, p. 264)

Again, this is Shakespeare not as magnificent choice or freedom, but Shakespeare as register of loss, ambivalence, and failure.

In the passage with which I began Sonny stands in his burned-out house, mixed-race neighbors before him:

And then of course the old rhetoric took up the opportunity. We can't be burned out, he said, we're that bird, you know, it's called the phoenix, that always rises again from the ashes. Prison won't keep us out. Petrol bombs won't get rid of us. This street – this whole country is ours to live in. Fire won't stop me. And it won't stop you.

Flocks of papery cinders were drifting, floating about us – beds, clothing – his books?

The smell of smoke, that was the smell of her.

The smell of destruction, of what has been consumed, that he first brought into that house. (*MSS*, p. 274)

In those slightly odd "cinders" are the ashes of Shakespeare's "The Phoenix and the Turtle":

Beauty, truth, and rarity,
Grace in all simplicity,
Here enclosed, in cinders lie.

And Will decodes this for us:

> It's an old story – ours. My father's and mine. Love, love/hate are the most common and universal of experiences. But no two are alike, each is a fingerprint of life. That's the miracle that makes literature . . .
> (*MSS*, p. 275)

Shakespeare then emerges as a sign of literature's mastery of commitment and ambivalence over time, reduced to a brilliantly terse formula: "Love, love/hate." And Will makes Shakespeare, in this case Hamlet, his signature of triumph over time:

> I've learned what he didn't teach me, that grammar is a system of mastering time; to write down "he was", "he is", "he will be" is to grasp past, present, and future.
> Whole; no longer bearing away.
> All of it, all of it.
> *I have that within which passeth show.* (*MSS*, p. 276, italics Gordimer's)

In *My Son's Story*, the classic survives the State of Emergency and indeed to some extent prevails over it. Gordimer creates in Will a mixed-race inheritor of the political efforts of the independence movement who testifies to the continuing utility of Western classics, a utility that has to do both with sponsoring desires for freedom and, more importantly, with recognizing ambivalence at the core of love-relations, both personal and political. One might, perhaps presumptuously, read into the way Gordimer brings Shakespeare into the end of the novel a covert suggestion that white art (including Gordimer's own) will continue to be useful in South Africa's black-governed future, and will be useful partly by expressing ambivalence.

* * *

Age of Iron, on the face of it a book far more deeply involved with classical literature – the dying narrator, Mrs. Curren, is a retired Classics lecturer from the University of Cape Town – is also less sanguine about the survival of classic literary traditions, just as she is less sanguine about the political future of South Africa than any character in *My Son's Story*. Mrs. Curren is "Trying to keep the soul alive in times not hospitable to the soul" (*AI*, p. 130). She has the privilege of the old, the female, the sick, the clearly non-combatant, of saying what she pleases without its being either a challenge to immediate violence or an erotic challenge. What she says is also thereby dismissable, the words of someone who does not matter, who is not a player. (In this, of course, she speaks not only for old ladies with bad hips, but for liberal white South African English-speakers, who were from the 1950s through the 1980s in a position of increasing political marginality in South Africa.) "Keeping the soul alive" involves speaking her truth not only to her exiled daughter, to whom the book is addressed as a letter, and to the white authorities, but also to the black children of whose heroic militancy she also disapproves.[5] She argues with her African housekeeper

Florence and with Florence's son Bheki about the school boycott which is one of the major forms of political action on the children's side (a form of action that, in effect, aligns the classics and indeed all schooling with the white government). And, as mentioned above, she speaks of the lessons of the Pelopponesian War to Bheki's comrade John, who lies bandaged and sedated in hospital after being knocked off his bicycle by white policemen as part of their war against young blacks:

> "Be slow to judge. . . ."
>
> "If you had been in my Thucydides class . . . you might have learned something about what can happen to our humanity in time of war. Our humanity, that we are born with, that we are born into."
>
> . . . he . . . knew who I was, knew I was talking to him. He knew and he did not listen, as he had never listened to any of his teachers, but had sat like a stone in the classroom, impervious to words, waiting for the bell to ring, biding his time.
>
> "Thucydides wrote of people who made rules and followed them. Going by rule they killed entire classes of enemies without exception. Most of those who died felt, I am sure, that a terrible mistake was being made, that, whatever the rule was, it could not be meant for them. 'I!—': that was their last word as their throats were cut. A word of protest. I, the exception.
>
> "Were they exceptions? The truth is, given time to speak, we would all claim to be exceptions. For each of us there is a case to be made. We all deserve the benefit of the doubt.
>
> "But there are times when there is no time for all that close listening, all those exceptions, all that mercy. There is no time, so we fall back on the rule. And that is a great pity, the greatest pity. That is what you could have learned from Thucydides. It is a great pity when we find ourselves entering upon times like those. We should enter upon them with a sinking heart. They are by no means to be welcomed."
>
> Quite deliberately he put his good hand under the sheet, in case I should touch it again. (*AI*, pp. 79, 80–1)

This is a dense passage that participates in a number of the strategies of the novel. It invites recognition first, and perhaps rather unexpectedly, of the extent to which Coetzee is a quite reverent participant in a Western literary and philosophical tradition deriving from Athens, a tradition under attack (in North America as well as in South Africa) precisely because its rationalism is intimately linked with the very imperialism and ethnic pride that undid Athens in Thucydides' Athenian account. Coetzee, through Mrs. Curren, insists that the words of Virgil and Thucydides be uttered in contemporary South Africa, thus suggesting we take seriously their potential value in this context even to people like John who for their own sufficient reasons cannot and will not hear them.

I do not think the novel's ironies attach to Mrs. Curren's feelings for Bach or for Greek and Latin literature, but other readers feel differently. David Attwell, granting Mrs. Curren "the authority of irrelevance," calls her "a retired professor of classics whose canon means little to anyone except herself,"[6] but begins and ends his excellent book with an epigraph in which J. M. Coetzee describes his work in terms virtually quoted from Plato's Parable of the Cave: "I am someone who has intimations of freedom (as every chained prisoner has) and constructs representations – which are shadows themselves – of people slipping their chains and turning their faces to the light" (*SAPW*, vol. x, p. 125). John Coetzee is clearly not someone for whom Mrs. Curren's canon means little. In fact, while much in the novel may seem to support the idea that Mrs. Curren's classics fail in the face of the Emergency, there is considerable external evidence that for Coetzee these very classics are part of what the Emergency is testing; there is also evidence that Mrs. Curren, in her partial, classically-inflected answer to the question "what is to be done?" stands in Coetzee's mind for himself and for other white South African writers.

During the 1980s, Coetzee was active as a reviewer, and Coetzee and David Attwell collect and reprint important reviews in *Doubling the Point*. In a review of Athol Fugard's *Notebooks, 1960–1977*, Coetzee comments that

> the *Notebooks* are . . . the autobiography of a man of intelligence and conscience who chose to remain in South Africa at a time when many fellow writers were opting for (or being forced into) exile. Fugard's choice meant, among other things, that he would . . . continually be brought face to face with the question of his relationship with a ruling order characterized by a remarkably loveless attitude toward its subjects (or some of them), an attitude of lovelessness that sometimes extends to atrocious callousness.[7]

Mrs. Curren sees the central problem before her, perhaps by extension the problem for people like her, to love those with whom they have no immediate sympathy, in this case Bheki's friend John:

> I do not want to die in the state I am in, in a state of ugliness. I want to be saved. How shall I be saved? by doing what I do not want to do. That is the first step: that I know. I must love, first of all, the unlovable. I must love, for instance, this child. Not bright little Bheki, but this one. He is here for a reason. He is part of my salvation. I must love him. But I do not love him. Nor do I want to love him enough to love him despite myself. (*AI*, p. 136)

Coetzee finds this imperative in Fugard:

> The route he follows out of his crisis of conscience is to take upon himself (following Sartre) the task of *bearing witness*. "The truth [must] be told . . . I must not bear false witness." "My life has been given its order: love the little grey bushes," by which he means, love the insignificant, the forgotten, the unloved. Against a system whose own degradation he measures by the degradations it imposes on others (at one point he goes further

> and suggests that the ultimate and unwitting victims of a regime of degradation are its perpetrators), Fugard opposes an ethic of love. "South Africa's tragedy is the small, meager portions of love in the hearts of the men who walk this beautiful land." "People must be loved." . . . "What is Beauty? The result of love. The ugliness of the unloved thing."
> (*DP*, p. 370)

It is clear that Mrs. Curren, in her own self-writing, has accepted the same "order" heard by Fugard; indeed, I cannot read this passage without seeing Mrs. Curren temporarily *as* Fugard, as a perhaps parodic but by no means sketchy embodiment of the humanist artist in the South Africa of the 1980s. Similarly, though in a more barbed idiom (perhaps the slight edge of a competitor), Mrs. Curren offers a scaled-down version of something Coetzee finds in Nadine Gordimer's essays:

> Without necessarily being egocentric, she is more interested in herself than in other writers: in herself as the site of a struggle between a towering European tradition and the whirlwind of the new Africa. (*DP*, p. 386)

I argue above that Sonny and Will in *My Son's Story* are the site of such a struggle (though framed less grandly than this). Coetzee, discussing Gordimer as an essayist and commentator, suggests that she sees such a struggle between the towering accomplishments of European literature and the centrifugal energies of the liberation struggle in herself and her own work – with perhaps a hint that she casts herself as a Moses trying to follow these signs. Mrs. Curren is, in her reduced way, the site of exactly such a struggle.

To push the argument further and involve a third important white contemporary author, Mrs. Curren's plan to immolate herself in her ancient Hillman in front of Parliament House may be an echo, from Coetzee's viewpoint, of Breyten Breytenbach's "quixotic foray into the fortress of the enemy" (*DP*, p. 379) – the doomed attempt to infiltrate South Africa under a false name that led to Breytenbach's conviction and nine-year sentence as an enemy of the state. Coetzee finds the most valuable aspect of *True Confessions of an Albino Terrorist* (1985), Breytenbach's account of his political mission, trial, incarceration, and release, to be the passages in which Breytenbach "tries to feel his way into the experience of the condemned man, into the experience of death itself" (*DP*, p. 379), which is very much what Mrs. Curren is doing. In the essay on Breytenbach in *Giving Offense*, Coetzee's recent book on censorship – an essay originally published in 1990 – Coetzee comments of Breytenbach's *Mouroir* (1984), a prison text published after Breytenbach's eventual release, that "Text becomes coextensive with life: text will not end till writing ends; writing will not end till breath ends."[8] Mrs. Curren of course enacts this arrangement in *Age of Iron*, a narrative in the form of an unfolding letter to her daughter which will only be sent when she dies of the cancer which is destroying her, if then. As she says:

> For as long as the trail of words continues, you know with certainty that I

> have not gone through with it: a rule, another rule. Death may indeed be the last great foe of writing, but writing is also the foe of death.
> (*AI*, pp. 115–16)

Thus, very evidently in the case of Fugard, and plausibly in the cases of Gordimer and Breytenbach, Mrs. Curren offers a view, desperate in its political impotence, but not I think a satire, of the role of the literary artist and the bearer of literary traditions in the South African State of Emergency.

This makes her also, as I commented above, a partial self-portrait on Coetzee's part. She writes, in a passage that is both funny and moving, of Bach as one of the immortals – thus extending, perhaps strategically, the book's idea of the classic to include great music. (The auditor she senses halfway through the passage is her derelict tenant Vercueil, a homeless alcoholic, probably of mixed race, whom she brings into her home in the course of the novel.)

> Then at last I went back to Bach, and played clumsily, over and over again, the first fugue from Book One. The sound was muddy, the lines blurred, but every now and again, for a few bars, the real thing emerged, the real music, the music that does not die, confident, serene.
>
> I was playing for myself. But at some point a board creaked or a shadow passed across the curtain and I knew he was outside listening.
>
> So I played Bach for him, as well as I could. When the last bar was played I closed the music and sat with my hands in my lap contemplating the oval portrait on the cover with its heavy jowls, its sleek smile, its puffy eyes. Pure spirit, I thought, yet in how unlikely a temple! (*AI*, p. 24)

In a brilliant but little-known essay, "What is a Classic?" originally delivered at a symposium at Michigan State University, which begins with a re-examination of T. S. Eliot's essay of that name and its relation to Eliot's own move from periphery to metropolis, Coetzee narrates the story of his own first encounter with Bach – a story which casts him in somewhat the role of Vercueil:

> One Sunday afternoon in the summer of 1955, when I was fifteen years old, I was mooning around our back garden in the suburbs of Cape Town, wondering what to do, boredom being the main problem of existence for me in those days, when from the house next door I heard music. As long as the music lasted, I was frozen, I dared not breathe. I was being spoken to by the music as music had never spoken to me before.
>
> What I was listening to was a recording of Bach's *Well-Tempered Clavier* played on the harpsichord. I learned this name only some time later, when I had become more familiar with what, at the age of fifteen, I knew only – in a somewhat suspicious and even hostile teenage manner – as "classical music." The house next door had a transient student population; the student who was playing the Bach record must have moved out soon afterwards, or lost his/her taste for Bach, for I heard no more, though I listened intently.
>
> I don't come from a musical family. There was no musical instruction offered at the schools I went to, nor would I have taken it if it had been

> offered: in the colonies classical music was sissy. . . . At home we had no musical instrument, no record player. There was plenty of the blander American popular music on the radio . . . but it made no great impact on me. . . .
>
> And then the afternoon in the garden, and the music of Bach, after which everything changed. A moment of revelation which I will not call Eliotic – that would insult the moments of revelation celebrated in Eliot's poetry – but of the greatest significance in my life nevertheless: for the first time I was undergoing the impact of *the classic*.[9]

I have quoted at considerable length, though I have nonetheless scanted the careful ways in which Coetzee contextualizes this personal experience. He goes on to ask several questions, questions that I think we find Mrs. Curren also asking and attempting to answer:

> The moment in the garden was a key event in my formation. Now I wish to interrogate that moment again, using as a framework both what I have been saying about Eliot – specifically, using Eliot the provincial as a pattern and figure of myself – and, in a more skeptical way, invoking the kinds of question that are asked about culture and cultural ideas by contemporary cultural analysis.
>
> The question I put to myself, somewhat crudely, is this: Is there some non-vacuous sense in which I can say that the spirit of Bach was speaking to me across the ages, across the seas, putting before me an ideal of form; or was what was really going on at the moment that I was symbolically electing high European culture, and command of the codes of that culture, as a route that would take me out of my class position in white South African society and ultimately out of what I must have felt, in whatever obscure and mystified terms, as the dead-end of that society itself – a road that would culminate (again symbolically) with me on a platform here addressing a cosmopolitan audience on Bach, T. S. Eliot and the question of the classic? In other words, was the experience what I understood it to be – a disinterested and in a sense impersonal aesthetic experience – or was it really the masked expression of a material interest? (*WC*, p. 14)

Note Mrs. Curren's related meditation in *Age of Iron*:

> Pure spirit, I thought, yet in how unlikely a temple! Where does that spirit find itself now? In the echoes of my fumbling performance receding through the ether? In my heart, where the music still dances? has it made its way into the heart too of the man in the sagging trousers eavesdropping at the window? Have our two hearts, our organs of love, been tied for this brief while by a cord of sound? (*AI*, p. 24)

Coetzee in his essay attempts to answer these related questions – the question posed by what we might call the rampant *cuibono*ism of modern cultural criticism which assumes that Coetzee must have been sensing an interpellative call to a material social advantage – sensing the possibility that he might acquire cultural capital – when he heard Bach in the backyard, and the question posed by Mrs. Curren about where the spirit of Bach may be said to reside if it is not in the cultural capital which has accrued to him over time. In his essay on the classic, Coetzee historicizes the most famous aspect of the transmission of Bach through time – the supposed "rediscovery" of Bach by Mendelssohn – and shows that in fact the huge increase in Bach's reputation in the nineteenth century was connected with the projects of German nationalists. Does this, he asks, undermine the notion of the classic as the timeless? And how does it bear on his own first experience?

> If the notion of the classic as the timeless is undermined by a fully historical account of Bach-reception, then is the moment in the garden – the kind of moment that Eliot experienced, no doubt more mystically and more intensely, and turned into some of his greatest poetry – undermined as well? Is being spoken to across the ages a notion that we can entertain today only in bad faith? (*WC*, pp. 17–18)

"To answer this question," Coetzee continues, "to which I aspire to give the answer No, and therefore to see what can be rescued of the idea of the classic, let me return to the story of Bach" (*WC*, p. 18). And he then points out that in fact Bach was not entirely forgotten in the eighteenth century, but was rather in continuous, though not very prominent, use by a small community of professional musicians in Berlin and Vienna. Mendelssohn did not find the choral music of Bach wrapped around a fish, he heard about it from a friend of his banker father's, C. F. Zelter, director of the Berlin *Singakademie*, who however "regarded the Passions as unperformable and of specialist interest only" (*WC*, p. 18). Thus, according to Coetzee, Bach survives through the experience of continual examination that comes of being part of the material worked on by an expert community. Here Coetzee may implicitly endorse the retention of classics in university curricula – or he may simply assert that true classics will remain part of the material experts need to know whatever the political climate in which the experts work:

> If there is anything that gives one confidence in the classic status of Bach, it is this *testing* process that he has been through within the profession. Not only did this provincial religious mystic outlast the Enlightenment turn toward rationality and the metropolis, but he also survived what turned out to have been a kiss of death, namely, being promoted during the nineteenth-century revival as a great son of the German soil. And today, every time a beginner stumbles through the first prelude of the "48," Bach is being tested again, within the profession. Dare I suggest that the classic in music is what emerges intact from this process of day-by-day testing? (*WC*, p. 18)

It is the associated fugue, "the first fugue from Book One," that Mrs. Curren plays for herself and Vercueil. I think we are encouraged by this context in

Coetzee's essay to see the moment as part of the testing of the classic. But if so, we should also see the reference to her professional life as a classicist at the beginning of Mrs. Curren's hospital visit to John cited above as another such reference to testing: "If you had been in my Thucydides class . . ."

Moreover, in the context of *Age of Iron*, we need to invoke Coetzee's final words in his essay on the classic, words that come after he has, ultimately, suggested that he did have a relatively disinterested encounter with Bach in the garden (while also finessing the autobiographical question to some degree):

> I hope I have allowed the terms *Bach, the Classic* to emerge with a value of their own, even if that value is only in the first place professional and in the second place social. Whether at the age of fifteen I understood what I was getting into is beside the point: Bach is some kind of touchstone because he has passed the scrutiny of hundreds of thousands of intelligences before me, by hundreds of thousands of fellow human beings. (*WC*, p. 19)

And Coetzee goes on to invoke Zbigniew Herbert's view of the classic as that which survives its confrontation with barbarism (a confrontation which, as we have seen throughout, includes the appropriation of the classic by the barbarian for barbaric purposes):

> It is not the possession of some essentialist quality that, in Herbert's eyes, makes it possible for the classic to withstand the assault of barbarism. Rather, what survives the worst of barbarism, surviving because generations of people cannot afford to let go of it and therefore hold on to it at all costs – that is the classic. (*WC*, p. 19)

From this, Coetzee concludes, criticism (or fiction) which interrogates the classic and appears to endanger it is in fact part of the mechanism of testing by which it survives:

> Thus the fear that the classic will not survive the decentering acts of criticism may be turned on its head: rather than being the foe of the classic, criticism, and indeed criticism of the most skeptical kind, may be what the classic uses to define itself and ensure its survival. Criticism may in that sense be one of the instruments of the cunning of history. (*WC*, p. 19)

While Mrs. Curren does not exactly have this view, her work within the novel enacts it, and her articulation of views largely identical to Coetzee's on Bach and other classics suggests, again, that we should regard her as something of a self-portrait. Coetzee does not explicitly raise the obvious question hovering over this particular close to his essay, which has elsewhere scrupulously followed the directions of a materialist critical practice which seeks to demystify the classic: should criticism wish to ally itself with Herbert's barbarian, or should it ally itself with a tradition of classics which have survived? Coetzee seems to say: if the classics are real, criticism will not be able to help itself. A classic demystified is not shorn of strength. But his novel is more partisan, ethical, and desperate in its approach to this issue, since it offers an account of a woman for whom the classics partly constitute the bonds of love that may link a failing human life to "what does not die," as she says of Bach.

Let me return in closing to the Thucydides passage yet again. Like her description of the spirit of Bach linking her to Vercueil, Mrs. Curren's hospital lecture to John attempts to use the classic to get out of the isolation in which she finds herself: to speak, to touch, and to love in a process of intergenerational transmission that is both personal and cross-cultural. Mrs. Curren recognizes her failure, the failure of her people, and the failure of her daughter (who has left South Africa in anger) as a failure to love, to be present as an eye, a voice, a hand, a body in the lives of others. Yet she cannot do anything except attempt to be such a presence, to see, touch, and speak. Nor does she wish her intervention in the horrors she witnesses to mitigate her guilt or make us sorry for her. This is a point she stresses, and here she clearly speaks for her author, who wants from us something other than our sympathy: "I tell you this story not so that you will feel for me but so that you will learn how things are" (*AI*, p. 103).

Despite its commitment to life, this text is narrated by a dead woman – either a woman who dies in Vercueil's cold embrace at the novel's end or the woman whose package he has taken to the post office. Here again, like Coetzee's *Foe* though less obviously, *Age of Iron* rewrites a canonical subtext from a more or less subaltern viewpoint: it is retelling *The Aeneid* – the story of the death of one city and the struggle to found another – from the viewpoint of Creusa, who, abandoned by Aeneas and killed by the Greeks, nonetheless returns as a ghost to urge him to set aside his grief, get on with his divinely-appointed mission, and live on for the sake of their child and the displaced future of their community.[10] Needless to say, in the unreassuring context of *Age of Iron* the ghost of Creusa does not bring such an encouraging message. Such a narrator produces many uncanny effects. The Aeneas to whom she would speak has no definite identity: her own daughter is absent, her own "defenders" are bloodstained criminals, the young blacks she defends and admonishes get killed, Vercueil, her one faithful listener, is so politically unencumbered, so immune to the summons of history, that he can dance to the old South African national anthem, "Die Stem" (*AI*, p. 180). Yet she must speak her truths even from death, awaiting a hearer.

This, I suggest, is Coetzee's pared-down and uncanny version of the classic humanist tradition in the South Africa of the Emergency. He presents the classics, and those writers like himself who have been shaped by their call, as poised between being abandoned despised ghosts, tossing on the shore of Styx without passage beyond (the ghosts described in the Latin passage Mrs. Curren recites for Vercueil [*AI*, p. 192]), and being so to speak a ghost with a future. That future will only happen if this Creusa can find a true Aeneas, a man or woman destined to establish new cities willing to be both a political parent and a cultural child. Thus Coetzee, unlike Gordimer, makes the survival of the classics in the State of Emergency a matter for future politics to decide, yet suggests, like Gordimer, that if truly classic, they will find an Aeneas who hears their call.

PART FOUR

EASTERN EUROPE AFTER COMMUNISM

INTRODUCTION

John Burt Foster Jr.

Because "Eastern Europe" was accepted terminology during the Iron Curtain decades, when it seemed to make the political status quo a geographical inevitability, it has not been popular in the border lands between the Germans and Italians to the west and the Russians and Turks to the east. "Central Europe" and "East Central Europe" have been floated as alternatives, but neither term has passed into common speech. However, the "Eastern Europe" in our title to this part is no tribute to the communist past; it is rather a way to highlight some cultural tensions in this area's relations with the West after communism. Despite the urge to affirm its connections with Europe after the lifting of old barriers, this nearest of Near Easts remains separated from the West by major divisions.

Marcel Cornis-Pope's vignette of a poet-rebel leading a crowd alongside a political conspirator strikes a keynote for these four essays. Potential for cultural renewal mingles ambivalently with sinister forces of ethnic difference, whose pseudo-Cartesian motto might be "I hate, therefore I am." On the one hand, as Cornis-Pope shows by relating Romanian developments to counterparts throughout the region, it was inevitable that movements of cultural resistance from the post-war Stalinist regimes to the events of 1989 and beyond should interweave philosophical and literary innovation. Since Soviet-style Marxism in Eastern Europe was a philosophy in power, with socialist realism as its artistic doctrine, it invited opposition along a spectrum from literary experimentation, through new forms of criticism and theory, to congruent styles of philosophical speculation. Contemporary trends in Western philosophy and literature did have an influence, but often after major reworking and certainly with more immediate application to the public sphere, as seen in Vaclav Havel's career or in Derrida's bemusement (cited in Cornis-Pope's epigraph) at notions that the Russian word for deconstruction was "*perestroika*." Nikita Nankov's essay updates these creative reworkings of Western art and thought. Marshaling performance art, semiotic theory, and other recent trends, he uses satire and audacious humor to demystify postcommunist Bulgarian anxieties about cultural identity, based on a location at the edge of Europe.

However, both authors do allow for countercurrents. Though Cornis-Pope calls on Eastern Europeans to replace reified, agonistic ideas of culture with "transactive" ones that recognize and negotiate differences (his own discussion being a case in point), he acknowledges the fragility of the literary/ philosophical resistance after 1989. Nankov worries about a tradition of terror in Bulgarian politics, and both authors note the new authority of the media, whose welcome liberation from party control also opened the way for divisive stereotypes from a pre-communist past. For Western observers, however, such problems have been eclipsed by the break-up of Yugoslavia and the Bosnian crisis, treated here by Tomislav Longinović and Caroline Bayard, whose essays predate the 1999 events in Kosovo.

These two chapters complement each other as an insider's and outsider's view of tragedy in Eastern Europe, but both also emphasize a certain bad faith on the part of the West. For Longinović, ethnic cleansing is not simply a frightening revival of the Nazi Final Solution, but harks back to more respectable Western ideas of the cohesive nation-state. It also draws on one set of current assumptions about culture, a separatist model that seems to mirror earlier racial dogma and that Balibar calls "the racism of cultural differences." Bayard shares these concerns, but also stresses the discrepancy between lofty Western ideals and an almost Munich-like failure to act on them. The failure is especially striking when contrasted with Cold War mobilization against danger in this part of the world.

Bayard's polemic includes the work of Jean-François Lyotard, who could analyze the aporias of irreconcilable public differences so incisively when handling denials of the Holocaust, but whose response to events in Bosnia was more muted. Ultimately, however, her "re-audit" moves beyond Lyotard to question relativist tendencies in current Western thought, which in effect would dismiss even ethnic cleansing with the never openly spoken comment: "It's in their culture." Against such fatalism, Bayard pleads for international responsibility, as argued in the writings of philosophers like Paul Ricoeur and Hannah Arendt as well as in the activities of human rights workers and other concerned people. She also invokes a renewed commitment to basic ethico-political universals, in the spirit of Michiel Heyns's essay in Part Three.

Reading Longinović with Bayard also provocatively juxtaposes Yugoslav and Western insights into the South Slav tragedy. Focusing on the encoded ethnopolitical affiliations of cultural artifacts and performances, Longinović; analyzes the nation's dissolution, moving from the integrative community of suffering proposed by Nobel Laureate Ivo Andrić to the widening dilemmas of late Titoism, then on to the implicit cultural allegiances of the *Laibach* rock group and the "turbo-folk" phenomenon. In the spirit of Bayard's remarks on Lyotard, he also undertakes an "audit" of Slavoj Žižek, probing the meaning of his influential "return to Freud" in the context of Yugoslav events. Bayard, meanwhile, brings together an impressive array of Western responses to the Bosnian crisis, from many different disciplinary and national perspectives. Yet with so much commentary yielding such meagre results, readers of her painful account can only hope that something has been learned for dealing with future crises. Bayard does consider various possible lessons, both philosophical and practical, yet reminds us that the West had already vowed, "Never again."

Delving into the deeper past, one could argue that some of the West's ambivalence and confusion during the Yugoslav tragedy depended on its very sense of geocultural identity. As pointed out in the general introduction, this is a culture that historically has resisted identification with any one place; rather, it has been a vector – and one with northern as well as western elements. The south and east by contrast have been problematic, often intensely so, for the Eurocentric gaze. In today's postcolonial environment, of course, this Eurocentric compass no longer holds the same authority in Africa or Asia. Yet Longinović and Nankov show that it still flourishes close by, as the southern parts of Eastern Europe, left behind by the northwesterly progress of the West yet undeniably connected with some of its past positions, struggle to get their bearings after decades of communist rule. Nankov rightly notes that this tangle of symbolic geographies and interwoven histories has close affinities with center-periphery issues in postcolonial theory. But as Longinović observes, turmoil in Eastern Europe also offers Westerners an exaggerated, unflattering, but not grossly inaccurate image of some key exclusions in their own tradition.

Thus the artistic hoax described by Nankov depends upon an intense need to give Bulgaria a place in Western culture. As a result, the well-known debt of Italian Renaissance painting to Byzantine frescoes can become the pretext for an invented Bulgarian intermediary who, emulating the originary role of classical Greece, initiates a northwestern migration of art that leads to Giotto. Similarly, but in a tragic setting where such fantasies can become driving motives, Longinović analyzes the breakup of Yugoslavia along a northwest to southeast axis. He suggests a story that, without exonerating the Serbs, is more complex than standard media accounts. Slovenia, at one extreme, could identify with Europe to the point of stressing its historical ties with the German world. But the Serbs, whose oral battle narratives once yielded precious insights into the origins of Western literature in Homeric epic, until the revival of these ancestral themes in Bosnia aroused the indignation of the world, had already been de-Westernized within Yugoslavia – as Eastern Orthodox in religion, as onetime vassals of the Turks, and as users of the Cyrillic alphabet. A "nasal racism" that sensed bad odors in everything southeastern gave a final touch to this drawing of boundaries. Even the demonization of this south Slavic people echoes, no doubt unconsciously, a double pejorative already embedded in Western languages when Africa and Asia were just distant rumors. For if "slave" borrows from "Slav," "Serb" comes from "servus," a Latin root for the same state of abjection.

Taken together, these four essays pair off with each other in several ways to give a many-sided overview of cultural exchange and conflict in Eastern Europe. On the one hand, its intellectuals have learned much from intellectual and artistic ferment in the West during the past generation, and have gone on to give creative new accents to that cultural movement. But, on the other, they face daunting challenges in turning from dissidence to finding new roles that would help their nations move productively beyond the communist era. And if reflection on the region's varied heritages could yield new insights into the postcolonial condition and transnationalism, the revival of old antagonisms warns of a future fraught with deadly cultural controversy. For the West, as it considers this region at the other side of a shared European homeland, and linked to the West's own identity by a long, intricate history, honesty should compel a sober awareness of tragic repetition – both of its own recent failures and of certain long-term prejudices. But a more hopeful observer might welcome a potential source of insight into an emerging global network of culture, which promises to interweave so many influences from so many directions that the old vectors will no longer serve.

9

CREATOR VERSUS CONSPIRATOR IN THE POSTCOMMUNIST REVOLUTIONS

Marcel Cornis-Pope

> Certain Soviet philosophers told me in Moscow a few years ago: the best translation of *perestroika* was still "deconstruction." . . . And this deconstruction is not . . . only the critical idea or the questioning stance . . . It is even more a certain emanicipatory or *messianic* affirmation, a certain experience of the promise that one can try to liberate from any dogmatics and even from any metaphysico-religious determination, from any *messianism*. . . . [T]his responsibility appears today . . . to return *more imperatively* . . . to those who, during the last decades, managed to *resist* a certain hegemony of the Marxist dogma, indeed of its metaphysics, in its political and theoretical forms. And still more particularly to those who have insisted on conceiving and on practicing this resistance without showing any leniency towards reactionary, conservative and neoconservative, anti-scientific or obscurantist temptations, to those who, on the contrary, have ceaselessly proceeded in a hyper-critical fashion, . . . in the name of a new Enlightenment for the century to come. Jacques Derrida[1]

> . . . The greatest menace *to* dictatorships lies in the fact that, through their "efficiency" in silencing the enemy, they deprive themselves of competitive collaboration. Their assertion lacks the opportunity to mature through "agonistic" development. By putting the quietus upon their opponent, they bring themselves all the more rudely against the *unanswerable opponent* who cannot be refuted, the nature of brute reality itself.
>
> Kenneth Burke[2]

The drama of the East European intellectual, Dorin Tudoran wrote two years before the December 1989 uprising, "is that he has all too many ideas, and no faith whatsoever! Reconquering faith would mean for the [East European] intellectual a moral resurrection, it would adjust his life experience to the ideas professed in his works. . . . The first non-bloody barricade for the contemporary

[East European] intellectual would have to be this rediscovery of self, without which he is doomed to remain a prisoner of the present crisis."[3] Whether "velvety" as in Czechoslovakia, or bloody as in Romania, the anti-communist revolutions of 1989 attempted to bridge the wide gap that had divided words from deeds, self from world, culture from politics. What these civic projects enacted, even if briefly, was a convergence between political and poetic imagination, between thinkers and doers.

In a key scene of the anti-Ceauşescu saga, beamed in daily installments on the American networks, a rowdy crowd led by two notable figures broke into the fortified headquarters of the Romanian National TV station to proclaim Ceauşescu's overthrow. The first figure could be easily identified as dissident poet Mircea Dinescu. To many participants and sympathetic observers, Dinescu's presence at the head of that insurgent crowd appeared as a historical reparation, a success story for the formerly ignored and disoriented Romanian intelligentsia. The mysterious second figure, mistaken briefly by the Western media for the new president of postcommunist Romania, was Sergiu Nicolaescu, film director and actor, well known for his lavish, semi-propagandistic screenings of Romanian history. The presence side by side of an emaciated, wild-eyed poet, looking like some fugitive from the communist gulags, and a flashy, histrionic film director towering over him, strikes me as a significant metaphor for the anti-communist uprisings. Let me explore briefly this revolutionary "primal scene" which brought together – in an improbable and volatile alliance – poet and master of ceremonies, dissident thinker and compromiser, creator and conspirator. I realize that the poles of my metaphor are not always clear cut: there is an adventuresome, histrionic side to Mircea Dinescu, which cost him his presidency of the post-1989 Writers' Union; just as there has been an occasional moral stir in Sergiu Nicolaescu's politics, which made him resign temporarily his Senate seat after he had been accused of betraying the ideals of the anti-Ceauşescu revolution.[4] More recently, Nicolaescu chaired a commission of inquiry into the repressive role played by the old party hierarchy, the Army and the Securitate in the December 1989 uprising, but his commission produced no significant revelations.

The poet's presence on that revolutionary stage was justified by a tradition of literary and cultural radicalism which had fed into that historical moment. For twenty some years the literatures of Eastern Europe had tried to match words to social realities in a "very serious game of anti-totalitarian doublespeak and newthink."[5] The philosophic and sociocultural issues that writers had been debating for two decades contributed to a significant ideological overhaul in pre-revolutionary Eastern Europe. In particular, novelists became acutely aware of the prohibitive boundaries set up by power around social "truth" and of their need to challenge them, first by insinuating a strong element of subjectivity and mythopoïesis into the prescriptive realism of the fifties (Mikhail Bulgakov, Ştefan Bănulescu, Géza Ottlik); then by sharpening their political focus in the anti-Stalinistic fiction of the following two decades (Aleksandr Solzhenitsyn, but also Jurek Becker, Augustin Buzura, Kazimierz Brandy, Stephan Heym, György Konrád, Milan Kundera, Miklós Mészöly, Anatoly Rybakov); finally, by attacking the very foundation of consensus reality in bolder experimental fiction, exposing Eastern Europe's paternalistic immobility (Gabriela Adameşteanu, Vasily Aksyonov, Péter Esterházy, Danilo Kiš, Mircea Nedelciu, Christa Wolf, Liudmila Petrushevskaia, Alexandr Zinoviev). Not only genres with a clear political commitment (debate dramas, ideological novels), but even private ones like lyrical poetry became vehicles of cultural and "moral resistance," opening "the doors and windows of poetry to life, reality, to history; to street language."[6] Literary and philosophic thought also played a liberating role: the various critical practices and arguments developed in the margin of official ideology challenged the centers of ideological production, promoting alternative visions and discursive modes.[7]

Recent political analyses have tried to explain the relative success of this critical-artistic "resistance" in hypercentralized Eastern Europe by emphasizing socialism's tendency to create dispersed states rather than monolithic power systems as previously thought. Even in countries where the process of de-Stalinization remained superficial, affecting artistic culture but leaving intact the economic and political base (the Soviet Union, Czechoslovakia, East Germany, Romania, Bulgaria), the communist system was to a certain degree "permeated with anarchy and competition," illustrating for Katherine Verdery the essential paradox of "socialism's 'weak state' . . . in which excessive centralization was yoked with extreme anarchy."[8] As a result of cultural de-Stalinization, political power worked according to a Foucauldian rather than Weberian definition, exerting insidious pressures on cultural symbology and ideological truth. By turning "language and discourse . . . [into] the ultimate means of production" (*NIS*, p. 91), communism colonized the political imagination of its people, but also created a cultural surplus, more intellectual work than the system could absorb or control. This excess managed over time to threaten the system, "reinvigorating and reframing . . . social imagination," "articulating kinds of social consciousness other than the authoritarian ones."[9] In Ceauşescu's Romania the *Glasnost* phenomenon began within the cultural and artistic superstructure: in a country where, until recently, historiography and political philosophy were not allowed to question official ideology, literature had to perform that function under the cover of its metaphors.[10] Literature and critical thought provided almost the only available forms of oppositional discourse also in Czechoslovakia, East Germany, and to some extent in the Soviet Union. The *Glasnost* phenomenon can be regarded as a successful convergence of transformative energies, in which the intellectual and artistic radicalization spearheaded by Jacek Kuron and Adam Michnik in Poland, György Konrád and Miklós Haraszti in Hungary, Jurek Becker and Wolfgang Biermann in East Germany, Paul Goma, Dorin Tudoran, and Mircea Dinescu in Romania, Alexandr Solzhenitsyn, Vladimir Bukovsky, and Alexandr Zinoviev in the Soviet Union, led finally to a genuine process of political reformation.

The product of this literary and cultural emancipation was twofold: a) the creation of a dialogic context in East European cultures, more tolerant towards innovative, reformulative discourses; b) the outlining of an alternative model of intellectual and social interaction for postcommunist "civic societies," based on creative "disagreement" rather than blind consensus. The second project often had to disguise itself to escape censorship. In Romania, an attractive but rather arcane version of civic society was outlined by the post-Heideggerian school of philosopher Constantin Noica who argued the redemptive value of culture and proposed a Socratic model of socio-cultural exchange outside the channels controlled by the communist state. This project rallied around it not only professional philosophers, but also literary and art critics with views that often looked postmodern. Departing from their master's proud assertion of marginality as a preserver of true cultural values, Noica's followers (Gabriel Liiceanu, Andrei Pleşu, Sorin Vieru) advocated an "ethics of engagement" and "cultural resistance" against the party's encroaching ideology. According to Verdery, "the Noica School came closest to articulating both the confrontation of culture with power and the possibility of an alternative vision – the foundation of a diversified ideological field and, through this, of transforming society from within" (*NIS*, p. 259). Other dissident thinkers tied their idea of an "open society" to notions of political pluralism, human solidarity, and European integration (Adam Michnik, Vaclav Havel, Zbigniew Bujak, Andrei Sinyasky, Paul Goma, Dorin Tudoran), as well as to the principle of "self-determination for individuals, groups, and for the nation" (George Konrád).[11]

At the same time, we must remember that for every victorious discourse in pre-1989 Eastern Europe there were others which never managed to break the silence. With the cultural space carefully colonized by the inflationary discourse of power, there was little room for whole-scale experimentation. New trends would emerge only when older ones would weaken or break up. The explorative work of Milan Kundera and Milos Forman found only a brief window of opportunity in pre-1968 Czechoslovakia; the innovative fiction of Danilo Kiš could emerge only when the "specific Yugo-hybrid of socialist realist doctrines" receded, and even then it continued to struggle with a xenophobic Serbian culture which "rejected foreign literary influences as unauthentic," preferring instead "realism with a specific national flavor."[12] In Romania, alternative modes of fiction (self-reflexive, psychological, feminist) gained attention only after the political novel which had successfully interrogated the Stalinistic fifties began to appear outdated. In criticism, stronger theoretical approaches emerged after the anti-systematic, paradoxical forms of "new criticism" had run their course.

And yet, in spite of its numerous hesitations and compromises, the literary-philosophic revival of the last three decades has played a transformative function in East European cultures, encouraging innovation and norm-breaking. Writers and philosophers were in the forefront of the process of cultural and political rethinking which led to the 1989 movements. Their theories and moral example found practical applications in the early days of the anti-communist uprisings: as each resister and dissident re-emerged from his or her own form of "internal exile," the crowds adopted them as leaders. But if poets and philosophers were projected to the center of the 1989 movements, they were also forced to share that revolutionary stage with professional conspirators trained to replace the collapsed first tier of communist power. This semi-dissident "second shift" of party activists and publicity-hungry intellectuals, deftly manipulated the revolutionary transition, insinuating itself back into the power structures. In retrospect, the Romanian revolution appears to have relied more on the theatrical, manipulative talents of its various plotters than on the creative imagination of its poets. The partnership between the free intelligentsia and those anti-Ceauşescu elements in the top party and army echelons that had established the governing "National Salvation Front" did not last beyond the first months of 1990. Prominent pro-democracy activists (Doina Cornea, Ana Blandiana, followed later by Mircea Dinescu) resigned from the National Salvation Front, protesting its "crypto-communist" tactics. The new publications associated with these democratic intellectual forces denounced the appropriation of power by the "caretaker" NSF. Literary imagination and political power were working again at cross-purposes, weaving two different narratives: one idealistic, reformulative, the other reactionary, interested in safeguarding the old infrastructure.

And Romania was not alone in choosing political expediency over poetic imagination, at least through the early years of "transition." While it is true that the post-1989 restructuring has produced a few poet-presidents, animated by the inclusive ideals of an "open," pluralistic society, they are outnumbered by political "conspirators" who have been busy dreaming up ethnically "pure" countries and new political empires (Yugoslavia's president Miloševič, Hungary's former vice president István Csurka, Russia's ultra-nationalistic maverick Vladimir Zhirinovsky, or presidential candidate Gennadi Zyuganov, Romania's National Unity Party president, Gheorghe Funar, and so on). While the transition governments of these countries (Yugoslavia excepted) reacted with embarrassment or criticism towards such nationalistic excesses, they have been known to use the politics of ethnic fear themselves, discovering in it an effective principle of self-legitimation: "I hate, [I fear], therefore I exist" (*FF*, p. 4). More importantly, a number of transition governments have learned almost instantaneously how to use postmodern tele-technics to revamp their own image. As Jacques Derrida reminds us, mass-media culture has contributed significantly to, and profited from, the collapse of communism: the power of the media channels "has grown in an absolutely unheard-of fashion at a rhythm that coincides precisely . . . with that of the fall of regimes on the Marxist model" (*SM*, pp. 52–3). While celebrating the return to market values, the techno-mediatic complex has also allowed postcommunist governments to consolidate their power by exploiting the ingrained paternalism, xenophobia, and anti-intellectualism of their voters.

Perhaps this was to be expected of a transition period coming after an ideology which for Derrida (*SM*, pp. 40–8) epitomizes the very definition of the French word "conjuration": conspiring, conjuring, exorcizing one form of power and socio-economic organization in order to replace it with the deferred promise of another. The irreducible paradoxes of the communist conjuration continue to haunt us as so many ghosts; we can thus say, with Vladislav Todorov, that the postcommunist period "demobilizes communist ideology and rehabilitates the conspirators."[13] The political culture of this period unfolds like a postmodern spectacle which has replaced self-promoting totalitarian ideologies with more insidious, local *mise-en-scènes*. Though the new plotters of division have not, with few exceptions, gained mass following, their increasing popularity threatens the fragile balance between politics and cultural emancipation achieved in 1989. This raises the question of whether the encounter between poetic imagination and political pragmatism has ever really taken place. And if it has, does the current resentment against the dissident thinkers and writers who had prepared the 1989 revolutions in East Germany (the Christa Wolf case), Czechoslovakia, Poland or Romania, signal the end of oppositional thought as we know it? Are aesthetic "resistance" and critical innovation viable strategies in the postcommunist restructuring? Can literary discourse challenge and mediate between the monologic, ethnocentric concepts of culture that have re-emerged in many places? Or should the radical intelligentsia simply retire, leaving the stage to political conspirators?

The answer to this last question can only be negative. The Eastern European cultures are undergoing at present an identity crisis whose causes are largely ideological, having to do with an unsettled conflict of theories and mentalities. The postrevolutionary landscape of Eastern Europe is strikingly incoherent, traversed by remnants of pre-socialist and socialist ideologies which have not been properly re-examined. An Enlightenment rhetoric of cultural emancipation coexists with some form or other of nationalism; a nineteenth-century notion of market capitalism overlaps with a distrust of mass consumerism; over-politicized modes of cultural production vie with aestheticism and cheap entertainment. The demise of the communist regimes did not bring instantaneous democracy: as Vladimir Tismaneanu correctly argues, the "slow pace of the national purification" needs to confront resilient communist "customs – all the habits, mentalities, attitudes, symbols, and values that had permeated social life for decades"; but also "resentful [precommunist] myths" of an ethnic kind[14] that have lain dormant in Eastern Europe through four decades of forced national amnesia. The input of a creative and critical intelligentsia is especially needed in such periods of transition, torn between transformative and restorative trends. Innovative literature and criticism can now play the role of a "democratic laboratory":[15] rethinking divisive socio-cultural issues and exposing the vestiges of totalitarianism in whatever guise they may appear.

At the same time, however, the creative thinker must be prepared for his confrontation with the political conspirator. The magnitude of the issues being decided today on the battlefield of cultural ideology no longer allows the writer-thinker to withdraw to the margin of politics, in an attitude of subversive expectancy. The strategies of aesthetic and cultural "resistance" worked well under the centralized power of the communist state. The sharp divisions and conspiratorial plots of the postcommunist phase require a pragmatic breed of critic-poet who can connect his/her intellectual function as a critical consciousness to an active political role. As Nicolae Manolescu, Romania's premier literary critic and president of the Party of Civil Alliance, has argued, the two activities are not conflicting but complementary: the politician draws on the analyses of the critic who can always return to his writing to rethink his responsibilities in a rapidly changing cultural and political environment.[16] Neither superciliously distanced from the fray of politics, nor unreflectively immersed in it, the politician-poet can continually move in and out of the political structures, reimagining these structures and his role in them. It may well be that his main role should remain that of a critical interlocutor of power, responding to its divisive tactics with his discourse of restructuring and mediation. But this oppositional role should be used in a politically effective way to set much of the country's agenda for democratization.

There are encouraging signs of this new type of collaboration between political and cultural imagination. The input of a pluralistic, mediative type of thought is reflected today in the political programs of the democratic governments which have managed to replace (in Romania as recently as the November 1996 elections) the more ambiguous transition governments of the "postcommunist" phase (1989–95). The growing influence of this pluralistic-mediative imagination is obvious even in the area of national ideologies. If the nationalistic propaganda has so far had less success than anticipated in most East European countries, it is also because the critical opposition has managed to discredit a self-assertive form of nationalism, denouncing its old tactics of class and ethnic division. The work of literary and cultural pluralists has had a positive impact on the civil Imaginary, "reducing the national idea to manageable size" and replacing the discourse of the Nation with "persuasive discourses on pluralism and democracy" (*NIS*, p. 318). But their role in the process of postcommunist democratization is far from finished. The ideals of intercultural and interethnic communication are even more important today, in the shifting contexts of Eastern Europe, tempted simultaneously by globalist and localist interests. The task of East European literatures is to continue their creative brainstorming, finding more imaginative ways for reconciling ethnocultural differences with global emphases. Literary and philosophic thought need to confront openly, and with more effective tools, the agonistic process of nation- and culture-building in Eastern Europe, which started with the post-World War I ideal of a self-determined and democratic Central Europe conceived in the interstices between collapsed empires. This project was often interrupted and detoured between 1918 and 1989, both by right-wing nationalisms and left-wing (pseudo)-internationalism until it was recovered more recently by dissident intellectuals in the former Soviet bloc. The "Joint Declaration from Eastern Europe" (October 1986), signed by 123 pro-democracy activists, proclaimed a "common determination to struggle for political democracy in our countries, for their independence, for pluralism founded on the principles of self-government, for the peaceful unification of Europe and for its democratic integration, as well as for the rights of minorities" (quoted in *RP*, pp. 188–9). But these notions of ethnic tolerance, cultural pluralism, and human solidarity are being threatened again by a return of postcommunist societies to older myths and definitions of national identity.

A perceptive analysis of these national myths can be found in Livezeanu's 1995 book, *Cultural Politics in Greater Romania*.[17] Taking advantage of the post-1989 re-evaluative mood, Irina Livezeanu submits the cultural myths of the 1920s to a critical scrutiny, arguing that the history of East Central Europe before communism was marked by political and ethnic problems which often put the ideal of democratic restructuring in jeopardy. The autonomous civil society conceptualized between the wars was not as genuinely pluralistic as that reimagined by recent dissident thinkers from Czechoslovakia, Hungary, Poland, Romania, or the Soviet Union. The legitimate aspiration to national self-determination often translated into nationalistic-integrative tactics rather than into a concept of multicultural coexistence. Richly documented from East European and Western archives, Livezeanu's book makes a convincing effort to explore the historical antecedents of the interwar process of nation-building in Eastern Europe and occasionally points to the confusion of national issues under communist ideological practices; but the very fact that her investigation is confined primarily to the period between 1918 and 1930 tends to isolate and reify the study of East European nationalism.

A critical re-examination of the interwar cultural ethos, such as that undertaken by Livezeanu, can help prevent East European postcommunist societies from falling back on idealized pre-communist models of nationhood. But in order to be truly effective, this analysis must consider the "postcolonial" conditions that enabled the emergence of nationalistic ideologies in the aftermath of World War I and their reappearance after the collapse of the Soviet Empire. In 1918, the emancipated nationalities of Eastern Europe were confronted with the enormous challenge of rapidly modernizing, democratizing, and consolidating their culture after several centuries of colonial domination (Turkish, Russian, Austrian) or limited state sovereignty. In 1989, questions of ethnicity and nation-building re-emerged with a vengeance after being repressed for several decades by "internationalist" Soviet ideology. The striking parallelisms between these two moments call for a comparative analysis that would acknowledge the retarding effect that traditional as well as revamped forms of imperialist domination (such as the Soviet) had on the process of nation-building in East Central Europe; this analysis should further consider the role played by both right-wing nationalism and communist internationalism in obfuscating any serious analysis of our concepts of ethnic and national identity.

The consensus among analysts is that the post-totalitarian restructuring of Eastern Europe must include the creation of a new civil society that will function as a catalyst for broad intellectual and social exchanges; but this enterprise depends on a successful re-examination of the conflictive notion of difference inherent in Central European ideas of ethnicity and race. This process should not lead to a disregard of ethno-cultural differentiations (something like the socio-cultural "leveling" pursued by the former totalitarian societies), but rather to the development of a non-conflictive (transactive) socio-cultural space that would allow each ethnic group to contribute its own interests and traditions. As Mihai Spariosu has suggested in a series of studies culminating with *The Wreath of Wild Olive: Play, Liminality, and the Study of Literature* (1997), we need to question both our totalistic notions of identity inherited from the Enlightenment, and the agonistic conceptualizations of difference embodied in Nietzsche and his heirs, Derrida, Foucault, and Deleuze.[18] As faces of the same "mentality of power" that has dominated Western thought (*GMN*, p. xviii), such reified conflictive notions fragment culture, organizing it around nationalist, racist, and ethnocentric interests.[19] The appropriate response to them is neither a simplistic eradication of difference from cultural transactions, nor some sort of transcendental leap to an integrative, "universal" consciousness, but rather the recovery and consolidation of those interactive, multicultural spaces within which ethnic differences are recognized and negotiated. Clearly, this task cannot be accomplished by adepts of either the class-party or race-party systems who continue to hide behind their nationalistic rhetoric. The articulation of a truly democratic social body can only come from an uncompromised, politically imaginative intelligentsia, willing to take Eastern Europe through a "purgatory" of self-reevaluation.

10

YUGOSLAVISM AND ITS DISCONTENTS

A CULTURAL POST-MORTEM

Tomislav Z. Longinović

Slavoj Žižek's 1996 book *The Indivisible Remainder* opens with a statement of national belonging: "As a Slovene."[1] This embrace of Slovene national identity seems to be at odds with the writings of the philosopher whose Marxist-Lacanian meditations have earned him the reputation of being one of the "hottest" poststructuralist thinkers in the West. It is especially unsettling to read this simple declaration of what is, without a doubt, a form of "postmodern nationalism" from a philosopher whose work had until recently been part of a broader cultural space, that of the former Yugoslavia.

According to the Croatian weekly *Start*, Žižek's Slovenism was articulated when the Yugoslav People's Army tried to stop the secession of its northwestern republic and he responded with the following exclamation: "Today I have become a Slovene." Žižek constructs this embrace of his particular brand of ethnic belonging as a direct result of the aggression of the imploding socialist state. Slovenism is offered as an escape from the Balkans, towards the promise of *Mitteleuropa* and perhaps in the distant and ever-elusive future of Western Europe or Europe itself. In the late 1980s, Slovene hunger for Europe was expressed with the slogan "Europa zdaj!" (Europe now!), as if Yugoslavia was not already a geographical part of Europe. However, a special brand of symbolic geography was at work in this strategy of separating the Slovenes and later the Croats as members of a different civilizational tradition, from the "east" and the "south" which were associated with yet another label in the emergent racist discourse of the former Yugoslavia – the Balkans.

Slovene escape from Yugoslavia was indeed a response to the rise of "the serbs" under the guidance of Slobodan Milošević, who were marked as belonging to an inferior culture due to their double orientalization, both as postcolonial subjects of the Ottoman Empire and as bearers of an Orthodox Christian cultural heritage tied to the heritage of Byzantium.[2] "The serbs" were a threat to the Slovene "European identity" because they had the power of numbers and weapons, which could coerce the Slovenes to remain part of the abject cultural space of "the Balkans." The concrete political response to this threat was Slovene adoption of a national flag which was identical to the flag of the European Union. Belonging to Europe and the West was defined by a Roman Catholic cultural heritage, a separate Slovene language, and nationalism based on civil society.

The racism of the Slovene position was not immediately perceivable to the proverbial "Western observer," since whiteness, technological superiority, and universalist humanism have all been incorporated into the specter of Europe itself, as the symbolic foundation of the West. The German push for the political recognition of Slovenia and Croatia by the European Union was a symptom of this civilizational recognition of the northwestern Yugoslav republics as belonging to Europe, while the rest were forced back south and east into the realm of political immaturity, cultural inferiority, and social abjection.

One of the most interesting cultural manifestations of Slovene racism was the rise of the rock group *Laibach* in the early part of the 1980s, which featured the performance of totalitarian imagery in the context of the emergent punk and new wave scene of the former Yugoslavia. Performing in dark Nazi-like uniforms, with stern expressions on their faces and mechanical bodily movements, the members of the group evoked an uneasy and nervous laughter from their audiences. Since *Laibach* is a German name for the capital of Slovenia, the first reactions of the official communist establishment usually denounced the use of its German instead of its Slovene name, Ljubljana. The rock group was part of a hierarchically organized artistic movement that called itself *Neue Slowenische Kunst* and that included theatrical, dance, and visual art components. The names of the individual artists were very intentionally suppressed so that the collective could be placed in the absolute foreground of this New Slovene Art movement.

Although most of their performances were received by contemporary culture critics as a parody of the totalitarian legacy of both the left and the right, *Laibach* foregrounded the desire for order, cleanliness, health, and beauty inherent in the tacit racism of the newly emergent Euro-American culture which foregounded the "West" as the ultimate achievement of world civilization. *Laibach*'s parody of the socialist state through a post-punk performance of overidentification with its inherent totalitarian logic was an early manifestation of a Slovene desire to distance themselves from the object of their parody, fleeing the union with those other peoples who did not belong to the same civilizational tradition. The formation of the artistic collective around *Laibach*, which significantly bears a German and not a Slovene name, *Neue Slowenische Kunst* (NSK), was one of the first symptoms of the Yugoslav cultural dissolution that began in the 1980s. Here is how the program of this group was formulated to the Japanese magazine "Takarajima":

> NSK (*Neue Slowenische Kunst*) is an organized cultural and political movement and school established in 1984, . . . as an organization active in the area between ideology and art. NSK unites the total experience of Slovene art and politics. Our cultural and political groundwork is the Slovene nation and its history . . .[3]

The cynical blending of politics and art in the Yugoslav context, which had overcome its own version of socialist realism by the early 1950s, achieves a double-edged effect. On the one hand, it exposes the trappings of Tito's soft totalitarianism and its effect on art and culture, not through critical distancing, but by parodic identification with its theoretical assumptions. On the other hand, Slovene allegiance to and endorsement of Germanic *Mitteleuropa* are present as tacit acknowledgments of the European white supremacist discourse.

Žižek's placement of *Laibach*'s cultural mission is quite different. Coming from the same Slovene culture, he presents his compatriots as psychoanalysts who manipulate the transference by performing the underside of the obscene superego of the socialist state: "By means of the elusive character of their desire, of the undecidability as to 'where they actually stand,' *Laibach* compel us to take up our position and decide upon *our* desire."[4] On the contrary, *Laibach*'s performances of totalitarian imagery were far from undecidable and elusive for those who stood on the Eastern side of the symbolic boundary that began to divide Yugoslavia after Tito's death in 1980. Their parodic performance clearly articulated Slovene supremacy within the disintegrating socialist state, provoking both laughter and pity. The confusion arose in the field of reception, since many intellectuals could not directly confront their performance, exactly because it was so blatantly racist. And if they had a hard time deciding upon their desire, it was not so hard for the political elites in the eastern part of Yugoslavia to decide upon their own version of ethnic suprematism and cultural superiority, and upon military means for its achievement.

Although the *Laibach* phenomenon played a tiny role in the former Yugoslavia at that moment, it became one of the symptoms of the emergent ethnic-based culture that was to dominate that country in the eighties and lead to the war in the early nineties. Since the very name of the Slovenes proclaims their Slavic origin, the new nationalist leadership chose a new strategy which replaces the "genetic" identity of a people with its "culture," which then assumes the central place in this new form of racism. *Laibach*'s intentional or unintentional participation in this project was manifested in the choice of German names in order to claim affiliation with *Mitteleuropa*, thus playing into the Germanic dream of geopolitical domination of the "Other" Europe. According to this reading of the Balkans, Slovenes and Croats belong to the West because of a culture rooted in Roman Catholicism and a postcolonial status as former Habsburg territories, while the rest of the Yugoslavs are culturally inferior due to their domination by the Ottoman Empire and a culture rooted in either Christian Orthodoxy or Islam. South Slavic identity is consequently subdivided according to these new criteria of civilizational belonging.

Here is how Petar Tancig, the Slovene Minister of Science and Technology at the time of the outbreak of the Yugoslav war in 1991, expressed this new form of racism based on cultural differences:

> The basic reason for all the past/present mess is the incompatibility of two main frames of reference/civilization, unnaturally and forcibly joined in Yugoslavia. On one side you have a typical violent and crooked oriental-bizantine (sic!) heritage, best exemplified by Serbia and Montenegro . . .

> On the other side (Slovenia, Croatia) there is a more humble and diligent western-catholic tradition . . . Trying to keep Yugoslavia afloat . . . is also very bad geostrategic thinking, as independent (and westernized) Slovenia (and Croatia) could and would act as a "cordon sanitaire" against the eastern tide of chaos.[5]

Is it then strange that Slavoj Žižek begins *The Indivisible Remainder* with a statement of national belonging, especially since that belonging is later accompanied by the vision of Freud's discovery of his most vivid and influential metaphor for the unconscious after wandering through the Škocjan caves in Slovenia? For if the father of psychoanalysis saw in the Slovene landscape the concealed foundation of the entire Western European civilization, is it then so strange that one of Slovenia's proudest sons has taken it upon himself to continue the "return to Freud," initiated by Jacques Lacan? Žižek's vision of Freud in the native landscape serves to authenticate and essentialize the position of the Slovene philosopher in psychoanalytic theory by playing the double role of a tourist guide for proper Europeans and of a civilized, "Westernized" Slav.

Žižek as a figure and a symptom of the Yugoslav implosion is certainly less apparent to the "Western observer" than the Bosnian bloodshed and the role of "the serbs" as designated aggressors. The look at Žižek's "narcissism of minor differences" is *Unheimlich* exactly because it brings to the fore questions that the West is not willing to confront regarding the destruction of Yugoslavia.[6] It is especially in regard to "the serbs" that the Euro-American West has refused to see its own enlarged and distorted image in the atrocities committed in the name of a territorialized collective identity which calls itself "the nation." If aggression by "the serbs" was the cause of Žižek's transformation into a Slovene, isn't that process of becoming part of a larger entity revealing of all identifications, individual or collective? And inversely, aren't then "the serbs," especially in the incarnation constructed and disseminated by the Western media, manifesting the behavior that forms the very core of Western identity and which Europe no longer wants to consider its own?

In *Civilization and its Discontents*, Freud sees "inclination to aggression" as a profoundly human phenomenon which the work of civilization regularly fails to contain and eradicate (*CD*, p. 61). If we consider the Yugoslav implosion as one of the cases where the civilizational framework of the multiethnic state has failed, then the foregrounding of particular ethnic identities which followed this implosion will necessarily bear the mark of this aggression. The struggle for the territorial division of Yugoslavia followed the logic of aggression, whereby the land figured as the metaphor of ethnic identity which needs to be defended in the name of acculturated religious differences. Since the ideological framework of Titoism did not survive Tito's death, the military-party complex which was left in his wake tried to anchor itself in a different symbolic frame. As the fear of bipolar nuclear confrontation faded, class interest was gradually replaced by ethnic pride as the main ideological category within Yugoslavia. The ideology of official Yugoslavism, symbolized by the slogan of "brotherhood and unity," had been in decline since the 1974 Constitution transformed the country into a virtual confederation. Instead of following the Leninist model of "democratic centralism" present in other socialist countries, this constitution decentralized the governmental power and control over every aspect of political and economic life, giving the six constitutive republics and two autonomous provinces much virtual independence in decision-making. One of the results of this decentralization was the nationalist perception that ethnic minorities (particularly Albanians, Bosnian Moslems, and Hungarians) had been strengthened at the expense of "the serbian" majority. Slovene Edvard Kardelj, who was the spiritual father of the 1974 Constitution and Tito's right-hand man, was later accused by "the serbs" of designing it with a future decomposition of Yugoslavia in mind. Tito's death in 1980 only accelerated this process of splitting, since there was no paternal metaphor of comparable symbolic and political authority to act as a substitute for the power exerted by his name.

Slobodan Milošević's attempt to insert himself into Tito's position with the help of the military-party complex of the disintegrating state and "the serbs" resulted in the cloning of the paternal metaphor within the boundaries of a particular ethnicity: while Milošević became a totalitarian substitute for "the serbs," Tudjman was invented as his counterpart for "the croats," Kučan for "the slovenes," Izetbegović for "the moslems," etc. This authoritarian cloning created a political climate which completely delegitimized Yugoslavism as an overarching conceptual framework within which the common state of "the South Slavs" could function. The failure of Yugoslavism represents a failure of civilization precisely because it marks the rise of a new type of exclusivist discourse which Etienne Balibar has called "the racism of cultural differences."[7] This new form of racism is not as blatant as the one promoted by the German Nazis or the KKK; its exponents try to normalize their racism by insisting on the incompatibility of different cultures and the impossibility of their dialogue. According to this view, each ethnic group should stay within the boundaries of its own civilizational framework, without attempting to bridge the gaps and understand its "others." Since Yugoslavia had been founded at the intersection of a multitude of civilizational currents brought about by the colonial subjugation of its ethnic groups, these cultural differences were part of the historically constructed reality incorporated into the ideology of Yugoslavism. Therefore, the tacit collaboration of the Euro-American West with the homegrown nationalists in ex-Yugoslavia has been evolving exactly along the lines of this new racist discourse that does not tolerate cultural incompatibility, while conflating it with the premises of classical racism.

Apart from the official "brotherhood and unity" sloganeering, the community of different ethnicities had been imagined by some of the most prominent intellectuals as a multicultural entity based on the common experience of foreign political domination and subjugation. The foundation of Yugoslavism in the class interest of workers and peasants that had been promulgated by the communist party was supplemented by the notion of cultural Yugoslavism based on the experience of common postcolonial suffering. When the ideological foundations of the state vanished, this cultural notion of a common destiny based on the absence of fulfillment was obviously not enough to keep the state together, but gradually evolved into a racism of cultural differences.

Ivo Andrić imagined the community of co-sufferers in his novels *The Bridge on the Drina* (1945) and *Bosnian Chronicle* (1945) as a model for this type of multiethnic community. Published right after the end of World War II, these novels provided a literary context for the newly created "second Yugoslavia," led by Tito and his communist partisans. But Andrić's ambiguous portrayals of his native Bosnia could never escape the echo of historical traumas which were naturalized in his novels. Using the metaphor of the "great flood," Andrić posits the times of the misfortune as the only channel for interethnic communication available to the Bosnians:

> After the interval of fifteen or twenty years in which they had once more restored their fortunes and their homes, the flood was recalled as something great and terrible, near and dear to them; it was an intimate bond between the men of that generation who were still living, for nothing brings men closer together than a common misfortune happily overcome. They felt themselves closely bound by the memory of that bygone disaster. They loved to recall memories of the hardest blow dealt them in their lives. Their recollections were inexhaustible and they repeated them continually, amplified by memory and repetition; they looked into one another's eyes, sclerotic and with yellowing whites, and saw there what the younger men could not even suspect.[8]

The common memory of misfortune that binds men together is presented as the model of collective identity upon which Andrić imagines his version of Yugoslavism. At the bottom of this negative identity is the self-perception of victimization by forces which are outside the sphere of the individual's grasp and control. While the "socialist realist" writers from the same period featured the "positive" Yugoslav identity through the triumph of Tito's partisans over the forces of Fascism, Andrić found unity in the shared negative historical experience of all three Slavic communities, otherwise divided by religion. This paradox of unity in negativity expresses the universal nature of collective and individual suffering rooted in the colonial and postcolonial condition of Yugoslavs. The repetition of misfortune through narrative remembering serves to reinforce the common bond between men, founded on the secret knowledge of the victim which can never be fully recounted, but remains fixed in the glances exchanged between the old men. The horror and silence of those who endure natural disasters are equated with the misfortunes which originate in human behavior as well.

Wars, invasions, occupations, and colonizations which come from both the East and the West have the same fatalistic origin and purpose as the "great flood." While writing about the beginning of World War I and the persecution of "the serbs," Andrić invokes a mechanism of destruction which underlies civilization:

> The people were divided into the persecuted and those who persecuted them. That wild beast, which lives in man and does not dare to show itself until the barriers of law and custom have been removed, was now set free. The signal was given, the barriers were down. As so often happened in the history of man, permission was tacitly granted for acts of violence and

> plunder, even for murder, if they were carried out in the name of higher interests, according to established rules, and against a limited number of men of a particular type and belief. (*BD*, p. 282)

The violence is naturalized by a fatalistic sense of the universal course of the "history of man," where the beast within is awakened by the new political situation and its destructive instincts given free rein.

Falling in love with one's collective reflection requires the hatred and extermination of the simplified, reified other. The emergence of the "wild beast" is not incompatible with civilization, since murder, plunder, and violence in general can be committed "according to established rules" and "in the name of higher interests." One could also argue that the failure of humanism as an ideology is predicated on the ceaseless struggle against other species of "wild beasts" which occupy a lower place in the scheme of evolutionary classification. Is it then strange that a woman who endured the siege of Sarajevo tried to explain the Bosnian war to me by saying that it was a sort of divine punishment for slaughtering and eating so many little lambs and piglets? Balibar's analysis of universalist humanism leads him to conclude that "the problematic quality of *difference between humanity and animality* is re-utilized to interpret conflicts within society and history" (*RNC*, p. 57), reinforcing a kind of racism that dehumanizes religious and ethnic others by ascribing animality to them. The inability of civilization to see aggression as its own foundation, leads it to use the animal as the metaphor both for those who transgress its prohibitions by killing and those who fertilize its foundations by being killed. This is the paradoxical realm which appears to Freud as the working of Thanatos, the "death drive" which is supposed to collaborate with Eros in the homeostatic regulation of civilization. Aggression is civilization's irreducible other, which is nevertheless built into its very foundations. Or in the words of Walter Benjamin: "There is no cultural document that is not at the same time a record of barbarism."[9]

If Yugoslavism managed to sublimate the inner workings of its "animals," personified in the various ethnic identities locked within their respective "narcissisms of minor differences," it did so by instilling a sense of guilt in the major protagonists of the conflict. During the Titoist period, both Serbs and Croats were constantly reminded that not all of them had fought alongside the communists during World War II and the German occupation, but were instead drafted into the ranks of Royalist Chetniks and Nazi Ustashes. Anyone diverging from the official ideologies of the communist party could have been accused of "nationalist deviation" and therefore cast in the role of the "domestic traitor" to Yugoslavia. The figure of Tito functioned as a strict super-ego within the public sphere, preventing the eruptions of nationalism by maintaining a constant level of collective guilt over the two most dominant ethnic groups. Being a Croat himself, Tito came to power by leading "the serbs" to establish the new order and "liberate" the country from foreign occupation, breaking the imaginary boundaries of civilizational separation between the two groups, while reinforcing his version of Yugoslavism. The desperate attempt of the communists right after his death in 1980 to hold onto power in the name of the father was expressed in their adoption of the slogan with surreal overtones: "I posle Tita – Tito." (After Tito – also Tito.)

The belief that the dead father will continue to function as the metaphor which guarantees the life of Yugoslavia was predicated on the same guilt that was supposed to keep the ethnic conflicts from spreading. Cast in a role that apparently transcended ethnicity through power politics of the new Yugoslavia, Tito functioned as a screen onto which each ethnic group could project its own collective guilt. The existence of this guilt, paired with the military-party apparatus of the communist state, was the main guarantee of the existence of the common state of the South Slavs. The absence of Tito signaled the moment when the burden of guilt could be transposed into its horrifying analogue – aggression and violence between the ethnic groups. One of the cultural manifestations of love for the dead father was embodied in the attempt to continue celebrating the "Day of Youth." This holiday, which marked Tito's birthday, involved a relay race around Yugoslavia which culminated with the "baton of youth" being handed to the president-for-life at the central event in Belgrade on May 25. In the absence of Tito, the baton was placed in the position where he used to stand, its phallic shape reminiscent of the imaginary nature of all power. The structure of this event was staged as if it was meant to parody the psychoanalytic theories of both Freud and Lacan, revealing the underside of the symbolic order which was soon to collapse under its own weight.

This type of cultural demonstration of loyalty to the dead father did more damage to the idea of Yugoslavism in the early eighties than the riots of Kosovar Albanians that began to destabilize the country politically around the same time. The emptiness of the supreme signifier of political Yugoslavism became painfully obvious through another popular cultural practice initiated at the same time: street vendors began selling aluminum pins in the shape of Tito's signature. Another sign of loyalty that was supposed to alleviate the collective guilt of Yugoslavs for past crimes against each other was enacted by wearing the signature of the dead father on their bodies.

Ultimately, none of the cultural projects which tried to sustain Titoism worked because the gestures of collective identity were as empty as the signifiers that were supposed to embody them. Milošević's attempt to act as a father substitute failed because he could appeal only to "the serbs," due to the nationalist rhetoric he embraced in the late 1980s. The reaction of Slovenes to the "serb-rising" rhetoric was predictably in tune with the age-old European practice of "nasal racism" which had been applied to those outside the magical circle of *Mitteleuropa*: the thumb and the index finger preventing the unpleasant odor of those Balkan "orientals" from reaching their refined nostrils. One's proximity to Europe was measured by the quality of that odor, whose unpleasantness increased along the northwest–southeast axis. Bosnians, Albanians, and Macedonians ranked the worst on that scale, but the Slovenes did not have to worry about them as much, since they had the Croats and the Serbs as territorial intermediaries, or, as Petar Tancig had put it, their own *cordon sanitaire*.

Atrocities tied to the name of Bosnia and "the serbs," who emerged as designated aggressors, seconded by "the croats," against the postcolonial/

neocolonial assertion of an independent identity by the Bosnian Moslems, cannot be separated from the name of the Slovenes. Their desire for independence and for Europe was intimately tied to a version of soft, cultural racism, based on the idea of ethnic separation which runs along the lines instituted by the former colonial masters. The supposed cultural superiority of the former Habsburg subjects emerged after communism lost its ideological validity, manifested in Slovene calls for a "civil society" which would of course exclude most of the rest of Yugoslavia. Other Yugoslavs figured in Slovene nationalist discourse as "dirty Bosnians," transforming the desired "civil society" into a return to a claustrophobic vision of the ethnically homogeneous nation state. Žižek recognizes the multiplicity of possible meanings inherent in the individual's relationship to the state, which however functions under the same name and constitution: "When the signifier 'our Nation' starts to function as the rallying point for a group of people, it *effectively* co-ordinates their activity, although each of them may have a different notion of what 'our Nation' means" (*IR*, p. 142).

As we have seen earlier, Žižek co-ordinates his own intellectual activity with that of other Slovenes by symbolically descending into the Škocijan caves with Freud in order to claim the realm of unconscious exploration for himself and his nation. "As a Slovene," the postmodern Lacanian philosopher finds himself confronted with the same figure which Freud met in the depths of the caves. Žižek analyzes Freud's encounter with the right-wing, anti-Semitic mayor of Vienna, Dr. Karl Lueger, as if Freud was recounting a dream and not a real event from his life. According to this interpretation, the mayor's last name associates with the *Lüge*, which is a German word for lie. *Ditto*, "what we discover in the deepest kernel of our personality is a fundamental, constitutive, primordial *lie*" (*IR*, p. 1).[10]

This lie which constitutes "our personality" is also what we find at the bottom of both the individual and collective identity embraced by Žižek. If our personality is constituted by this primordial lie, then the ethical concerns of those psychoanalytic theorists who believe in this finding need not conform to anything else but this lie. If the unbearable inconsistency of the symbolic order forces the subject to constantly falsify his own sense of personal identity, isn't the extrapolation of the lie to the "national" level a logical next step? Therefore, the fundamental lie has been responsible not only for the successful operation of the institution of psychoanalysis, but also for the Western perception of the Yugoslav implosion which has been considerably influenced by the narratives manufactured by the Slovene Ministry of Information.

Here's how National Public Radio reporter Sylvia Poggioli analyzes her experiences at the beginning of the Yugoslav Wars, after the Slovene secession:

> Starting with the 10-day war in Slovenia in June and July of 1991, one of the most difficult tasks for reporters has been to protect themselves from the propaganda offensive. The Slovenia Information Ministry organized a media center in a modern underground conference hall in Ljubljana. Here troops of young multilingual Slovenes constantly churned out reams of war bulletins. [. . .] We were supplied with excruciatingly detailed

accounts of battles too far away to check personally before deadline. Often we learned the next day that the battles had never taken place.[11]

Freud's underground caves were replaced by an underground media center for the dissemination of lies which have colored perceptions of the Yugoslav wars ever since. The United States were drawn into the role of the protector of those civilized peoples of the Yugoslav northwest that used to be played by the Habsburg Empire during the nineteenth century. Acting as the agent of Western "democracy and justice" on the basis of Slovene "fundamental lies," it set out to impose civilization and order on those less civilized peoples of the Balkan southeast.

This certainly does not mean that the governments of Serbia and Montenegro were justified in their own campaign of lies, which stemmed from their traditional cultures rooted in heroic epic poetry. Western scholars have long regarded Balkan epic poetry as the source of the "Western" literary heritage, a paradox which made popular oral verse-making of the "East" into a cult object in the "West." In his monumental study *The Singer of Tales* which researches the Serbo-Croatian oral tradition, Albert Lord posits the formulaic theory of verse-making as the remnant of the Homeric epic that can be traced to the roots of the "West" in classical Greece.[12] By stressing the formal side of particular oral formulas, Lord moves away from the postcolonial context in which his and Perry's research took place. In fact, the Balkan tradition of epic verse-making represents the perpetual resurrection of past traumas, which are mourned in male company, and represent at least two contradictory interpretations of the Ottoman Turkish rule in the Balkans.

In order to be modern, a nation has to prove both to its members and to its others that it is ancient, older than time itself. This desire to posit its origins on the side of the old in time and the present in space, finds its expression in the epic tradition stored and transmitted mainly by "the serbs," but also by "the moslems" and others who sung for Milman Perry and Albert Lord in the postcolonial Yugoslav Sandžak region. The centrality of the epic formula is for Lord a purely literary concern that he has cultivated as a student of the Ancient Classics of the Western Tradition. He chose to research the voices and memories of the singers trained by the division of Balkan Slavs into Christian slaves or *rayah* placed into the apartheid-like "millets" formerly ruled by the Greek Orthodox colonial theocracy and by the Moslem Slavic feudal owner class of "beys," "agas," "pashas," "spahis," and so on.

The uncomfortable questions of history and politics were laid aside as a matter of temporal banality which does not belong to the study of the oral tradition and its formal properties before the advent of literacy. Displaying the identity of the Western scholar-sage, Lord developed his formulaic theory of verse-making as a timeless expression of the classical Greek epic which has been preserved in the Dinaric region of the former Yugoslavia. On the other side of the West, both "the moslems" and "the serbs" who sang and listened to the heroic epics lived in a different kind of Europe which had endured colonization by an Asian power well into the nineteenth century. The 1462 execution of the last Bosnian king by Mohammed II is a perfect metaphor for the Turkish colonization of the Balkans, since this Ottoman ruler demonstrated a fascination with Italian Renaissance doctrines of human freedom, which he embraced to repeat in reverse the military performance of Alexander the Great and conquer the West of Europe. Although the last Bosnian king surrendered after written assurances that the sultan would not harm him, Mohammed considered a promise to an infidel the same as a promise to a dog and had him decapitated.[13]

For "the serbs," resistance to the Turk as a religious colonizer activated medieval narrative models embodied in the figures of the Orthodox Christian priest and the blind singer of tales whose epic formulas performed the ritual of mourning for the injured "manhood and honor" of their nation. These epic performances by old men put into circulatation the dominant codes of the "community of birth and faith," which is itself constituted by what Bakhtin had conceptualized as the "single and unified world view" of the epic imagination.[14] Lord's formulaic theory provides a context for theorizing a collectivity prior to the "nation," which is performed by the oral word recalled from imagined centers of signification which circulate through the bodies of singers. Their performance of the epic enables the audience to relive the trauma of conquest by wailing and crying as it remembers and mourns the days of slavery to the Turks. At the same time, the literary devices of exaggeration and mythologization of the past provide a perfect metaphor for the postcolonial imagination of "the serbs." Their nationalism is indeed based on epic formulas which have been effectively transposed into their own media campaigns against the contemporary representatives of Islamic culture: Bosniaks and Albanians.

What is bothersome is the Western distinction between the "angelic" nationalisms which were perceived in the northwestern republics of Slovenia and to a certain extent Croatia, and the "demonic" ones which were soldered to the name of "the serbs." While there was the willingness of the West to look the other way in cases where those "diligent Catholic nations" were abusing human rights and fomenting hatred of those "culturally inferior" nations of the Yugoslav southeast, there was a great need to demonize "the serbs" and make them the target of one of the most vicious campaigns devoted to foreign policy issues in the Western media at the end of the twentieth century.

"The serbs" have been collectively tried by the most powerful global institutions and the media and found guilty of ethnic intolerance, forced ethnic displacement, mass rapes, massacres of civilians, use of detention camps, and creation of an endless stream of refugees. The transformation of Serbian national identity into a tool of ethnic totalitarianism has resulted in political, economic, and cultural exclusion from the global community. Very few "experts" stressed the fact that the war for territorial division of Yugoslavia came as the result of the diplomatic de-recognition of that state, transforming "the serbs" into a population without a common state, the supreme guarantee for the functioning of the collectivity within the present political system. The passion and violence with which "the serbs" lashed out at their former "brothers" were at least partly a reaction to the perceived betrayal of the common Yugoslav state. It was especially those members of the newly reimagined community of "the serbs" who lived outside the administrative boundaries of the Republic of Serbia and who found themselves in the newly independent states of Croatia and Bosnia-Herzegovina that have displayed the "uncivilized" forms of behavior condemned by the international community. They were faced with the bleak choice of going back to Serbia three centuries after they had been "ethnically cleansed" from its territory by the Turks, or "ethnically cleansing" either those who embodied the return of Moslem colonial rule in Bosnia or those who exterminated them in the name of ethnic purity in Croatia. By now, more than half "the serbs" no longer inhabit the territories they settled in the eighteenth century as the "border guards" of the Habsburg Empire.

"The serbs" who remained in Bosnia have been forced to assume the role historically played by the Ottoman Empire until the nineteenth century, acting out their own postcolonial "identification with the aggressor" in Bosnia and Croatia, by expelling all non-Serbs from the territories they hold. At the same time, their political behavior was fully in tune with the Austro-German rationality of *Realpolitik* based on the territorial expansion of the stronger at the expense of the weaker. This paradoxical identification with former colonial masters is most obvious in the popular culture which is dominated by the melodies of the emerging turbo-folk culture of the Milošević-Marković era, which features "orientalized" popular music combined with the rise of the new criminal class, known as *dizelaši* (the Diesel Boys). Turbo folk is the sound of an unacknowledged postcolonial culture that has been dormant under the communist veil of forgetfulness until the latest war. The techno rhythms from the Germanic colonizing cultures to the North and the West (Europe proper) are embraced as markers of racial/cultural superiority, while the wailing voice of the singer articulates a suppressed, shameful legacy of one's slavery to the Turks, who are regarded as a part of the inferior cultures and races of the Islamic East and South. At the same time, this music reveals the emptiness of myths of racial and ethnic authenticity, since turbo folk features a hybrid culture produced by combining musical importations from past and present colonial masters. Turbo folk fit perfectly into the emergent nationalist culture of the late eighties and the war culture of the early nineties, since it foregrounded a zero-degree identity of "Western" technological dynamism and the performance of "Oriental" emotional depth, which could not be easily blended with the political rhetoric about the age-old Serbian pride and desire for independence.

This new identity is defined by the desire for inclusion into the symbolic realm of European "whiteness" which is manifested in the presence of the adjective "turbo" in the name of the musical genre. The incessant repetition of the techno beat is a ritual meant to insure their belonging to the West, which has never recognized them as its own part. The place of the Serbs within the West is defined by the Latin etymology of their proper name (*servus*, meaning servant, serf, or slave). This abject position makes them "black" despite their genetic "whiteness" in the eyes of the West. In order to entice the gaze of the West, new Serbian singers engage in musical performances rooted in the combination of the most archaic and the most modern. On the one hand, the Serbian treatment of its Ottoman colonial heritage comes from the Christian crusading mythology which manifests a European fear of contamination by an alien, "oriental" civilization. At the same time, turbo folk features the "oriental" sound as the essence of racial being and belonging, which it appropriates from the culture of the Ottoman invaders as a metaphor of its own colonial power over other Yugoslav ethnic groups. This postcolonial moment, reactivated by the disappearance of Titoism as a Pan-Yugoslav discourse, brings back collective identities which imagine their medieval origins as the essence of time and being. The victims and torturers are placed within stories which originate within the imaginary of their birth communities, predicated on an agonistic vision of the past and the future as they participate in the breakdown of old state structures and the creation of new totalitarian ethnic territories.

11

BOSNIA AND THE ETHICAL LIMITS OF CULTURAL RELATIVISM

RE-AUDITING LYOTARD

Caroline Bayard

The issue of the importance, boundaries, and limits of Lyotard's political philosophy needs to be confronted explicitly in the wake of the nineties, since *The Differend*, one of the profound and pivotal texts of the eighties in France, has to be re-examined in light of a decade which witnessed the revival of ethnic cleansing and human rights violations.[1] Some commentators have referred to the latter developments as "the resurrection of an evil in Europe which many had assumed had been extinct since the defeat of Nazi Germany"; others have looked upon them as "a philosophical problem"; others still have depicted them as "Europe's death in Sarajevo." It appears reasonable today to submit that a re-examination of Lyotard's discourse analysis – once enacted in the eighties in front of the worst case of historical revisionism – is called for. Because, since 1991, Europe has witnessed catastrophic resurgences of nationalistic turmoil and civil war, its citizens may well be interested – and rightfully so – in re-auditing Lyotard's philosophical intervention.

But what had this text proposed? In 1983 how had it looked into the clamor, uproar, and ultimate silence of the Shoah? *The Differend*, as an inquiry into or appraisal of the impossibility of phrasing that which could not possibly be phrased, had fulfilled a particular expectation, or responsibility in France of the early eighties.[2] It had responded to a specific anxiety when that country, a Western European nation among other European polities, had experienced its own period of dangerous revisionism. However marginal such excesses had been at the time, they had caused substantial distress – and still rightfully do so today – in a culture never remembered for defending its own Jewish citizens with the same courage or decency that other Western European nations (Denmark, or Italy in this context) had demonstrated during World War II.[3]

I, for one, must concede that I find it harder to be persuaded of the philosophical significance of this text today than in 1983. Why? Why should one be entitled to be disappointed today? Why could one suggest that "the honor of thinking" which Lyotard was proposing to save, has not in fact been saved? In part, it may well be due to the unfair assumption that words should have made a difference, i.e., that Lyotard's reminder of the Holocaust might at least have made it problematic for other genocides to unfold *exactly* in the vicinity of those which had taken place some fifty years earlier. As it turned out, the tragic entreaty of Lyotard's words did not make one iota of difference to the European incapacity to act while there was still time to save civilian lives, or to protect those principles they had stood by when recognizing the legitimacy of national self-determination for Slovenia, Croatia, and Bosnia.[4] When Lyotard wrote in 1983 that differends "are reborn from the very resolution of supposed litigations" (*D*, #263), his accuracy was then seen to be just as presciently cruel as it turned out to be pragmatically and politically futile in the 1990s. Although Lyotard's accurate diagnosis does not necessarily provide a healing of past sins, neither did it prevent an eerie re-enactment of European genocidal passions, as recently noted by many political analysts,[5] except that in the nineties we could all watch those passions on television and – if we had the time – meditate upon Lyotard's *Differend*, or simultaneously "reflect upon our sorrow when faced with the incommensurability between Ideas and realities" (*D*, #260). Sadly, that humble epistemological knowledge which *The Differend* had bestowed upon us in 1983 contributed very little to an ethical, moral, or practical resolve to salvage or protect those ideas we Europeans had thought we believed in (democratic process, pluralism, constitutional rights, human rights, individual rights), while Europe staged and enacted, through various bungling operations, its own differend for the nineties. So that it was not so much a drama of culture as an ethical shame. I would argue that what both this European shame and drama of culture specifically invoke is a sharp reminder of the importance of ethical norms in international relations, norms taking explicit precedence over extreme cultural relativism.

Clearly, Lyotard cannot be faulted for his own community's sins. Yet one wishes he had addressed the issue. Others did and did so to political leaders, while Lyotard remained – to my knowledge – silent.[6] Of course it should be noted that the European community as a whole, as well as the West, were complicitous in encouraging hopes for a multicultural, multiethnic Bosnia in 1991, while knowing that little would be done to foster such principles, or to enact supportive measures to ensure that such a state would indeed be viable. If, as Anthony Lewis put it, "Bosnia was an example of multiculturalism in the fine sense, an instance of different cultures finding common ground rather than the separatism some American multiculturalists want the word to mean," then it would follow that Western policy makers and democratic citizens should have limited the proliferation of what was to take place: extensive civilian strife, rape, and war crimes.[7] Hence, *the sorrow amongst spectators and actors, in this end of the twentieth century*, since Lyotard's ethical mediations in *Le Différend* (1983) and *Le Postmodernisme expliqué aux enfants* (1986) actually made little difference.[8] All appearances suggest that they – as philosophical reflections available to both witnesses and actors enacting the modes of specific polities –

did not facilitate any conflict resolution, nor did they encourage political players to reflect upon the massive differend which was taking place in their own backyard (if one may refer to the former Yugoslavia as Europe's backyard). By August 1995 all efforts to mediate a conflict resolution between the warring parties, or to protect civilian populations caught in the cross-fire, appeared null and void. Massive human rights abuses had been taking place within the so-called "safe havens" circumscribed by the EU and other Western nations (Canada being one of the parties involved in this case), and the whole of Bosnia Herzegovina was, as David Rieff has recently and succinctly put it, a slaughterhouse.

While a respect for contrasting cultures and historical narratives is relevant, while liminalities and difference need to be taken into account in post-1989 Europe, it is nevertheless crucial to remind readers of this essay that ethical issues should take precedence over discursive differences, that the horror of a human slaughterhouse has precedence over the obsession of discourse analysts with narrative freedom. Two decades ago I had assumed that a scrutiny of a shared European experience, an *anamnesis* of our collective and individual pasts, would enable us to learn from our respective grievous histories. Today, I am less sure than I was – when I was younger – that such a process has been meaningful. In fact, looking at the uses of history by the very defenders of liberal democracy, the so-called protectors and watchguards of human rights, one does have strong doubts about the justification scholarly historiography has sometimes, albeit unwillingly, provided to human rights abusers. Also, describing a culture as anthropologically mired in hatred and prejudice (i.e., to describe its human rights abuses as a drama of culture) has made intervention look unworthy and essentially futile.[9] "Sauver l'honneur de penser" was explicitly on Lyotard's agenda in 1983. As he wrote then, "Given 1) the impossibility of avoiding conflicts (the impossibility of indifference) and 2) the absence of a universal genre of discourse to regulate them . . . [let us try] then at least to save the honour of thinking" (*D*, p. xii). And I have always respected this entreaty. But I find it difficult now to see how he specifically tried to salvage such honor when the only consensus the European community achieved on Bosnia was precisely to do as little as possible, as belatedly as possible. I also find it hazardous to determine how even the possibility of thinking with integrity will ever be rescued for Western Europeans watching this Balkan morass.[10]

In fairnesss to Lyotard, the world changed considerably (and he with it) between 1983 and 1996. In 1994, in *Moralités postmodernes*, he signalled that his mega-mistrust of the "economic genre" had been replaced by the recognition of liberalism as that system "which is performative, open, and faced with the entropy of closed systems, Marxist or fundamentalist, both of which are inevitably condemned to ultimate disappearance."[11] Indeed, the lament of 1983 on the oppressive nature of "capital," where he wrote "the economic genre of capital requires the suppression of the heterogeneity of genres of discourse" (*D*, #253), did give way to a very different critical analysis of our shared benefits: a conviction that the "commandments of liberal democracies were good," since they allowed the existence of such organizations as Amnesty

International as guardians for minority rights (*MP*, p. 108). Yet, the ambiguity Lyotard nurtures vis-à-vis these same liberal democracies re-emerges in an essay dedicated to Gilles Deleuze, titled "Ligne générale," which reflects upon the *dangerous abuses* (emphasis mine) of the definition of "liberal democracy," as well as upon the disquieting emergence, in North America at any rate, of "special rights and minority rights." While stressing that rules of liberal democracy are as essential as the defense of those rights is vital in polities where such rights are – by definition – not even recognized, Lyotard insists that the constant policing of conformity to such rights can ultimately culminate in total and radical oppression. When one moves from the position of *vigilante* to that of proxy for a totalitarian order one has crossed that line.[12]

Thus the intractable region Lyotard was earlier speaking about, or what he earlier called also "l'inhumain, la région inhumaine qui échappe tout à fait à l'exercice des droits" (*MP*, pp. 108–10), appeared also *to be* that about which no democracy, liberal or other, can or should legislate . . . lest it become a totalitarian order. This did not mean that the author of *Moralités postmodernes* failed to express a certain melancholy about the appropriate use of rights and responsibilities in such liberal societies, or about the disquieting removal or excision of this "inhuman region . . . which radically escapes and lies beyond the notion of rights." To the contrary, as he put it succinctly, rights are only meaningful when they salvage that which exceeds them: misery, sin, passion, energy, inspiration.[13]

While it is easy to understand why and how Lyotard chooses complexity and conflict over any utopian temptation to dispose of evil, when he makes it his duty to remind us that "just as much as terror (and abjection, its mirror image) must be excluded from any community structure, it must be accepted and endured in the domain of writing (écriture), as its singular condition of existence" (*MP*, p. 180), I would also maintain that the distinction he sketches between "community" on the one hand, and "writing" on the other, needs to be challenged. It is acceptable to see how one needs to establish – meaningfully and thoughtfully one hopes – distinctions between terror in the community as opposed to terror and abjection in writing. But, one will stress equally that it is important to recognize the correlations and connections between the two. Ethnic strife and hate-discourse are not, most of us would agree, as we look at recent genocides in the former Yugoslavia or Rwanda, as thoroughly disconnected as Lyotard seems to imply. What is more, to affirm that terror and abjection *have to be* "subies et assumées" (accepted and borne) would not and should not impress human rights activists as a thoughtful coda to such ordeals. One could add, human rights workers – in their quotidian struggles – would not at all be daunted by the risk of evil disappearing in the near future, or by the peril of a quick disposal of the inequities and crimes present in this world. When one acknowledges the futile, tragically numbing battles human rights activists wage daily, in Bosnia in particular, Lyotard's concept of risk does seem inappropriate; and any suggestion that our shared European polities are in danger of ever acceding to a semblance of eternal bliss on the human rights front seems outright unreasonable.

A careful observer of Lyotard's work in the later nineties will suggest that if a Marxist teleology of history has been extinct in his work since his early days (*Socialisme ou Barbarie*, 1956), nonetheless later on, he chose to replace such a teleology with his own poetic, romantic wager centered upon the inhuman. Strangely, this inhuman has shown a tendency to fulfill the role of the proletariat of old, "l'étranger inhumain" becoming that which saves us from the dangers of consensus (as he puts it in *MP*, p. 110), where he re-reclaims this "inhuman region which radically escapes the exercise of rights, or that which incites us to resist" (as he reminds us in *I*, p. 88).[14]

The silence to which Lyotard exhorts us to listen may be tempting if we have the luxury to savor such privileges.[15] If we enjoy the entitlements common to "normal European nations," then indeed in such a world Lyotard's call has full currency. If, in other words, we belong to polities which have effected the transition from "an emerging nation-state of the modern period" to that of "a matter-of-fact, economically institutional body, focused on establishing co-operative international communities and determined to cooperate *and* compete with other nations," then by all means Lyotard's exhortation may well be in order. In other less fortunate, or "less normal" European nations (to use political scientist Peter Schwarz's definition), Lyotard's anxiety about protecting "the silence of the other" comes off as a pure irresponsibility, as thoughtless extroverted recklessness.[16] Worse than this, seen from the Balkans today, it throws into serious doubt Lyotard's civic and ethical responsibility as much as it reflects the geo-political incompetence and abysmal inadequacy of the Maastricht nations between 1991 and 1996.[17] And in the latter case this is exactly what a number of commentators, critical theorists, and legal experts have maintained.[18]

PHILOSOPHY'S LIMITS IN FACING A HUMAN SLAUGHTERHOUSE

The question the same observer will ask is: are Lyotard's entreaties of any use to aggrieved Europeans attempting to participate in a minimal re-establishment of human rights in Bosnia? Curiously in a French context, Lyotard in the early sixties had made valiant efforts to confront his own government's human rights abuses, in Algeria and in France. Indeed when there was political, civic danger his interventions were significant.[19] Also, in the early eighties he was indubitably listened to when he confronted the ugly face of revisionism regarding the Holocaust amongst his compatriots, although in this case the outcome of the battle was already predetermined, easily won, and never acute, except as a historical/ethical duty. No historian in France, provided he is not a fringe lunatic of the Ernst Zundel Canadian category, would think today of disputing the reality of the Holocaust.[20] Possibly, one could object that correcting a historical misinterpretation (however hideous it may be) is a small proposition. Impacting on one's own government's incapacity to act is another. But "Sauver l'honneur de penser" is also inherently linked to – although clearly distinct from – those specific, punctual, "defensive and local interventions" which, as Lyotard had reminded us in 1984, intellectuals will still have to wage, year after year, even in an era when the heroics of yesteryear are obsolete (*PW*, pp. 6–7).[21]

The questions one will be obliged to ask at this point, therefore, are these: how local? how defensive, how outraged should the average citizen be when facing the Sarajevo slaughterhouse, as well as the broader context one could call the Yugoslav tragedy? How much European shame can a private citizen withstand after these years of violence? While one may need to heed Lyotard's reminder of the importance of acting as "a night watchman," as a "careful listener to what is spoken, to what is not yet spoken," nevertheless it is difficult not to experience an uneasy sense of *his* incapacity to address what, on the other hand, did occupy the minds of Euro-citizens. These might have been the culpable witnesses of ethnic cleansing, to which they offered little or only belated resistance, explained by someone like Baudrillard as a drama of culture (*LCP*, pp. 188–9); but the same citizens were also explicitly troubled by those national communist regimes, as neighbors.[22]

It is interesting in this context to interrogate with care the Lyotardian disquiet, or suspicion if you will, expressed in 1984 to David Carroll about universality as this "horizon to attain from the starting point of an immanent, singular situation."[23] While accepting Lyotard's attention to the difficulty present when one translates, not only from one language to another, but *also* from one culture to another – what he calls "this complex agglomerate of contexts" – it is equally relevant to challenge the validity of Lyotard's hesitation in an International Relations context. Furthermore it seems pertinent to look to other philosophical reminders capable of extricating Lyotardian principles from such difficult aporia.[24] Strangely enough, in other circumstances he did not hesitate to cross this line. In 1991 for instance, precisely in the context of the Iraqi invasion of Kuwait, he chose to support Allied intervention in the Gulf war, a position he took, not only as a citizen, but also as a philosopher.[25] At that time Lyotard, along with Pierre-André Taguieff, Alain Touraine, and Jacob Rogocinski, rejected Gilles Deleuze's and Pierre Bourdieu's interpretation of this massive military intervention. It was not, he insisted, a war of the rich against the poor, of the North against the South, but "a defense of the Rule of Law in a Post-Yalta World suddenly destabilized by the disappearance of its former binary balance" (*GR*, p. 12). While neither he nor any of the other signatories denied the immense responsibility of Western nations who had constructed, abetted, and shaped Saddam Hussein (a position Lyotard was to elaborate upon in a subsequent essay, "The Wall, The Gulf, the Sun: a Fable"), he recognized the need to attend to those exacting demands enunciated by an ethical politics in the nineties.[26]

Lyotard's position on the Gulf war is not my subject here, yet the rich contradictions it emphasized in ethical and International Relations terms should be looked at within the framework he himself established on the issue of justice in his earlier texts. In *The Differend* and *Le Postmoderne expliqué aux enfants* one found a philosophical argument waged on two opposing, contradictory tracks. On the one hand, he had insisted as early as the late seventies upon the reality of legitimation crises in advanced societies. On the other, in the eighties he stressed the impossibility of accepting foundationalism and emphasized the danger of a utopian faith guaranteeing immutable, immovable laws. In each of these successive contexts he reiterated the preposterousness of countering the irremediable opacity of language itself.[27] Without confronting Lyotard with either/or binary solutions, one cannot avoid proposing that first his radical rejection of foundationalism, then his subsequent, last-stand position on the Iraqi invasion of Kuwait, in effect an ultimate defense of the Rule of Law . . . do not exactly offer a consistent pattern. Today, to save the honor of thinking in the context of European politics – and after our lamentable collective performance on the Yugoslav front – he may have to tackle the issue of political and civic answerability differently. If he could have found it within himself to warn Europeans in 1991 against both "the combined temptations presented by moral angelism and cynical realism" in order "to preserve the exacting demands of an ethical politics" [la voie difficile d'une politique morale, cf. endnote 27], one wonders where he was between the bombing of Vukovar and Dubrovnik and the slow destruction of Sarajevo. Equally, one needs to understand *why* he did not join his other compatriots when they asked the French government to "play a more direct role in resolving this conflict." One will necessarily wonder also why he did not recognize the destruction of a specific national group (i.e., the Muslims in Bosnia), as numerous other French intellectuals like Pierre Bourdieu, Jacques Derrida, Ariane Mnouchkine, and Etienne Balibar had with no hesitation.

APPEALING TO OTHER THEORISTS?

Other texts, by younger philosophers such as French Myriam Revault D'Allones or long-departed philosophers such as Hannah Arendt or even Aristotle seem to me to address issues of what Arendt had called "a reconstruction of the ethico-political" in a more persuasive way than Lyotard has been able to, in either 1983, 1991, or 1993. I would also add that Paul Ricoeur, another contemporary of Lyotard, has interrogated such obligations and responsibilities. Specifically in the context of the economically advanced economies of Western nations, in that of well-established democracies operating through the rule of law (or "Etats de droit"), when Ricoeur proposed that the quest and the promise of rationality contained in the definition of a rightful democracy were indeed the sustenance and extension of ethics, he was not afraid of taking ethical and philosophical stands. Taking Ricoeur's text *Autour du politique* (1991) into consideration, along with his thoughtful 1994 reminder about the interactions and intersections between politics and ethics, in the context of democratically established states operating within the Rule of Law, may help European citizens assess their ability to deal with future conflicts in a more persuasive way.[28] The effectiveness of ethics in Ricoeur's eyes was precisely to have provided politics with a dignity which it had lost through various catastrophic regimes (a reminder which *The Differend* serenely avoids, but which Europe since the 1990s may want to confront). Re-establishing ethics in the practice of politics, in Ricoeur's eyes, is also precisely the capacity to re-establish "the *reasonable*," as opposed to "the *rational*," within the concrete universal which defines the political as such.[29] Similarly, in the 1990s another philosopher, Myriam Revault D'Allones, although her point of departure is more territorially based than Ricoeur, calls to our attention the ethical necessities today facing the citizens of a democracy (Maastricht's voters in this case). Such subjects, recalls d'Allones, will have to face those demands put upon them by what she calls "a democracy which should not be exclusively, or smugly satisfied with the management of its own entropy," and she urges her readers to be aware of such needs and expectations.[30]

The ordeal of Bosnia – seen by its inhabitants (at least until 1994) as a European site, hence as part and parcel of European culture and so deserving a level of support from Europe that never materialized when Bosnia faced virtual annihilation – raises two issues. The first is the question of reflecting upon the "unthinkable"; the second is a response to the need, as Arendt had also urged her readers after the Eichmann trial, to be reconciled with reality, to accept – once horror and shame have been confronted – the challenge of participating in a transformation of this heritage. When we reflect upon the unthinkable (Arendt's term), or the inhuman (Lyotard's) – which has operated as the ground-zero meaning of showing one's respect for minority and democratic rights crushed through the fire and hell of ethnic cleansing – we may subsume a particular experience (first the Bosnians', then ours) within a general rule, within a bedrock of sense. If we fail to do so, then we may well have to abandon the purpose of civic reponsibility, period. As Hannah Arendt recalled in her reading of Kant's *Critique of Pure Reason* and his *Critique of Judgment*, it is possible to propose that singular events be deciphered as particular events which reveal the definite within the general.[31] Once such translation is effected, then answerability or responsibility must be brought in.[32] Pertinent to a reading of our present situation are the specific reminders of Ricoeur, Arendt, and Kant applied to the precise context of Bosnia. Those reminders apply to European disarray when faced with the destruction of a legitimate, fully fledged multicultural society, initially gifted with all the trappings of so-called European normalcy.[33]

What can Hannah Arendt, Ricoeur, and Revault d'Allones tell us which Lyotard could not? Simply, all three of them help us face this question from two separate, although connected conceptual levels. The first one appears to be the infinite, yet necessary danger of living with, of co-existing with, the inhuman. Lyotard is not as alert as one would like him to be on this issue. In the area of individual and civic responsibility, he has not said anything which can facilitate even a provisional settlement of conflicts. His emotional fatigue concerning international relations, political upheavals, and ultimate betrayals since *Le Différend* in 1983, *Le Postmodernisme expliqué aux enfants* in 1986, or his intervention during the Iraqi–Kuwait war in 1991, has not decreased, but only grown deeper. As a philosopher, he has either retreated into the position of last resort (a position he would have preferred not to find himself in, but had to face in the end – his position on the Iraqi–Kuwait war), or into an embrace of the benefits of liberalism. Both positions will inevitably be viewed as resigned acquiescence to the inevitable. And this became evident in his *Moralités postmodernes*, when it has become increasingly clear that the Cold War has been won by one side. His critical stance then consisted in identifying – unenthusiastically, of course – with the benefits of liberalism. But this was done not in a Ricaldian spirit (i.e., because he wished to proceed to a methodical exposé, or analysis of both liberalism's merits and the need of controlling its operations), but primarily because there were *no other options left*, and to his surprise history had not turned out the way he obscurely had expected some decades ago.[34]

One point should be emphasized: Lyotard stresses in the 1990s that there *are no alternatives* after 1989 beyond liberal democracy. On this particular terrain he defends himself from any nostalgia smacking of leftist irredentism.[35] Nonetheless, Lyotard's position is not totally convincing. If the Rule of Law appeared defensible in 1991 during the invasion of Kuwait, it is difficult to see why recent European history has not awakened comparable commitment from Lyotard's philosophical agenda. Furthermore, recent re-examinations of the concept of responsibility, along with Ricoeur's extensive re-examinations of this concept in "Ethique et politique" and "Le Concept de responsabilité," have forced a number of European philosophers and legal scholars today to challenge its undue extension and propose a different, ethical interpretation of its expectations. Emmanuel Lévinas and Hans Jonas, for instance, recompose Lyotard's concept of responsibility on moral grounds. In both Lévinas and Jonas, Ricoeur points out that we witness a narrowing of the juridical sphere, along with an extension of its moral counterpart. Ricoeur insists that, in the case of Hans Jonas, one notes the application of responsibility as an imperative. With Lévinas he recalls that one notices a widening of the issue of responsibility, a broadening which transforms fragile and vulnerable beings as objects of responsibility.[36] Such a displacement of the subjects of our responsibilty also fits in with a distinct moral sensitivity and the promotion of intersubjectivity as a major philosophical theme.

PRAGMATIC LESSONS FROM BOSNIA

Commentators, International Relations theorists, and legal experts have written extensively on ways to limit political and civilian damage in a future European conflict, as well as in civil and ethnic wars.[37] Contingency planning for major humanitarian disasters appears increasingly relevant to both policy makers and military attachés. But more importantly, policing (on the part of NATO in this case), and discarding a *Realpolitik* approach in favor of a permanent International criminal court, freed from the criticism that dogged the Nüremberg war crimes trials of 1946 (where victors imposed their justice on the vanquished), is called for by a number of different voices. Morris B. Abram and Václav Havel have independently reached such conclusions.[38] The notion of collective guilt would be the shortest way to accepting the ideology of ethnic fanatics, and both Abram and Havel reject the concept of "warring parties" which amounts to an unwitting acceptance of the ethnic principle while ignoring the difference between aggressor and victim.

To learn from the past and to attempt better humanitarian interventions next time would seem to be in order. Ethicists might be well-advised to take note of

International Relations scholars' inquiries both into human rights and into concerns formulated by human rights organizations, specifically about changing definitions of the notion of national sovereignty and especially vis-à-vis international bodies such as the United Nations, which have had a long tradition of codifying the principle of non-intervention.[39] While non-intervention has also had a long-standing tradition in international jurisprudence, one primarily based upon the sanctity of national sovereignty, it has become increasingly evident in the past decade that such paradigms are being challenged.[40] Thus policy reversals reflect the way the international community views human rights and also the controversy within the UN over allowing armed intervention to reduce human suffering. In the past, however, this did not necessarily entail a pragmatically efficient and protective international response in Bosnia. It is true that this change might have contributed to the destruction of the Muslim population of Bosnia, for example, when peacekeepers were stationed where there was no peace to keep and in effect allowed to be passive witnesses, if not unwitting participants, in another genocide.[41] It is also true that the lamentable narrative of the United Nations' incompetence, lack of vision, and obstinately impervious attitude regarding the disaster looming over Bosnia-Herzegovina, as early as 1991, was never put as clearly as when Boutros-Ghali termed it a "rich man's war," which did not really require a strong United Nations response against evident abuse.[42] But equally, it is becoming extremely clear that Bosnia should teach us what Lyotard began to scrutinize in *Le Différend* in 1983, although he failed to do so in the 1990s when another genocide took place in Europe.

What is there among Western Europeans today which may allow them to interpret their failure to meet their responsibility to a neighbor, their obligation to act in the midst of full-blown genocidal realities? As Ricoeur has bravely put it and Lyotard failed to discern, understanding our past – which is, as Timothy Garton Ash put it in a reference to the historical complexities of Eastern and Central Europe that also applies to the West, "a present past, a distant past"[43] – is more than an important hermeneutic exercice. More to the point, it represents an ethical and moral duty. Presumably "never again" will be another mantra for Europeans to clamor, some eighty years after they initially uttered it in 1919, only to have to repeat it in 1945. Presumably also such expectations will strictly depend upon the civil societies of so-called normal Europe, whether they remain ritualistic, virtual mantra, or whether they will teach citizens, if not what to do, at least what *not* to do in times of strife and uncivil discord. As a contemporary editorial in *The Economist* concluded, a complete withdrawal of the NATO implementation force – or IFOR – after October 1996 would be a clear recipe for disaster. So, "if Europeans cannot persuade the United States to stay in IFOR there is only one solution. They should have the courage to lead IFOR's successors themselves."[44]

Although cultural elements are clearly present in most genocidal situations, clearly also in 1996, such elements cannot be invoked as even minimally explanatory. A drama of culture explains little. Worse, it can become an excuse for exonerating oneself from minimal accountability. Ethical expectations, on the other hand, became by the 1990s explicit hermeneutic exercises as much as practical International Relations operations. As the editorial in *The Economist* sternly put it, they oblige even distant witnesses to take a stand and to face the reality of a long haul rather than abstracting themselves from concrete materiality.

12

CULTURAL CO-ORDINATES OF A BULGARIAN ART-HOAX

"DRAFTS" BY VIRGINIA, A *TRAGEDIA DELL'ARTE*

Nikita Nankov

[To Dzhinko Terpentinko]

> i moite veseli risunki sa mnogo tâzhni risunki . . . Iliia Beshkov[1]

> Politics again? Why can't they just hear it as a piece of beautiful music?
> David Henry Hwang[2]

PROLOGUE

Signore e Signori, welcome to the show!

I mean the one-man show *"Drafts" by Parthenos/Virgo Restored and Presented by Virginia Stoianova* or, more briefly, *"Drafts" by Virginia*. As you see, it consists of 35 sketches by the young Bulgarian artist Virginia Stoianova ("Virzhiniia," in Bulgarian) and a concept by me. The exhibition takes place in March 1994 in the *Lessedra* gallery in Sofia, Bulgaria, which was ranked as the best private gallery in the country for 1991, 1992, and 1993 by *Kultura*, the leading weekly newspaper for culture. The show is a hoax: the obviously contemporary drawings are accompanied by purported scholarly documents which present them as Protorenaissance works. Taken in by the concept, the visitors and the media become involuntary participants in and propagators of the mystification, thus turning it into a piece of performance art on a national scale. The exhibition, which entwines visual art, performance, literature, and philosophy, both artistically challenges and critically analyzes some mental, social, and cultural paradigms in postcommunist Bulgaria. Its success comes from the fact that some widespread Bulgarian fantasies and assumptions about their national cultural identity are enacted as real.

In Act One, I present the concept of the exhibition as outlined in the pseudo-scholarly documents which frame the drawings. In Act Two, I review the reaction of the public and the media. Finally, in Act Three, I offer a revised English version of an article I wrote in Bulgaria, which analyzes the meaning of the show and its cultural repercussions, and which ends the performance.[3]

ACT ONE

The concept, which I am sending to the media, consists of four parts, allegedly excerpts from top-tier scholarly publications. Watch carefully, ladies and gentlemen!

*Scene 1: The Discovery (*Art History*)*
"In the summer of 1990, Professor Ivan Iordanov[4] of the University of Sofia, while studying the manuscripts and the frescoes in the Bulgarian monastery Zographou[5] in Athos, Greece, came across unknown drawings which he assumed dated from the second half of the thirteenth century. . . . They remind one of some of the famous frescoes in the Boiana Church in Sofia (considered the paramount exemplars of Protorenaissance art in Bulgaria) as well as some frescoes in the churches of Athos. A marginal note [*pripiska*] in the famous thirteenth-century *Draganov minei* (*Menaeon of Dragan*), considered unclear before this discovery, relates the drawings beyond any doubt to the most valuable frescoes in these churches. . . .

"In the spring of the following year, in the Archivio segretto vaticano [the secret archives of the Apostolic library of the Vatican], Professor Iordanov discovered drawings similar to Giotto's mosaic *Navicella* in St. Peter's Church in Rome. . . . The most astounding discovery, however, was that of the preparatory sketches for the decoration of the monastery of Santa Chiara by the same master. Giotto executed the decoration while working in the service of King Robert, but his paintings had been considered irrevocably lost. . . . The likeness between the Zographou and the Vatican drawings was so striking that Professor Iordanov presumed that they belonged to one and the same artist and were, very likely, drafts. His hypothesis was further supported by the fact that texts on the sketches – in Greek and Latin – shared much of the same content and seemed to be parts of a treatise that Professor Iordanov named *On the 'Drafts.'* The author signed both the Athos and the Vatican drawings 'Parthenos' or 'Virgo,' that is, 'Virgin.' This is why Professor Iordanov called the unknown master Parthenos/Virgo or, simply, 'Virginia.'"

Scene 2: The Feminist Twist
(Samantha Krukowski, The Old [Women] Masters: Women in the Protorenaissance *[Cambridge, Mass.: Harvard U P, 1994]*[6]*)*
"The scholarly opinions on Parthenos/Virgo or Virginia can be summarized in the following manner: she was born *circa* 1240 in Bulgaria. . . . The second Bulgarian Empire took up the high artistic traditions of Byzantium after the fall of Constantinople to the Venetians and Crusaders in 1204. After working on the frescoes in the Boiana Church near Sredets – today's Sofia – around 1259, Virginia parted for Athos. Despite the interdict on women and female animals

entering the Mount of Athos, the most important monastic center of the Eastern Orthodox Church, Virginia, disguised as a man, became a monk first in the Serbian Chilandar and later in the Bulgarian Zographou, and succeeded in working her way up to a position in the Epistasia, the body composed of five representatives exercising executive power over all the Athos monasteries. After Catalonian pirates plundered Zographou and set it on fire in 1275, Virginia concealed herself in the Latin cloister *Coenobium Amalfitanorum* near Chilandar, and later secretly left for Italy. There she changed her identity for a second time and became Giotto di Bondone. . . . Virginia's genius and comprehensive education, as well as her successful financial undertakings and her unprecedented social and artistic success, ensured her a prestige that was unthinkable for her female contemporaries in the field of art."

Scene 3: The Exhibition "Drafts" by Virginia *and Ms. Stoe*
*(*The Burlington Magazine*)*
"The Zographou and the Vatican drafts by Virginia have been restored and prepared for exhibition by Ms. Virginia Stoe, a famous American painter, gallery owner, restorer, art historian, philanthropist, and art expert for corporations such as Chrysler and Motorola. Ms. Stoe . . . was born in Bulgaria as Virginia Stoianova. In 1956, in protest against the Soviet invasion of Hungary, she defected to France. Since 1960 she has been living in the US, in New York City and Chicago. In a lengthy interview for *The New York Times Book Review*, Ms. Stoe says that she has taken to heart the 'drafts' of the enigmatic Virginia for several reasons. First, they are 'an extremely important bridge' between Eastern European and Western art and culture. Second, the treatise *On the 'Drafts'* more than seven centuries ago 'anticipated ideas which are at the very core of today's postmodernism.' Third, the hypothesis that the anonymous Boiana Master and Giotto were one and the same person who, beyond any doubt, was a woman, is 'an inspiration for the feminist cause.'

"The exhibition *'Drafts' by Virginia* was made possible in part through the generous financial assistance of the Patriarch's Institute for Patristic Studies in Thessaloniki, Greece, Banco di Santo Spirito Vaticano, and the Rockefeller Foundation. . . .

"The exhibition was shown for the first time at the Art Institute of Chicago (May–July 1993) and after that at the Grand Palais in Paris (August–October 1993) and the Kunsthistorisches Museum in Vienna (December 1993–February 1994). After its stop in Sofia, Bulgaria, the exhibition will travel to the Pushkin Museum of Fine Arts in Moscow. In accordance with Ms. Stoe's wishes, *'Drafts' by Virginia* are exhibited in Sofia in the *Lessedra* gallery by her protegee, the Bulgarian artist Virginia Stoianova, who is now pursuing her master's degree in Fine Arts at the Parsons School of Design in New York City. The work of the young Virginia, according to Ms. Stoe, reminds her of her own paintings when she first came to America."

Scene 4: From the Treatise On the "Drafts"
*(*GESTA*, translation from Greek and Latin)*
"But, lying to themselves, some say: 'The draft presupposes a fair copy, an

original. The drafts are only the stepping stones leading from the initial idea to the image incarnate. But these stages are ascended only by him who knows, in other words, by him who is skillful in the rules of the artistic craft. . . . The rules describe what the finished work has to be like in order to be perfect, and what skills [*techne*] one has to apply. The drafts, therefore, are duration and history. They provide the meaning of the final image: this image is beautiful because it is ripe. The same holds true for the painter: before becoming a master he must be an apprentice. The academy serves precisely this purpose – to create masters from apprentices.'

"To these madmen we respond with the words of the venerable apostle Peter, who teaches that there are 'drafts and "drafts".' With the 'drafts' we do not go anywhere because we have already reached our destination. The 'draft' does not presuppose a fair copy because it denies both the draft and the original. The 'draft' is born solely of this innervation in the hand that cannot be taught or exercised. The 'draft' is not a fruition but an instant. It is not an apprenticeship but mastery in itself. The 'draft' does not lead to the beautiful but to the sublime, which cannot be represented and which relishes the heart only because the 'draft' is here, it happens. The 'draft' is perfect not because it follows the rules but because it overwhelms him who beholds it. The 'draft' is an angel who announces its own annunciation. The 'draft' does not have any other meaning. Or is it not, ignoramuses, the wonder-working icon of St. George in Zographou, which painted itself in one night, that is the best example of a 'draft'? Or will you, unbelievers, deny that every creation is perfect, and will you insist on the old fable of the deluge and Noah, which proves God's imperfect creation? Wretched madmen, if this were so, the spider would have been a more magnificent creator than God, for no spider destroys its own intricate web as God allegedly did by sending the Flood."

ACT TWO

Scene 1: Numerous Signs

Mesdames et Messieurs! Numerous signs hint at the jocular character of the exhibition. The opening is on March 8, a day which in communist Bulgaria was celebrated as the Woman's Holiday comparable with Mothers' Day in the US; after 1989, however, it was ridiculed as an institutionalization of women's lower status in society. Two weeks before the opening, an article in a major newspaper announces the forthcoming *"Drafts" by Virginia*.[7] At the opening Virginia/Virzhiniia appears wearing a theatrical thirteenth-century costume and a mustachio, indicating the parodic verve of this ostensibly historical and feminist exhibition. All these signs, however, are totally neglected by the media and the audience. Too bad.

Scene 2: The Viewers

The viewers fall into three groups. Our friends are enjoying the artistic joke which intertwines present-day drawings with a Protorenaissance concept. They are the ideal viewers for whom this is just a piece of beautiful music, and we,

Figure 1: The Boiana master, signed by Parthenos. Study for a fresco decoration "Virgin and Child" at the Boiana church, near Sofia, *c.* 1258–1259. 24 × 17 cm. Drawing in ink and wash. Monastery of St. George, Mount Athos.

Figure 2: Giotto, signed by Virgo. Study for a fresco decoration "Annunciation of the Virgin" at the Church of the Badia in Florence, *c.* 1280–1298. 65 × 48 cm. Drawing in pen and chalk. The Vatican, Archivio Segretto Vaticano, Ms. F. 214 inf., fol. 10 recto. The work is described by Giorgio Vasari and is considered one of Giotto's first independent works; it has been destroyed.

the authors, think that everybody will interpret the exhibition in the way they do. The artists, indifferent to verbal concepts, are focused on the works. The third and largest group consists of the journalists and the ordinary viewers. They believe the concept and never feel any discrepancy between it and the sketches, which clearly are not what the concept maintains (see Figures 1–4). Too bad.

Look to the left, *Seniores y Senioras*! This is Mr. X, the Head of the Cultural Heritage Program of the richest foundation in Bulgaria, a professional who has spent fifteen years working on the Boiana Church frescoes as a historian. He is asking Virginia/Virzhiniia's assistance in connecting him with Ms. Stoe. Now look to the right. This is a young Bulgarian film director, dreaming of "making it" in the US. He is encouraging Virginia/Virzhiniia and me to write a script about Parthenos/Virgo, which he will sell to Hollywood. And in the center is an associate professor of art history at the National Art Academy in Sofia. He has brought his students to the gallery and is lecturing on the Boiana Master and Giotto. The *Lessedra* gallery is frequented by the intelligentsia, who leave content with what they have seen. In order to make the exhibition even more a shrine of national pride, Virginia/Virzhiniia and I start selling expensive tickets, and ask a friend of ours of impressive physique to play guard with a toy gun and to scold every curious viewer who dares to come too close to the drawings.

Figure 3: Boiana master, signed by Parthenos. Study for the fresco decoration "Christ Euergetes (the Benefactor)" at the principal church of the monastery of Chilandar, Mount Athos. *c.* 1260–5. 50 × 70 cm. Drawing in chalk. Monastery of Chilandar, Mount Athos.

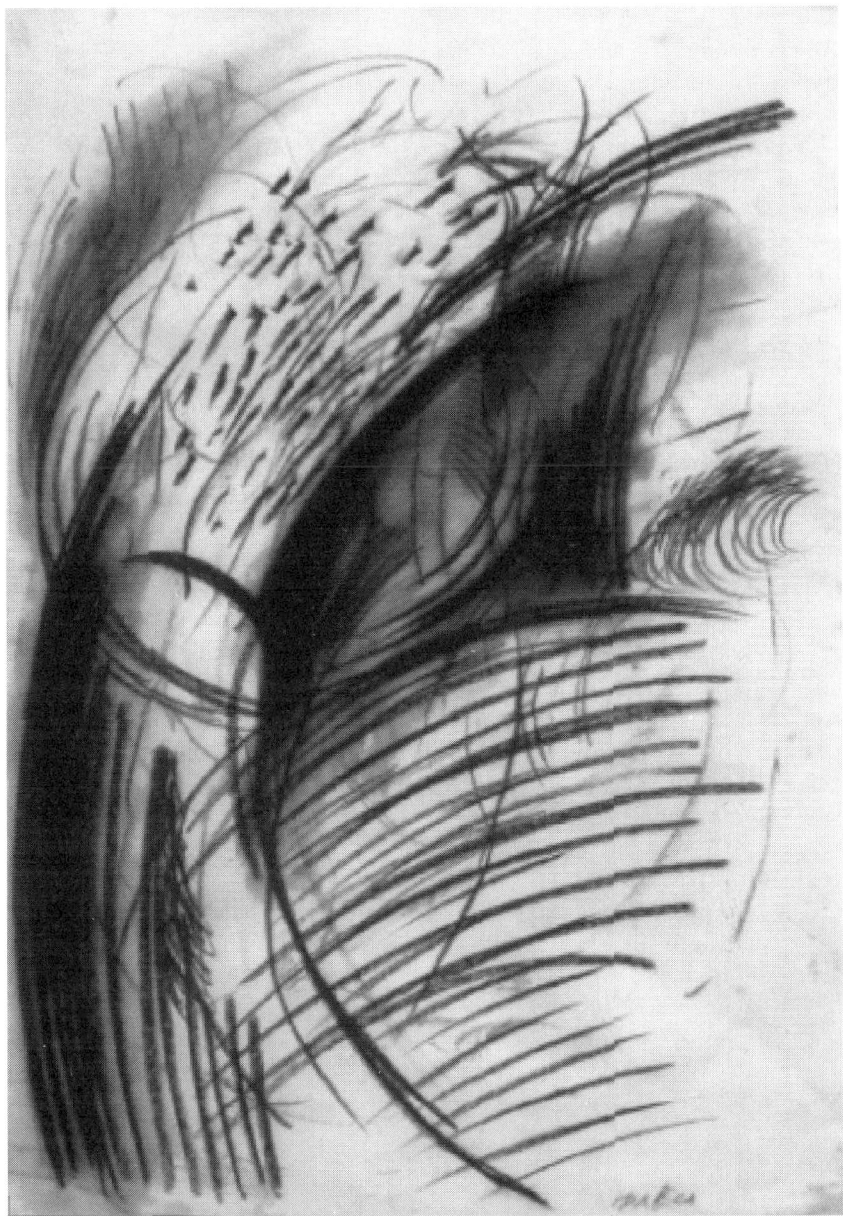

Figure 4: Giotto, signed by Virgo. Study for the fresco decoration "Crucifix" at the Church of Santa Maria sopra Minerva, Rome. *c.* 1298. 50 × 70 cm. Drawing in chalk. The Vatican, Archivio Segretto Vaticano, ms. F. 216 inf. fol. 11 verso. The work is mentioned by Vasari but has been destroyed.

Scene 3: The Media
And now comes the juiciest part of our show, ladies and gentleman! What turns the exhibition into a large-scale hoax is the media. Several of the national newspapers, the national television and radio, and some private newspapers and radio stations take the concept at face value, and create the fame of Parthenos/Virgo.[8] An article by Mila Vacheva, the art critic of the major socialist newspaper *Duma*, demonstrates concern for national values: "Viarna ili ne, hipotezata e liubopitna i povdiga natsionalnoto ni samochuvstvie." ("True or not, the hypothesis [of Parthenos/Virgo being the Boiana Master/Giotto] boosts our national self-esteem.") After enumerating the powerful foreign institutions which have sponsored and exhibited the show, Vacheva accuses the political opponents of the socialists, who are in power at that time, of neglecting national interests: "Uchudvashto e, che v Bâlgaria i domakinstva malkata chastna galeriia 'Lesedra' . . . a ne institut ot ranga na izbroenite po-gore." ("It is amazing that in Bulgaria the show is hosted by the small private *Lessedra* gallery . . . and not by an institution whose rank is commensurate with those enumerated above.")

To begin the process of demystification we involve more newspapers in the hoax, informing them of the short-sightedness of their competitors. In her article, Nadia Medneva praises the drawings by Virginia/Virzhiniia, not by Parthenos/Virgo, and castigates the naivety of the new-fangled art critics, who degrade the standards of the profession with their ludicrous ignorance.[9] In the April Fool's Day issue of *Kultura*, the elitist newspaper promoting postmodern tastes in Bulgaria through *ex cathedra* dicta, Diana Popova, the art critic of the paper, delivers a didactic lecture on conceptual art overseas and in the fatherland. *Kultura* publishes a half-page photograph of a fresco from the Boiana Church with an ironic comment: "Kompozitsiia po chernovi na Virginiia" ("A composition based on Virginia's drafts").[10]

The best proof that the show has exposed the manipulative mechanisms of the media is provided in July 1994, when Virginia/Virzhiniia and I open her next exhibition *Virginia Stoianova in Quotation Marks*, also at the *Lessedra* gallery. It comprises 12 imaginative self-portraits by her and a concept by me, a self-ironic collage of enthusiastic newspaper quotes about *"Drafts" by Virginia*. The media, which has regularly produced a dozen or so reviews for each of Virginia/Virzhiniia's previous shows, this time remains silent. Too bad, indeed.

ACT THREE

Scene 1: The Sign and the Magic
Meine Damen und Herren, what is the significance of *"Drafts" by Virginia?* Let me begin my answer by recalling some well-known premises, which, however, provide the semiotic and social prerequisites for the meanings of the exhibition. The sign, if we may oversimplify things, is a unity of signifier and signified. In modern times, that is, during the last five centuries, our civilization has been aware that the connection between these two elements is not natural, as was previously thought, but conventional.[11] Today, if conventionality is dealt with

as if it covered the whole of reality, we speak of ideological manipulation.[12] The disclosure, first, of the pretense of natural connection between signifier and signified and, second, of the pretense on the part of ideology to give a total semantic interpretation of the world, is demystification and denunciation of the ideological manipulation. When the media claims that it presents news "objectively," "such as it is," it resorts to ancient semiotic magic in order to manipulate the audience. Conversely, when *"Drafts" by Virginia*, on the one hand, with its drawings (as signified) perspicuously demonstrates that they are works by a contemporary artist and, on the other hand, with its concept (as signifier) affirms that these sketches are the works of the enigmatic Protorenaissance Virginia, it takes aim at the very heart of manipulation, and tests the audience's immunity to manipulation. The exhibition is widely reviewed by the national media but in a way that naively reiterates that the works belong to the Boiana Master/Giotto. This demonstrates two things: first, through semiotic magic, the media manipulates not only their audience but themselves as well; second, an artistic mystification is an effective means of demystifying mass communication.

Scene 2: Hyperrealism, Manipulation, and Terror

"Drafts" by Virginia is a play of hyperrealism, a juggling of signifiers with no signifieds.[13] However, the exhibition is not only an exercise in fashionable postmodernism in a country hypnotized by American values, but it also acquires concrete Bulgarian meanings by pointing to socio-political and cultural traditions that flourished in this Balkan country during the last one hundred and twenty years. These traditions have consisted in an alternation between manipulation and terror. If manipulation is a form of semiotic and ideological magic, terror is a quasi-alternative imposed by brute force. In Bulgarian cultural history manipulation has been thought of as something civilized, progressive, democratic, and European, whereas terror has been thought of as primitive, conservative, autocratic, and Bulgarian.[14]

In the 1890s, the dawn of the modern Bulgarian state, the unscrupulous parvenu Bai Gan'o, the notorious character created by Aleko Konstantinov, the greatest Bulgarian satirist, proclaimed that he could elect even a donkey as a parliamentary deputy if he had at his disposal a bunch of drunken "prangadzhii" ("jail-birds").[15] Bai Gan'o opts for terror, not for manipulation. For him, the newspaper as a means of mass communication is first of all an instrument of violence – "psuvai naliavo i nadiasno" ("curse everybody and his mother") (*BG*, vol. 1, p. 126) – and, then secondarily, an implement of manipulation. At the beginning of the twentieth century, in the era of Bulgarian modernism, manipulation was extolled as coming from the civilized West, whereas coercion was despised as something typically Bulgarian: one of the characters in Peio Iavorov's play *V polite na Vitosha* (*In the Skirts of Vitosha*, 1911) sighs for Europe where they kill with "igla ot zlato" ("a needle of gold"), while lamenting a Bulgaria where they kill with "dârvarska sekira" ("a woodman's ax").[16] The book of the prominent sociologist Ivan Khadzhiiski *Avtoritet, dostoinstvo i maska* (*Authority, Dignity, and Mask*, 1933)[17] is perhaps the first Bulgarian attempt at a detailed analysis of manipulation.

However, Bulgarian history does not consist simply of the advent of manipulation replacing terror but, alas, of the alternation between the two. Geo Milev, one of the most versatile Bulgarian modernists, brilliantly defined this in his poem *Septemvri* (*September*, 1924): " 'Otechestvoto / e v opasnost!' / Prekrasno: / no – shto e otechestvo? – / I iarostno laiat / kartechnitsi . . ." (" 'The fatherland / is in danger!' / Very fine: / but – what is the fatherland? / And the machine-guns / are furiously barking . . .").[18] In other words, in the first two lines of the quote, the fatherland is a manipulative notion; in the second two lines, it is demystified; in the last two lines, the debate is silenced by machine guns. During the last fifty years or so the situation has not changed much. Up to the beginning of the 1960s constraint predominated over manipulation, whereas during so-called "ripe" socialism (1970s–the early 1980s) manipulation came to the forefront. *Perestroika* and *Glasnost* in the late 1980s exemplified the demystification of communist mass communication. The boom in the media after the fall of communism in 1989 ushered in not only the heyday of new manipulations, but also the period of using party newspapers in the fashion of Bai Gan'o, i.e., as a means of party terror.[19]

Scene 3: (Anti)performance

The show *"Drafts" by Virginia* is, in many respects, an (anti)performance. It critically echoes classical Western – predominantly American – performances, as well as the proliferation of their Bulgarian imitators immediately after 1989. Xanti Schawinski described his performance *Circus* (1924) as a "visual theatre"; in the late 1930s, grafting his Bauhaus experience onto American soil, he used the same phrase for his performance *Spectrodrama*.[20] In 1959, Allan Kaprow wrote of his *18 Happenings in 6 Parts*: "Some guests will also act" (quoted in *PAFP*, p. 128). In 1970, Yoko Ono, in her contribution to the show "Information" at MOMA, instructed the reader to "draw an imaginary map . . . go walking on an actual street according to the map. . . ." (quoted in *PAFP*, p. 154). Summarizing such examples and somewhat oversimplifying things, we can say that the classical performance is, first, a visual-theatrical spectacle which is restricted in time and space, and in which the performers are separated from the viewers. Second, the borderline between the author and the viewers is trespassed according to instructions given by the author. Third, the viewer, who is also a participant, consciously challenges his or her stereotypes and undergoes a change of his or her identity following the prescriptions of the author. In this, the viewer may succumb to chance and nonsense (as in the case of Ono) or to rituals which are alien to him or her (as in performances based, for instance, on Native American customs which represent a form of foreign collective memory).

"Drafts" by Virginia challenges this poetics in more than one respect. To begin with, the confluence of art and reality – one of the ultimate goals of the classical performance[21] – is achieved at one stroke in the case of our exhibition. It does not confront its viewers and the media with chance, nonsense, or alien rituals but with their own enacted dreams and myths, and in this way it artistically denounces these dreams and myths as nonsensical, fortuitous, and alien. In other words, the show achieves its effect through the Hermetic

principle *post hoc, ergo ante hoc*, that is, a consequence is assumed and interpreted as the cause of its own cause.[22] To use the vocabulary of hermeneutic circularity, the viewer sees what he or she wants to see (but, as the exhibition demonstrates, to see what one wants to see is also to see that he or she cannot see at all).

Next, *"Drafts" by Virginia* is not restricted in social time and space as its classical predecessors were, for it begins at this unannounced and unpredictable moment when the viewers and the media start believing that they are going to see the drawings of the Boiana Master/Giotto and actually see them. The concept of the exhibition generously offers the viewers and the media their own expectations and prejudices: all of a sudden it turns out that in times of yore Bulgarian culture substantially augmented Western culture; all at once Western scholars of the highest rank and mighty Western institutions hold their breath en masse when encountering Bulgarian genius; all of a sudden, in a patriotic paroxysm, Ms. Stoe sets in motion her multi-faceted talents and almighty connections . . . The very kernel of the illusions of the Bulgarian intelligentsia and the media is expressed by these innumerable and hypnotically sweet – but poisonous – "all of a sudden(s)." The miraculous importance of these mirages in the years after the fall of communism has grown in a geometrical progression paralleling the day-to-day growth of impoverishment, humiliation, and loss of self-confidence. Ironically, the matrix of this postcommunist phenomenon was formulated in the early 1940s by Bulgaria's greatest communist poet Nikola Vaptsarov (no longer taught in school after 1989, ladies and gentlemen!), who wrote in his poem "Ne boite se, detsa" ("Don't Be Scared, Children"): "I az, ponezhe niamam khrana . . . shte vi nakhrania / sâs vera" ("And I, because I have no food . . . I will feed you / with faith").

"Drafts" by Virginia parodically models the way Bulgarian viewers and the media identify themselves aesthetically, and demonstrates that if they have ever entered the realm of Kant's aesthetics at all, that is to say have ever contemplated art intransitively, after 1989 they have already left this domain.[23] Art in postcommunist Bulgaria matters, if at all, chiefly as a prop for a deeply hurt national and cultural identity[24] (and also as an investment, of course). This explains why more people visited this exhibition than any other in the history of the *Lessedra* gallery. By marching away from the politicized art of communism,[25] Bulgarian art and viewers enter the province of cultural nationalism, which characterized the Bulgarian Renaissance in the second half of the eighteenth and the first three quarters of the nineteenth century. The reward – or the consolation prize? – for this paradoxical aesthetic movement forward into the past is the possibility of interpreting contemporary Bulgarian art by using a postmodern vocabulary, insofar as transitive aesthetics and cultural chauvinism color the cultural policy of every minority and periphery struggling for recognition by the majority and the center.[26]

The paradox of the "forward = intransitive" versus "backward = transitive" needs historical clarification. From the mid-1940s to the mid-1960s, due to the dominance of orthodox Marxism, the prevalent aesthetics in Bulgaria was transitive, in the sense that it served an overt ideological doctrine. From the mid-1960s till 1989 (and after) the struggle against the ideological indoctrination of culture and scholarship proceeds under the banner of intransitive aesthetics and has two major forms. In terms of methodology, this involves on the one hand the introduction of formalist and structuralist approaches, and on the other a growing thirst for Western scholarship; thematically this is the scholarly rediscovery of Bulgarian and European modernism. To sum up: in Bulgaria's new cultural history, the alternation of transitive and intransitive aesthetics defines five periods: (i) 1760s–1880s, transitive anti-Ottoman and pro-Russian/European nationalistic aesthetics; (ii) 1890s–1940s, intransitive period, modernism, universal values; (iii) mid-1940s–1960s, transitive communist aesthetics; (iv) 1960s–late 1980s, intransitive era of formalism(s) and resurrection of modernism; (v) 1990s, the beginning of yet another transitive epoch, new cultural nationalism, and post???ism. *"Drafts" by Virginia* voices the shift from the fourth to the fifth era, and satirizes the utilitarian verve of every transitive age.

Scene 4: "Who Am I, in Fact . . ."
At the entrance of the *Lessedra* gallery Virginia/Virzhiniia has placed an autobiographical drawing: a nude woman without a face, hiding her pubic area with a fan, in a bird cage. The inscription on the drawing reads: "Koia sâm az vsâshtnost . . ." ("Who am I, in fact . . .").

"Drafts" by Virginia ironically cements the collective narrative identity of the Bulgarian intelligentsia by indefinitely deferring and displacing (or misplacing) the individual narrative identity of its author.[27] According to the concept, Virginia/Virzhiniia Stoianova – the virtual author of the drawings – attends the show in Bulgaria upon the insistence of her patron Ms. Stoe. The deferral then continues through the following stages: the Bulgarian-American Ms. Virginia Stoe, who is the ex-Bulgarian Virginia Stoianova (in the virtual reality of the national and nationalistic reverie, Ms. Stoe stands for the ideal intellectual-political dissident who, alas, is nonexistent in Bulgarian cultural history of the last fifty years or so);[28] Giotto who is the unknown Boiana Master; the Boiana Master who is Parthenos; Parthenos who is Virgo; Parthenos/Virgo who is Virginia; Virginia who is no more than a set of mysterious signatures in Greek and Latin; finally, all this is only scholarly hypothesizing. On the one hand, the reluctance to acknowledge one's authorship is the last gasp of the "dying" postmodern author, textual "signifiance," and "jouissance,"[29] an index of the openness of the modern art work,[30] a tribute to the interpretive activity of the viewer. On the other hand, however, this is an allusion to, first, the paradise lost of the former communist identity of Eastern Europe after 1989, and, second, to the slipping, unidentified identity of the generation of Bulgarian intellectuals who, at the time of the breakdown of communism, were between 25 and 45. In this latter sense, Virginia/Virzhiniia's exhibition is essentially autobiographical: it mocks the impossibility of a legitimate intellectual biography or, what amounts to the same thing, the impossibility of a coherent narrative identity.

"Koia sâm az vsâshtnost . . ." – "that is the question . . ."

Scene 5: Comedia *as* Tragedia
Last but not least, ladies and gentlemen, *"Drafts" by Virginia* and our modest

drama based on this real case do not just ironize today's Bulgarian and East European realities. They also parody some of today's Western stereotypes of the postcommunist era in Eastern Europe and the way the West thinks of itself in this respect. To begin with, the very form of our histrionics challenges the possibility of perceiving what is happening in Eastern Europe after – and before – 1989 only by means of pedantic charts, diagrams, graphs, and "works cited." The West views Eastern Europe as the Other and describes it, let us assume, objectively. But in our production we want to blow up this crumb of the Old World by staging it passionately because, for us, it is not an object of examination but our Own World: "those things about which we cannot theorize, we must narrate."[31] And we narrate them even at the price of theorizing. Next, *meine Damen und Herren*, despite the shared prefix "post-," postmodernism and postcommunism are different. What works in Alabama does not work in Albania, and what is good for Portland is not good for Poland, be it the purest specimen of democracy or postmodern art. Listen attentively! *Comedia dell'Arte* reverberates as *Tragedia dell'Arte* across the Adriatic Sea. If the Grand Narrative is dead, as we all agree, why are we so reluctant to realize that there is no Grand Narrative of Democracy or Grand Narrative of Postmodernism either? Finally, *Mesdames et Messieurs*, *"Drafts" by Virginia* pokes fun at feminism (and through it at resurgent Bulgarian nationalism)[32] because transitive aesthetics are political no matter what banner they fly, whether of socialist realism or of gender/minority/periphery/etc. -isms. With all these old and new real-isms we re-enter the kingdom of ideology, only now not by its manipulative but its teleological gate.[33]

Scene 6: Aesthetic Theory of the Draft/"Draft"

The treatise *On the "Drafts"* offers a theory of the draft, an aesthetic category which is often in limbo. The text, stylized as an Orthodox medieval polemic, juxtaposes the two leading paradigms in contemporary Bulgarian art. The first paradigm (where the notion draft is used without quotation marks) was constituted during the Renaissance and legitimized through institutions such as the Academy, the Museum, the Connoisseur, the Expert, the Market, and so on. Its presupposition is the exercise of *techne* in the form of an individual style; in the path from the sketch to the original, it creates beauty according to certain rules. The second paradigm (in which the term draft is used within quotation marks) is postmodern. In it, the "draft" is viewed as aesthetically and artistically meaningful because it happens,[34] that is, it condenses the time-span between the draft and the masterpiece into a single moment, annuls the classical Renaissance-academic duality of sketch versus masterpiece and, as a corollary, subverts the institutions connected with it. This is how, thanks to a shift from the draft to the "draft," the *Lessedra*, a small private gallery in Sofia, can compete with the Grand Palais in Paris. In the former paradigm, the draft and the masterpiece belong to the aesthetics of the beautiful. In the latter paradigm, the "draft" partakes of the aesthetics of the sublime as elaborated by Longinus, Burke, Kant, and Lyotard. The hoax *"Drafts" by Virginia* is possible solely in the twilight domain where the sublime is taken for the beautiful.

Scene 7: Diasparactive Theory of the Draft
The mystifying mechanism of *"Drafts" by Virginia* can be elucidated not only within a socio-cultural and aesthetical framework but also within a theory of the draft *per se*.[35] The notion used in my analysis is diasparaction. It designates, first, an existential modus: our lives are defined by a permanent incompleteness (Heidegger's *ständige "Unganzheit"*); second, it is an umbrella term for incompleteness, fragmentation, and ruin, which is derived from Greek and means "torn to pieces." The draft is a diasparact: it presupposes a whole, which is the final work. Depending on the type of the whole, we can define four types of draft:

(i) The nominal whole is a phenomenological notion, "a part or portion in a field of perception" (*RFR*, p. 51). Correspondingly, the nominal draft is one perceived as a part of a nominal whole. For instance, we view as a draft a preparatory sketch, which we can compare with a work that we think of as complete. The nominal draft is a comparison between two stages of completion in our field of cultural perception.
(ii) The contingent whole depends upon the syntactic implication of its parts: "Each conception takes its being from and is defined by the complementarity of the other" (*RFR*, p. 52). In the case of the contingent draft, we have a series of drafts, which we compare with a finished oeuvre. Every such draft is a part in relation to the contingent whole of the final work. The final work is the stages of the successive drafts. Thus, every draft after the first one in the series is also a potential complete work.
(iii) The whole of faith is "assumed rather than perceived or imagined," for it is "too large for cognitive perception" (*RFR*, p. 53). The draft of faith relates to a whole of faith, in other words, we assume a connection between the two phenomena because we cannot verify it with certainty. In practice, such drafts exist by themselves, and it is impossible to compare them directly with the whole, which, for some reason, is absent.
(iv) The true whole is "a transcendentally constituted whole" (*RFR*, p. 409). The true draft, consequently, is the epiphany, the intuition of the true whole. Such drafts pertain only to a certain type of art – art, which deliberately deals with meontic true reality (Platonic, as in Romanticism, or communist, as in socialist realism).[36]

In *"Drafts" by Virginia*, the drafts are presented as nominal and contingent, that is to say as single drawings or a series of drawings directly comparable with well-known Bulgarian, Byzantine, and Italian frescoes, whereas, in fact, they are drafts of faith – preparatory works for nonexistent oeuvres. Most importantly, the exhibited drafts pretend to be true drafts, while, actually, they are parodies of such drafts.

Scene 8: Who Is She, in Fact?
Virginia/Virzhiniia's drawings fit comfortably into both the academic and the postmodern paradigms, into the aesthetics of the beautiful and into the aesthetics of the sublime; and this is their basic artistic quality. However, their

ambivalence becomes palpable only if they are perceived simultaneously as both classical and postmodern. The works of this artist are neither original nor imitative. She draws not objects but styles – often with virtuosity – from late medieval to classical French modernist. Virginia/Virzhiniia is defiantly eclectic in her use of style viewed as an aesthetic and artistic category. Her own style is an apostrophe of styles winking at the Style. To devote an entire exhibition to the styleless style and to offer theories of its significance in the guise of drafts/ "drafts" is an artistic novelty – at least in Bulgaria.[37]

EPILOGUE

After indulging in the conference version of this show, a shrewd colleague asked me whether my presentation of the hoax *"Drafts" by Virginia* was not itself a hoax. "What do you think?" I answered.

Well, if there are no other questions, our *Tragedia dell'Arte* is over. Good-bye, *Signore e Signori*!

PART FIVE

FAR EAST/FAR WEST

INTRODUCTION

John Burt Foster Jr. and Wayne J. Froman

In turning to East Asia, Part Five greatly widens the East–West split that was a major issue in Part Four. Given that region's lack of direct contact with Western Europe over several millennia, it makes sense to think not just of a familiar "far East," but of a "far West" as well. Yet if this language sharpens a well-worn slogan for cultural incompatibility, and thereby promises to give louder global resonance to the Balkan warning, this part ultimately suggests a certain irrepressible force to transnational exchange, even across such great cultural distance.

Rolf Goebel's essay on *Madame Chrysanthème*, Pierre Loti's late nineteenth-century account of Japan, shows how Hans-Georg Gadamer's hermeneutic theory can be extended to issues of cross-cultural interpretation. Gadamer held that the transmission of tradition depends upon a dynamic of "effective historical consciousness," a dialogic interaction that allows for a "fusion of horizons" between the current age and previous ones, one that goes back through the successive layers of earlier interpretations to when art works, institutions, or texts in a tradition originated. Goebel extends Gadamer by adopting anthropologist Robert Ulin's proposal that this account of tradition be applied to cultures other than one's own. A further sign of the fruitfulness of this dialogical approach would be Clifford Geertz's influential analyses of cultural interaction in ethnographic writing. Goebel applies these insights to the issue of Western understanding of Japanese culture, as reflected in Loti's "novelistic travelogue."

In the dialogic interaction of reader with text, according to Gadamer, authorial intention is not the final measure of interpretation. Rather it is the crucial content at its core, the text's *Sache*, which tends to exceed the author's intention. In *Madame Chrysanthème*, a Western traveler to Japan adopts the late nineteenth-century European attitude known as *japonisme* in order to relate to his unfamiliar surroundings. This view of Japan as exotic and mysterious serves the conscious purpose of capturing surface sensuous experience in a way that aestheticizes Japanese culture while depriving it of any intrinsic significance; Loti thus seems to convey a condescending, ethnocentric attitude. However, as Goebel shows, Loti's traveler repeatedly faces major obstacles to applying *japonisme* to Japan. The result of these difficulties is a reflexivity that challenges Eurocentric categories and attitudes, and that is sufficiently active to render the novel deeply ambivalent. This ambivalence stands out at places where language itself becomes inadequate to the traveler's experiences, or when Japanese art challenges his sense of reality and illusion.

This triumph of self-reflexivity over the aestheticizing intent illustrates Gadamer's thesis regarding core elements in a text that exceed an author's reach. Further, the role of *japonisme* in sparking self-reflexivity supports Gadamer's provocative contention that prejudice, or pre-judgment, is not an altogether negative factor in increasing understanding of another historical setting. It can, in fact, be pivotal in developing insight. Goebel finds, moreover, that Loti's *japonisme* accords with Homi Bhabha's reinterpretation of Edward Said's critique of Western Orientalism, when Bhabha argues that its ambiguous "median" status is the very quality that can help to open up a new, contentious site within Western attitudes toward Asia. While this site does not amount to a cross-cultural "fusion of horizons" on the order of Gadamer's insights into tradition, it can lead to a "hybrid" form of interaction and inclusion that may anticipate fruitful forms of cultural creation in an increasingly transnational world.

Eugene Eoyang's essay explores a set of major contrasts between the traditional cultures of East Asia and attitudes which, though evident throughout the Western history, have become especially salient in today's United States. His remarks spring from the thoughtful observations of a lifetime, and thus go beyond current debates about transnationalism. However, precisely because East Asia and the West developed in isolation from each other for so long, comparisons of this kind do have the capacity to put the contingency of certain Western trends in high relief.

Eoyang pursues this strategy with items from both elite and popular culture. Thus he can consider the Western ideal of logical clarity that favors polarized oppositions and its legal system that assumes division and conflict between the contending parties. But he also examines the "winner-take-all" mentality fed by a burgeoning obsession with sport, as well as a religious life that perhaps never completely outgrew the early Manichean heresy and that stresses fidelity to one exclusive creed. To learn that East Asia by contrast could develop an alternative "both-and" logic, a legal tradition that tried to promote consensus, an attitude of ironic detachment toward all-out competition, and a religious syncretism that could fuse Confucius, Taoism, and Buddhism could open doors in Western perceptions. It might even encourage Westerners to reconsider what Eoyang, like Cornis-Pope in Chapter 9, calls their agonistic mindset. Are the harsh divisions that surfaced in the Holocaust, apartheid, or the agony of Bosnia, as discussed earlier in this book, merely unfortunate exceptions, or are they an ever-present possibility in a culture that has put so much stress on polarization, divisiveness, exclusivity, and the impulse to be "Number One"? An East Asian alternative, which holds that "differences of viewpoint cannot be overcome by contention," dates back to an interpretation of the Sung hexagram in the *Book of Changes*, a picture of which is included with this essay.

Eoyang does not address the vast transformations of East Asia over the past fifty years, nor the question of how well the traditions that he describes have weathered them. Instead, though clearly intent on advancing cross-cultural understanding in an emerging transational world, his essay shifts to another, even more basic issue. Looking beyond East–West contrasts in and for themselves, Eoyang considers the assumptions that motivate such contrasts, and raises doubts about the value of culture as a master term when used just as a principle of classification and division. In this spirit, Eoyang slyly reveals the paradox inherent to his approach, namely that the practice of making systematic contrasts is itself agonistic, so that his argument against agonism becomes self-undermining if taken in its most literal sense. At another level, he defuses the Manichean logic of bipolar opposition by showing that dualities themselves can differ, by analyzing a vocabulary that distinguishes "contradictories," "contraries," and "sub-contraries."

Above all, Eoyang allows for "conflations" as well as contrasts, thereby opening a space for overlap and interplay beyond cultural distinctions. In a suggestive example, he considers the odd coincidence which allows the pun between the two Chinese words "li" to repeat itself in English as "right" and "rite." Along with a similar link between "property" and "propriety," this parallel projects readers into a bilingual zone that mimics, in little, the possibilities for richer insight that come from entering a liminal space between cultures. In this case Eoyang invites Western readers to think their way past a major expression of agonism today, the apparently unqualified endorsement of laissez-faire individualism; here, it will be noticed, Eoyang returns to an issue raised by the reassessment of Western subjectivity discussed in Part One.

13

CULTURAL HERMENEUTICS AND ORIENTALIST DISCOURSE

LOTI'S SELF-REFLEXIVE *JAPONISME*

Rolf Goebel

I

Pierre Loti's novelistic travelogue *Madame Chrysanthème* (1887),[1] combines considerable popularity with a fairly dubious reputation as a text deeply entrenched in exoticism and colonial power.[2] It depicts the author's arranged "marriage" in the Japanese port of Nagasaki; the affair is really nothing more than a summer-long exploitation of the eponymous young girl whom he meets through the offices of a certain Mr. Kangarou, "interpreter, washerman, and confidential agent for the intercourse of races" (*MC*, p. 29/18). The work's immediate or indirect influence extends from Lafcadio Hearn's decision to leave Philadelphia for Japan to Giacomo Puccini's *Madame Butterfly*, from George Orwell's novel *Burmese Days* to films like Alain Resnais's *Hiroshima Mon Amour*, and has even left traces in the James Bond movie *You Only Live Twice*.[3] In critical terms, however, Loti's impressionistic depiction of Japan as an elusive farce of fragile beauty, ridiculous social customs, and grotesque religious rituals has always elicited deep suspicion. While praising Loti's impressionistic descriptions, Hearn complains about the decadent dandy's "worn-out *blasé* nerves" and calls Loti "a little morbid modern affected Frenchman."[4] This judgment is understandable given Hearn's own advocacy of a cultural hermeneutics that sought to liberate the poetic self from Eurocentric entrapments through an empathetic immersion in Japan's indigenous traditions.

In the context of the turn-of-the-century encounter between East and the West, I regard cultural hermeneutics as a project of deciphering the cultural signs of the other through a fusion of the horizons of the Western visitor and the foreign self-understanding; as an empathetic willingness to allow other realities, traditions, and histories to revise one's own cultural prejudgments and ethnocentric ideology; and as a strategy of writing that seeks to represent the non-West within the categorical framework of truth, authenticity, and plenitude of meaning. According to Hans-Georg Gadamer's philosophical hermeneutics, from which I borrow some of these concepts, the fusion of the reader's and the text's horizons allows the truth claim of a text to retain its significance for the present through the reader's effective-historical consciousness; conversely, the interpreter's prejudgments or prejudices (the German *Vorurteile* encompasses both) are questioned in the encounter with the otherness of the text.[5]

For Gadamer, this process of understanding is primarily predicated on the continuity of a single cultural tradition and shared linguistic resources that encompasses past text and present interpreter alike. But as Robert Ulin has argued, hermeneutic theory can also be applied to the ethnographic interpretation of other cultures. He argues that anthropologists must recognize the productive function of their own prejudgments because they anticipate the potential meaning of the other culture; in the encounter with foreign reality, these anticipations are corrected and reformulated, thus enabling the articulation of further ethnographic questions in a continual search for the other culture's meaning. If anthropologists "are truly interested in understanding other societies both cross-culturally and historically, they must be prepared to allow the otherness of the object/subject to assert itself."[6] Regarding Gadamer's claim that the hermeneutic experience always takes place as a dialogue mediated by language, Ulin explains that Gadamer does not ignore the existence of different languages and world views; rather, "[t]he universality of language means that all that has been said or will be said is potentially understandable to every language speaker and hence all language communities" (*UC*, p. 102).

The translatability of diverse experience, the dialogic encounter between ethnographer and foreign realities, and the problem of representing the viewpoint of the other stand at the center of Clifford Geertz's interpretive anthropology as well. He insists that cultural interpretation needs to be "actor-oriented," that is, descriptions of other cultures "must be cast in terms of the constructions" which the ethnographer imagines other peoples "place upon what they live through, the formulae they use to define what happens to them." Although composed from the presumed perspective of the other, such descriptions, Geertz stresses, are not the direct, authentic self-articulations of the subjects in the foreign cultures but the "fictions" (meaning self-consciously fashioned, rather than simply "false" texts) of the anthropological writer.[7]

This intersection of hermeneutics and ethnography, which I can only sketch here, has wide implications for a writer like Loti. In his text, the anthropological sense of the term "fiction" and the aesthetic connotation (fiction as poetic invention) blur inseparably into one another. Moreover, while Loti is deeply trapped in ethnocentric prejudices, he self-consciously reflects, like a modern ethnographer, on the constitutive role of his prejudgments and anticipations in the construction of Japanese culture, and even allows Japan's otherness to challenge his own cultural position. This conflict immediately raises the question whether Loti can forge a discursive space for Japan to articulate its own authentic meaning within a Westerner's representation. If Gadamerian hermeneutics constitutes one of the starting-points of my discussion of these issues, aspects of Edward Said's critique of orientalism and Homi Bhabha's (post)colonial theories will allow me to situate Loti's work in the context of the interpretation of the non-West that Gadamer himself could not have addressed.

Compared to the position of Hearn and others like him, Loti's "self-centered, unsympathetic attitude," as Basil Hall Chamberlain writes, may well seem to make him "unfit for the comprehension of a highly complex subject" like Japan.[8] This harsh claim suggests that Chamberlain – like Hearn one of the most perceptive observers of Japanese culture at the turn of the century – works essentially within the hermeneutic paradigm of cultural understandability and truth even while remaining aware of the difficulties that beset the Westerner in seeking to understand Japan. What Chamberlain underestimates, however, is that a writer like Loti is not simply hostile or indifferent to Japan's cultural complexity, but rather assumes a self-reflexive position that wrestles with what he perceives as the limits of hermeneutic understanding, the unreadability of the signs of the other, and the inherent insufficiency of ethnographic discourse. Certainly, Loti's misogyny, racism, and Eurocentrism are undeniable, and his reading of Japan is replete with stereotypes. But I also think that it can be argued that his discourse itself persistently problematizes the very attitude – the aestheticist focus on sensuous surface signifiers of Japanese culture – that seems to account for his snobbishness, prejudices, and clichés.

In his illuminating critique of Said's notion of orientalism as a homogenous regime of imperial power and knowledge, Bhabha works out the far-reaching implications of Said's suggestion that Western constructions of the East employ a "median category." This maneuver allows for a view of the Orient as something new yet recognizable as a version of something previously encountered in travel writings, fables, stereotypes, and other such discursive preformations. The Orient, Said argues, thus appears as neither "completely novel" nor "completely well known."[9] As Bhabha argues, the orientalist or colonial stereotype resembles the Freudian fetish in being "predicated as much on mastery and pleasure as it is on anxiety and defense, for it is a form of multiple and contradictory belief in its recognition of difference and disavowal of it."[10] A comparable ambivalence also characterizes Loti's discourse. His text is deeply self-divided, discontinuous, and contradictory; his construction of Japan continually oscillates between fascination and hatred, between aesthetic preconceptions and new experiences, between interpretive blindness and self-critical insight into the rhetoricity of his own orientalist fantasy.[11] It is this paradoxical double-movement of his writing that allows us to criticize Loti's ideological biases and yet to take him seriously as a writer who explores the inevitable conflicts between Western subjectivity and Asian reality in the mediating space of cultural representation. In other words, I propose to read Loti dialectically by seeking to locate a highly significant moment of poetic struggle, self-awareness, and even self-revision within the complacency of exotic fantasy; in my estimation, this conflict continually, and productively, destabilizes the interpretive authority of his discourse.

II

From the beginning, Loti self-consciously questions the validity of traveling, traditionally conceived as the exploration of new geographic vistas as a source for subjective self-exploration and self-renewal. In the modern period, he argues, this topos may have exhausted itself. *Fin-de-siècle* ennui, solitude, and the quest for new experiences have driven him to visit Japan, but upon arriving in Nagasaki harbor, he realizes that Asian reality is already affected by homogenizing signs of Western modernity that disturb the exotic space. Nagasaki looks just "like any other commonplace town," and its port is "a tangled mass of vessels, carrying all the flags of the world," a "banal" scene of ugly steamboats, quays, and factories, which one has "already seen everywhere." This view inspires Loti to speculate about a future modernity when all cultural differences will have been obliterated and the earth will be a terribly "tedious" place to live in. Consequently, he maintains, traveling will become useless for the (Western) subject seeking distraction in faraway locales (*MC*, p. 16/6–7).

Haunted by this vision, Loti tries to counteract the realities of modernity's mercantile hegemony by fictionalizing traditional Japan as a country of exaggerated difference, as the West's desired yet incommensurable other, as a mysterious, if contemptible fairy tale filled with doll-like women, picturesque streets, unfathomable customs, and other disjointed, free-floating, but poetically intriguing surface impressions. In his discourse, the political forays of Western colonialism into the East are turned around and reappear, aesthetically sublimated, as the Orient's theatrical effect on the visitor: torn between revulsion and fascination, Loti feels "invaded" by the "mercantile, bustling, comical Japan" (*MC*, p. 17/7). The author plays this rhetorical game in the self-consciously ironic mode that pervades his entire construction of the Orient; indeed, as Todorov has indicated, Loti does not claim to describe the real Japan or to tell the truth about it; rather, the actual country serves as the occasion for recording effects, impressions, and subjective responses.[12]

Pursuing this orientalist fantasy outside the traditional parameters of a hermeneutic search for ethnographic verisimilitude, Loti's preferred strategy is to read Nagasaki's street life by evoking the aestheticist categories of what has come to be called *japonisme*. This term refers to the nineteenth-century craze for Japanese wood cuts, hanging scrolls, and screens in fashionable Parisian salons as well as to the productive imitation of Japanese subject-matter and painting techniques by artists like Degas, Manet, Toulouse-Lautrec, Van Gogh, and Whistler. Writers, too, were influenced by this movement, developing a style of fragmentary sentences, evocative images, and subtle colors to render their subjective impressions of evanescent reality.[13] In 1868, the Goncourt brothers claimed that they were among the first to have developed a "taste for things Chinese and Japanese," which "is now spreading to everything and everyone, even to idiots and middle-class women," thanks mainly to their own efforts.[14] Already in 1864 the Goncourts had contended that, although appearing "incredibly fantastic to bourgeois eyes," Chinese and particularly Japanese art offers direct copies of nature, while Greek art, "except for sculpture, is false and invented" (*PA*, p. 91).

A corrective to classical Western aesthetics, Japanese art also expands the horizon of the European imagination to include the exotic other: "I really believe that when you know how to look at a picture, how to discover all there is in it, you do not have to visit the country it depicts," the Goncourts' entry for April 4, 1891 reads. It continues to assert:

> Thus today, having under my eyes a picture by Toyokuni representing the office of a Green House, a house of prostitution, and being given a Japanese explanation of all the large and small objects adorning the office, I was convinced that by my description I could give the reader a feeling for the place with as much photographic accuracy as one of Loti's descriptions made on the spot. (*PA*, pp. 287–8)

Here the Goncourts formulate a radically aestheticist program. Japanese art, because it is held to involve highly mimetic representation, provides the Western audience with expectations, images, and preconceptions that create a reality-effect seemingly as truthful as, but more poetic than, the mechanical reproductions of nature made possible by the camera. To some extent, Japanese art produces a set of hermeneutic prejudgments that open up a new perspective on a foreign culture, but its reception by the West also has a counter-hermeneutic effect. For in replicating the radical separation of art and life typical of *fin-de-siècle* aesthetics, *japonisme* defers the actual Japan and marginalizes travel as a mode of exploration and ethnographic understanding. Ironically, what the Goncourts may have seen as Loti's quasi-photographic realism, as empirical observation and truthful recording of exotic details, was itself heavily dependent on the preformative power of *japonisme.*

III

In Loti's subversion of cultural hermeneutics, reality and fiction, illusion and truth continually and contradictorily intermingle, questioning each other's ontological status. Watching the consular residences, custom-house offices, and manufactories, the European concession and American bars on the quays, Loti records a keen sense of unreality and dislocation caused by the inscription of these Western sights in the Japanese port city. But behind these "commonplace objects," Loti hopes, he will probably find the "true old Japanese Nagasaki which still exists" and the "little woman" he wants to marry (*MC*, pp. 19–20/9–10). If this passage contrasts the inauthenticity of colonial institutions with the apparent truth of the traditional Japan unaffected by Westernization, this initial binarism cannot be maintained once the author finds himself in the midst of the other culture. Taking a *ricksha* ride to the teahouse where he is to meet his future "wife," Loti examines the "sullen, muddy, half-drowned Japan" as it presents itself on this rainy day:

> All these houses, men or beasts, hitherto only known to me by drawings; all these, that I had beheld painted on blue or pink backgrounds of screens or vases, now appeared to me in reality, under a dark sky, with umbrellas and wooden shoes, with tucked-up skirts and pitiful aspect. (*MC*, p. 29/18)

He passes by "a lady, struggling with her skirts, unsteadily tripping along in her high wooden shoes, looking exactly like the figures painted on screens, tucked up under a gaudily daubed paper umbrella" (*MC*, p. 30/19). In these statements, the hermeneutic function of prejudgments guide the visitor's experiences of Japan without allowing the new vistas to assert their own meaning and to have a redefining influence on the Westerner's anticipations. The experience of Oriental art encountered in France literally precedes – temporally as well as cognitively – the reality of Japan; but the tangible actuality of the foreign country exerts merely a postponed, belated effect on the writer's perception. Having arrived at the tea-house, Loti virtually collapses reality and artistic representation, original and copy. He contends that the sights of the actual Japan before him – maids, tea-service, landscape, and pagoda – offer no really new experiences but merely confirm the prior image which he had created for himself from artifacts contemplated at home: "I feel myself fairly launched upon this tiny, imagined, artificial world, which I felt I knew already from the paintings of lacquer and porcelains. It is so exact a representation [C'est si bien cela]!" (*MC*, p. 42/30).

Listening to a woman singing behind a paper screen, he believes that this was "so evidently the way they should sing, these musicians I had so often seen painted in amazing colors on rice paper, half closing their small, dreamy eyes in the midst of impossibly large flowers." Thus Loti's mixture of decadent aestheticism and melancholic alienation betrays its hegemonic desire to turn Japan into a secondhand, inauthentic artifice that fails to live up to the expectation of exotic beauty held by European subjectivity and poetic imagination:

> Long before I came to it, I had perfectly pictured this Japan to myself. Nevertheless perhaps, in reality it seems to be smaller, more finicking, and also much more mournful, no doubt by reason of that great pall of black clouds and this incessant rain. (*MC*, p. 43/30–1)

Here, Loti's position resembles what Said has called the orientalist's "textual attitude" toward the East. Seeking to make sense of a diverse and elusive reality, the Westerner relies on knowledge gleaned from previous writings about the Orient. Projecting these prejudgments and expectations onto the foreign reality, the interpreting subject constructs a schematic, reductive, but reassuring image of the Orient. As Said writes, "the book (or text) acquires a greater authority, and use, even than the actuality it describes."[15]

Although for Loti, this authority comes from Japanese artifacts rather than from written texts,[16] the effect is similar: Japanese actuality, stereotyped, diminished, and ridiculed, is granted lesser truthfulness and significance than the aestheticist preconceptions and expectations formed in France. Performing a self-conscious doubling and reversal of *japonisme*, Loti asserts that Japanese reality is little more than an inauthentic semblance, an orientalized reproduction of the European imitation of genuine Japanese arts, the failed copy of a copy. The traveler believes it is his self-appointed role to explore and exploit this third-hand cultural construct as an intriguing source for the collection of thrilling, diverse, if fragmented sense-impressions as well as for authoritative ethnographic explanations. In this sense, *japonisme* emerges as an aestheticist version of what Said calls "exteriority," the Westerners' moral and existential non-involvement in the Orient which they purport to render familiar and understandable through their strategies of representation.[17]

IV

This very "exteriority," however, also enables Loti to foreground language and aestheticist preconceptions as privileged objects of discursive self-examination. He remarks that the silhouette-like outline of Chrysanthème corresponds exactly to the figures of women depicted on Japanese porcelain or silk paintings that one can find in Western bazaars. Literally content with resting on the outer contours, on the surfaces of the Japanese female body, the gaze of the male Western visitor reads the women around him as "little Nipponese dolls" in whose thoughts he is not interested at all (*MC*, pp. 73–4/59–61). But at night, triggered by the sight of his "wife" sleeping on a wooden pillow designed to preserve her elaborate head-dress and of the cozy, tent-like mosquito net dyed in the traditional colors of Nagasaki custom, this typically orientalist attitude takes a characteristically self-critical turn. In Oceania or Stamboul, it had seemed to Loti "as if mere words could never express all I felt, and I vainly struggled against my own incompetence to render, in human language, the penetrating charm surrounding me." Here, the hermeneutic dialogue between the interpreter and the foreign culture breaks down as the paucity of Western words vis-à-vis the affective plenitude of the other reveals itself. In Japan, however, the problem is not the incapacity of the French language to capture the surplus of exotic sensations; rather, Loti writes, "words truthful in themselves are always too grand, too thrilling; the words embellish" (*MC*, p. 76/63). Implying that Japanese reality is too minute and meaningless to be represented adequately in the Westerner's language, this statement is yet another expression of Loti's ethnocentric arrogance. Moreover, as Todorov notes, the "central paradox of exoticism" is that the "strangeness of the experience would disappear if it were expressed in the familiar words of the French language" (*OHD*, p. 311). But Loti also acknowledges Japan's resistance to this homogenizing power of ethnographic discourse. For in the writer's eyes, the Asian country figures as a kind of catalyst that brings about the decomposition of the Western language's claims of truth into mere surface beauty and decorative semblance. The ethnocentric conception equating Loti's French with "human language" in general while asserting Japan's insignificance backfires, as it were. Meant to ridicule the country as a "completely pitiful and banal comedy," the author's stereotype actually reveals his fearful awareness of the hegemonic power, stylistic superficiality, and mimetic insufficiency of his own excessively impressionistic and purely ornamental orientalism. In other words, while orientalist discourse has traditionally sought to master an unruly, evanescent Eastern reality, in Loti's case, it is the referent itself that undermines the supposedly autonomous, dominating sign of the West.

Loti's relentlessly self-reflexive exploration of the limits of cultural interpretation recognizes, and to some extent even welcomes, the fact that Japan unsettles the very language conventions and ethnocentric stereotypes that he projects onto the Orient. But his travelogue does not go so far as to open up a discursive space in which Japan's indigenous and contentious *political* voice is allowed to articulate itself authentically as the country struggles to redefine its identity during the transition from feudalistic self-seclusion to Westernized modernity. In this sense, Loti's Nagasaki resembles Roland Barthes's Japan, Julia Kristeva's China, and similar writings, where, as Bhabha argues, "the Other text is forever the exegetical horizon of difference, never the active agent of articulation"; as a result, the other "loses its power to signify, to negate, to initiate its historic desire, to establish its own institutional and oppositional discourse."[18] In Loti's text, such loss of agency occurs most notably in the scene where the Japanese police object to Loti's landlords letting rooms outside the European concession to a Frenchman married to a Japanese. Presenting himself to the register office, the author mimics the polite, formalized style of Japanese speech but mixes it with terrible insults heaped upon the registry officials: "In order that *thou shouldest* leave me in peace in the suburb I am inhabiting, what bribe must I offer *thee*, set of little beings more contemptible than any mere street porter?" Scandalized and totally puzzled by the foreigner's bizarre behavior, the officials first maintain "silent consternation" and finally try to be conciliatory, reminding him that his proper registration is really all that is needed (*MC*, p. 165/146). Here the Westerner literally seeks to silence the potentially oppositional self-articulation of the other by parodying the native subjects' speech characteristics, by incorporating them in a ridiculing, distorted manner into his own dominant discourse.

Yet Loti himself is self-critically aware of his tendency to silence the social agency of Japan without going so far as to use this insight as the first step toward changing the hegemonic trajectory of his discourse. After remarking that the chief diversion of the Japanese seems to be hunting and bargaining for curios in the many little antique-sellers' booths, he comments:

> I really make a sad abuse of the adjective *little*, I am quite aware of it, but how can I do otherwise? In describing this country, the temptation is great to use it ten times in every written line. Little, finickal, affected, – all Japan is contained, both physically and morally, in these three words. (*MC*, p. 242/220)

Not merely in a physical and moral, but in the widest possible political sense, Loti's discourse explicitly reveals its desire to reduce the heterogeneity of Japanese society, to suppress the individual subjectivities of its inhabitants, and to marginalize the nation's emerging position in the global history of modernization which Japan had aspired to since the internationalizing impulse of the Meiji restoration.

The very discourse of miniaturizing Japan fails to render the foreign reality comprehensible and describable. Hence Loti experiences the country as a space of radical discontinuity with his native culture. Whereas in his childhood "the smallest trifles" possessed "an unfathomable and infinite profundity" (*MC*,

p. 171/152), Japan offers the adult traveler little harmony with the world and certainly no experience of the sublime and the sacred. Attending a major religious festival in Nagasaki, he observes: "In the religious amusements of this people it is not possible for us to penetrate the mysteriously hidden meaning of things. . . ." The customs, symbols, and masks, he believes, "proceed from sources utterly dark and unknown to us; even the oldest records fail to explain them to us in anything but a superficial and ineffectual manner, *simply because we have absolutely nothing in common with this people*" (*MC*, p. 184/163–4). An extreme case of cultural relativism, Loti's stark, unmediated binarisms seem to deny any possibility of an interpretive mediation, of a hermeneutic fusion of cultural horizons, between his own Western subjectivity and Japan's spiritual self-understanding.

V

It is in the area of Japanese aesthetics, however, that Loti discovers possibilities of appreciation which he cannot find in the realms of the political and the sacred. Commenting on the artful arrangements of rare flowers and common plants in the open houses along the streets leading up to a temple, he gives his favorite topos of the culture's artificiality a positive connotation. Some vases, he remarks, are "complicated and twisted," others "graceful and simple, but of a simplicity so studied and exquisite that to our eyes they seem the revelation of an unknown art, the subversion of all acquired notions on form" (*MC*, p. 186/165). Artistic expression is allowed to broaden the visitor's cultural horizon even if he self-consciously rejects the possibility of understanding the larger social, spiritual, and historical contexts of Japanese life.

Toward the end of his stay, he seeks to develop a more appreciative perception and a refined terminology that allows the Japanese *aesthetic* (as opposed to the *political*) self-understanding to assert itself as an oppositional force within the visitor's conceptual framework. Visiting his "mother-in-law," Loti, though bored with the idle conversation on the verandah and finding her garden melancholy, constricted, and antiquated, also recognizes that a "true feeling for nature has inspired this tiny representation of a wild spot." The intricate placement of rocks and dwarf cedars over a miniature valley is meant to create the impression of a real landscape; the small plants' "look of *big trees* perplexes one and falsifies the perspective." Seeing Japanese garden design as a subtle play with the spectator's conventional sense of proportions, he interprets the view from the verandah as an aesthetically productive blurring of the boundaries between studied illusion and the reality principle. Perceiving this "dimly lighted" landscape at a "certain distance," Loti wonders "whether it is all artificial, or whether one is not oneself the victim of some morbid illusion; and if it is not indeed a real country view seen through a distorted vision out of focus, or through the wrong end of an opera-glass" (*MC*, p. 200/178). Paradoxically, he recognizes the imitation of a Japanese landscape by this tiny garden as the "real," as an actually existing, not merely imagined, referent, while the Western visitor's apparatus of perception must concede its deceptive – and theatricalizing – optic, its decadent misrepresentation of the other.

If Loti construes Japan as a small and artificial country in order to minimize its importance on the world-political map, this topos reverses itself in the domain of the aesthetic. It is the European practice of *japonisme*, rather than Japanese culture itself, that he now condemns as pretentious and superficial: "I cannot help smiling when I think of some of the so-called *Japanese* drawing rooms, overcrowded with knick-knacks and curios and hung with coarse gold embroideries on exported satins, of our Parisian fine ladies" (*MC*, p. 202/179).[19] By contrast, the actual "Japanese manner of understanding interior luxury," while itself not without artificial aspects, expresses itself in the "scrupulous and excessive cleanliness, white mats and white woodwork" of the Japanese house; the Japanese custom strikes Loti as favoring an "appearance of extreme simplicity" and as an "incredible nicety in infinitely small details" (*MC*, p. 202/179–80). This simple elegance offers him a rare instance of something close to an authentic experience, at least when opposed to the purely decorative assembly of exotic collectors' items in the Parisian salons, where these artifacts have been wrenched out of their natural, original context.

Later contemplating the golden rays of the evening sun pouring into his room and illuminating the Buddha statues and flower arrangements in their antique vases, Loti acknowledges the "real charm" of feeling that his living quarters and Chrysanthème playing the guitar are an emotional part of himself. Certainly this sense of affinity with Japanese domestic life is not free from orientalist condescension, but it also offers an opportunity for self-critical introspection:

> On the whole, I have perhaps been unjust to this country; it seems to me that my eyes are at last opened to see it in its true light, that all my senses are undergoing a strange and abrupt change; I suddenly have a better perception and appreciation of all the infinity of the dainty small things amongst which I live; of the fragile and studied grace of their forms, the oddity of their drawings, the refined choice of their colours.
>
> (*MC*, pp. 276–7/253–4)

Although the conventional vocabulary of exoticism continues to permeate his discourse, Loti allows the stereotype of Japan's smallness to reverse itself. Subverting what he recognizes as the crudity of his own generalizations, "smallness" now connotes attractive delicacy and subtle taste, rather than ludicrous insignificance. Thus, even while continuing to construct a stereotypical image of Japan's essence, the foreigner's discourse also turns self-reflexively against its own originator, the orientalist subject himself, urging him to reconsider his own self-distancing contempt for Japan and to adopt, if only as a temporary and artificial pose, an attitude of hermeneutic openness and empathetic inquiry toward the other.[20]

The fact that no letters have arrived from Europe signifies for Loti the disappearance of conventional, old habits and the experience of self-accommodation to the different scale and proportions of Japanese space, both in the architectural and in the symbolic, cultural sense. He thinks that he is becoming used to things like the "tiny and ingenious furniture" and the "immaculate monotony" of the floor mats, and he believes that he is shedding his "Western prejudices" (*MC*, pp. 279–80/255–6). He even tries to conceptualize the foreign reality in its authentic language, calling the traditional string instrument *samisen*, rather than "guitar" or mandolin. He also decides to call his wife by her Japanese name, Kikou-san; although it literally means "Madame Chrysanthème," the native appellation does not carry the obviously exoticist and condescending connotations of the French translation. The use of such indigenous terms is not only, as Todorov argues, a strategy of expressing exotic otherness,[21] but also an attempt to take a, however limited, "insider's" look at the foreign culture. Listening to Kikou's playing, Loti admits that "her gaze has no longer the vacant stare of a doll." Affirming his "wife's" individual personality beyond her mere function as a provider of sexual pleasure – her subjectification rather than mere subjection – Loti indicates an important shift in his attitude toward Japan. Recognizing it as a site of comprehensible signification, he finally develops some empathetic affinity for the *genius loci*, feeling "almost at home in this corner of Japan" (*MC*, pp. 280–2/256–8). Here Loti is temporarily able to engage in a hermeneutic dialogue that acknowledges the possibility of a linguistically mediated communality between different cultures that transcends the differences between specific languages and their indigenous world views. Thus he tentatively approaches the fusion of his own subjectivity and the cultural horizon of Japan that he usually rejects as an unattainable, even undesirable, position.

Ironically, his decision to abandon some of his indifference toward Japan coincides with the rumor that he will soon have to leave the country for China. It is as if the visitor's ideological and aesthetic self-critique is possible only as belated experience, as a fragile and transitory insight that depends on the fading away from the author's consciousness of the very reality that his newly gained sensitivity has begun to appreciate. If for Said, the attitude of exteriority, the Westerner's distance from the East, precludes the possibility of authentic understanding, Loti, at this point of his journey, offers a different, more productive version of this category. Paradoxically, as long as he obtains actual experiences in the daily life of Nagasaki, as long as he has a real – though largely unused – chance of encountering its people, customs, and values, he makes few efforts at overcoming his cultural distance, thus attaining only the barest and most superficial of understanding. It is only in the midst of expecting his departure that Loti is able to employ this sense of inevitable exteriority to some hermeneutic advantage. It is as if in his discourse, cross-cultural understanding is possible only through temporal and geographic distance, as if a sense of nostalgia is called for to promote a less biased, though not necessarily more sympathetic view of the foreign country.

He decides to make a drawing of his room before leaving Nagasaki, a plan confirming his sense that all his activities in Japan are but a "bitter mockery" of his life in Stamboul. The sketch is to be an interesting souvenir but not, as he emphasizes, a sign that he really cares for his Japanese dwelling. Again, Loti's discourse is replete with ambiguities. At first he boasts of his ability "to draw from nature," which he opposes to the "entirely conventional" style of Japanese art, and he proudly mentions that even the Japanese are "amazed at the air of *reality* thrown in my sketch" (*MC*, p. 298/272–3). But once the drawing is finished, he realizes that Japanese space defies his strategies of Western mimetic representation. He feels that his sketch "has an ordinary, indifferent, *French* look which does not suit"; lacking in "sentiment," it fails to render accurately and truthfully the "fragile look" and "sonority" of his room, the "minute delicacy," "extreme antiquity," and "perfect cleanliness" of its woodwork. Thus, he muses, he may "have done better" had he been "falsifying the perspective, – Japanese-style"; this approach would have exaggerated the strange outlines of the space in front of him and hence, as Loti implies, would have provided a more authentic rendition. Ironically, it is the presumed inferiority of Japanese artistic technique to the Western aesthetic norm that unmasks that norm's limited translatability into the context of the non-West.

Suggesting that only the indigenous mode of representation is adequate for depicting the space of the other, Loti concludes that his Japanese surroundings "cannot be drawn, cannot be expressed, but remains untranslatable and undefinable" (*MC*, pp. 299–300/274–5). On the one hand, Japan figures as a mystified space of the ineffable that energizes the self-critique of Western representation, even though the foreign domain is literally taken into his possession as an object, as a souvenir for the Western exoticist imagination. But Loti's text also opens up a space of "hybridity" in which the self-assertion of the indigenous aesthetics of Japanese architecture *competes with*, and actively *opposes*, the ethnocentric trust in the supposedly "natural," universal adequacy of Western perception and artistic technique. This form of hybrid cultural encounter is comparable to the process of "the opening up of another contentious political and cultural site at the heart of colonial representation" that Bhabha describes in the context of discussing how in India the Western Christian missionary's discourse on the necessity of being reborn or twice-born is subtly invaded and subverted by the Brahmanic counter-version of this religious doctrine: "Here the word of divine theology," Bhabha explains, "is deeply flawed by the assertion of the indigenous sign, and in the very practice of domination the language of the master becomes hybrid – neither the one thing nor the other."[22] While in Bhabha's example, the Western text actually quotes parts of the Indian counterdiscourse *verbatim*, the categories that Loti uses to conceptualize Japanese culture – extreme simplicity, dainty smallness, fragility, grace, and refined colors – reflect his affiliation with Western aesthetic movements such as aestheticism, impressionism, and decadence, rather than, as it may seem, the authentic voice of classical Japanese aesthetics.[23] But nonetheless, as in the case of Bhabha's missionary, Loti's text must incorporate the unsettling power of the very signs of the other culture that the West tries to conceptualize and affect through its hegemonic strategies. Simplicity, fragility, grace, and so forth are part of a vocabulary that is Western and yet read off the sights of Japanese culture; given positive connotations, these expressions of Japan's beautiful "smallness" manage to destabilize the "grand" narrative of Eurocentric power and patriarchal chauvinism that lies at the center of Loti's discourse.

VI

The hybridizing inscription of the disturbing signifier of the other in the dominant discourse of the West is particularly visible in Loti's pronouncements about the importation of Japanese art into Europe. He believes that Japanese crafts are bizarre and spiritually preposterous but acknowledges that they are the products of long traditions and extreme dexterity on the part of even the most insignificant artist. But once this authentic art "threatens to invade us in France, in this epoch of imitative decadence," it deteriorates into *japonisme*, which Loti now rejects as a movement complicit with capitalist commodification and mass-production; Japanese art, he complains, "has become the great resource of our manufacturers of cheap '*objects of art*'" (*MC*, p. 327/298).

If the commercialization of Japanese art reveals the artificiality of European orientalist fashion, then the West itself, according to Loti's melancholy interpretation, reveals its inauthenticating effect on Japan:

> Is it because I am about to leave this country, because I have no longer any link to bind me to it, any resting-place on its soil, and that my spirit is ready on the wing? I know not, but it seems to me I have never as clearly seen it as today. And more than ever, do I find it little, aged, with worn-out blood and worn-out sap; I feel more fully its antediluvian antiquity, its centuries of mummification, which will soon end in grotesquerie and pitiful buffoonery, as it comes into contact with Western novelties.
>
> (*MC*, pp. 327–8/298–9)

"Mummification" as an image of ahistorical stagnation, superannuated culture, and proud self-seclusion is a recurrent topos in the writing on China by authors like Herder, Schelling, and Marx.[24] As used by Loti in the context of Japan, the image is highly ambivalent. On the one hand, it replicates the author's ethnocentric ideology, his stereotypical views of the Orient as a marginal, historically stagnant farce. But this dubious metaphor contains a grain of truth, for it draws attention to the visitor's own insight that what strikes him as Japan's ridiculous and anachronistic appearance is not an intrinsic aspect of Japanese cultural essence but merely the direct conceptual product of Western modernity, whose political power and hegemonic idea of progress enable the writer to deploy the image of mummified Japan in the first place.

Here, as throughout his book, Loti exhibits a strangely bifurcated, self-divided vision of Japan, oscillating between stereotype and rhetorical self-critique, between ethnocentric prejudice and the search for aesthetic understanding, between orientalist discourse and meta-discursive reflection. It is in these breaks, doublings, and conflicts of ethnographic writing, I suggest, that we may discover Loti's continuing significance for a renewed understanding of orientalism. If Said has emphasized the inextricable connection between imperialist ideology or colonial power and cultural representation in the Western constructions of the Eastern other, a writer of Loti's stature – despite his obviously deluded misogyny and racism – shows that this connection does not necessarily mark the conceptual boundary of orientalism. His writings remain of compelling interest in the present debates on the discursive construction of cultures because Loti articulates the experience that the signifying power of non-Western cultures always exceeds the confining parameters of Eurocentric essentialism, sexist arrogance, or exotic idealizations; that the voice of the Eastern other can be suppressed but never entirely silenced in Western discourse; and that resistance to Western hegemony (re-)asserts itself even in the most totalizing conceptualizations.

For this reason Loti's deeply problematic travelogue may be regarded as a necessary supplement or counter-expression to writings such as Lafcadio Hearn's. Like his French precursor, Hearn was conscious of his exteriority as a Westerner and the limits of cross-cultural interpretation, but nonetheless attempted to position himself *within* the foreign culture of Japan. As a result of this ambivalent perspective, he tended to promote an idealizing view of Oriental essence, beauty, and moral tradition that needs to be read side by side with the aesthetics of surface impressions promoted by Loti. Perhaps it is in the comparative space opened up by considerably different writers like these two that the ideological and rhetorical spectrum of the Western literary discourse on Japan around the turn of the century becomes visible. If cultural hermeneutics, like all other branches of interpretive discourse, is intrinsically characterized by conflicts, impasses, blindness, and the temporality, even transitoriness, of all insights, then voices like Hearn's and Loti's, articulating these problems in a particularly self-conscious fashion, still deserve to be heard today.

14

WESTERN AGON/EASTERN RITUAL

CONFRONTATIONS AND CO-OPTATIONS IN WORLDVIEWS

Eugene Eoyang

INTRODUCTION

"Agon" vs. "Ritual" is a contrast I wish to draw of a mindset in the Western tradition (epitomized by the culture of the United States), with a mindset familiar in Asia (represented predominantly by the cultural traditions of China – though variations can be found in Japan, as well as in Korea). By "agon," I refer to "the Greek term for 'assembly associated with contests' ";[1] and by ritual, I mean the performance of "a custom or practice of a formal kind."[2] I shall not make the monolithizing fallacy and pretend that there are no "rituals" in the United States (or the West in general), nor do I suggest that there are no agons in China (or in Asia).[3] What I propose is not a blanket generalization of Western culture as agonistic and Eastern culture as ritualistic: my purpose is to examine those areas of "agon" in the West perhaps not always found in the East, and those areas of "ritual" perhaps not totally comprehensible in the West.

Invariably, the word "agon" conjures up what Thomas Scanlon has characterized decisively as "the vocabulary of competition." He points out that "most societies have special terms for sports contests," but he observes that the English word "sport," as originally conceived in English, "merely indicated one form of leisure diversion." Nowadays, when sports, in every sense of the word, is a serious business, a source not so much of diversion as of anxiety and stress, and athletes have to work to be competitive – while spectators get worked up before, during, and after a game, diversion and amusement seem only etymologically relevant to the meaning of sports. Indeed, in modern day sports, sportsmanship has been overwhelmed by an all-consuming emphasis on winning at all costs.

By contrast, the cultures of the Far East are more concerned with relationships over time rather than with competitiveness in an instant of time, and their concern is not so much on ephemeral winning as it is on establishing a non-ephemeral harmony. A sense of balance and ceremony, rather than an instinct for combativeness, is what informs the cultures of the Far East.[4] Where the culture of agon strives toward the annihilation of the other, the culture of ritual strives for communion with the other. Where one seeks victory by eliminating the enemy, the other strives for hegemony by co-optation. What I want to do is to examine the underlying premises between these two viewpoints, and to analyze the potential misunderstandings that may result in exchanges between individuals representing these opposing viewpoints.

At the root of the problem is a difference in logic. Aristotelian logic is a form of agonistic thinking: it is based on the assumption that "Nothing is X and non-X." Yet, effective as this deductive strategy may be for certain propositions (digitial machines, for example), its universality can be easily challenged. The following examples have been proposed (by Gödel, among others) as meaningful exceptions to Aristotle's categorical rule:

> "This sentence is not true."
> "I am lying."

In either case, the proposition is – logically – both X, and non-X. In the first instance, if the sentence is true (X), then the sentence must be untrue (non-X): in other words, if what the sentence claims is true, then its assertion must be untrue; if what it claims is untrue, then its assertion must be true. Similarly, the statement "I am lying" cannot be either true or untrue: it must be both, because if it is true that "I am lying," then the assertion must be untrue, and if it is not true that "I am lying," that must mean that I am telling the truth. In both instances, the proposition asserts both "X" and "non-X."[5]

An alternative logic suggests a four-fold rather than a binary model, and allows for the following possibilities: (1) that something can be X but not non-X; (2) that it can be non-X but not X; (3) that it can be both X and non-X; and (4) that it can be neither X nor non-X. In more concrete terms, this form of logic can be made more recognizable. To use only the most familiar example, in the last generation we have come to recognize that it is possible not only to be (1) masculine or (2) feminine, it is also possible to be (3) both masculine and feminine (bisexuals, for instance), and that some may be (4) neither masculine nor feminine (eunuchs, for example).

The clearest exposition of this "four-cornered" logic occurs in the Chuang-tzu (Zhuangzi):

> Suppose that you and I debated and you bested me, would it mean that you were naturally right and I was naturally wrong? Or even vice versa? Or would one be partially right and one partially wrong? Or would both be right and wrong?[6]

Plato, whose thinking was more dialectical, less categorical than Aristotle's, defined "becoming" from a more ontological rather than a logical perspective: Lloyd recalls Plato trying to establish a general law of becoming "that 'opposites come to be out of opposites,' greater from less, less from greater, weaker from stronger, stronger from weaker. . . . As each of these processes may be reciprocal, he concludes, by analogy, that not only does death follow life, but life death."[7] Nevertheless, Aristotle has generally prevailed in history over Plato, and radical oppositions rather than dialectical polarities predominate in Western culture. Lloyd may reflect a Western bias when he observes: "the evidence for comprehensive dichotomous classifications of reality is widespread and relates to societies of many different types in many different parts of the world" (*P&A*, p. 31).

If logic and the premises of logic are a foundational form of rhetoric or persuasion, then it becomes clear why Western cultures tend to formulate their vision of the world in categorical terms that specifically exclude the middle. "Love it or leave it" was the chauvinistic sixties version of this thinking in the United States; the current attack on immigrants in a US vs. THEM confrontation stems from the same impulse, in defiance of the inconvenient fact that some Americans are immigrants. If one adds to this notion of reality of mutually exclusive categories the rhetoric of faith,[8] which sees good and evil in black and white terms, one can appreciate the power of persistently agonistic thinking. This dualistic vision of the world was promoted by the third century Persian prophet, Mani, "the Apostle of Light," in the religious movement known as Manicheism. Even though this sect was attacked by both Christianity and the Roman state, the Manichean mindset nevertheless left an indelible mark on Christian thinking[9] and vestiges persist to the present day. But the agonistic view of the world codified by Mani did not originate with him: the seeds were planted in the Bible itself, and in Christ's own words. As Father Walter Ong points out, in

> one of its principal aspects of Jesus' work is diaeretic, differentiating, field breaking, as the masculine agon and style are. "I come into this world to divide it" (John 9:39). . . . "He who is not with me is against me" (Matthew 12:30).[10]

"The concept of Satan," Ong reminds us, "takes form in this agonistic milieu – the name Satan means adversary" (*FL*, p. 169).

CONTRASTS

This intolerant, monolithic requirement of absolute allegiance creates inevitably its own agon. "Thou shalt have no other gods before me" (Exodus 20:3); "For the Lord thy God is a jealous God" (Deuteronomy 6:15); "No man can serve two masters. . . . Ye cannot serve God and mammon" (Matthew 6:24). It is axiomatic in the West that faith requires exclusive allegiance to one deity and to one set of doctrines, even if different religions share portions of the same tradition, such as Judaism, Christianity, and Islam. One cannot even be an adherent of two sects of Christianity; no one is, for example, Catholic and Protestant at the same time. One cannot even belong to two subsets of Protestantism at the same time: no one is, for example, both a Methodist and a

Baptist. One could, as Robert Bork did, claim he was "a generic Protestant"; but we assume that he had several Protestant denominations in his family background, not that he was a member of several churches.

Contrast this with the practice of religions in China which do not demand such exclusive allegiances. Of the Chinese, W. E. Soothill observed in 1923, that "they belong to none of the three religions, or, more correctly, they belong to all three. In other words, they are eclectic, and use whichever form best responds to the requirement of the occasion for which they use religion."[11] Henrik Kraemer put it another way: "One of the best-known features of Chinese Universism is that the three religions – Confucianism, Buddhism, and Taoism – are virtually treated as one. The religious allegiance of the average man is not related to one of the three religions. . . . He participates unconcerned as to any apparent lack of consistency, alternatively in Buddhist, Taoist, or Confucian rites. He is by nature a religious pragmatist."[12] There are memorable metaphoric celebrations of this doctrinal eclecticism:

> The teachings are three, but the Way is one.
> Confucianism is the sun; Buddhism is the moon; Taoism is the stars.
> Confucianism governs the state; Taoism governs the body; Buddhism governs the mind.

In addition to this eclectic view of choosing between religions, the Chinese believe in the ambivalent nature of their gods, who "may be good and evil."[13] In Christianity, it would be inconceivable, the most outrageous blasphemy, to believe that God is both good and evil. The very ontology of Western belief in the supernatural, its concept of divinities, contrasts with Chinese beliefs: where one is absolutist, abstract, and categorical, the other is relativist, pragmatic, and complementary.

To the rhetoric of reason and the rhetoric of faith, one can add the further reinforcement of social sanction in the adversarial character of the practice of law as it has evolved since the Middle Ages. Even though the tradition of trial by combat, where the intercession of the Almighty was supplicated in determining the innocence of the accused, was condemned in the thirteenth century, the practice continued through the fourteenth and fifteenth centuries, and its paradigm has been continued in the modern institution of the trial. The word "trial" preserves its etymological meaning of "ordeal," which Huizinga reminds us meant "nothing more or less than divine judgment" (*HL*, p. 81). Speaking of Greek tradition, Huizinga says, "The lawsuit had in fact once been an agon in the strict sense of the word" (*HL*, p. 73). The drama of a court trial and the drama of a sports contest stem from the same adversarial tension: "the juridical process," to quote Huizinga again, "started by being a contest and the agonistic nature of it is alive even today" (*HL*, p. 76).

The most famous trial of recent years – the criminal trial of O. J. Simpson – might be accurately characterized as "trial by ordeal." However, while many would defend the process as consistent with the procedures and principles of the practice of law, few believe that the verdict reflected the judgment of God, let alone the purposes of justice. Unfortunately, the legal system reflects a legalistic mindset, for it presents us with an either/or choice: it does not allow us to admit both possibilities – that Mark Fuhrman was a racist who tainted the evidence and O. J. Simpson was guilty.[14] There is a vestige of the Manichean belief in unadulterated good pitted against unmitigated evil in modern jurisprudence when it insists that the side of the "good" (the prosecution) cannot be tainted with "evil" (the racism of Mark Fuhrman).

Indeed, in the past thirty years, libertarian laws and Supreme Court decisions protecting the rights of the individual – from the Miranda law to the principle of "the fruit of the poisoned tree," where evidence illegally secured can be excluded – have given criminals wide latitude, further distancing the law from justice in the minds of many. The protection of the individual (regardless of who that individual is) reflects the highest principles of civil rights in the West; yet it also reflects an idealistic and categorical worldview that requires that the side of the right be pure and free of taint. The officers of the law must be procedurally flawless if convictions are to stand up in court. The fastidiousness on the part of law enforcement in the arrest and indictment of the Unabomber suspect Theodore Kaczynski reflects the enormous pressure on those who apprehend suspected criminals to be without taint in following due process. The miscreant in criminal cases can ignore his or her culpability in erecting a defense, since defense counsel need only show that the practice of the law is at fault to enhance the chances of an acquittal. It is both an irony of Western jurisprudence, and its sense of nobility, that the side of the "right" must always be more magnanimous than the side of the "wrong": the enforcers of the law must be more fastidious than the violators of the law.

Contrast this with the non-adversarial paradigm in the traditional Chinese court system, where the accused was considered guilty until he was exonerated; where the propensity of the guilty to lie was assumed, which justified torture to extract confessions as a consequence; where the magistrate was also the judge and the prosecutor. As for civil suits and tort trials, Chinese are influenced by Confucius's injunction against litigiousness: to publicly air one's grievances cast as much shame on the litigant as on the defendant. "In hearing litigations," the Master said, "I am like anyone else. What should happen, however, is to make litigations unnecessary" (*Analects*, 12:13).

The justice system in Japan cannot always guarantee a fair trial: defendants with notorious reputations have difficulty finding adequate counsel because lawyers in Japan are reluctant to associate with social pariahs – unlike the United States, where the most heinous crimes appear to attract the most celebrated lawyer. (Timothy McVeigh was represented by twenty lawyers costing the US taxpayer millions of dollars.) The head of the Aum Shinrikyo sect, "Shoko Asahara" (Chizuo Matsumoto), when he was indicted for releasing sabin gas in the Tokyo subway on March 20, 1995, was reported to have had difficulty finding a lawyer in Japan.

Combative images dominate our discourse: we must have a "war on drugs"; we must wage a campaign against pornography, inflation, corruption, or what have you. The underlying assumption is that the ultimate solution is destruction of the enemy: extirpation and annihilation are the only guarantors of victory. Cauterization – a physiological burning and pillaging – is considered the only method of cure. As successful as the Gulf War against Iraq was, many Americans felt that, because Saddam Hussein was not eliminated, it fell far short of total victory. George Bush was perceived as having snatched defeat from imminent triumph. Unconditional surrender is the only "win" worth boasting of. Martial metaphors abound: when Louis Farrakhan advocates his cause, he says, "And literally, going to Washington to seek justice for our people is like going to war." Even a balanced discourse devoted to resolutions of conflict cannot avoid agonistic rhetoric, as when Paul Gilroy, in his lecture at the "Dramas of Culture" conference, referred to "the crusades of tolerance." At the same time, Gilroy could recognize that, in comprehending the need to "set afoot a new man," Frantz Fanon met "this urgent obligation via a binary code almost as pernicious as the manichean dualisms that he sought to supplant."

The oppositional paradigm was, indeed, what led US foreign policy into the quagmire in the Middle East in the first place. That paradigm suggests that one can only be one thing or its opposite, that one cannot be both; by that logic, a friend of a friend – commutatively – must be a friend, and an enemy of an enemy – distributively – must also be a friend. In the seventies, symbolized by US citizens who were taken as hostages, Iran was the arch-enemy. In the same decade, Iran had been waging a bloody war with Iraq. In the eighties, Iraq and the US were alike enemies of Iran. But the difficulty with US policy was precisely that it did not appreciate that, despite its opposition to Iran, Iraq was not an ally either. Doubtless many Americans were confused and could not follow the disputes between two countries whose name in English differed only in the last letter: a "q" or an "n."

The muddle derives from a paradigm of simplistic agon applied to a reality of complex dialectics. The unwillingness to consider multivalent logics or multiple perspectives, or disconcerting ambivalences and ironies, stems from the same impulse that abhors indeterminacy despite its pervasiveness; it stems from the anti-intellectualism in the United States that sees complexity as casuistry and needless convolutedness, Machiavellian constructs of "effete intellectuals." The distinction between the schematic simplicity of sport and the untidy complexity of reality becomes important when sports dominate national mythology, when the "ultimate" is not peace on earth, but the winning of a championship – whether the Super Bowl, the World Series, the NBA title, or the NCAA tournament. (It is, of course, not without its commercial advantages that these "ultimates" are repeated annually.)

But sports are one thing, life is another. Yet, if one wishes to understand how Americans deal with reality, it is necessary to understand the increasingly agonistic character of sports. Sports are not only an occupation for its now wealthy practitioners, they have become a preoccupation for millions of fans, and for many they have turned into nothing less than the driving raison d'être for living.

Increasingly, in the modern era, sports have assumed a more than recreational purpose: they have provided, almost more than political or religious ceremony, the dominating paradigm for our times. Richard Nixon, for example, was fond of sports analogies when he was planning strategy, whether manipulating party politics or managing geopolitical diplomacy. An important part of the American ethos starts with Vince Lombardi's famous, oft-quoted dictum: "Winning isn't everything, it's the only thing."[15] The emphasis on winning is part of the media hype that dominates modern life in the United States.

This penchant for winning has become so overwhelming that games that allow for an outcome where there might be no winner have been revised to force a winner. American football has instituted its "sudden death"; basketball has added overtimes until the issue is decided; baseball has always had extra innings to determine the victor; tennis has installed the tiebreaker; soccer uses overtimes at the college level, and "penalty kicks" in the World Cup (which infamously resulted in Brazil's triumph over Italy in 1994). We can understand why the media insists on a winner, despite the fact that two teams or two players are comparably competitive, but the assumption that every game has a winner misleads many into thinking that, in life also, there must always be a winner and a loser.

There is a way, however, to deconstruct winning and losing in a manner that may make it less simplistic for the media to manipulate, but which accords more accurately with realities. If one conceives of winning not as a decisive outcome in favor of one combatant over another, but as a victory of the spirit and of the soul, then most games, if truth be told, are not so much about winning as about competitive or non-competitive losing. The winning-is-everything concept assumes that the desire to win is universal, and that the value of winning is uncontested. However, in real life, the outcome is often decided randomly, not from a contest of wills, but from luck, circumstance, or a disparity in degrees of indifference. The win–lose dynamic makes more sense if it were deconstructed into four possibilities instead of two, following the pattern of four-cornered logic introduced earlier. To (1) A wins, B loses, or (2) A loses, B wins, we add (3) A wins, B wins; (4) A loses, B loses. For the discerning spectator of the sport, it is alternative (3) – A wins, B wins – which is the most satisfying, because no matter who emerges technically victorious, the game has been played at its best when the combatants perform at their highest potential. The other three possibilities interest partisans of the combatants – fans – more than the connoisseurs, because partisans care more for their side winning or losing than they care about the aesthetics of the sport. "Winning," indeed for them, "is the only thing, even winning ugly." Partisans only care about winning, whereas aesthetes of the game, to say nothing of the true athletes of the sport, care more about the quality of the competition.[16]

To the American aversion to ties, we may contrast the Japanese tendency in favor of ties. As Robert Whiting has shown in *You Gotta Have Wa*, baseball in Japan not only allows for ties, players actively strive for a tie. The objective of the game is not to beat the opposition into submission, but to create a competitive harmony – *wa* – with the people one plays with. I offer a personal experience as corroboration: when I was a visiting scholar in Beijing, I looked for someone to play tennis with. I happened to chance on a Japanese player, who was, unfortunately, not much more than a beginner: though I tried hard to make the game competitive, I ended up beating him pretty soundly. Whether out of humiliation or consideration for me, he never played with me again. In winning decisively, I lost a tennis partner.

One can lose even while winning, which the Greeks recognized early on in the concept of "Pyrrhic victories." Victories are never final; neither are losses. The two countries that, fifty years ago, offered unconditional surrenders, Germany and Japan, are now at the top of the economic heap, among the wealthiest nations on earth. One can equally win even while losing. Huizinga has observed, justly, that "Competition for honour may also take, as in China, an inverted form by turning into a contest in politeness," where "one demolishes one's adversary by superior manners, making way for him or giving him precedence" (*HL*, p. 66).

CONCEPTUAL DECONSTRUCTIONS

In the literature on oppositions, unfortunately, many crucially different paired concepts are lumped together to prove the inherent duality of things. Actually, what the universality and pervasiveness of dualities indicate is not so much the inherent duality of things, but the inherent tendency of the human mind to understand things better when they are presented as dualities. "Opposites," G. E. R. Lloyd has written, "provide a simple and apparently comprehensive framework by reference to which other things may be described or classified" (*P&A*, p. 86). Here are a list of the ten pairs that the Pythagoreans considered "fundamental oppositions in the universe":[17]

Limited and Unlimited
Odd and Even
Unity and Multiplicity
Right and Left
Masculine and Feminine
Quiescence and Motion
Straight and Curved
Light and Darkness
Good and Bad
Square and Rectangle.

If we look at these juxtaposed pairs closely, we find that they are verbal opposites but not ontological opposites. Right and left, for example, are opposites in direction, but they are meaningless without a central deictic reference from which rightness and leftness can be determined; unity and multiplicity are not mutually exclusive opposites because one can subsume the other – as in the famous motto of the United States, "e pluribus unum"; and there are what I call pseudo-dualities, dualities that are not really two separate entities, but rather one thing and its absence – darkness, for example, is merely the absence of light, quiescence is the absence of motion, unlimitedness is merely the lack of limits.[18] On the other hand, light without darkness is conceivable (as in overlit supermarkets), just as motion without quiescence is not only conceivable in the modern world, it's all too familiar, and limitations do not logically require a notion of the infinite or the eternal. (Square and Rectangle are hard to conceive of as opposites at all, since one is a sub-species of the other.) Aristotle was not entirely unaware of the implicit single nature of some of the oppositions he posited, as Lloyd reminds us: "Indeed, although . . . there appear to be certain inconsistencies in Aristotle's attitude to certain pairs, it is clear from repeated statements in the *Metaphysics* that he believed it to be true of contrary terms as a whole, that one of each pair is a positive term, the other a (mere) privation" (*P&A*, pp. 64–5).[19]

One needs to distinguish between pairs that are mutually exclusive, like "odd and even" (a number cannot be odd and even, assuming we're dealing with whole numbers); pairs that are merely different aspects of the same thing, like "right and left," and "unity and multiplicity," that may be more complementary than oppositional; and pairs that are just different, but not categorically opposite, such as "straight and crooked" and "masculine and feminine."[20] Logicians have labeled the first class of pairs "contradictories" because they are mutually exclusive: one cannot be the one and the other; the second class they have characterized as "contraries" because the presence of one does not preclude the presence of the other (my "left," for example, may be your "right");[21] the third class they have labeled "sub-contraries," which are not real oppositions: they are distinctions rather than contrasts in substance or in aspect (*P&A*, pp. 86–7; *OLPA*, pp. 54–5).[22] As Ogden rightly points out: "Difference, however great, does not create opposition" (*OLPA*, p. 37).

As an example of indiscriminate lumping together of pairs, I cite Walter Ong's assertion that

> Various kinds of adversativeness have been exploited to deal intellectually with the world and with being itself from as far back as we can trace human thought up to the present . . . Mother Earth and Father Sky . . . the Chinese *li* [reason, order of things] and *ch'i* [spirit or life force], yin and yang, Empedoclean attraction and repulsion, the Platonic dialectic, matter and form, Abelard's sic et non, essence and existence, Hegelian dialectic, and countless other binary modes of analysis. (*FL*, p. 16)

The lumping together of essentially different pairs reflects the convenience of conceiving of things in pairs, but it is unhelpful to view these pairs as being equally opposite, i.e., mutually exclusive. Only one of the pairs cited by Ong, Abelard's *sic et non*, may be justly characterized as contradictory: the other pairs are not mutually exclusive. Some – Mother Earth and Father Sky, yin and yang, attraction and repulsion, the Platonic dialectic, matter and form – are "contraries," representing contrastive aspects; while others, *li* and *ch'i*, essence and existence, are "sub-contraries," contradistinctions rather than radical opposites.

These distinctions are not the mere quibbles of the fastidious pedant, for how we analyze paired concepts, whether as "contradictories" or as "contraries," and what logic we use to understand them, will decisively affect not only our understanding, but also our behavior. For example, is "pain and pleasure" a contradictory or a contrary pair? Aestheticians who define pleasure as the absence of pain obviously consider the pair as contradictory, of the kind I have characterized as a pseudo-duality: the pair really acknowledges the existence of only one thing, pain, and signals its presence or its absence. However, others might insist that pain exists separate from pleasure: in this case, the pair would be contrary, not contradictory. This would allow for concurrent pleasure and pain, as well as the absence of either pleasure and pain. Work and play would be another pair in the same class, contraries rather than contradictories. The negation of play does not necessarily constitute work, and the negation of work need not constitute play; it is possible to be neither playing nor working, just as it is possible to play at the same time we work and work at the same time we play. Professional athletes and professional musicians are perfect illustrations of those who are working and playing at the same time.

Some pairs are not easy to characterize, because whether they represent real oppositions, contrasting aspects, or mere contradistinctions, depends on how one regards them. The notion of sickness and health, for example, might be viewed as: (1) contradictory – if one regards either sickness or health (but not both) as real, so that sickness is conceived of as the absence of health, or health is viewed as the absence of sickness; (2) contrary – if one regards sickness and health as merely the two extremes in a continuum, so that one may think of health as minimally sick or sickness as minimally healthy; or (3) sub-contrary – if one conceives it possible to be neither sick nor healthy, or both sick and healthy (as in dying patients with robust bodies but cancer in the brain).

To provide a test case for contradictory, contrary, or sub-contrary definitions of health, consider the native populations of the New World before the arrival of the Conquistadors, wiped out within a few generations with diseases to which the Europeans were themselves immune. If health is survival, then the Europeans were healthy; if the presence of disease is an indication of sickness, the Europeans were sick; on the other hand, if responsiveness to the environment is one index of health, the Amerindians were certainly healthy; but if the ability to defend against new viral invasions is a warrant of health, the Amerindians were sick. It is clear that in this instance, sickness and health cannot be conceived of as either contradictory or contrary. Only a sub-contrary definition of sickness and health would apply: the Europeans were healthy by their standards, and the Amerindians were healthy by their (different) standards; and they were both, each in a different way, sick.

Among the dualities most persistently viewed in the West as contradictory are the notions of Good and Evil: what is good cannot be evil; what is evil cannot be good. Taoists, however, when they are not dismissing "good and evil" as human constructs imposed on a neutral reality, would be able to see good coming out of evil, and evil coming out of good.[23]

In his book *Fighting for Life*, Walter Ong attributes the agonistic impulse to oral cultures; with the advent of a print culture, he contends, "the agonistic edge of oratory is dulled" (*FL*, p. 142). I agree with Ong in his identification of the "agonistic impulse," but I am dubious about his implicit assertion that print cultures have "outgrown" the proclivities of earlier oral cultures. Vestiges of the "agonistic edge of oratory," far from being dulled, persist in the continuing "face-downs" between management and labor that result in strikes where no one is the winner; between the baseball owners and the players which damaged a hallowed American institution and cancelled half of the 1995 season; between a Democratic President and a Republican Congress over the 1996 budget, which resulted in two government shutdowns. Perhaps these are the results of our entering into a phase of what Ong calls "secondary orality," one which is fostered by modern electronic technology. The oral cultures of the East are not as agonistic as those in the West; on the contrary, their often non-verbal, non-textual sense of ceremony and ritual nurture a sense of balance rather than contestation, of harmony rather than conflict.

CONFLATIONS

It will not have escaped the notice of the astute that my formulation of the topic – "Agon vs. Ritual" – is itself unwarrantedly agonistic in form. Surely, contests and conflicts, whether those in politics, sports, or religion, constitute a kind of ritual, a ceremony, a "custom or practice of a formal kind." Indeed, given the seriousness with which one takes these activities, and surrounded as contests are with ritual (the Olympic games are a regular reminder), agon and ritual can be seen as not opposed but contiguous and complementary. One could stipulate that there is a difference between the formality of agon and the formality of ritual: it may be useful to see agon as advertently spontaneous and inadvertently ceremonial whereas ritual is advertently ceremonial and inadvertently spontaneous. In contests, whether gladiatorial or recreational, there are formal rules, but these rules are merely the framework for improvisations and spontaneities; in rituals, on the other hand, whether funerals or weddings or commencements, the individual and improvisational is subordinated to the conventional: the ceremony is, in a sense, both conventionalized for, and "customized" to, the occasion. Rituals are no less meaningful because they are repeated over and over again. Christmas does not touch the heart any less for being ceremonially like every previous Christmas; indeed, ritual derives its power to move us precisely from its familiarity, not its novelty. Nevertheless, the agon vs. ritual juxtaposition is a contradistinction rather than an ontological dichotomy: they are not diametrically opposed; to the logician agon vs. ritual belongs to the category of sub-contraries rather than of contradictories.

What we offer here by way of conclusion are conflations of agon and ritual, ways by which we can avoid the agonistic error of choosing either/or by admitting the possibility of both/and.

Robert Oliver's exegesis on the trigram sung in the *Book of Changes* (see the diagram on the facing page) offers a perspective on conflict that emphasizes its futility:

> The kind of communication to be sought is suggested in the Sung hexagram, an intermixture of two broken lines and four solid lines, which warns that differences of viewpoint cannot be overcome by contention. The utmost sincerity, if expressed argumentatively, simply arouses increased opposition. Convictions should be set forth with "apprehensive caution." It is not advantageous to urge ardently acceptance of one's views. "Contention is not a thing to be carried on to extremity." (*CC*, p. 159)

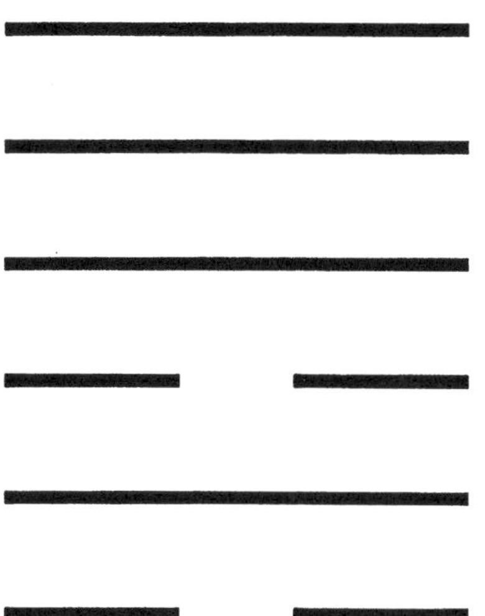

The Sung hexagram from the *I-ching*, illustrating the ancient Chinese position that contentiousness is "not a thing to be carried to extremity."

The dialectic nature of Chinese logic always sees the ambivalence of things, evinced in irony, paradox, reversal, reciprocity, multivalency: nothing is clearly one thing or its opposite; it is sometimes neither or both.[24] But this perception of reality goes beyond binary logic: its premises are ontological as well. Everything is both itself and something else (even, at times, something opposite).

One last conflation involves a fortuitous pun in both English and in Chinese. In Chinese the word for "principle and reason" is a different character from the word for "rite and ceremony," but they are homophonous and are both pronounced *li*. To the oral ear, there is no difference in Chinese between what is "right" and what is "rite." No one who has read Confucius's *Analects* in English translation will have missed the *a*ppositeness in the ancient belief, and the *o*ppositeness in modern practice, of the link between "propriety" and "property." In ancient philosophy what was "proper" is what conformed to the rules of "propriety," and "propriety" responded to the dictates of harmony, the dialectics of the situation, and the demands of communion in a culture.[25] It is perhaps time to restore what was once one and the same, the rightness of ritual, the ceremoniousness of what is right. For truth has no meaning absent of context, and reason has no relevance in the abstract.

Along with the emphasis on "property" as commercial – the bias of capitalism – there is also the decline in one's respect for "propriety" – the bias of individualism. Indeed, the rights of the individual have been elevated – at least since Rousseau – to absolutist levels: "human rights," as it is advanced by Western countries, and with which it criticizes Asian regimes, is a totalized version of the rights of the individual disguised as a presumed universal love of freedom (it was Bakunin, among others, who has argued that humans have an "instinct for freedom" – an assertion that is rarely challenged). But, totalized individualism leads not only to hegemonic politics but also, on a personal level, to murder. Whether motivated by selfishness, autism, or anarchy, the cases of O. J. Simpson, Ted Kaczynski, or Timothy McVeigh, each in its way, illustrate the perils of extreme individualism. The rights of the individual cannot be total: they can be exercised only in the context of the rights of a just and orderly society. Freedom can only be appreciated when there is freedom from as well as freedom to. Extreme individualism, at least in the cases of Ted Kaczynski and Timothy McVeigh, leads not to democracy, but to the tyranny of terrorism.

The rights of the individual may have too often superseded the rights of society in our time. The growing movement of victim's rights is an assertion that society has rights as well: legislation against stalkers before an actual crime is committed and against pederasts after they have served their terms for crimes committed, are but two examples of the assertion of society's rights against the unbridled exercise of individual freedom. Saluting the flag, communal prayer, funerals, inaugurations, commencements, etc. – these are merely society's way of exercising its rights by requiring the rigorous observance of its rites. The post-Romantic mindset, so bent on novelty and originality and spontaneity, so opposed to seemingly mindless conformities of ritualized behavior, so oppositional and anti-traditional in its revolutionary stance, misunderstands the meaning of what a "rite" means. A "rite" is not an empty and insincere show of piety, but an affirmation of the individual's allegiance to the collective and to tradition. Society defines its "rights" in its "rites." Rites are part of the "liminal" reality that Victor Turner has explored so productively. It is perhaps time to restore what was once one and the same, the rightness of ritual and the ceremoniousness of the right. For meaning is not possible absent of context, and reason has no relevance unless it is seen in perspective. In the Confucian tradition, this symbiosis is exemplified by the ideal of the cultured literatus, whose understanding of the right impels him to observe rigorously the demands of ritual. Rites are the price one pays to society for the rights that one enjoys. Observing the rites of society derives from a sense of responsibility which alone makes freedom possible.

The recognition of a "both/and" in preference to an "either/or" paradigm enables us to resolve complexities without casuistry or hypocrisy: we can love our country and yet criticize it; we can, despite the proverbial injunction, have our cake and eat it too. In the mantra of the modern entrepreneur, one should be able to envision a "win–win" scenario, where the rights of the individual and the welfare of the collective are concurrently enhanced, where the benefits to management and to labor do not have to be at the other's expense, where patriotism and love of country do not necessarily involve closing one's borders to new immigrants. One's identity can be based on both how different one may be from everyone else, and, at the same time, how much humanity one shares with everyone else. Identity stems as much from commonality as difference.

Our examination of the conceptual underpinnings of the logic and rhetoric of thought has, I hope, exposed certain limitations and fallacies in the paradigms we use. We share the same objective as Lloyd, when he wrote: ". . . important though the analysis of the different modes of opposition was from the point of view of formal logic, the effect of the advances we have considered was not so much to preclude the use of certain types of argument on opposites, as to enable a dividing line to be drawn between those that have a claim to be demonstrative, and those that are at best persuasive, or at worst frankly misleading" (*P&A*, p. 171). In the concerns about "hegemonies of language," "essentializing thought," and "totalizing ideologies," perhaps we need to be skeptical of rhetorics that are presented as logics.

Some claims to universality may be no more than cultural convictions. While no one would doubt the universal validity of certain propositions (like the Pythagorean Theorem, an example of what Plato thought was "Real"), there are many "pseudo-universals" – scientisms, "self-evident truths," empirical positivisms – that are culturally bound. Categorical thinking may have the aura of objectivity and neutrality, but it may be the most deceptive cultural imperialism. Westerners often invoke "the rule of law" as axiomatic and foundational (particularly in crossroads cultures like Hong Kong). But the law is a human institution that evolved in the West; the emphasis on the law, therefore, reflects a cultural bias ("ex oriente lux, ex occidente lex" – "out of the East, light; out of the West, law"). Even notions of justice and fairness are not immune to cultural preconceptions, particularly with different cultural assumptions on the importance of the individual vis-à-vis the importance of the collective (which is the question that makes Sophocles' *Antigone* perennially fascinating).

The multiculturalism of Benjamin Lee Whorf serves us better, in this case, than the essentialism of Chomsky's universal grammar. But Chomsky is by no means alone in claiming pseudo-universals on the basis of the hegemony of one's own thought. Aristotle, no less than any other, was also guilty of this logocentricity: "His complete dependence on one language," C. K. Ogden writes, "before grammatical distinctions had even been systematized, was hardly less of a handicap than the primitive state of Greek science" (*OLPA*, p. 24).

Without falling into the trap of "relativity," the meaninglessness where everything can mean anything, and anything can mean everything, we must nevertheless be wary of falsely extrapolated paradigms, to which our culture and our language tend to inure us. To use a homely image, it is as if, seeing the world through prescription lenses, one assumes that everyone must wear prescription lenses in order to see. "We must always be on our guard," Huizinga reminds us, "against the deficiencies and differences of our means of expression" (*HL*, p. 25). To which I would add that there are deficiencies and differences not only in our means of expression, but also in our means of perception and conception. Indeed, our solutions to problems of all kinds will be forever undermined if we do not first examine the limitations and the fallacies of the conceptual instruments by which we approach those problems.

ABBREVIATIONS

A	Kate Chopin. *The Awakening and Selected Short Stories*. New York: Bantam, 1981.
AA	A. Irving Hallowell. "Ojibwa Personality and Acculturation," in *Acculturation in the Americas*, ed. Sol Tax. New York: Cooper Square, 1967.
AI	J. M. Coetzee. *Age of Iron*. New York: Penguin, 1998 [1990].
AR	Arthur Abraham. *The Amistad Revolt*. Freetown, Sierra Leone: USIS, 1987.
BD	Ivo Andrić. *The Bridge on the Drina*, trans. Lovett F. Edwards. Chicago: University of Chicago Press, 1977.
BG	Aleko Konstantinov. *Bai Gan'o, Sâchineniia v dva toma*. Sofiia: Bâlgarski pisatel, 1970.
BH	Raymond Desouza George. *The Broken Handcuff or Give me Free*. Unpublished manuscript. Freetown, Sierra Leone: 1994.
CC	Robert Tarbell Oliver. *Communication and Culture in Ancient India and China*. Syracuse: Syracuse University Press, 1971.
CCP	Steven Collins. "Categories, concepts or predicaments? Remarks on Mauss's use of philosophical terminology" in *CP*.
CD	Sigmund Freud. *Civilization and its Discontents*. Trans. James Strachey. New York: Norton, 1962.
CI	David Bromwich. *A Choice of Inheritance: Self and Community from Edmund Burke to Robert Frost*. Cambridge: Harvard University Press, 1989.
CMM	Anthony Ashley, Earl of Shaftesbury. *Characteristics of Men, Manners, Opinions, Times*. Ed. John M. Robertson. Indianapolis/New York: Bobbs Merrill, 1964.
CP	Michael Carrithers, Steven Collins, and Steven Lukes (eds.). *The Category of the Person: anthropology, philosophy, history*. Cambridge, UK: Cambridge University Press, 1985.
CPD	Anya Taylor. "Coleridge on Persons in Dialogue." *Modern Language Quarterly*, 50, 1989.
CR	Paul Ricoeur. "Le Concept de responsabilité: Essai d'analyse sémantique," *Esprit*, 11, November 1994.
CS	Michel Foucault. *The Care of the Self (The History of Sexuality, Volume 3)*, trans. Robert Hurley. New York: Pantheon, 1986.
D	Jean-François Lyotard. *The Differend: Phrases in Dispute*, trans. Georges Van Den Abbeele. Minneapolis: University of Minnesota Press, 1988.

DC J. M. Coetzee. "Into the Dark Chamber: The Writer and the South African State (1986)," in *Doubling the Point: Essays and Interviews*, ed. David Attwell. London: Harvard University Press, 1992.

DHP Dick Veerman. "Développer l'honneur de penser," *Les Cahiers de philosophie*, no. 5, 1988.

DL Diogenes Laertius. *Lives of Eminent Philosophers*, trans. R. D. Hicks. 2 vols. London/Cambridge: William Heinemann and Harvard University Press, 1925.

DP J. M. Coetzee. *Doubling the Point: Essays and Interviews*, ed. David Attwell. Cambridge: Harvard University Press, 1992.

DS Francis Jacques. *Difference and Subjectivity: Dialogue and Personal Identity*, trans. Andrew Rothwell. New Haven: Yale University Press, 1991.

EMA Abdul JanMahomed. "The Economy of Manichean Allegory: The Function of Racial Difference in Colonialist Literature," *Critical Inquiry*, 12, 1985.

EP Paul Ricoeur. "Ethique et politique," in *Du texte à l'action: essais d'herméneutique II*. Paris: Seuil, 1986.

ER Joseph A. Opala. *Ecstatic Renovations: Street Art Celebrating Sierra Leone's 1992 Revolution*. Freetown: Ro-Marong Industries, 1994.

EWB Bill Ashcroft, Gareth Griffiths, and Helen Tiffin. *The Empire Writes Back: Theory and Practice in Post-Colonial Literatures*. London: Routledge, 1989.

F Gabriele D'Annunzio. *Fedra*, ed. and intro. Pietro Gibellini. Milan: Mondadori, 1989.

FC Michael André Bernstein. *Foregone Conclusions: Against Apocalyptic History*. Berkeley: University of California Press, 1994.

FF Dorin Tudoran. *Frost or Fear? Reflections on the Condition of the Romanian Intellectual*, trans. Vladimir Tismaneanu. Daphne, AL: Europa Media, 1986.

FH Kwame Anthony Appiah. *In My Father's House: Africa in the Philosophy of Culture*. London: Methuen, 1992.

FL Walter J. Ong. *Fight for Life: Contest, Sexuality, and Consciousness*. Ithaca: Cornell University Press, 1981.

FMP David Couzens Hoy. "Foucault: Modern or Postmodern?" in *After Foucault: Humanistic Knowledge, Postmodern Challenges*, ed. Jonathan Arac. New Brunswick, NJ: Rutgers University Press, 1988.

FPPC Lawrence D. Kritzman (ed.). *Michel Foucault: Politics, Philosophy, Culture. Interviews and Other Writings*. New York/London: Routledge, 1988.

FR Michel Foucault. *The Foucault Reader*, ed. Paul Rabinow. New York: Pantheon, 1984.

GMN Mihai Spariosu. *God of Many Names: Play, Poetry, and Power in Hellenic Thought, from Homer to Aristotle*. Durham: Duke University Press, 1991.

GR Jean-François Lyotard, Alain Finkielkraut, Elisabeth de Fontenay, Jacob Rogozinski, Pierre André-Taguieff, and Alain Touraine. "Une Guerre requise," *Libération*, February 21 1991.

HD Joseph Conrad. *Heart of Darkness and The Secret Sharer*, intro. Albert J. Guerard. New York/London: Signet, 1983.

HL Johan Huizinga. *Homo Ludens: A Study of the Play Element in Culture*. Boston: Beacon Press, 1955.

HT Lawrence Langer. *Holocaust Testimonies: The Ruins of Memory*. New Haven: Yale University Press, 1991.

I Jean-François Lyotard. *The Inhuman: Reflections on Time*, trans. Geoffrey Bennington and Rachel Bowlby. Stanford, CA: Stanford University Press, 1991.

IA Mario Morasso. *L'imperialismo artistico*. Torino: Fratelli Bocca, 1903.

IN Jean-François Lyotard and David Carroll. "Interview," *Diacritics*, 14, no. 1, Fall 1984.

IR Slavoj Žižek. *The Indivisible Remainder*. London: Verso, 1996.

JA Henry Fielding. *Joseph Andrews*, ed. Martin C. Battestin. Boston: Houghton Mifflin, 1961.

LA Slavoj Žižek. *Looking Awry: An Introduction to Lacan Through Popular Culture*. Cambridge: MIT Press, 1991.

LC Homi K. Bhabha. *The Location of Culture*. London: Routledge, 1994.

LCP Jean Baudrillard. *Le Crime parfait*. Paris: Galilée, 1995.

MB Lewis Nkosi. *Mating Birds*. Braamfontein: Ravan Press, 1987.

MC Pierre Loti. *Madame Chrysanthème*. Paris: Calmann-Lévy, 1893. English translation: *Madame Chrysanthème*, trans. Laura Ensor, intro. Terence Barrow. Rutland, VT: Tuttle, 1973.

MM Martin Hollis. "Of masks and men," in *CP*.

MP Jean-François Lyotard. *Moralités postmodernes*. Paris: Galilée, 1993.

MS Cynthia Ozick. *The Messiah of Stockholm*. New York: Vintage, 1987.

MSK David R. Maines, Noreen M. Sugrue, and Michael A. Katovich. "The Sociological Import of G. H. Mead's Theory of the Past," *American Sociological Review*, 48, April 1983.

MSS Nadine Gordimer. *My Son's Story*. New York: Farrar Straus Giroux, 1990.

NIS Katherine Verdery. *National Ideology Under Socialism: Identity and Cultural Politics in Ceauşescu's Romania*. Berkeley/Los Angeles: University of California Press, 1991.

NV Geoff Smith and Nicola Walker Smith (eds.). *New Voices: American Composers Talk About Their Work*. Portland: Amadeus, 1995.

O Edward W. Said. *Orientalism*. New York: Vintage, 1979.

OHD Tzvetan Todorov. *On Human Diversity: Nationalism, Racism, and Exoticism in French Thought*, trans. Catherine Porter. Cambridge: Harvard University Press, 1993.

OLPA C. K. Ogden. *Opposition: A Linguistic and Psychological Analysis*. Bloomington: Indiana University Press, 1967.

OR Edward W. Said. "Orientalism Reconsidered," in *Europe and its Others*, ed. Francis Barker *et al.* 2 vols. Colchester: Essex University Press, 1985.

OWA Martin Heidegger. "The Origin of the Work of Art," in *Poetry, Language, Thought*, trans. Albert Hofstadter. New York: Harper & Row, 1972.

PA George Becker and Edith Philips (ed. and trans.) *Paris and the Arts, 1851–1896: From the Goncourt Journal*. Ithaca: Cornell University Press, 1971.

P&A G. E. R. Lloyd. *Polarity and Analogy: Two Types of Argumentation in Early Greek Thought*. Indianapolis: Hackett, 1992 [1966].

PAFP RoseLee Goldberg. *Performance Art: From Futurism to the Present*. New York: Abrams, 1988.

PC Homi K. Bhabha. "Postcolonial Criticism," in *Redrawing the Boundaries: The Transformation of English and American Studies*, eds. Stephen Greenblatt and Giles Gunn. New York: MLA, 1992.

PE Jean-François Lyotard. *Postmodernism Explained to Children*, trans. Don Barry, Bernadette Maher, Julian Pefanis, Virginia Spate, and Morgan Thomas. Minneapolis: University of Minnesota Press, 1993.

PLD Anthony Kenny (ed. and trans.). *Descartes: Philosophical Letters*. Minneapolis: University of Minnesota Press, 1970.

PP George Herbert Mead. *The Philosophy of the Present*. Chicago: Open Court Publishing, 1932.

PW Jean-François Lyotard. *Lyotard: Political Writings*, trans. Bill Readings. Minneapolis: University of Minnesota Press, 1993.

PWD René Descartes. *Discourse on the Method of Rightly Conducting One's Reason and Seeking the Truth in the Sciences . . .*, in *The Philosophical Writings of Descartes*, trans. John Cottingham, Robert Stoothoff, and Dugald Murdoch. 2 vols. Cambridge: Cambridge University Press, 1985.

RFR Thomas McFarland. *Romanticism and the Forms of Ruin: Wordsworth, Coleridge, and the Modalities of Fragmentation*. Princeton: Princeton University Press, 1981.

RI Thomas C. Heller, David E. Wellbery, and Morton Sosna (eds.). *Reconstructing Individualism*. Stanford: Stanford University Press, 1986.

RL Rosemary Jolly. "Rehearsals of Liberation: Contemporary Postcolonial Discourse and the New South Africa," *PMLA*, 110, 1995.

RNC Etienne Balibar and Immanuel Wallerstein. *Race, Nation, Class: Ambiguous Identities*, trans. Chris Turner. London: Verso, 1991.

RP Vladimir Tismaneanu. *Reinventing Politics: Eastern Europe from Stalin to Havel*. New York/Toronto: Free Press, 1992.

SAPW David Attwell. *J. M. Coetzee: South Africa and the Politics of Writing*. Cape Town/Berkeley: David Philip and University of California Press, 1993.

SCCM Barry Schwartz. "Social Change and Collective Memory: The Democratization of George Washington," *American Sociological Review*, 56, April 1991.

SM Jacques Derrida. *Specters of Marx: The State of the Debt, the Work of Mourning, and the New International*, trans. Peggy Kamuf. New York/London: Routledge, 1994.

SO Slavoj Žižek. *The Sublime Object of Ideology*. London: Verso, 1989.

SPS Barry N. Olshen. "Subject, Persona and Self in the Theory of Autobiography." *a/b: Auto/Biography Studies*, 10, 1995.

SR Judith Berling. *The Syncretic Religion of Lin Chao-en*. New York: Columbia University Press, 1980.

SS Diana Tietjens Meyers. *Subjection and Subjectivity: Psychoanalytic Feminism & Moral Philosophy*. New York: Routledge, 1994.

SZB Barry Schwartz, Yael Zerubavel, and Bernice Barnett. "The Recovery of Masada: A Study in Collective Memory," *The Sociological Quarterly*, vol. 27, no. 2, 1986.

TCW Shoshana Felman and Dori Laub. *Testimony: Crises of Witnessing in Literature, Psychoanalysis, and History*. New York: Routledge, 1992.

TEBB Mongane Serote. *To Every Birth Its Blood*. Braamfontein: Ravan Press, 1981.

TFR John Ardoin. *The Furtwängler Record*. Portland: Amadeus, 1994.

TOS Luther H. Martin, Huck Gutman, and Patrick H. Hutton (eds.) *Technologies of the Self: A Seminar with Michel Foucault*. Amherst: University of Massachusetts Press, 1988.

TS Robert Brinkley and Steven Youra. "Tracing *Shoah*," *PMLA*, 111, 1996.

UC Robert C. Ulin. *Understanding Cultures: Perspectives in Anthropology and Social Theory*. Austin: University of Texas Press, 1984.

WC J. M. Coetzee. "What is a Classic?" *Current Writing*, vol. 5, no. 2, 1993.

WRH James E. Young. *Writing and Rewriting the Holocaust*. Bloomington: Indiana University Press, 1988.

NOTES

GENERAL INTRODUCTION: THRESHOLDS OF WESTERN CULTURE (JOHN BURT FOSTER JR. AND WAYNE J. FROMAN)

1 T. S. Eliot, "Tradition and the Individual Talent," in *Selected Prose of T. S. Eliot*, ed. Frank Kermode (London: Faber, 1975), pp. 38–9; Adrienne Rich, "When We Dead Awaken: Writing as Re-Vision," in *On Lies, Secrets, and Silence: Selected Prose, 1966–1978* (New York: Norton, 1979), p. 35.

2 Edward Said, *Culture and Imperialism* (New York: Knopf, 1993), pp. 18, 66–7.

3 Mihai Spariosu, *The Wreath of Wild Olives: Play, Liminality, and the Study of Literature* (Albany: SUNY Press, 1997). Spariosu credits Turner's "Liminal to Liminoid in Play, Flow, and Ritual," in *From Ritual to Theatre: The Human Seriousness of Play* (New York: Performing Arts Journal Publications, 1982), ch. 1.

4 Matthew Arnold, *Culture and Anarchy*, in *The Portable Matthew Arnold*, ed. Lionel Trilling (New York: Viking, 1949), pp. 482–3; also Jonathan Swift, *The Battle of the Books*, in *Jonathan Swift: Selected Prose and Poetry*, ed. Edward Rosenheim, Jr. (New York: Rinehart, 1959), p. 167. In the "Ancients and Moderns" debate around 1700, Swift contrasted the ancient/bee as a cultural agent with the modern/spider; the latter was basically sterile, but the former's honey and wax yielded "sweetness and light," the phrase Arnold borrowed a century and a half later.

5 Walter Benjamin, "Theses on the Philosophy of History," in *Illuminations*, ed. Hannah Arendt, trans. Harry Zohn (New York: Schocken, 1969), p. 256.

6 Gaetano Salvemini, *The Origins of Fascism in Italy*, trans. Roberto Vivarelli (New York: Harper, 1973), p. 297; George Steiner, *Language and Silence* (New York: Atheneum, 1974), p. ix.

7 Paul Gilroy, *The Black Atlantic: Modernity and Double Consciousness* (Cambridge: Harvard University Press, 1993), especially ch. 1, "The Black Atlantic as a Counterculture of Modernity."

8 Steven Tötösy de Zepetnek, "Configurations of Postcoloniality and National Identity: Inbetween Peripherality and Narratives of Change," *The Comparatist*, 23 (1999), pp. 89–90, 92–4.

PART ONE: THE CRISIS OF MODERN SUBJECTIVITY

INTRODUCTION (WAYNE J. FROMAN AND JOHN BURT FOSTER JR.)

1 Martin Heidegger, *Hegel's Concept of Experience*, ed. J. Glenn Gray (New York: Harper & Row, 1970).

2 Georg Wilhelm Friedrich Hegel, "Self Alienated Spirit. Culture," in *Phenomenology of Spirit*, trans. A. V. Miller, with an analysis and foreword by J. N. Findlay (Oxford: Oxford University Press, 1977), pp. 294–364.

CHAPTER 1

INTERIORITY, IDENTITY, KNOWLEDGE: UNRAVELING THE CARTESIAN COGITO (ROBERT STROZIER)

1 Michel Foucault, "On the Genealogy of Ethics: An Overview of Work in Progress," in *The Foucault Reader*, ed. Paul Rabinow (New York: Pantheon, 1984), p. 341. Henceforth cited as *FR*.

2 *Michel Foucault: Politics, Philosophy, Culture. Interviews and Other Writings*, ed. Lawrence D. Kritzman (New York/London: Routledge, 1988), pp. 125–7, 137. Henceforth cited as *FPPC*.

3 Diogenes Laertius, *Lives of Eminent Philosophers*, trans. R. D. Hicks, 2 vols. (London/Cambridge: William Heinemann/Harvard University Press, 1925), Book 7.49. Henceforth cited as *DL*.

4 *DL*, Book 7, pp. 45–6, 50–1; Sextus Empiricus, *Adversos Mathematicos*, in *Sexti Empirici Opera*, ed. H. Mutschmann *et al.*, 4 vols. (Leipzig: Teubner, 1905–24), pp. 228, 229ff. and *passim*.

5 René Descartes, *Discourse on the Method of Rightly Conducting One's Reason and Seeking the Truth in the Sciences . . .*, in *The Philosophical Writings of Descartes*, trans. John Cottingham, Robert Stoothoff and Dugald Murdoch, 2 vols. (Cambridge: Cambridge University Press, 1985), vol. 1, p. 116. Henceforth cited as *PWD*.

6 *Descartes: Philosophical Letters*, ed. and trans. Anthony Kenny (Minneapolis: University of Minnesota Press, 1970), pp. 177ff. Henceforth cited as *PLD*.

7 David Couzens Hoy, "Foucault: Modern or Postmodern?" in *After Foucault: Humanistic Knowledge, Postmodern Challenges*, ed. Jonathan Arac (New Brunswick, NJ: Rutgers University Press, 1988), pp. 18, 36–7. Henceforth cited as *FMP*.

8 H. D. Harootunian, "Foucault, Genealogy, History: The Pursuit of Otherness," in *FMP*, p. 119.

9 Anthony Ashley, Earl of Shaftesbury, *Characteristics of Men, Manners, Opinions, Times*, ed. John M. Robertson (Indianapolis/New York: Bobbs Merrill, 1964), vol. 2; pp. 286–7. Henceforth cited as *CMM*.

10 Henry Fielding, *Joseph Andrews*, ed. Martin C. Battestin (Boston: Houghton Mifflin, 1961), p. 167. Henceforth cited as *JA*.

11 Wallace Martin, *Recent Theories of Narrative* (Ithaca: Cornell UP, 1986), p. 136ff.; also Dorrit Cohn, *Transparent Minds: Narrative Modes for Presenting Consciousness* (Princeton: Princeton University Press, 1978).

12 Charles Dickens, *Great Expectations*, ed. R. D. McMaster (New York: Odyssey, 1965), ch. 1, pp. 1–5.

13 Michel Foucault, *Power/Knowledge*, ed. Colin Gordon, trans. Colin Gordon *et al.* (New York: Pantheon, 1980), p. 83.

14 James Joyce, *A Portrait of the Artist as a Young Man* (New York: Viking, 1964), pp. 185–90.

15 Joseph Conrad, *Heart of Darkness and The Secret Sharer*, intro. Albert J. Guerard (New York/London: Signet, 1983), pp. 99–102. Henceforth cited as *HD*.

16 Kate Chopin, *The Awakening and Selected Short Stories* (New York: Bantam, 1981), p. 36. Henceforth cited as *A*.

17 I. A. Richards, *Principles of Literary Criticism* (New York: Harcourt, Brace & World, 1925).

18 Roy Pascal, *The Dual Voice: Free Indirect Speech and its Functioning in the Nineteenth-Century French Novel* (Totowa, NJ: Rowman and Littlefield, 1977).

19 Ann Banfield, *Unspeakable Sentences: Narration and Representation in the Language of Fiction* (Boston/London: Routledge and Kegan Paul, 1982).

20 See, for example, Jürgen Habermas, "Modernity versus Postmodernity," *New German Critique*, 22 (1981), pp. 3–14 and *The Philosophical Discourse of Modernity*, trans. Frederick Lawrence (Cambridge: MIT Press, 1987), vol. 1, pp. 294–326.

CHAPTER 2

SUBJECT, SELF, PERSON: MARCEL MAUSS AND THE LIMITS OF POSTSTRUCTURALIST CRITIQUE (ANTHONY JOHN HARDING)

1 Francis Jacques, *Difference and Subjectivity: Dialogue and Personal Identity*, trans. Andrew Rothwell (New Haven: Yale University Press, 1991), pp. 5, 13. Henceforth cited as *DS*.

2 Diana Tietjens Meyers, *Subjection and Subjectivity: Psychoanalytic Feminism & Moral Philosophy* (New York: Routledge, 1994), p. 35. Henceforth cited as *SS*.

3 Marcel Mauss, "A category of the human mind: the notion of person; the notion of self" ("Une catégorie de l'esprit humain: la notion de personne, celle de 'moi' "), trans. W. D. Halls, in *The Category of the Person: anthropology, philosophy, history*, ed. Michael Carrithers, Steven Collins, and Steven Lukes (Cambridge: Cambridge University Press, 1985), pp. 1–25. Information about the lecture and its previous appearances in print comes from the preface, pp. vii–viii. Henceforth cited as *CP*.

4 See *CP* for the major critiques of Mauss's lecture. On the "modern self," see Felicity Nussbaum, *The Autobiographical Subject: Gender and Ideology in Eighteenth-Century England* (Baltimore: Johns Hopkins University Press, 1989) and David Saunders and Ian Hunter, "Lessons from the 'Literaratory': How to Historicise Authorship," *Critical Inquiry*, vol. 17, no. 3 (1991), pp. 479–509.

5 Quoted in Steven Collins, "Categories, concepts or predicaments? Remarks on Mauss's use of philosophical terminology," in *CP*, p. 50. Henceforth cited as *CCP*.

6 J. B. Schneewind, "The Use of Autonomy in Ethical Theory," in *Reconstructing Individualism*, ed. Thomas C. Heller, David E. Wellbery, and Morton Sosna (Stanford: Stanford UP, 1986), pp. 64–75. Henceforth cited as *RI*.

7 Werner Hamacher, "'Disgregation of the Will': Nietzsche on the Individual and Individuality," trans. Jeffrey S. Librett, in *RI*, p. 108.

8 Felicity Nussbaum, "Toward Conceptualizing Diary," in *Studies in Autobiography*, ed. James Olney (New York/Oxford: Oxford University Press, 1988), p. 131.

9 David Bromwich, *A Choice of Inheritance: Self and Community from Edmund Burke to Robert Frost* (Cambridge: Harvard UP, 1989), p. 274. Henceforth cited as *CI*.

10 Anya Taylor, "Coleridge on Persons in Dialogue," *Modern Language Quarterly*, 50 (1989), pp. 357–74. Henceforth cited as *CPD*.

11 Michel Foucault, "Technologies of the Self," in *Technologies of the Self: A Seminar with Michel Foucault*, ed. Luther H. Martin, Huck Gutman, and Patrick H. Hutton (Amherst: University of Massachusetts Press, 1988), p. 89. Henceforth cited as *TOS*.

12 Michel Foucault, *The Care of the Self (The History of Sexuality, Volume 3)*, trans. Robert Hurley (New York: Pantheon, 1986), p. 51. Henceforth cited as *CS*.

13 Rux Martin, "Truth, Power, Self: an interview with Michel Foucault, 25 October 1982," in *TOS*, p. 15.

14 See the works in note 4 as well as Nancy Armstrong and Leonard Tennenhouse, *The Imaginary Puritan: Literature, Intellectual Labor, and the Origins of Personal Life* (Berkeley: University of California Press, 1992).

15 Barry N. Olshen, "Subject, Persona and Self in the Theory of Autobiography," *a/b: Auto/Biography Studies*, 10 (1995), p. 5. Henceforth cited as *SPS*.

16 For how the Romantics tried to identify the self with the conscious mind, and, in their writing, brought the authorial consciousness, or "subject," closer to the textual "persona," see Charles J. Rzepka, *The Self as Mind: Vision and Identity in Wordsworth, Coleridge, and Keats* (Cambridge: Harvard UP, 1986), especially p. 24: "The Cartesian assumption that the self is identical to mind provided, ultimately, the condition of the possibility of Romanticism."

17 Edward Said, "Orientalism Reconsidered," in *Europe and its Others*, ed. Francis Barker *et al.*, 2 vols. (Colchester: Essex UP, 1985), vol. 1, p. 15. Henceforth cited as *OR*. For the connections between poststructuralism and postcolonialism, see Robert Young, *White Mythologies: Writing History and the West* (London: Routledge, 1990), especially pp. 11, 44.

18 Martin Hollis, "Of masks and men," in *CP*, pp. 232, 230. Henceforth cited as *MM*.

19 Gerald Vizenor, "The Ruins of Representation: Shadow Survivance and the Literature of Dominance," *American Indian Quarterly*, 17 (1993), pp. 7–30.

20 A. Irving Hallowell, "Ojibwa Personality and Acculturation," in *Acculturation in the Americas*, ed. Sol Tax (New York: Cooper Square, 1967), pp. 105–12, henceforth cited as *AA*; Basil H. Johnston, *Ojibway Heritage* (Toronto: McLelland and Stewart, 1990 [1976]); Richard J. Preston, "Towards a General Statement on the Eastern Cree Structure of Knowledge," in *Papers of the Thirteenth Algonquian Conference*, ed. William Cowan (Ottawa: Carleton University Press, 1982), pp. 299–306.

21 Kathryn T. Molohon, "Notes on a Contemporary Cree Community," *Actes du quatorzième congrès des Algonquinistes*, ed. William Cowan (Ottawa: Carleton University Press, 1983), p. 195.

PART TWO: SHADOWS OF FASCISM AND WESTERN CULTURE

CHAPTER 3

AESTHETIC FASCISM AND MODERN TRAGEDY: D'ANNUNZIO'S *FEDRA* (MARY ANN FRESE WITT)

1 Umberto Eco, "Ur-Fascism," *New York Review of Books*, vol. 42, no. 11 (June 22 1995), pp. 12–15.

2 Roger Griffin, "Staging the Nation's Rebirth: The Politics and Aesthetics of Performance in the Context of Fascist Studies," in *Fascism and Theatre*, ed. Gunter Berghaus (Providence: Berghahn, 1996), p. 13.

3 Emil Ludwig, *Colloqui con Mussolini*, trans. Tommaso Gnoli (Milan: Mondadori, 1932), pp. 125, 219. All translations into English are mine unless otherwise indicated.

4 "The Work of Art in the Age of Mechanical Reproduction," in *Illuminations*, ed. Hannah Arendt, trans. Harry Zohn (New York: Schocken, 1968), p. 242.

5 See Russell Berman, "Written Right Across Their Faces," in *Modern Culture and Critical Theory: Art, Politics, and the Legacy of the Frankfurt School* (Madison: University of Wisconsin Press, 1989), pp. 105–6.

6 Edouard Berth, *Les Méfaits des intellectuels*, 2nd edn. (Paris: Rivière, 1926), p. 355; cited in Zeev Sternhell, *The Birth of Fascist Ideology*, trans. David Maisel (Princeton: Princeton UP, 1994), p. 89.

7 "La Violence [syndicaliste] appelle l'ordre, comme le sublime appelle le beau; Apollon doit completer l'oeuvre de Dionysos." Edouard Berth, *Les Méfaits des intellectuels* (Paris: Rivière, 1914), p. 329.

8 Mario Morasso, *L'imperialismo artistico* (Torino: Fratelli Bocca, 1903), p. 27. Henceforth cited as *IA*.

9 D'Annunzio to Luigi Lodi, July 15 1897, cited by Paolo Alatri, *Gabriele D'Annunzio* (Torino: Unione tipografica-editore Torinese, 1983), p. 193.

10 Gabriele D'Annunzio, "Arte e politica non furono mai disgiunte nel mio pensiero," interview in *La Tribuna*, June 20 1902, in *Scritti politici di Gabriele D'Annunzio*, ed. Paolo Alatri (Milan: Fetrinelli, 1980), p. 11.

11 Gabriele D'Annunzio, "La Rinascenza della tragedia," *La Tribuna*, August 3 1897, in Valentina Valentini, *La Tragedia moderna e mediterranea: sul teatro di Gabriele D'Annunzio* (Milan: FrancoAngeli, 1992), p. 80.

12 See Paolo Valesio, *Gabriele D'Annunzio: The Dark Flame* (New Haven: Yale University Press, 1992), and Giorgio Barberi Squarotti, *La Scrittura verso il nulla: D'Annunzio* (Torino: Genesi, 1992), as well as Antonucci's introduction to the anthology of D'Annunzio's theater cited here. However, a recent book by an American scholar, Jared M. Becker, *Nationalism and Culture: Gabriele D'Annunzio and Italy after the Risorgimento* (New York: Peter Lang, 1994), argues forcefully for the poet's contributions to Fascism. As Becker notes, foreign scholars, including George Mosse and Zeev Sternhell, have tended to associate D'Annunzio more closely with Fascism than Italians.

13 Giovanni Antonucci, "Il linguaggio politico nel teatro di Gabriele d'Annunzio," in *D'Annunzio e il suo tempo*, ed. Francesco Perfetti (Genoa: SAGEP, 1992), vol. 2, pp. 157–67.

14 Renzo de Felice, *D'Annunzio politico 1918–1938* (Bari: Laterza, 1978).

15 Gabriele D'Annunzio, interview by Renato Simoni, *Corriere della sera*, April 9 1909, cited by Pietro Gibellini, "Introduzione" to *Fedra* (Milan: Mondadori, 1989), p. 12. Henceforth cited as *F*.

16 D'Annunzio to Nathalie de Goloubeff, December 10 1908, cited in *F*, p. 9.

17 This is suggested by Anna Meda in her interesting Jungian study of myth in D'Annunzio's theater, *Bianche statue contro il nero abisso: Il teatro dei miti in D'Annunzio e Pirandello* (Ravenna: Longo, 1993), p. 140.

18 Barbara Spackman, "The Fascist Rhetoric of Virility," *Stanford Italian Review*, vol. 8, nos. 1–2 (*Fascism and Culture*), pp. 81–101.

19 Maria Iolanda Palazzolo has discussed the function of the play's two worlds, identified with different systems of law: that of Theseus, marked by obedience to the gods and respect for clarity, civil law, and order; and that of Fedra, marked by revolt against law and gods and the attempt to create a law of "supermen." See "Le due leggi: La *Fedra* di D'Annunzio," in *Transgressione tragica e norma domestica: Esemplari di tipologie femminili dalla letteratura europea*, ed. Vanna Gentile (Rome: Edizioni di storia e letteratura, 1983), pp. 211–39. Nietzsche surely influenced D'Annunzio's "Dionysian" concept of Fedra and "Apollonian" concept of Theseus.

20 *Fedra* was revived in a spectacular outdoor production on the Palatine, October 10–22 1922. The review in question, however, was published on October 29, the day after the March on Rome. The original reads: "quella perfetta fusione tra scena e platea che sembra trasformare effettivamente lo spettacolo stesso in un rito, in una 'celebrazione.'" G. M. Andriulli, in *Il Secolo*, October 29 1922, reprinted in Laura Granatella, *"Arrestate l'autore!" D'Annunzio in scena (Cronache, testimonianze, illustrazioni, documenti inediti e rari del primo grande spettacolo del '900)* (Rome: Bulzoni, 1993), vol. 2, p. 734.

CHAPTER 4

OF MUSICAL HEADINGS: TOSCANINI'S AND FURTWÄNGLER'S *FIFTH SYMPHONIES*, 1939–54 (HERMAN RAPAPORT)

1 The main Derridean texts mentioned in this paragraph are *De l'esprit* (Paris: Galilée, 1987) and "Geschlecht I and II" in *Psyché* (Paris: Galilée, 1987). See also *Glas* (Paris: Galilée, 1974); "Like the Sound of the Sea Deep Within a Shell" in *Responses* (Lincoln: University of Nebraska Press, 1988); and "Limited Inc," *Glyph*, 1 (1977).

2 Herman Rapaport, *Heidegger and Derrida: Reflections on Time and Language* (Lincoln: University of Nebraska Press, 1989).

3 According to Derrida, the French word *cap* refers, among other things, to heading, but also to a cape and, in particular, to Europe as a cape, to the head or prow of a ship, to capital, to an aim, to an appendix, etc. In short, *cap* is a complex condensation that takes in a fairly wide-ranging vocabulary.

4 Theodor Adorno, *Introduction to the Sociology of Music*, trans. E. B. Ashton (New York: Continuum, 1989), p. 155.

5 *New Voices: American Composers Talk About Their Work*, ed. Geoff Smith and Nicola Walker Smith (Portland: Amadeus, 1995), p. 6. Henceforth cited as *NV*.

6 This Web Site currently is maintained by Peter Krapp of the University of Konstanz at computer server Hydra.lake.de

7 Theodor Adorno, *Philosophy of Modern Music*, trans. Anne G. Mitchell and Wesley V. Blomster (New York: Continuum, 1994), p. 142. Adorno's example is actually *Petroushka*; had Adorno known *Les Noces* he would have found it much more suitable, since it thematizes more overtly his criticisms of Stravinsky.

8 Jacques Derrida, *The Other Heading*, trans. Michael Naas and Pascale-Anne Brault (Bloomington: Indiana University Press, 1992), p. 15.

9 Yehudi Menuhin's political defense of Furtwängler is well known and contrasted sharply with repudiation of Furtwängler by Artur Rubinstein and many other American Jewish performers who deplored his actions during the Nazi period. See John Ardoin, *The Furtwängler Record* (Portland: Amadeus, 1994), pp. 57–8. Henceforth cited as *TFR*.

10 The recordings of these performances are: Wilhelm Furtwängler, *Symphony No. 5*, by Ludwig van Beethoven, Berlin Philharmonic (June 27–30, 1943), Music and Arts CD–824; Wilhelm Furtwängler, *Symphony No. 5*, by Ludwig van Beethoven, Vienna Philharmonic (1954), EMI CD–76980324; Arturo Toscanini, *Symphony No. 5*, by Ludwig van Beethoven, NBC Symphony Orchestra (1939), RCA Victor CD–09026–60270–2; and Arturo Toscanini, *Symphony No. 5*, by Ludwig van Beethoven, NBC Orchestra (1952), RCA Victor CD–60255–2RG. Also see Wilhelm Furtwängler, *Symphony No. 5*, by Ludwig van Beethoven (1937), Biddulph Recordings CD–WHL 006–7; this recording has more in common with Toscanini's recordings than with the wartime ones Furtwängler made.

11 After having noticed this for myself in listening to the recordings, I came across the following in Furtwängler's *Notebooks*: ". . . that the tutti is precisely the usual Toscanini tutti, on which the sonata form relies, and that evidently not the slightest attempt is made to turn it into a real musical and psychological connection of contrasts." Furtwängler, *Notebooks 1924–1954* (London: Quartet Books, 1989), p. 41. The notation is already from the year 1930.

12 My source here is the Internet where Henry Fogel has come into dialogue with music buffs on Usenet. He also writes columns for a journal called *Fanfare*.

13 Ardoin notices that the famous conductor Arthur Nikisch once said of the young Furtwängler, "he doesn't conduct; he seems to surrender himself to some mysterious, magic force" (*TFR*, p. 127). Nowhere is this more true than during the war years.

14 Martin Heidegger, "The Origin of the Work of Art" in *Poetry, Language, Thought*, trans. Albert Hofstadter (New York: Harper & Row, 1972), p. 19. Henceforth cited as *OWA*.

CHAPTER 5

HOLOCAUST TESTIMONY AND POST-HOLOCAUST FICTION: CYNTHIA OZICK'S *THE MESSIAH OF STOCKHOLM* (JAMES BERGER)

1 Faurisson (quoted in Lyotard): "'I have analyzed thousands of documents. I have tirelessly pursued specialists and historians with my questions. I have tried in vain to find a single deportee capable of proving to me that he had really seen, with his own eyes, a gas chamber.'" Lyotard responds, "The plaintiff complains that he has been fooled concerning the existence of gas chambers. . . . His argument is: in order for a place to be identified as a gas chamber, the only eyewitness I will accept would be a victim of this gas chamber; now according to my opponent, there is no victim who is not dead; otherwise this gas chamber would not be what he or she claims; there is, therefore, no gas chamber." Jean-François Lyotard, *The Differend: Phrases in Dispute*, trans. Georges Van Den Abbeele (Minneapolis: University of Minnesota Press, 1988), pp. 3–4. See also Pierre Vidal-Naquet, *Assassins of Memory: Essays on the Denial of the Holocaust*, trans. Jeffrey Mehlman (New York: Columbia University Press, 1992).

2 Primo Levi, *The Drowned and the Saved*, trans. Raymond Rosenthal (New York: Vintage, 1989), pp. 83–4.

3 Elie Wiesel, *Night*, trans. Stella Rodway, in *The Night Trilogy* (New York: Noonday Press, 1987), pp. 17, 119.

4 Paul Ricoeur, "The Hermeneutics of Testimony," *Anglican Theological Review*, 61 (1979), pp. 435–61; Emmanuel Levinas, *Otherwise Than Being or Beyond Essence*, trans. Alphonso Lingis (The Hague: Martinus Nijhoff, 1981).

5 Terrence Des Pres, *The Survivor: An Anatomy of Life in the Death Camps* (New York: Oxford University Press, 1976), pp. 177, 176.

6 Lawrence Langer, *Holocaust Testimonies: The Ruins of Memory* (New Haven: Yale University Press, 1991), p. xi. Henceforth cited as *HT*.

While discarding literary representation, Langer nevertheless continues the line of thinking begun in *The Holocaust and the Literary Imagination* (New Haven: Yale University Press, 1975). This book also relies on a theory of radical, non-representational "mimesis" in which shattered and grotesque aesthetic forms stand as models for unimaginably horrific events, thus making claims for the dislocating power of avant-garde art techniques. But so, surprisingly, does *Holocaust Testimonies* in proposing oral testimony as an anti-art. Both books assume that a particular aesthetic form (or anti-form) can reveal the essence of an inconceivable event.

7 Robert Brinkley and Steven Youra, "Tracing *Shoah*," *PMLA*, 111 (1996), p. 115. Henceforth cited as *TS*.

8 Shoshana Felman and Dori Laub, *Testimony: Crises of Witnessing in Literature, Psychoanalysis, and History* (New York: Routledge, 1992), p. 219. Henceforth cited as *TCW*.

9 James E. Young, *Writing and Rewriting the Holocaust* (Bloomington: Indiana University Press, 1988), p. 24. Henceforth cited as *WRH*.

10 Young would add, contra Brinkley and Youra, that the testimonial text is, like any text, open to interpretation. He concludes: "Our aim here then is to sustain both the privileged status of these testimonies and their invitation to critical interpretation" (*WRH*, p. 170).

Michael André Bernstein is the only theorist I've read who unequivocally rejects the privileged position of testimony, calling it "one of the most pervasive myths of our era." *Foregone Conclusions: Against Apocalyptic History* (Berkeley: University of California Press), p. 47. Henceforth cited as *FC*. There is, he argues, "no single order of memorable testimony, no transparent paradigm of representation, that can address the different narrative needs of all those gripped by the subject" (*FC*, p. 50). I agree, but this essay tries to explain, unlike Bernstein, the persistent recurrence of testimonial texts within fictional texts that would seem to have, in Bernstein's words, "different narrative needs."

11 James E. Young, *The Texture of Memory: Holocaust Memorials and Meaning* (New Haven: Yale University Press, 1993).

12 Alvin Rosenfeld, *Imagining Hitler* (Bloomington: Indiana UP, 1985); Saul Friedländer, *Reflections of Nazism: An Essay on Kitsch and Death* (New York: Harper & Row, 1984).

13 William Styron, *Sophie's Choice* (New York: Random House, 1979); George Steiner, *The Portage to San Cristobal of A. H.* (New York: Simon & Schuster, 1981).

14 The use of atomic weapons against Japan was, of course, another catastrophe that has reshaped modes of feeling and thinking. For the cultural effects in America of possible nuclear war, see Paul Boyer, *By the Bomb's Early Light: American Thought and Culture at the Dawn of the Atomic Age* (New York: Pantheon, 1985).

15 Philip Roth, *The Ghost Writer*, in *Zuckerman Bound* (New York: Farrar, Straus, Giroux, 1985), pp. 1–180; D. M. Thomas, *The White Hotel* (New York: Penguin, 1981); Emily Prager, *Eve's Tattoo* (New York: Vintage, 1991); David Grossman, *See Under: Love*, trans. Betsy Rosenberg (New York: Farrar, Straus, Giroux, 1989).

16 See both Robert Jay Lifton, *The Broken Connection: On Death and the Continuity of Life* (New York: Simon & Schuster, 1979) and Slavoj Žižek, *The Sublime Object of Ideology* (London: Verso, 1989) and *Looking Awry: An Introduction to Lacan Through Popular Culture* (Cambridge, MA: MIT Press, 1991) on the ghost or living-dead as traumatic symptom. Žižek's books are hereafter cited as *SO* and *LA*.

Lifton describes trauma as a symbolic death, and the survivor as "one who has come into contact with death in some bodily or psychic fashion and has remained alive" (p. 269). Lifton remarks on our tendency to associate the survival of trauma "not only with pain but also with value – with a special form of knowledge . . ." (p. 170). Žižek describes the ghost as a pure and horrifying fragment of the Lacanian Real, a symptom of repressed trauma who exists in a realm "between two deaths," that is, between the original trauma and its eventual repetition in a heightened, apocalyptic form (*SO*, pp. 131–6). Žižek later refers to imagery of the living-dead as "the fundamental fantasy of contemporary mass culture" (*LA*, p. 22). Compare Freud on "The Uncanny" as a return of the repressed, *Standard Edition of the Complete Psychological Works of Sigmund Freud*, trans. James Strachey (London: Hogarth, 1955), vol. 17, pp. 217–56.

17 Elie Wiesel, *Night*, trans. Stella Rodway, *The Night Trilogy* (New York: Noonday Press, 1987), p. 43.

18 On the incompatibility between trauma and language, see Elaine Scarry, *The Body in Pain: The Making and Unmaking of the World* (New York: Oxford University Press, 1985), who argues that pain unmakes language and the conceptual worlds that language produces. Scarry also theorizes on how wounding nevertheless does enter language to become central to the development of theology and ideology. Geoffrey Hartman has written on the relations between trauma and literary language, how "words are the wounds that are always, again, words," *Saving the Text: Literature/Derrida/Philosophy* (Baltimore: Johns

Hopkins University Press, 1981), p. 156. Criticism must learn how to "read the wound," and thereby discover how "the original text, itself vulnerable, addresses us, reveals itself as a participant in a collective life, or life-in-death, one sign of which is tradition or inter-textuality," "On Traumatic Knowledge and Literary Studies," *New Literary History*, 26 (1995), p. 549.

19 This is Cathy Caruth's point on using trauma to reinterpret history, in *Unclaimed Experience: Trauma, Narrative, History* (Baltimore: Johns Hopkins University Press, 1996), pp. 10–24. The necessary delay in narrating trauma enables new historical understandings that both acknowledge trauma's shattering effects on previous narratives and permit some healing of its contemporary symptoms.

Dominick LaCapra, *Representing the Holocaust: History, Theory, Trauma* (Ithaca: Cornell University Press, 1994), makes a similar point in warning against discourses of the Shoah that attempt to reach a complete narrative closure of traumatic events or exist in a realm of pure "acting out" of traumas. A discourse that in any degree "comes to terms" with historical trauma must do both, and neither. See also Eric Santner on the "narrative fetish" in "History Beyond the Pleasure Principle: Some Thoughts on the Representation of Trauma," in *Probing the Limits of Representation: Nazism and the "Final Solution,"* ed. Saul Friedländer (Cambridge: Harvard University Press, 1992), pp. 143–54, and Slavoj Žižek on the relations between ideology and trauma in *SO*.

20 See Geoffrey Hartman, *The Longest Shadow: In the Aftermath of the Holocaust* (Bloomington: Indiana University Press, 1996), on the position of the bystander – "what others suffer, we behold" (p. 88) – and on the "kakangelic impulse" of contemporary mass media. Hartman is less optimistic about the effects of what he calls "secondary trauma" (p. 152) than either Caruth or LaCapra.

21 My thinking here comes closest to Marianne Hirsch's idea of "post-memory," in "Family Pictures: *Maus*, Mourning, and Post-Memory," *Discourse*, 15 (1992), pp. 3–29. Post-memory is the memory of someone else's memories, stories, and physical memorabilia. It is "distinguished from memory by generational distance and from history by deep personal connection" (p. 8). For Hirsch, the photograph is the most representative object of post-memory, as, in my thinking, the testimonial text forms the basis for writing after the end of testimony. There is, however, a closer connection between post-memory and memory than I find between post-testimony and testimony.

Michael André Bernstein uses the term "third generation" for recent Holocaust representation. "Since the generation of survivors will soon die out," we need to keep alive the "tribal story" as "part of communal memory" that "needs regularly to be retold and reinterpreted" (*FC*, p. 45). For me, Bernstein gives too much weight to conscious motives and not enough to the traumatic compulsion to retell the story.

22 Cynthia Ozick, *The Messiah of Stockholm* (New York: Vintage, 1987). Henceforth cited as *MS*.

23 Cynthia Ozick, "Interview," with Elaine M. Kauvar, *Contemporary Literature*, 34 (1993), p. 391. See also her *Art and Ardor: Essays* (New York: Knopf, 1983). For an intelligent reading of *Messiah* that follows from Ozick's professions of iconoclasm, see Elisabeth Rose, "Cynthia Ozick's Liturgical Postmodernism: *The Messiah of Stockholm*," *Studies in American Jewish Literature*, 9 (1990), pp. 435–61.

PART THREE: AFRICA AT THE PASSING OF WHITE SUPREMACY

CHAPTER 6

REVISITING THE *AMISTAD* REVOLT IN SIERRA LEONE (IYUNOLU OSAGIE)

1 In 1787, the Sierra Leone Company, made up of men like Granville Sharpe, Thomas Clarkson, William Wilberforce, and Zachary Macaulay, formed an anti-slave-trade movement in England. Concerned about increasing numbers of poor blacks in England, they helped found a settler community in the West African nation of Sierra Leone. For a comprehensive history of the Sierra Leone Company, read Christopher Fyfe's *A History of Sierra Leone* (London: Oxford University Press, 1962), chs. I–V. See also Francis Utting's *The Story of Sierra Leone* (New York: Books for Libraries Press, 1971 [1931]), Part III.

2 Barry Schwartz, Yael Zerubavel, and Bernice Barnett, "The Recovery of Masada: A Study in Collective Memory," *Sociological Quarterly*, vol. 27, no. 2 (1986), p. 148. Henceforth cited as *SZB*.

3 See George Herbert Mead, *The Philosophy of the Present* (Chicago: Open Court, 1932), p. 81. Henceforth cited as *PP*. Also Maurice Halbwachs, *On Collective Memory*, ed. and trans. Lewis Coser (Chicago: University of Chicago Press, 1992), p. 40.

4 Barry Schwartz, "Social Change and Collective Memory: The Democratization of George Washington," *American Sociological Review*, 56 (April 1991), p. 221. Henceforth cited as *SCCM*.

5 David R. Maines, Noreen M. Sugrue, and Michael A. Katovich, "The Sociological Import of G. H. Mead's Theory of the Past," *American Sociological Review*, 48 (April 1983), p. 161. Henceforth cited as *MSK*.

6 For more on the Symbionese Liberation Army and Patty Hearst, see *Trial of Patty Hearst* (San Francisco: Great Fidelity Press, 1976), with the complete proceedings of the Patty Hearst case, and Patty Hearst, *Every Secret Thing* (New York: Doubleday, 1982).

7 For more on the *Amistad* story, see Christopher Martin, *The Amistad Affair* (London: Abelard-Schuman, 1970); Mary Cable, *Black Odyssey: The Case of the Slave Ship Amistad* (New York: Viking, 1971); and Howard Jones, *Mutiny on the Amistad* (New York: Oxford University Press, 1987).

8 Arthur Abraham, *The Amistad Revolt* (Freetown: USIS, 1987), p. 23. Henceforth cited as *AR*.

9 David Driskell, *Amistad II: Afro-American Art* (New York: United Church Board for Homeland Ministries, 1975), p. 15.

10 George Herbert Mead, "The Nature of the Past," in *Essays in Honor of John Dewey*, ed. John Coss (New York: Henry Holt, 1929), p. 238.

11 A. B. C. Sibthorpe, *The History of Sierra Leone*, 4th edn. (London: Frank Cass, 1970), p. 125.

12 Joe Alie, *A New History of Sierra Leone* (New York: St. Martin's, 1990), pp. 145, 146.

13 The italicized words are sung in Temne, Bai Bureh's tongue, to poke fun at how he

supposedly surrendered. They mean: "He hollered, 'Master, I beg; oh, Master, I beg, oh, Master, It's enough.' He hollered, 'Master, I beg.' "

14 The youth of Sierra Leone today remain the noticeable exception to the self-cynicism that plagued earlier generations. They have rejected the all-too-familiar portrait of Bai Bureh in a meditative and defeatist posture, in favor of a dynamic, conquering hero. Like the *Amistad* hero Sengbe Pieh, Bai Bureh is a hero in the present cultural awakening, and is portrayed on the one thousand Leone bank note.

15 Frantz Fanon argues that the cultural imposition of whiteness on blackness (through slavery and the colonial encounter) produces psychopathology; see *Black Skin, White Masks* (London: Pluto Press, 1986 [1952]), p. 141.

16 Raymond Desouza George, *The Broken Handcuff or Give me Free*, unpublished manuscript (Freetown, Sierra Leone: 1994), p. 32. Henceforth cited as *BH*.

17 Cited in the foreword to Joseph A. Opala, *Ecstatic Renovations: Street Art Celebrating Sierra Leone's 1992 Revolution* (Freetown: Ro-Marong Industries, 1994). Henceforth cited as *ER*.

18 Charlie Haffner, "An Interview with Charlie Haffner by Iyunolu Osagie," unpublished material (April 18 1994), p. 4.

19 John R. Cartwright, *Political Leadership in Sierra Leone* (Toronto: University of Toronto Press, 1978), p. 266.

20 The words, "unity, freedom, justice," appear on the Sierra Leone coat-of-arms. Ironically, these watchwords for the nation's development have been barren of their true realization. Until recently, the nation has been politically divided along ethnic lines, and the continued looting of the national treasury, and the government's consequent moral degeneration, have denied the people any true sense of freedom and justice.

21 For another version of this review of street art see *African Affairs: The Journal of the Royal African Society*, vol. 93, no. 371 (April 1994), pp. 195–218.

22 Barry Schwartz, "The Social Context of Communication: A Study in Collective Memory," *Social Forces*, vol. 61, no. 2 (December 1982), p. 377.

23 The statue of Sengbe Pieh to which Opala refers is the *Amistad* monument in front of New Haven City Hall, the same site where, in 1839, the *Amistad* captives were jailed.

CHAPTER 7

AN ETHICAL UNIVERSAL IN THE POSTCOLONIAL NOVEL – "A CERTAIN SIMPLE RESPECT"? (MICHIEL HEYNS)

1 John Burt Foster, Jr., "Cultural Multiplicity in Two Modern Autobiographies: Friedländer's *When Memory Comes* and Dinesen's *Out of Africa*," *Southern Humanities Review*, 29 (1995), p. 205.

2 Robert Thornton, "Culture: A Contemporary Definition," in *South African Keywords: The Uses and Abuses of Political Concepts*, E. Boonzaaier and J. Sharp, eds. (Cape Town: David Philip, 1981), p. 22.

3 Mongane Serote, *To Every Birth Its Blood* (Braamfontein: Ravan, 1981), p. 71. Henceforth cited as *TEBB*.

4 Homi K. Bhabha, "Postcolonial Criticism," in *Redrawing the Boundaries: The Transformation of English and American Studies*, Stephen Greenblatt and Giles Gunn, eds. (New York: MLA, 1992), p. 438. Henceforth cited as *PC*.

5 Edward Said, *Culture and Imperialism* (London: Chatto and Windus, 1993), pp. xiii, xiv.

6 Bill Ashcroft, Gareth Griffiths, and Helen Tiffin, *The Empire Writes Back: Theory and Practice in Post-Colonial Literatures* (London: Routledge, 1989), p. 2. Henceforth cited as *EWB*.

7 Annamaria Carusi, "Post, Post and Post. Or, Where is South African Literature in All This?" in Ian Adam and Helen Tiffin, eds., *Past the Last Post: Theorizing Post-Colonialism and Post-Modernism* (Calgary: University of Calgary Press, 1990), p. 95. Carusi explains why the label is (or was when she wrote, before majority rule in South Africa) especially problematic here:

> . . . there is a large part of the (white) population, for whom the label "post-colonialism" is not an issue at all. Post-colonialism . . . has been accomplished, de facto, and in a most successful manner. The South African nation exists because of the success of the construction of Afrikanerdom. The only problem is how to defend it.
>
> This is no small problem, especially when one considers the numbers for whom post-colonialism is not an issue, not because it is a fait accompli, but because it never happened. For the black majority, . . . to speak of post-colonialism is pre-emptive . . . What then is the use of the term "post-colonial" in a context where it is not seen as applicable by either one in the customary colonizer/colonized opposition, and where the terms themselves are in question? (p. 96)

The problem is also discussed by Cherry Clayton in "White Writing and Postcolonial Politics," *Ariel*, vol. 25, no. 4 (1994), who argues that "South Africa's intransigent position with regard to postcolonial theory . . . has made it an illuminating case within critical debates over the political purchase of postmodernism and postcolonialism generally" (p. 157).

8 See Rosemary Jolly, "Rehearsals of Liberation: Contemporary Postcolonial Discourse and the New South Africa," *PMLA*, 110 (1995), p. 22, henceforth cited as *RL*. "It is impossible to understand the psychology of nationalist Afrikaners as colonizers without understanding that they continued to see themselves as victims of English colonization and that the imagined continuation of this victimization was used to justify the maintenance of apartheid."

9 See *EWB*, p. 83: "South Africa is a society in which control of the means of communication is still held by the colonial authority of the racist state. In this sense, it is a society caught between two phases, manifesting the dynamic of colonial domination but producing both white and black writers whose engagement with the processes of abrogation and appropriation is part of a continuing struggle for survival. South African writing clearly demonstrates the fact that the political impetus of the post-colonial begins well before the moment of independence."

10 See, for instance, Neil Lazarus, *Resistance in Postcolonial African Fiction* (New Haven/London: Yale University Press, 1990), p. ix: "[R]adical African writers tended drastically to overvalue the emancipatory significance of independence. One consequence was that, as their hopes were punctured in the years following decolonization (as they invariably were), a rhetoric of disillusion began to replace the earlier utopian rhetoric in their work: it emerged as fatalism or despair or anger or in the accusation that postcolonial leaders had betrayed the 'African revolution.'"

11 Kwame Anthony Appiah, *In My Father's House: Africa in the Philosophy of Culture* (London: Methuen, 1992), p. 246. Henceforth cited as *FH*.

12 This broad and loose generalization is based on the post-election novels of, say, Nadine Gordimer (*None to Accompany Me* [London: Bloomsbury, 1994]), J. M. Coetzee (*The Master of Petersburg* [London: Secker & Warburg, 1994]), and probably the leading Afrikaans novelist, Etienne van Heerden (*Die Stoetmeester* [Cape Town: Tafelberg, 1993]). The first and last of these deal overtly and uneuphorically with the problems confronting South Africa in its transition to democracy; Coetzee's novel, set in 1869 Russia, seems to find little comfort or function for the writer in a time of change: towards the end Dostoevsky muses on the place of his craft and his own role as moral guide: "He knows now the answer he should have given: 'I write perversions of the truth. I choose the crooked road and take children into dark places. I follow the dance of the pen' " (p. 236).

13 A partial State of Emergency was declared in South Africa on July 20 1985, lifted on March 7 1986, and reimposed in more stringent form in June 1986, to be lifted only in June 1990. I use the term fairly loosely to refer to writing produced during this whole period or in response to it.

14 An influential exception is best-selling Wilbur Smith: by 1990 he had published twenty novels which had sold fifty million copies; David Maughan-Brown, "Raising Goose-Pimples: Wilbur Smith and the Politics of *Rage*," in *Rendering Things Visible: Essays on South Africa Literary Culture*, ed. Martin Trump (Johannesburg: Ravan, 1990), p. 134. Maughan-Brown's article analyzes the "ideological baggage" of *Rage*, one of Smith's commercially most successful novels.

15 ". . . what I am calling humanism can be provisional, historically contingent, anti-essentialist (in other words, postmodern) and still be demanding. We can surely maintain a powerful engagement with the concern to avoid cruelty and pain while nevertheless recognising the contingency of that concern" (*FH*, p. 250).

16 J. M. Coetzee, *Age of Iron* (New York: Penguin, 1998 [1990]), p. 80. Henceforth cited as *AI*.

17 Abdul JanMahomed refers to "the domination, manipulation, exploitation, and dis-franchisement that are inevitably involved in the construction of any cultural artifact or relationship"; "The Economy of Manichean Allegory: The Function of Racial Difference in Colonialist Literature," *Critical Inquiry*, 12 (1985), p. 59. Henceforth cited as *EMA*.

This, of course, restates Walter Benjamin's famous dictum that "There is no document of civilization which is not at the same time a document of barbarism"; "Theses on the Philosophy of History," in *Illuminations*, trans. Harry Zohn (Glasgow: Fontana, 1973), p. 258. In the present context it is worth recalling that Benjamin is speaking specifically of "cultural treasures" which according to him "owe their existence not only to the efforts of the great minds and talents who have created them, but also to the anonymous toil of their contemporaries" (p. 258).

18 For a more optimistic reading, see Michael Marais, especially when discussing Mrs. Curren's "transcendence of the State's deformed relations through learning to love": Alluding to the herb that protected Odysseus from being transformed into a swine by Circe, Marais states of Mrs. Curren: "The moly by means of which this 'salvation' can be accomplished is love – learning to love that which appears unlovable. . . . And love, as Mrs. Curren later comes to learn, is an empathetic emotion which leads to insight capable of counteracting the State's power to blind. It enables her through a willed act of imagin-ation to see John" (" 'Who Clipped the Hollyhocks?': J. M. Coetzee's *Age of Iron* and the Politics of Representation," *English in Africa*, vol. 20, no. 2 (1993), p. 15). Marais bases his admittedly appealing reading on Mrs. Curren's "perception" that "I must love, for

instance, this child . . . He is part of my salvation" (*AI*, p. 136); but ignores the immediately following lines: "But I do not love him. Nor do I want to love him enough to love him despite myself."

19 Ovid, *Metamorphoses*, trans. Mary M. Innes (Harmondsworth: Penguin, 1955), p. 32.

20 J. M. Coetzee, "Into the Dark Chamber: The Writer and the South African State (1986)," in *Doubling the Point: Essays and Interviews*, ed. David Attwell (London: Harvard University Press, 1992), p. 367. Henceforth cited as *DC*.

21 Interestingly, Coetzee cites Serote's novel as "taking on the challenge of finding words adequate to represent the terrible space of the torture chamber itself" (*DC*, p. 365).

22 Doriane Barboure, "Mongane Serote: Humanist and Revolutionary," in *Momentum: On Recent South African Writing*, ed. M. J. Daymond, J. U. Jacobs, and Margaret Lenta (Pietermaritzburg: Natal University Press, 1984), p. 177. Barboure argues "that the two sections of the novel are balanced against each other, Part One exploring suffering, despair, and the helplessness of the individual, Part Two offering the hope of a different future through concerted political activity." Nick Visser sharply criticizes Barboure, seeing the shift as a move towards revolutionary commitment resulting from the 1976 Soweto uprising, which occurred during the novel's composition ("Fictional Projects and the Irruptions of History: Mongane Serote's *To Every Birth Its Blood*," *English Academy Review*, 4 (1987), pp. 67–75. Annie Gagiano, disagreeing with Visser, says that "It surely is and must always have been a predominantly political novel, and the 'nausée' of a figure like Tsi is throughout presented as the immediate consequence of the violations of dignity perpetrated by the present state and its agents and institutions" ("Serote's Novel and Visser's Criticism," *English Academy Review*, 6 (1989), pp. 87–8).

23 Ashcroft *et al.* attempt, to me unconvincingly, to show that "Sexual union with the tantalizing but unattainable woman is the metaphoric equivalent of the Black child's attempt to enter the world of white society (and therefore of power) through the wielding of the pen" (*EWB*, p. 87). Josephine Dodd, from a highly critical feminist perspective, calls this reading "dangerous nonsense" ("The South African Literary Establishment and the Textual Production of 'Woman': J. M. Coetzee and Lewis Nkosi," *Current Writing*, 2 (1990), p. 125). For the view that the novel "is not primarily about 'interracial sexual relationships' and 'the terrible distortion of love' in South Africa (as the dustcover comments would have us believe)," but that it is "primarily about the origin and nature and result of sexual obsession, the external development of which is complicated by the fact that the protagonist is a black man living in South Africa," see Tessa Welch, "Controlling the Story: Review of *Mating Birds* by Lewis Nkosi," *The English Academy Review*, 5 (1998), pp. 201–5.

24 André Brink, "An Ornithology of Sexual Politics: Lewis Nkosi's *Mating Birds*," *English in Africa*, 19 (1992), pp. 1–20.

25 Lewis Nkosi, *Mating Birds* (Braamfontein: Ravan, 1987), pp. 114–15. Henceforth cited as *MB*.

26 As an English phrase this is very obscure. The italics would seem to suggest, by analogy with his practice elsewhere, that Nkosi intends to quote an Afrikaans exclamation, but the phrase makes no sense in Afrikaans either.

27 Rosemary Jolly, in a different context altogether, describes the neo-colonial text in terms that fit Nkosi's novel:

> In a text that can be identified as neocolonial because of its nominal rather than

> structural anticolonialism, not only are colonial subjects denied knowledge of the construction of the Manichean opposition but also, more important, colonizers can induce themselves to forget the artificiality of that construction. Nominal dissidence becomes the stage for the colonizers themselves. (*RL*, p. 18)

My application of Jolly's statement to Nkosi's novel suggests that, paradoxically, he has absorbed and reproduced the process whereby the colonial subject becomes "complicit" in constructing the Manichean opposition.

28 Richard Kearney, "Ethics and the Postmodern Imagination," *Thought*, vol. 62, no. 244 (1987), p. 53.

29 She says later to Vercueil: "I raged at times against the men who did the dirty work – you have seen it, a shameful raging as *stupid* as what it raged against – but I accepted too that, in a sense, they lived inside me. So that when in my rages I wished them dead, I wished death on myself too" (*AI*, p. 164).

CHAPTER 8

WESTERN CLASSICS IN THE SOUTH AFRICAN STATE OF EMERGENCY: GORDIMER'S *MY SON'S STORY* AND COETZEE'S *AGE OF IRON* (LARS ENGLE)

1 Nadine Gordimer, *My Son's Story* (New York: Farrar Straus Giroux, 1990), p. 247. Henceforth cited as *MSS*.

2 J. M. Coetzee, *Age of Iron* (New York: Penguin, 1998 [1990]), p. 80. Henceforth cited as *AI*.

3 See John Guillory, *Cultural Capital: The Problem of Literary Canon Formation* (Chicago: University of Chicago Press, 1993), Part One, pp. 55–63, "The School and the Reproduction of Social Relations."

4 Philip Larkin, *The Whitsun Weddings* (London: Faber & Faber, 1964), pp. 45–6.

5 For the novel's relation to epistolarity and the difficult necessity of communicating with others, see Derek Attridge, "Trusting the Other: Ethics and Politics in J. M. Coetzee's *Age of Iron*", *SAQ*, vol. 93, no. 1 (Winter 1994), pp. 59–82. Attridge anticipates my argument at several points, concluding that "Coetzee's work . . . does not hesitate to engage the dominating legacy of Western thought and culture and to stage, with remarkable results, the transformation that it undergoes, in a curious and conflicted living-on, in our postcolonial world" (p. 77).

6 David Attwell, *J. M. Coetzee: South Africa and the Politics of Writing* (Cape Town/Berkeley: David Philip/University of California Press, 1993), p. 121. Henceforth cited as *SAPW*.

7 J. M. Coetzee, *Doubling the Point: Essays and Interviews*, ed. David Attwell (Cambridge: Harvard University Press, 1992), p. 369. Henceforth cited as *DP*.

8 J. M. Coetzee, *Giving Offense: Essays on Censorship* (Chicago: University of Chicago Press, 1996), p. 230.

9 J. M. Coetzee, "What is a Classic?", *Current Writing*, vol. 5, no. 2 (1993), p. 13. Henceforth cited as *WC*.

10 See Allen Mandelbaum (trans.), *The Aeneid of Virgil* (New York: Bantam, 1971), II: pp. 1046–64. In *Age of Iron* (p. 192) Mrs. Curren quotes *Aeneid* VI: 337–40 for Vercueil in Latin, offering another scenario for her historical position if she does not manage, as Creusa does, to transmit her message to the next generation. Mandelbaum renders the lines as follows: "Before his bones have found their rest, no one / may cross the horrid shores and the hoarse waters. / They may wander for a hundred years and hover / About these banks until they gain their entry, / to visit once again the pools they long for" (VI: 430–4). Vercueil asks her to repeat:

> Later he came back. "Say the Latin again," he asked. I spoke the lines and watched his lips move as he listened. He is memorizing, I thought. But it was not so. It was the dactyl beating in him, with its power to move the pulse, the throat. (*AI*, p. 192)

Thus Coetzee stages another disinterested encounter between an innocent and the formal power of the classic, one similar in structure to his own youthful encounter with Bach.

PART FOUR: EASTERN EUROPE AFTER COMMUNISM

CHAPTER 9

CREATOR VERSUS CONSPIRATOR IN THE POSTCOMMUNIST REVOLUTIONS (MARCEL CORNIS-POPE)

1 Jacques Derrida, *Specters of Marx: The State of the Debt, the Work of Mourning, and the New International*, trans. Peggy Kamuf (New York/London: Routledge, 1994), pp. 89–90. Henceforth cited as *SM*.

2 Kenneth Burke, *The Philosophy of Literary Form: Studies in Symbolic Action*, 2nd edn. (Baton Rouge: Louisiana State University Press, 1967), p. 107.

3 Dorin Tudoran, *Frost or Fear? Reflections on the Condition of the Romanian Intellectual*, trans. Vladimir Tismaneanu (Daphne, AL: Europa Media, 1986), p. 56. Henceforth cited as *FF*.

4 Domniţa Ştefănescu, *Cinci ani din istoria României: O cronologie a evenimentelor Decembrie 1989–Decembrie 1994* (Bucharest: Editura maşina de scris, 1995), p. 108.

5 Adam J. Sorkin, "Hard Lines: Romanian Poetry, Truth and Heroic Irony Under the Ceauşescu Dictatorship," *The Literary Review* (Fall 1991), pp. 29–30.

6 Mircea Iorgulescu, "The Resilience of Poetry," *TLS* (January 19–24 1990), p. 61.

7 For more on the subversive-emancipatory role played by these discourses against the socioeconomic and ideological constraints of East European communism, see my book *The Unfinished Battles: Romanian Postmodernism Before and After 1989* (Iaşi: Polirom, 1996).

8 Katherine Verdery, *National Ideology Under Socialism: Identity and Cultural Politics in Ceauşescu's Romania* (Berkeley: University of California Press, 1991), pp. 236–7. Henceforth cited as *NIS*.

9 Edith Clowes, *Russian Experimental Fiction: Resisting Ideology after Utopia* (Princeton: Princeton University Press, 1993), pp. 4, 5.

10 See Cornis-Pope, "Critical Theory and the *Glasnost* Phenomenon: Ideological Reconstruction in Romanian Literary and Political Culture," *College Literature*, vol. 21, no. 1 (February 1994), pp. 133–5.

11 George Konrád, *Antipolitics* (San Diego/New York: Harcourt Brace Jovanovich, 1984), pp. 123–4.

12 Tomislav Longinović, *Border Line Culture: The Politics of Identity in Four Twentieth-Century Slavic Novels* (Fayetteville: University of Arkansas Press, 1993), pp. 109–10.

13 Vladislav Todorov, "The Birth of the Mummy from the Spirit of Ideology," *College Literature*, vol. 21, no. 1 (February 1994), p. 115.

14 Vladimir Tismaneanu, *Reinventing Politics: Eastern Europe from Stalin to Havel* (New York/Toronto: Free Press, 1992), p. 249. Henceforth cited as *RP*.

15 Nicolae Manolescu, "Literatură şi politică" [Literature and Politics], *România literară*, vol. 24, no. 39 (September 26 1991), p. 1.

16 Nicolae Manolescu, "Avantajul meu este că am unde să mă întorc din politică" [My Advantage Is That I Have Something to Return to When I Retire From Politics], interview with Dorina Băeşu, *Cuvîntul*, vol. 2, no. 36 (September 1991), p. 5.

17 Irina Livezeanu, *Cultural Politics in Greater Romania: Regionalism, Nation Building, and Ethnic Struggle, 1918–1930* (Ithaca: Cornell University Press, 1995).

18 Mihai Spariosu, *God of Many Names: Play, Poetry, and Power in Hellenic Thought, from Homer to Aristotle* (Durham: Duke University Press, 1991). Henceforth cited as *GMN*.

19 See Mihai Spariosu, *The Wreath of Wild Olive: Play, Liminality, and the Study of Literature* (Albany: SUNY Press, 1997), ch. 5.

CHAPTER 10

YUGOSLAVISM AND ITS DISCONTENTS: A CULTURAL POST-MORTEM (TOMISLAV Z. LONGINOVIĆ)

1 Slavoj Žižek, *The Indivisible Remainder* (London: Verso, 1996), p. 1. Henceforth cited as *IR*.

2 Emulating Jean-François Lyotard's *Heidegger and "the jews"* (Minneapolis: University of Minnesota Press, 1990), I use the common noun and quotation marks for the collective identity of the largest Balkan nation to emphasize that the nation in this case is no longer an essential, monumental, and historically stable category. The implosion of Yugoslavia deprived the Serbs of a common state and divided them into a series of subcategories associated with the new Balkan states they were forced to live in, i.e. Croatian Serbs and Bosnian Serbs. Once the efforts of Serbian leaders to create a nation-state degenerated into the "ethnic cleansing" of other ethnic groups, "the serbs" became a nation of outlaws for the American-led West. The ethnic cleansing of "the serbs" themselves from Croatia and Bosnia-Herzegovina was largely ignored by the international community. Both the self-glorification of the nation by some Serbian intellectuals and politicians and the "orientalization" of the entire Serbian population by the West have created this phantasmatic collective construct which I call "the serbs." Since all the other nations of the former Yugoslavia (Croats, Slovenes, Bosnians, Macedonians) have been recognized as such by the international community, I will use their proper names in this article, except when

referring to a comparable phantasmatic collectivity used to manipulate the identity of those ethnic groups. "The serbs" therefore emerge as a figure and a reflection of a new form of racism that demands distance and separation between the protagonists of different civilizations within the same symbolic territory of Europe.

3 New Collectivism, *Neue Slowenische Kunst*, trans. and ed. Mario Golobič (Los Angeles: AMOK Books, 1991), p. 53.

4 Slavoj Žižek, *The Metastases of Enjoyment: Six Essays on Women and Causality* (London: Verso, 1994), p. 72.

5 Quoted in Robert Hayden and Milica Bakić-Hayden, "Orientalist Variations on the Theme 'Balkans': Symbolic Geography in Recent Yugoslav Cultural Politics," *Slavic Review*, vol. 13, no. 1 (1992), p. 12.

6 The father of psychoanalysis famously described nationalism as a collective expression of narcissism in Sigmund Freud, *Civilization and its Discontents*, trans. James Strachey (New York: Norton, 1962), p. 61. Henceforth cited as *CD*.

7 Etienne Balibar and Immanuel Wallerstein, *Race, Nation, Class: Ambiguous Identities*, trans. Chris Turner (London: Verso, 1991), p. 21. Henceforth cited as *RNC*.

8 Ivo Andrić, *The Bridge on the Drina*, trans. Lovett F. Edwards (Chicago: Univeristy of Chicago Press, 1977), p. 75. Henceforth cited as *BD*.

9 Walter Benjamin, "Eduard Fuchs, Collector and Historian" in *One-Way Street and Other Writings* (London: New Left Books, 1979), p. 359.

10 According to German linguistic experts, Žižek's parallel is mistaken, since the "e" in Lueger, which is pronounced "Looayger," does not designate an umlauted "ü."

11 Sylvia Poggioli, "Scouts without Compasses," *Nieman Reports* (Cambridge: Harvard University, 1993), p. 4.

12 Albert Lord, *The Singer of Tales* (Cambridge: Harvard University Press, 1960).

13 Christopher Schevill, *A History of the Balkans* (New York: Dorset, 1991), p. 203.

14 Mikhail M. Bakhtin, *The Dialogic Imagination*, trans. Caryl Emerson and Michael Holquist (Austin: University of Texas Press, 1981), p. 35.

CHAPTER 11

BOSNIA AND THE ETHICAL LIMITS OF CULTURAL RELATIVISM: RE-AUDITING LYOTARD (CAROLINE BAYARD)

1 Mujeeb R. Khan, "Bosnia-Herzegovina and the Crisis of the Post-Cold War International System," *East European Politics and Societies*, vol. 9, no. 3 (Fall 1995), p. 459. See also Dunja Melčić, "The Balkans and Europe – A Philosophical Problem?" in the last issue of *Praxis International: Special Issue on the Rise and Fall of Yugoslavia: Stations of a European Tragedy*, vol. 13, no. 4 (January 1994), pp. 322–8. Seyla Benhabib and Andrew Arato in "The Yugoslav Tragedy," *Praxis International*, vol. 13, no. 4 (January 1994), p. 330, write, "Europe is dying in Sarajevo," in a scathing attack on European incompetence before ugly ethnic strife. The entire article is sharply critical of both European policy makers and intellectuals.

2 Originally published as *Le Différend* (Paris: Minuit, 1982). The English translation is *The Differend: Phrases in Dispute*, trans. Georges Van Den Abbeele (Minneapolis: University of Minnesota Press, 1988). The passage in question reads: "In the differend, something 'asks' to be put in phrases and suffers from the wrong of not being able to be put into phrases right away . . . what remains to be phrased exceeds what they can presently phrase" (#13). Henceforth cited as *D*; since the book consists of numbered paragraphs, all quotations will be referenced by paragraph rather than page number.

3 On revisionists, such as Faurisson, see *D* #2, 26, 27, 33, 48, 49.

4 On the limits of a Security Council mandate and the cruel fate of the so-called safe-havens (Srebrenica, Goražde), see David Rieff, *Slaughterhouse: Bosnia and the Failure of the West* (London: Vintage, 1995), pp. 173–96. As Fred Cuny, the envoy sent by George Soros (from the Open Society Foundation in Bosnia), told Rieff: "The UN would not have been very effective in dealing with Hitler in the 30's" (p. 172); he later added: "The UN agencies all lacked both the operational doctrine and the operational experience that would have allowed them to come up with an overall plan in Bosnia. . . . As a result, an agency as the UNHCR reacted to events, rather than trying to shape them" (pp. 198–9). On the need to protect specific principles once recognition has been made official, see David Kresock, "Ethnic Cleansing in the Balkans: The Legal Foundations of International Intervention," *Cornell International Law Journal*, 27 (1994), pp. 203–39.

5 Mujeeb R. Khan specifically refers to "Europe's First Post-Holocaust Genocide" (p. 459). Timothy Garton Ash, "Bosnia in Our Future," *New York Review of Books*, November 16 1995, adds: "We then saw the rapid descent to atrocities not seen in Europe for fifty years. Atrocities which do not merely reproduce but also, so to speak, elaborate upon the already formidable repertoire of European barbarism from 1939 to 1945" (p. 27). See also Laura Silber and Allan Little, *Death of a Nation: The Death of Yugoslavia* (New York: Penguin, 1995) on the frightening inadequacy of Europe's political and diplomatic corps between 1992 and 1995.

6 Several of Lyotard's contemporaries did intervene early against human rights abuses in Bosnia, and in some cases emphasized France's and Europe's explicit reluctance to defend Muslim survival in the Balkans, as Jean Baudrillard put it in *Le Crime parfait* (Paris: Galilée, 1995), pp. 181–90. Henceforth cited as *LCP*.

Other French intellectuals took a different approach from either Lyotard or Baudrillard; see the "Déclaration d'Avignon," signed July 29, 1995, by more than one thousand people, and the letter of Etienne Balibar, Hélène Cixous, Jacques Derrida, Philippe Lacoue-Labarthe, and Jean-Luc Nancy, "La Vérité?," *Le Monde*, August 14 1995, p. 9. For Ariane Mnouchkine's three-week fast in August 1995 during the worst killings after the "safe-havens" of Srebrenica and Zepa fell, see "Il y des causes qui valent des vies parce qu'elles engagent l'avenir de tous," *Le Monde*, August 25 1995, p. 16; and in the same newspaper the anonymous article, "Les grévistes de la faim de la cartoucherie de Vincennes continuent," p. 16.

7 Anthony Lewis, "War Crimes," *The New Republic*, March 29 1995, pp. 29–34. Here, specifically, see p. 29.

8 In fact the expression "Le chagrin des spectateurs en cette fin de siècle" is Lyotard's own as one will note in his "Dépêche, à propos de la confusion des raisons," *Le Postmodernisme expliqué aux enfants* (Paris: Galilée, 1987), p. 96. The English translation is *Postmodernism Explained to Children*, trans. Don Barry, Bernadette Maher, Julian Pefanis, Virginia Spate, and Morgan Thomas (Minneapolis: University of Minnesota Press, 1993), henceforth cited as *PE*.

9 See, in this context, how key military and diplomatic actors opposed intervention from 1991 on, even during massive abuses against civilians. Charles Boyd's rationale for

non-intervention while and after serving as Deputy Commander in Chief, US European Command, from November 1992 to July 1995, appears in "Making Peace With the Guilty," *Foreign Affairs: The Truth About Bosnia*, vol. 74, no. 5 (September–October 1995), pp. 22–38. On the responsibility of historians, see Timothy Garton Ash's debate with Robert Kaplan, whose *Balkan Ghosts*, according to Ash, gave support to those opposing forceful intervention. Kaplan defends himself by insisting, in "The Foul Balkan Sky," *New York Review of Books*, March 21 1996, p. 53, that *such was not his intention* and that some of his articles – as early as 1989 – had stressed his anxiety about ethnic strife in the Balkans. See "The Balkans Could Shape the End of the Century," *Atlantic Monthly* (July 1989), pp. 3–7. Ash rejects Kaplan's defense, blaming him for unduly "projecting the old saws about ancient hatreds and atavistic tribes," "Bosnia in Our Future," *New York Review of Books*, December 21 1996, p. 28.

10 See the last issue of *Praxis International*, specifically the essay by Dunja Melčič. See also Silber and Little, *Death of a Nation*.

11 Jean-François Lyotard, *Moralités postmodernes* (Paris: Galilée, 1993), p. 176 (translation mine). Henceforth cited as *MP*.

12 "Ligne générale" reminds us that "L'invite répétée à exercer les droits et à en surveiller l'observance peut être pressante jusqu'à l'oppression. . . . Que l'exercice des droits et la vigilance quant à leur respect soient requis comme des devoirs, il y a là une sorte d'évidence, aussi infaillible qu'une disposition totalitaire peut l'être" (*MP*, p. 108, translation in the main text mine).

13 *MP*, p. 110 (still untranslated). The French reads: "Le droit et le respect du droit ne nous sont dus que parce que quelque chose en nous excède tout droit reconnu. Celui-ci n'a de sens que pour sauvegarder ce qui se trouve au-delà ou en deçà, de lui. Misère, péché, inconscient, souffrance, honte ou bien inspiration, énergie, passion, grâce et talent, qu'en savons-nous?"

14 Lyotard writes: "Le consensus n'est pas la rédemption du crime, c'est son oubli. Nous sommes priés de contribuer au règlement des injustices qui abondent dans le monde, nous le faisons. Mais l'angoisse dont je parle est d'une autre trempe que le souci de civisme. Elle résiste à la République et au système, elle est plus archaique qu'eux, elle protège et fuit, à la fois, l'étranger inhumain qui est en nous, jouissance et terreur" (*MP*, p. 109). In *The Inhuman*, Lyotard had already reminded his readers that "as for the voice which prescribes, 'You must resist (to the extent that you must think or write),' it of course implies that the problem of the present time is in no way to communicate. What holds the attention and is a question is much rather what this prescription presupposes: 'what is or who is the author of this commandment? What is its legitimacy?'" See *The Inhuman: Reflections on Time*, trans. Geoffrey Bennington and Rachel Bowlby (Stanford, CA: Stanford University Press, 1991), p. 77. Henceforth cited as *I*.

15 *MP*, p. 110. See in particular: "Pourquoi aurions-nous droit à la liberté d'expression si nous n'avions rien à dire que le déjà dit? Et comment avoir la chance de trouver à dire ce que nous ne savons pas dire si nous n'écoutons pas le silence de l'autre en dedans?"

16 Peter Schwarz, "Germany's National and European Interests," *Daedalus*, vol. 123, no. 2 (Spring 1994), pp. 81–106. The key point for Schwarz is that such postmodern nations have long abandoned the idea of "national identity elevated to a mythological status." Germany became one such matter-of-fact entity *precisely* because it no longer understood nationhood in terms of absolute value and because it recognized, like other postmodern nations in the nineties, that it could *only* thrive if it surrendered some autonomy to regional *and* international bodies. Clearly, insists Schwarz, such agreements necessarily entail "all the ideological shadings, antitheses, and contradictions characteristic of

pluralistic societies." These Western European developments could not differ more strikingly from events in East and Central Europe.

17 The 1992 Maastricht Treaty had two main groups of provisions. The first sought to reform the old European Community by amending past provisions and adding new ones. The second was meant to establish a detailed framework for intergovernmental cooperation in foreign affairs, security, justice, and domestic policy. A major premise of Maastricht is that the new European Union will have a single institutional framework, although some political scientists have challenged this assumption.

18 On European inadequacies see Misha Glenny, *The Fall of Yugoslavia and the Third Balkan War* (London/New York: Penguin, 1992) and "Bosnia: The Tragic Prospect," *New York Review of Books* (November 4 1993), pp. 38, 48–9; also Michael Ignatieff, "The Missed Chance in Bosnia," *New York Review of Books* (February 26 1996), pp. 8–10. In a more international and legalistic framework, see Mark Weller, "The International Response to the Dissolution of the Socialist Federal Republic of Yugoslavia," *American Journal of International Law*, 86 (1992), pp. 569–607; Christine Ellerman, "Command of Sovereignty Gives Way to Concern for Humanity," *Vanderbilt Journal of Transnational Law*, vol. 26, no. 2 (May 1993), pp. 341–71; and Jordan J. Paust, "Peace-Making and Security Council Powers: Bosnia-Herzegovina raises International and Constitutional Questions," *Southern Illinois University Law Review*, 19 (1994), pp. 131–51. Because the last three articles challenge the Western nations' and Maastricht Europe's ability to abide by the United Nations Human Rights Declaration, they throw into serious doubt the validity of Lyotard's mistrust of consensual agreements.

19 See his "The Situation in North Africa" (1956), originally published in *La Guerre des Algériens* (Galilée: Paris, 1989) and partially translated in *Lyotard: Political Writings*, trans. Bill Readings (Minneapolis: University of Minnesota Press, 1993), pp. 171–8. Henceforth cited as *PW*.

20 See "A propos du Différend. Entretien avec Jean-François Lyotard. Introduction de Christine Buci-Gluksman," *Les Cahiers de philosophie*, 5 (1988), pp. 34–62; see also in the same issue Dick Veerman, "Développer l'honneur de penser," pp. 11–34, henceforth cited as *DHP*.

21 The original French text appears in *Le Tombeau de l'intellectuel et autres papiers* (Paris: Galilée, 1984), pp. 11–30.

22 On the night watchman, or the critic who keeps a vigil in the dark night of the soul, so that entire universes of names not be destroyed, see Lyotard's *Judicieux dans le différend* (Paris: Minuit, 1985), pp. 235–6. See also *DHP*, p. 14.

On the silence of European neighbors, see Annie Lebrun, *Les Assassins et leurs miroirs* (Paris: Terrain Vague, 1993); Velibor Čolič, *Les Bosniaques: hommes, villes, barbelés*, trans. Mireille Robin (Paris: Serpent à plumes, 1994); and Zlatko Dižderevič, *Le Silence et rien alentour* (Paris: Actes Sud, 1993).

23 Jean-François Lyotard and David Carroll, "Interview," *Diacritics*, vol. 14, no. 1 (Fall 1984), pp. 16–23. Henceforth cited as *IN*.

24 Lyotard insists that we make mistakes and that "misapprehensions are inevitable when we apply ideas elaborated from a simple situation. Ideas are not operators, or categories, but horizons of thought" (*IN*, p. 20).

25 On his own stance, with Alain Finkielkraut, Elisabeth de Fontenay, Jacob Rogocinski, Pierre André-Taguieff, and Alain Touraine, see "Une Guerre requise," *Libération*, February 21 1991, p. 12. Henceforth cited as *GR*. On the strength of open systems versus closed/

totalitarian ones and on the hiatus in the very definition of democracy, see *MP*, p. 76. For opposition to Lyotard on the Gulf War, see Etienne Balibar, Ben Jalloun, and Pierre Bourdieu, "Contre la guerre," *Libération*, February 21 1991, p. 13.

26 "The Wall, the Gulf, the Sun: A Fable," trans. Thomas Cochran, in Mark Poster, *Politics, Theory and Contemporary Culture* (New York: Columbia University Press, 1993), pp. 261–76. The original French, with the title "Mur, golfe, système," appears in *MP*, pp. 65–76. See also *GR*: "Against the combined temptations presented by moral angelism and cynical realism, it is essential to preserve the exacting demands ethical politics confer upon us all [la voie difficile d'une politique morale doit être préservée]. It is our duty to ensure that victory against Iraq promote democracy, justice as much as peace opportunities" (p. 12, translation mine).

27 See his stance on the intractable [l'intraitable] in 1982, when he insists on his respect for the very notion of gap, hiatus, pause, not just in a text or for his philosophical ear, but also inside political and cultural systems (*D*, #218). See also his definition of postmodernity as the end of the "peuple-roi des histoires," hence the end of any possibility for emancipation, revelation, or wisdom (*PE*, p. 39). On indeterminacy within democracy and the hiatus within it, see "Wall, Gulf, System" (*MP*, p. 270). On the irremediable opacity of language itself, see "A Svelte Appendix to the Postmodern" (*PW*, p. 27).

28 Paul Ricoeur, *Autour du politique* (Paris: Seuil, 1991). Also his "Le Concept de responsabilité: Essai d'analyse sémantique," *Esprit*, 11 (November 1994), pp. 28–48 (henceforth cited as *CR*), which does not hesitate to draw inspiration from both Hannah Arendt's *The Human Condition* (Chicago: University of Chicago Press, 1958) and Eric Weil's *La philosophie morale* (Paris: Vrin, 1961) in insisting that political categories need to be defined *first* vis-à-vis economics and social structures before they can be confronted with ethical expectations. But once this has happened, Ricoeur stresses the central flaw of Marxist analysis: to have overestimated the role of production modes within a given society. Conflating political and economic alienations was a catastrophic reduction in Ricoeur's view. Also pertinent is Ricoeur's *Finitude et culpabilité* (Paris: Aubier, 1988).

29 Paul Ricoeur, "Ethique et politique," in *Du texte à l'action: essais d'herméneutique II* (Paris: Seuil, 1986), pp. 393–406 and specifically p. 398. Henceforth cited as *EP*.

30 Myriam Revault d'Allones, "Vers une politique de la responsabilité," *Esprit*, 11 (November 1994), pp. 49–61, specifically p. 61.

31 "Vers une politique de la responsabilité" alludes (p. 49) to Hannah Arendt's "Postscriptum" in *The Life of the Mind* (New York: Harcourt Brace, 1971), pp. 213–6, which refers to Kant's two *Critiques*.

32 The validity of humanitarian intervention in the former Yugoslavia has caught the attention of many legal and human rights experts, in particular Ellerman and Paust (n. 17 in the article referenced above in n. 18).

33 Many commentators have reflected on Europe's need to face its responsibility in Bosnia. Georges Soros, for instance, has clearly outlined what was at stake there, for both the European community and the United Nations: "brutality has always existed, but continuing to tolerate it after it has been exposed can only weaken future attempts to resist it. The unspeakable brutality that we have witnessed in Bosnia is not simply the byproduct of mindless aggression: it has been committed in the name of a doctrine, the doctrine of the ethnic state, this is where lies the danger" ("Bosnia and Beyond," *New York Review of Books*, October 7 1993, pp. 15–16). Michael Ignatieff, on the other hand, has illuminated the effects of American *and* European reluctance to intervene: "National interests seem to require only that the Yogoslav problem be quarantined, not that it be resolved. . . . It is difficult to think of a recent conflict in which there was such moral unanimity in the face

of evil and so little determination to do anything about it. Outrage became a substitute for action: when inaction led to tragedy, there was recrimination. The Americans came to believe the Europeans were gutless; the Europeans thought the Americans were hypocritical. While Washington, London, Paris, and Bonn were arguing among themselves, 250,000 lost their lives, or were seriously wounded in the former Yugoslavia" ("The Missed Chance in Bosnia," *New York Review of Books*, October 7 1993, pp. 8–10).

34 Ricoeur, *EP*, p. 398. See also Lyotard, "The Wall, The Gulf, The Sun: A Fable," in *MP*.

35 Lyotard writes, "And I do not find it fair when Rorty, or others, take the liberty of reading into my defense of the differend, resonances of leftism, revolution, terrorism even. It is one thing to look upon a discussion, or even a conversation (whose aim is to extend consensus), as an important task. It is another to look upon this conversation as the only use we can derive from language" (*MP*, p. 119, translation mine). In "Un partenaire bizarre" (*MP*), Lyotard makes his political choices vis-à-vis liberalism very clear, specifically in exploring Donald Davidson's and Richard Rorty's different interpretations of dialogue and consensus when faced with contemporary conflicts. While it is true that this essay focuses on several Franco–American misunderstandings, Lyotard also rejects the reduction that both Rorty and Davidson perform upon the purpose and function of language (*MP*, pp. 119–20).

36 On Hans Jonas, see Ricoeur (*CR*, p. 43), who quotes the translation into French of *Le Principe responsabilité* (Paris: Cerf, 1990). When Ricoeur scrutinizes Jonas's extension of the notion of responsibility, he interprets it, following R. Spämann, as being placed under Hegelian *Sittlichkeit*. On Lévinas, see *CR*, pp. 45–8. The text referred to here is *Ethique et infini* (Paris: Fayard, 1982), where Lévinas defines reponsibility as that which is "an essential, primary and fundamental responsibility of subjectivity."

37 Humanitarian intervention has been discussed extensively in law journals and International Relations publications. See Kresock (n. 4), who considers the issues facing an international community that needs to re-evaluate its approach to individual state sovereignty. Also Deborah Z. Cass, "Re-thinking Self-Determination: A Critical Analysis of Current International Law Theories," *Syracuse Journal of International Law and Commerce*, 21 (1992), pp. 21–2; Nathaniel Berman, "Sovereignty in Abeyance: Self-Determination and International Law," *Wisconsin International Law Journal*, vol. 51, no. 70 (1988), pp. 11–17; and Ved Nanda, "Tragedies in Northern Iraq, Liberia, Yugoslavia, and Haiti – Revisiting the Validity of Humanitarian Intervention under International Law, Part I," *Denver International Law Journal and Polity*, 20 (1992), pp. 305–7.

38 Morris B. Abram, "Peace and Justice in Bosnia are Inseparable," reprinted in *The Globe and Mail*, February 19 1996, A15. Abram, who was Chairman of the Geneva-based monitoring group UN Watch and former US permanent representative to the United Nations in Europe, emphasizes: "Peace and justice are not irreconcilable, but inseparable. First is the deterrent effect of enforcing the rule of law, taken for granted as a condition of domestic civil society. . . . Second, war-crimes trials can facilitate interethnic reconciliation. Ethnic groups may be absolved of collective guilt by holding perpetrators individually responsible." For Abram ad hoc tribunals do not provide long-term solutions; only a permanent court can do so. Václav Havel, in his "Address in Conclusion of the Month of Bosnia Herzegovina in Prague," Spanish Hall, Prague Castle, October 13 1995, insists that the conflict was not ethnic in nature, but societal. "Two distinct concepts of state and society found themselves on a collision course. One was a modern, open, civil concept in which different nationalities, ethnic groups, traditions can live together and cooperate; the other an archaic, tribal state as 'a community of people of the same blood.' " Havel reminds us that the Bosnian conflict was never between the Serbs and the rest of the population, but pitted ethnic fanatics, the adherents of an authoritarian state based on national collectivism, against believers in civic principles.

39 Note for instance that Ellerman in "Command of Sovereignty" points to the slow emergence of necessary changes, even in such staunchly non-interventionist bodies as the United Nations. Ellerman argues that the UN stance on humanitarian intervention has increasingly justified intervention, provided it be carried out for humanitarian purposes.

On the need to separate war crimes issues from sovereignty issues, see David Martin's intervention at the "Symposium War Crimes: Bosnia and Beyond," titled "Reluctance to Prosecute War Crimes: Of Causes and Cures," *Virginia Journal of International Law*, 34 (1994), p. 255. As early as 1993 Daniel Eaton deplored American and European slowness to act on the War Crimes aspect of this conflict, in "Bosnia: the War Crimes Dimension," *New Zealand International Review*, July 7 1993, pp. 13–15.

40 Fernando Tesón, *Humanitarian Intervention: An Inquiry Into Law And Morality* (Dobbs Ferry, NY: Transactional Publishers, 1988). Ellerman notes, however, that the doctrine of non-intervention had already been challenged by Henry G. Hodges in *The Doctrine Of Intervention* (1915). Hodges defined intervention as "interference by a state, or states in the external affairs of another without its consent, or in the internal affairs of another state with or without its consent" (cited in n. 9 of Ellerman article referenced above, n. 18).

41 Robert Block accuses both General Ratko Mladić, described as criminally responsible for murdering thousands of Muslim men and boys in Potocari, *and* Dutch peacekeepers who were present but unwilling to keep the peace by intervening while organized murders occurred at the very spot where more than 28,000 refugees from Srebrenica had fled in July 1995. Furthermore, as Block puts it, the demand by the top UN military commander, General Janvier, that heavy guns be withdrawn from Sarajevo was rejected by General Mladić who responded, "The more you bomb us, the stronger we are." Block concludes that by then there had been a catastrophic miscalculation among the Western powers, and particularly French and British diplomats, who saw Mladić as the leader who might potentially bring peace to Bosnia. See Block's "The Madness of General Mladić," *New York Review of Books*, October 5 1995, pp. 7–9.

42 See Weller (n. 4 in article referenced above, n. 18), who examines UN Resolution 713 (1991) and 752 (1992), faulting them for failing either to stop Serbian aggression or to provide humanitarian assistance (pp. 600–2). Weller also criticizes the European Community for inefficiency, before concluding that EC recognition was never understood to constitute statehood or the *basic rights* (emphasis mine) associated with statehood (p. 605). See also Nigel Rodley, *To Loose the Bands of Wickedness: International Intervention in Defense of Human Rights* (London: Brassey's, 1992).

43 Timothy Garton Ash, "Central Europe: the Present Past," *New York Review of Books*, July 13 1995, pp. 21–3.

44 Editorial, "The Long Haul in Bosnia," *The Economist*, March 30 1996, p. 3.

CHAPTER 12

CULTURAL CO-ORDINATES OF A BULGARIAN ART-HOAX: "DRAFTS" BY VIRGINIA, A *TRAGEDIA DELL'ARTE* (NIKITA NANKOV)

1 The Bulgarian epigraph reads: "and my funny drawings are very sad drawings . . .," Iliia Beshkov, *Slovoto: Eseta razmishleniia, pisma, razgovori*. Stanislav Sivriev, *Do sâmnalo (Razgovori s Iliia Beshkov)* (Varna: Georgi Bakalov, 1981), p. 359. Taken from Beshkov's essay on Bai Gan'o and Aleko Konstantinov, it explains Beshkov's drawings of the relation

between the literary character (Bai Gan'o) and his author (Konstantinov). See below, note 19.

2 David Henry Hwang, *M. Butterfly* (New York: Plume, 1988), p. 19.

3 Nikita Nankov, "Nadpis 'Bivol' v kletkata na lâva" ("Inscription 'Buffalo' on the Lion's Cage"), *Literaturen vestnik*, April 11–17 1994, p. 3.

4 An anagram of Iordan Ivanov, a renowned Bulgarian medieval specialist.

5 The names for this monastery and the Chilandar monastery vary in English, with some authorities using "the Zograph monastery" and "the Hilendar monastery," while others prefer "Zographou" and "Chilandar."

6 Samantha Krukowski is (ostensibly) a Professor of Byzantine and Women's Studies and Sheridan Director of the Eisenhower Library at Harvard University, but in reality is a young American artist and art historian on whom I had a crush. Hi, Samantha, wherever you may be!

7 Nataliia Todorova, "Dushevno razkrepostiavane v svetli tonove" ("Spiritual Liberation in Bright Colors"), *Podkrepa*, February 22 1994, p. 10.

8 See "'Lesedra' predstavia 'Chernovi ot Virginiia'" ("*Lessedra* Exposes 'Drafts by Virginia'"), *24 Chasa*, March 9 1994, p. 23; "Dzhoto e bâlgarskata khudozhnichka Virginiia" ("Giotto Is the Bulgarian Artist Virginia"), *Novinar*, March 9 1994, p. 8; Sandrela Al Kadi, "Boianskiiat Maistor bil ot zhenski pol" ("The Boiana Master Was a Woman"), *Ekspres*, March 10 1994, p. 16; Mila Vacheva, "Boianskata cherkva e zografisana ot zhena" ("The Boiana Church Has Been Decorated by a Woman"), *Duma*, March 12–13, 1994, p. 12; "Khudozhestvenite galerii v Sofiia i ekspozitsiite v tiakh. Lesedra . . ." ("The Art Galleries in Sofia and Their Exhibitions. *Lessedra* . . ."), *Duma*, March 17 1994, p. 11.

9 Nadia Medneva, "Spontanen shtrikh, govoresht za strastnost" ("Spontaneous Strokes Testifying to Passion"), *Novo slovo*, March 19 1994, p. 9.

10 Diana Popova, "1. Nakhodkata. . . ." ("1. The Discovery. . . ."), *Kultura*, April 1 1994, p. 5.

11 Compare C. K. Ogden and I. A. Richards, *The Meaning of Meaning: A Study of the Influence of Language Upon Thought and of the Science of Symbolism* (New York: Harcourt Brace, 1923); Tzvetan Todorov, *The Conquest of America: The Question of the Other*, trans. Richard Howard (New York: Harper & Row, 1984).

12 Umberto Eco, *A Theory of Semiotics* (Bloomington: Indiana University Press, 1976), pp. 289–97.

13 Compare Umberto Eco, "Travels in Hyperreality," *Travels in Hyperreality: Essays*, trans. William Weaver (San Diego/New York: Harcourt Brace Jovanovich, 1986), pp. 1–58; Jean Baudrillard, *Simulations*, trans. Paul Foss *et al.* (New York: Semiotext[e], 1983); Jean Baudrillard, *America*, trans. Chris Turner (New York: Verso, 1988); Frederic Jameson, "Postmodernism, or the Cultural Logic of Late Capitalism," *New Left Review*, 146 (1984), pp. 53–92; Stephen M. Fjellman, *Vinyl Leaves: Walt Disney World and America* (Boulder: Westview Press, 1992).

14 For the Bulgarian intelligentsia in general, including their attitude to Western and Bulgarian values, see Roumen Daskalov, "Transformation of the East European Intelligentsia: Reflections on the Bulgarian Case," *East European Politics and Societies*, vol. 10, no. 1 (Winter 1996), pp. 46–84.

15 Aleko Konstantinov, *Bai Gan'o, Sâchineniia v dva toma*, 2 vols. (Sofiia: Bâlgarski pisatel, 1970), vol. 1, p. 105. Henceforth cited as *BG*.

16 P[eio] K[racholov] Iavorov, *V Polite na Vitosha, Sâbrani sâchineniia v pet toma*, 5 vols. (Sofiia: Bâlgarski pisatel, 1959–60), vol. 3, p. 111.

17 Ivan Khadzhiiski, *Avtoritet, dostoinstvo i maska, Sâchineniia v dva toma*, eds. Nesho Davidov and Efrem Karanfilov, 2 vols. (Sofiia: Bâlgarski pisatel, 1974), vol. 1, pp. 367–488.

18 Geo Milev, *September, The Road to Freedom*, trans. Ewald Osers (London and Boston: Forest Books/Unesco, 1988), p. 20.

19 This observation turned out to be prophetic, for in October 1996 after the initial draft of this essay, Andrei Lukanov, one of the most respected Bulgarian socialist politicians, was murdered in front of his home. The murderer was never found. The case recalls the end of Aleko Konstantinov (1863–97) who also fell victim to political terror. Iliia Beshkov (1901–58), one of Bulgaria's best draftsmen and cartoonists, who for decades had been thinking about and depicting the relation between Konstantinov and his hero Bai Gan'o as an historical, ethical, sociological, and aesthetic Bulgarian archetype, commemorated Konstantinov's tragic death with a series of drawings in which Bai Gan'o stands by the mortally wounded writer. The text to the drawings reads "Bai Gan'o ubiva avtora si" ("Bai Gan'o is murdering his author" [1947]). The pattern linking the media and politics in Bulgaria for more than a century is obvious: terror in the media goes hand in hand with physical terror.

20 Quoted in RoseLee Goldberg, *Performance Art: From Futurism to the Present* (New York: Harry N. Abrams, Inc., Publishers, 1988), pp. 109, 122. Henceforth cited as *PA:FP*.

21 Compare Allan Kaprow, *Essays on Blurring of Art and Life*, ed. and introduced Jeff Kelley (Berkeley and Los Angeles: University of California Press, 1993) and Frank Popper, *Art-Action and Participation* (New York: New York University Press, 1975), esp. pp. 13–32, 178–203.

22 See Umberto Eco, *Interpretation and Overinterpretation*, ed. Stefan Collini (Cambridge: Cambridge University Press, 1992), pp. 51, 56, 59–60 and Umberto Eco, *The Limits of Interpretation* (Bloomington: Indiana University Press, 1990), p. 19.

23 My terms "intransitive" and "transitive" are improvisations drawing on Tzvetan Todorov. "Intransitive" means noninstrumental, nonutilitarian, autotelic, dealing with the beauty of an expression for its own sake. "Transitive," in this *Tragedia*, stands for the opposite. Compare Tzvetan Todorov, "The Notion of Literature," *Genres in Discourse*, trans. Catherine Porter (Cambridge: Cambridge University Press, 1990), pp. 1–12, esp. pp. 2–6.

24 Bulgarian national radio prepared a special interview with Virginia/Virzhiniia for Bulgarians abroad, but it was cancelled once it became clear that the show was a mystification.

25 Compare Walter Benjamin, "The Work of Art in the Age of Mechanical Production," in *Illuminations*, trans. Harry Zohn (New York: Harcourt, Brace and World, 1968), p. 244.

26 Compare: "Out of these reexaminations of history and nature women drew material and inspiration for feminist rituals. . . . women's rituals of the 1970s should be read as attempts both to help create and to maintain a feminist culture. These feminist rituals began at the same time as autobiographical explorations in consciousness-raising groups and the development of the 'personal is political' concept" (Moira Roth, ed., *The Amazing Decade: Women and Performance Art in America 1970–1980* [Los Angeles: Astro Artz, 1983], p. 22). This topic is elaborated in Henry M. Sayre, *The Object of Performance: The American Avant-Garde since 1970* (Chicago: University of Chicago Press, 1989), pp. 66–100 and Lynda Hart and Peggy Phelan, eds., *Acting Out: Feminist Performances* (Ann Arbor: University of Michigan Press, 1993).

27 For narrative identity see Paul Ricoeur, *Time and Narrative*, trans. Kathleen Blamey and David Pellauer (Chicago: University of Chicago Press, 1988), vol. 3, pp. 186–9, 246–9.

28 To this statement, *Signore e Signori*, you may object: "But what about Tzvetan Todorov, Julia Kristeva, or Christo? . . ." Well, in Bulgaria, they are seen as luminaries with (almost) Bulgarian names who shine in the West but who are not linked with a Bulgarian cause (if such a cause exists at all).

29 Roland Barthes, "Theory of the Text," *Untying the Text: A Post-Structuralist Reader*, ed. Robert Young (Boston/London: Routledge and Kegan Paul, 1981), pp. 31–47.

30 Umberto Eco, *The Open Work*, trans. Anna Cancogni (Cambridge: Harvard University Press, 1989).

31 Umberto Eco, quoted in Peter Bondanella, *Umberto Eco and the Open Text: Semiotics, Fiction, Popular Culture* (Cambridge: Cambridge University Press, 1997), p. 95.

32 In an interview at the opening of the show, Virginia/Virzhiniia entwined nationalism and feminism: "Today some scholars and politicians maintain that there was, in fact, no Ottoman yoke in Bulgaria. Well, I declare that Giotto was, in reality, Virginia. What is the proof? My mustachio, of course!" Verily, verily, the personal is political.

33 For another amateur piece about the stereotypes of the West and Eastern Europe in relation to one another, see Nikita Nankov, "The Grand (Anti)communist Narrative Strikes Back: Five Postscripts on Bulgarian Past/Postcommunism," *Over the Wall/After the Fall: Post-Totalitarian Cultures East and West*, Sibelan Forrester and Magdalena Zaborowska, eds., forthcoming.

34 Compare Jean-François Lyotard, *The Inhuman: Reflections on Time*, trans. Geoffrey Bennington and Rachel Bowlby (Stanford: Stanford University Press, 1991), pp. 78–107, 135–43.

35 This Scene improvises on Thomas McFarland, *Romanticism and the Forms of Ruin: Wordsworth, Coleridge, and the Modalities of Fragmentation* (Princeton: Princeton University Press, 1981). Henceforth cited as *RFR*.

36 Mimetic art imitates what is there in reality, while meontic art imitates what is not there (*RFR*, p. 383). The mimetic and the meontic modes are not absolute opposites but the poles of an artistic continuum (*RFR*, p. 385).

37 Andrei Daniel, one of the most interesting contemporary Bulgarian painters, a teacher and supporter of Virginia/Virzhiniia, contested the very idea of exhibiting sketches. In his opinion, the drafts should remain in the studio, and only the final version of a work should be shown.

PART FIVE: FAR EAST/FAR WEST

CHAPTER 13

CULTURAL HERMENEUTICS AND ORIENTALIST DISCOURSE: LOTI'S SELF-REFLEXIVE *JAPONISME* (ROLF GOEBEL)

1 Pierre Loti, *Madame Chrysanthème* (Paris: Calmann-Lévy, 1893). The English translation is *Madame Chrysanthème*, trans. Laura Ensor, intro. Terence Barrow (Rutland, VT: Tuttle, 1973). Hereafter cited as *MC*, with page references given first to the translation, then to

the French original. Translation modified. In theory, of course, the novel's protagonist is not identical to Julien Viaud, its real-life author. Chris Bongie's *Exotic Memories: Literature, Colonialism, and the Fin de Siècle* (Stanford: Stanford University Press, 1991) discusses the shifting boundaries between author and romantic persona in Loti's *Aziyadé* and *Le mariage de Loti* (p. 92). *Madame Chrysanthème* blurs this boundary to such an extent that differences between fiction and actual travel experiences are almost impossible to detect. For the autobiographical background of Loti's views on Japan, see Lesley Blanch, *Pierre Loti: Portrait of an Escapist* (London: Collins, 1983), pp. 178–9, 195–6, 257.

2 Several recent critics insightfully address Loti's colonialism and exoticism. In *The Colonial Experience in French Fiction: A Study of Pierre Loti, Ernest Psichari and Pierre Mille* (London: Macmillan, 1981), Alec Hargreaves finds in Loti an ethnocentric fear that the exoticized non-West is disappearing as an object of writerly conquest and penetration (pp. 19–85). In "a kind of literary imperialism," Loti's "conceptual framework, preoccupations and value system were intensely personal, but they owed virtually nothing to non-European cultures" and did not change according to the realities he purports to describe (p. 80). Bongie discusses exoticism as "a discursive practice intent on recovering 'elsewhere' values 'lost' with the modernization of European society" (p. 5); its followers "register the exotic as a space of absence, a dream already given over to the past" (p. 22). While Hargreaves mentions *Madame Chrysanthème* just in passing (p. 81) and Bongie not at all, their treatment of Loti's ideological contexts and discursive strategies is pertinent to my argument. Tzvetan Todorov also emphasizes Loti's major place in exoticist French literature. See *On Human Diversity: Nationalism, Racism, and Exoticism in French Thought*, trans. Catherine Porter (Cambridge: Harvard University Press, 1993), pp. 308–23. Hereafter cited as *OHD*. For Loti's exoticist construction of women, see Todorov, pp. 314–18 and Irene Szyliowicz, *Pierre Loti and the Oriental Woman* (New York: St. Martin's, 1988), pp. 56, 75–6, 80.

3 For the book's cultural context and reputation, see Endymion Wilkinson, *Japan Versus the West: Image and Reality* (Harmondsworth: Penguin, 1990), pp. 110–19.

4 Cited from Jonathan Cott, *Wandering Ghost: The Odyssey of Lafcadio Hearn* (New York: Knopf, 1991), pp. 265, 284–5.

5 Hans-Georg Gadamer, *Wahrheit und Methode: Grundzüge einer philosophischen Hermeneutik*, 4th edn. (Tübingen: J. C. B Mohr [Paul Siebeck], 1975), pp. 250–360.

6 Robert C. Ulin, *Understanding Cultures: Perspectives in Anthropology and Social Theory* (Austin: University of Texas Press, 1984), pp. 96–7. Hereafter cited as *UC*.

7 Clifford Geertz, *The Interpretation of Cultures* (New York: Basic Books, 1973), pp. 14–15. Other such discussions include James Clifford and George C. Marcus, eds., *Writing Culture: The Poetics and Politics of Ethnography* (Berkeley: University of California Press, 1986) and Clifford's *The Predicament of Culture: Twentieth-Century Ethnography, Literature, and Art* (Cambridge: Harvard University Press, 1988).

8 Basil Hall Chamberlain, *Japanese Things: Being Notes on Various Subjects Connected with Japan* (Rutland, VT: Tuttle, 1971), p. 258.

9 Edward W. Said, *Orientalism* (New York: Vintage, 1979), p. 58. Hereafter cited as *O*.

10 Homi K. Bhabha, "The Other Question: Stereotype, Discrimination and the Discourse of Colonialism," *The Location of Culture* (London: Routledge, 1994), pp. 73–5. Hereafter cited as *LC*. Robert Young discusses Bhabha's theories in *White Mythologies: Writing History and the West* (London: Routledge, 1990), pp. 141–56.

11 Commenting on the Polynesian novel *Le Mariage de Loti*, Hargreaves notes similar

ambivalence and inconsistencies in Loti's authorial position, which oscillates between defending the indigenous culture against colonial intrusion and criticizing that culture for supposedly repugnant and terrifying wildness (pp. 45–67). Hargreaves traces such ambiguities to "loss of artistic control" (p. 67), thereby judging Loti by a poetic standard of organic wholeness that may be inappropriate for colonialist discourse. Responding to Hargreaves, Bongie emphasizes Loti's "duplicitous status as both an exotic and a colonial subject. As an exotic subject in search of the Other, he cannot fail to be anti-colonialist; as an exotic subject who finds himself in a situation of 'full colonialism,' however, he is inevitably disappointed by the indigenous culture since it can no longer furnish the geopolitical alternative that his ideological project requires . . ." (p. 97). While Japan, strictly speaking, was never a Western colony, Bongie's argument does apply to Loti's construction of Japan as the other of homogenizing Western modernity. Todorov also finds Loti's attitude toward Japan and his other exoticist explorations to be "ambiguous." On the one hand, Loti "submits to their charm, and finds a term of comparison that allows him to criticize European artifice and duplicity." On the other, "these primitivist reveries never really call into question the narrator's choice, which is to return, at the end of his sojourn, to the highly civilized countries he came from" (p. 312). This may be true, but in this ambiguity one can detect a self-critical impulse that questions the very hegemony of the culture and language to which Loti returns.

12 *OHD*, p. 310. Todorov concludes: "Such is indeed the logic of the egocentric voyage, which grants the dignity of subject to a single person – that is, the narrator himself" (rather than to the foreign country as well).

13 See Wilkinson, pp. 110–13 (who, following Baudelaire, refers to the imported art objects as *Japonaiserie*); Ingrid Schuster, *China und Japan in der deutschen Literatur 1890–1925* (Bern: Francke, 1977), pp. 9–17; and Inaga Shigemi, "A European Eye on Japanese Arts and a Japanese Response to 'Japonisme' (1860–1920): A Transcultural Interaction between Visual Arts and Critical Discourse," in *Literature, Visual Arts and Linguistics*, vol. 1 of *Rethinking Japan*, ed. Adriana Boscaro, Franco Gatti, and Massimo Raveri (New York: St. Martin's, 1991), pp. 131–6.

14 George Becker and Edith Philips (ed. and trans.), *Paris and the Arts, 1851–1896: From the Goncourt Journal* (Ithaca: Cornell University Press, 1971), p. 106. Hereafter cited as *PA*.

15 *O*, p. 93. In summing up Loti, Wilkinson cites Valéry's amusing advice: "[I]n order that the word Orient produces its complete and entire effect on someone's spirit, above all it is essential never to have been in the country which it so uncertainly indicates" (p. 119).

16 Said himself distinguishes between the preformative power of texts and that of artifacts: "[T]he Orient studied was a textual universe by and large; the impact of the Orient was made through books and manuscripts, not, as in the impress of Greece on the Renaissance, through mimetic artifacts like sculpture and pottery" (*O*, p. 52).

17 *O*, pp. 20–1. For Westerners, Said argues, the Orient is only important as an object of writing and ethnocentric explanation, not as a site of lived experience.

18 Homi K. Bhabha, "The Commitment to Theory," *LC*, p. 31.

19 On Loti's attitude toward *japonisme*, Blanch indicates that "it seems unlikely" that he "was blindly following the fashionable cult for all things Japanese, for his own instincts as a collector proved his fine sensibility." However, as Loti's own comparison between *japonisme* and actual Japanese culture suggests, Blanch's conclusion that Loti "never really responded to this people's fragile genius" as he did to "every aspect of Islamic culture" is somewhat overstated (p. 179).

20 See also Todorov's interesting point that Loti cannot truly identify with foreign countries

because he merely adds, in a self-consciously artificial manner, separate "Japanese" or "Turkish" lives to his Western identity, shedding them when leaving these countries (*OHD*, p. 313).

21 *OHD*, p. 311. As Todorov points out, the frequent use of terms like *étrange* (strange), *drôle* (ludicrous, curious), or *indicible* (unspeakable) further exoticizes Japan, although, one may add, they also indicate hermeneutic self-consciousness about the (un)readability of Japan.

22 Bhabha, "The Commitment to Theory," *LC*, p. 33. Further discussions of "hybridity" appear throughout Bhabha's book; see especially "Signs Taken for Wonders: Questions of ambivalence and authority under a tree outside Delhi, May 1917," *LC*, pp. 102–22.

23 See, for example, the notion of *yûgen*, which Makoto Ueda describes as "that elegant, delicate, graceful beauty which was the ideal of linked verse and of medieval Japanese culture at large." Especially with Noh theater, etymologically *yû* means "deep, dim, or difficult to see" while *gen*, "originally describing the dark, profound, tranquil color of the universe, refers to the Taoist concept of truth." See *Literary and Art Theories in Japan* (Cleveland: Press of Western Reserve University, 1967), pp. 59, 60. As Ueda explains, *yûgen* connotes "inner beauty manifesting itself outwards," as opposed to the "beauty of the outward appearance." In the present context, one may add that Loti, though reluctant to connect his image of Japanese culture with any kind of truth, would of course have preferred this latter form of surface beauty in Japan.

24 See Weigui Fang, *Das Chinabild in der deutschen Literatur, 1871–1933: Ein Beitrag zur komparatistischen Imagologie*, Europäische Hochschulschriften, Reihe I: Deutsche Sprache und Literatur 1356 (Frankfurt am Main: Lang, 1992), pp. 110, 137, 142.

CHAPTER 14

WESTERN AGON/EASTERN RITUAL: CONFRONTATIONS AND CO-OPTATIONS IN WORLDVIEWS (EUGENE EOYANG)

1 Thomas Scanlon, "The Vocabulary of Competition: Agon and Aethlos, Greek Terms for Contest," *Arete*, vol. 1, no. 1 (Fall 1983), p. 154.

2 *The Oxford English Dictionary*, 2nd edn., prepared by J. A. Simpson and E. S. C. Weiner (New York: Oxford University Press, 1989–).

3 Agons in Asia could include militarism in imperial Japan, conflict between Nationalists and Communists in China, the Korean War, the Vietnam War (though it might be argued that both North and South Korea and North and South Vietnam were partitioned as the result of Western decisions). Rituals in the United States are too numerous to recount; aside from weekly church-going or religious and semi-religious holidays – Christmas, Easter, Thanksgiving – one could also cite more secular examples like "Monday Night Football" or the New Year's habit of watching Bowl games.

4 Even exceptions, like imperial Japan's "Greater East Asian Co-Prosperity Sphere," were couched in co-optative language. Huizinga records that "after the capture of Canton in December, 1938, the Japanese commander proposed to Chiang Kai-shek that the latter should fight an engagement, which would be decisive, in the plains of Southern China for the purpose of saving his military honour, and then acknowledge the decision as terminating the 'incident.'" See Johan Huizinga, *Homo Ludens: A Study of the Play Element in Culture* (Boston: Beacon, 1955), p. 99. Henceforth cited as *HL*.

5 This is the "law of the excluded middle": "Aristotle appears to have affirmed the law of

excluded middle (for any proposition replacing 'p,' it is true that either p or not-p), but to have denied the principle of bivalence (that every proposition is either true or false). . . ." *Encyclopedia Britannica*, 15th edn. (Chicago: Encyclopedia Britannica, 1995), vol. 23, p. 264. Intuitional logicians, such as Arend Heyting and L. E. J. Brouwer, have challenged the universality of the law of the excluded middle.

6 Quoted by Robert Tarbell Oliver, *Communication and Culture in Ancient India and China* (Syracuse: Syracuse University Press, 1971), p. 250. Henceforth cited as *CC*.

7 Plato, *Phaedo* 70d–72a. Discussed in G. E. R. Lloyd, *Polarity and Analogy: Two Types of Argumentation in Early Greek Thought* (Indianapolis: Hackett, [1966] 1992), p. 24. Henceforth cited as *P&A*.

8 I specifically avoid "bipolar" in this context, because polarity suggests a continuum, a variation in degree, of distances between poles, whereas the mutually exclusive categories admit of no such continuum. A proposition is either true or false; a person is either good or evil; you are either for me or against me.

9 Augustine flirted briefly with Manicheism, whose doctrines he ultimately rejected; however, some of Mani's vision of the world, of its dualistic nature, and of good and evil, persisted in Augustine as well as later Christian thinkers. Among Mani's still persisting legacies to Christianity is the demonization of sexuality. It is curious that Mani's myth of history posited three stages: "a past with radically opposed substances – Spirit and Matter, Good and Evil, Light and Darkness; a middle period (corresponding to the present) during which the two substances are mixed; and a future period in which the original duality will be reestablished" (*Encyclopedia Britannica*, vol. 7, p. 776c).

10 Walter J. Ong, *Fight for Life: Contest, Sexuality, and Consciousness* (Ithaca: Cornell University Press, 1981), p. 178. Henceforth cited as *FL*.

11 William E. Soothill, *Three Religions of China: Lectures Delivered at Oxford* (London: Oxford University Press, 1923), p. 13. Quoted by Judith Berling, *The Syncretic Religion of Lin Chao-en* (New York: Columbia University Press, 1980), p. 1. Henceforth cited as *SR*.

12 Henrik Kraemer, *The Christian Message in a Non-Christian World* (London: Edinburgh House, 1938), p. 13. Quoted in *SR*, p. 1.

13 Francis Hsu, *Americans and Chinese* (New York: Doubleday Natural History Press, 1970), p. 244.

14 There was a dialectic in the turn of events, as it turned out: in the criminal trial, Simpson was acquitted, but was found guilty in the civil one. Doubtless most people believe that the verdicts in the trials can't both be true.

15 The actual quote reads: "Winning isn't everything, but wanting to win is," *Macmillan Dictionary of Quotations* (New York: Macmillan, 1989), p. 590.

16 Even imaginative partisans can take joy in a tie, as happened in the 1968 Harvard–Yale football game, in which Harvard scored three touchdowns in the last two minutes to tie the score at 29–29: the headline in *The Harvard Crimson* read: "Harvard Beats Yale, 29–29!"

17 C. K. Ogden, *Opposition: A Linguistic and Psychological Analysis* (Bloomington: Indiana University Press, 1967), p. 23. Henceforth cited as *OLPA*.

18 Hot and cold (presence or absence of heat); dry and wet (presence or absence of moisture);

"visible and invisible" (presence or absence of visibility); "possible and impossible" (presence or absence of possibility) are other examples.

19 Benjamin Lee Whorf identified the grammarian's version of these false dualities and gave them the name of "enantiomorphism, the pairing with every category of an opposite which is merely the lack of it," in *Language, Thought, and Reality: Selected Essays* (Cambridge: MIT Press, 1956), p. 100.

20 Others would be "young and old," "front and back," "top and bottom," "tall and short," "before and after" – all of which depend on the orientation of the subject.

21 Lloyd contradicts himself when he distinguishes between "the pairs black and white, and odd and even. . . . The first pair admits intermediates (grey and other colours) but the second does not. It is not the case that all colours are either black or white, but every whole number is either odd or even." Yet, he later asserts that "Odd and even, black and white, tall and short, are all pairs of contraries," thus disregarding the very distinction he has established (*P&A*, p. 87).

22 Plato's "matter and form" and Aristotle's "potentiality and actuality" would also be "sub-contraries," distinctions in conception rather than "contradictories," contrasts in substance, or "contraries," contrasts in aspect.

23 Good out of evil may be illustrated by the Christian motif of the fortunate fall which suggests that the catastrophe "Of man's first disobedience" might have been a blessing in disguise; evil out of good is more familiarly instanced by the observation that "the road to hell is paved with good intentions."

24 Deng Xiaoping's slogan "One country, two systems" for the reannexation of Hong Kong is but the most prominent recent instance of Chinese dialectical thinking.

25 It is perhaps emblematic that the meaning of "property" as a material or commercial commodity has eclipsed the sense of "property" as an innate attribute or characteristic.

BIBLIOGRAPHY

Adam, Ian and Helen Tiffin (eds.). *Past the Last Post: Theorizing Post-Colonialism and Post-Modernism*. Calgary: University of Calgary Press, 1990.

Adorno, Theodor W. *Introduction to the Sociology of Music*, trans. E. B. Ashton. New York: Continuum, 1989.

——*Philosophy of Modern Music*, trans. Anne G. Mitchell and Wesley V. Blomster. New York: Continuum, 1994.

Alcalay, Amiel. *After Jews and Arabs: Remaking Levantine Culture*. Minneapolis: University of Minnesota Press, 1993.

The Amistad Case, 2 vols.: *Africans Taken in the Amistad* [Doc. no. 185] and *The Argument of John Quincy Adams*. New York: Johnson Reprint, 1968.

Anderson, Benedict. *Imagined Communities: Reflections on the Origin and Spread of Nationalism*. London: Verso, 1983.

Appiah, Kwame Anthony. *In My Father's House: Africa in the Philosophy of Culture*. New York: Oxford University Press, 1992.

Apter, Emily S. *Continental Drift: From National Characters to Virtual Subjects*. Chicago: University of Chicago Press, 1999.

Arac, Jonathan (ed.). *After Foucault: Humanistic Knowledge, Postmodern Challenges*. New Brunswick, NJ: Rutgers University Press, 1988.

Arendt, Hannah. *Eichmann in Jerusalem: A Report on the Banality of Evil*. New York: Viking, 1964.

——*The Origins of Totalitarianism*. New York: Harcourt Brace, 1951.

Arnold, Matthew. *Culture and Anarchy* in *The Portable Matthew Arnold*, ed. Lionel Trilling. New York: Viking, 1949.

Ashcroft, Bill, Gareth Griffiths, and Helen Tiffin. *The Empire Writes Back: Theory and Practice in Post-Colonial Literatures*. London/New York: Routledge, 1989.

Assmann, Jan and Dietrich Harth. *Kultur und Konflikt*. Frankfurt am Main: Suhrkamp, 1990.

Attridge, Derek. "Trusting the Other: Ethics and Politics in J. M. Coetzee's *Age of Iron*," *SAQ*, vol. 93, no. 1, Winter 1994.

Bakhtin, Mikhail. *The Dialogic Imagination: Four Essays*, ed. Michael Holquist, trans. Caryl Emerson and Michael Holquist. Austin: University of Texas Press, 1981.

Balibar, Etienne and Immanuel Wallerstein. *Race, Nation, Class: Ambiguous Identities*, trans. Chris Turner. London: Verso, 1991.

Barker, Francis *et al.* (eds). *Europe and its Others*. 2 vols. Colchester, UK: Essex University Press, 1985.

Baudrillard, Jean. *Le Crime parfait*. Paris: Galilée, 1995.

Bauman, Zygmunt. *Postmodern Ethics*. Oxford: Blackwell, 1993.

Becker, Jared M. *Nationalism and Culture: Gabriele D'Annunzio and Italy after the Risorgimento*. New York: Peter Lang, 1994.

Benhabib, Seyla and Andrew Arato. "The Yugoslav Tragedy," *Praxis International*, vol. 13, no. 4.

Benjamin, Walter. *Illuminations*, ed. and intro. Hannah Arendt, trans. Harry Zohn. New York: Schocken Books, 1969.

Berling, Judith. *The Syncretic Religion of Lin Chao-en*. New York: Columbia University Press, 1980.

Berman, Russell. *Modern Culture and Critical Theory: Art, Politics, and the Legacy of the Frankfurt School*. Madison: University of Wisconsin Press, 1989.

Bernabé, Jean, Patrick Chamoiseau, and Raphaël Confiant. *Éloge de la créolité*. Paris: Gallimard, 1989.

Bhabha, Homi K. *The Location of Culture*. London/New York: Routledge, 1994.

Bhabha, Homi K. (ed.). *Nation and Narration*. London/New York: Routledge, 1990.
——"Postcolonial Criticism," in *Redrawing the Boundaries: The Transformation of English and American Studies*, eds. Stephen Greenblatt and Giles Gunn. New York: Modern Language Association, 1992.
Bjornson, Richard. *The African Quest for Freedom and Identity*. Bloomington: Indiana University Press, 1991.
Bloom, Harold. "Agon: Revisionism and Critical Personality," *Raritan*, vol. 1, no. 1, Summer 1981.
Bogue, Ronald and Marcel Cornis-Pope (eds.). *Violence and Mediation in Contemporary Culture*. Albany: SUNY Press, 1996.
Brink, André. "An Ornithology of Sexual Politics: Lewis Nkosi's *Mating Birds*," *English in Africa*, 19, 1992.
——*Reinventing a Continent: Writing and Politics in South Africa, 1982–95*. London: Secker and Warburg, 1996.
Bromwich, David. *A Choice of Inheritance: Self and Community from Edmund Burke to Robert Frost*. Cambridge, MA: Harvard University Press, 1989.
Brown, Marshall. *Turning Points: Essays in the History of Cultural Expression*. Stanford: Stanford University Press, 1997.
Cable, Mary. *Black Odyssey*. New York: Viking, 1971.
Cacciari, Massimo. *Geo-filosofia dell'Europa*. Milano: Adelphi, 1994.
Carrithers, Michael, Steven Collins, and Steven Lukes (eds.). *The Category of the Person: anthropology, philosophy, history*. Cambridge, UK: Cambridge University Press, 1985.
Carroll, David. *French Literary Fascism*. Princeton: Princeton University Press, 1995.
Carusi, Annamaria. "Post, Post and Post: Or, Where is South African Literature in All This?" in *Past the Last Post: Theorizing Post-Colonialism and Post-Modernism*, eds. Ian Adam and Helen Tiffin. Calgary: University of Calgary Press, 1990.
Caruth, Cathy, ed. *Trauma: Explorations in Memory*. Baltimore: Johns Hopkins University Press, 1995.
Caws, Peter. "Identity: Cultural, Transcultural, and Multicultural," in *Multiculturalism: A Critical Reader*, ed. David Theo Goldberg. Oxford, UK and Cambridge, MA: Blackwell, 1994.
Chanaday, Amaryll (ed.) *Latin American Identity and Constructions of Difference*. Minneapolis: University of Minnesota Press, 1994.
Chen, Xiaomei. *Occidentalism: A Theory of Counter-Discourse in Post-Mao China*. New York: Oxford University Press, 1995.
Chow, Rey. *Ethics after Idealism: Theory, Culture, Ethnicity, Reading*. Bloomington: Indiana University Press, 1998.
Clifford, James. *The Predicament of Culture: Twentieth-Century Ethnography, Literature, and Art*. Cambridge, MA: Harvard University Press, 1988.
——*Routes: Travel and Translation in the Late Twentieth Century*. Cambridge, MA: Harvard University Press, 1997.
Clowes, Edith W. *Russian Experimental Fiction: Resisting Ideology after Utopia*. Princeton: Princeton University Press, 1993.
Coetzee, J. M. *Doubling the Point: Essays and Interviews*, ed. David Attwell. Cambridge, MA: Harvard University Press, 1992.
——"What is a Classic?" *Current Writing*, vol. 5, no. 2, 1993.
Cornis-Pope, Marcel. *The Unfinished Battles: Romanian Postmodernism Before and After 1989*. Iaşi: Polirom Press & the Soros Foundation, 1996.
Culler, Jonathan. *Framing the Sign*. Ithaca: Cornell University Press, 1988.
Derrida, Jacques. *Dissemination*, trans., intro., and notes Barbara Johnson. Chicago: University of Chicago Press, 1981.
——and Mustapha Tlili (eds.). *For Nelson Mandela*. New York: Seaver Books, 1987.
——*Limited, Inc*, ed. Gerald Graff, trans. Samuel Weber and Jeffrey Mehlman. Evanston, IL: Northwestern University Press, 1988.
——*Mal d'Archive*. Paris: Galilée, 1995.
——*Of Spirit: Heidegger and the Question*, trans. Geoffrey Bennington and Rachel Bowlby. Chicago: University of Chicago Press, 1989.

Derrida, Jacques. *The Other Heading*, trans. Michael Naas and Pascale-Anne Brault. Bloomington: Indiana University Press, 1992.

——*Psyché: Inventions de l'autre*. Paris: Galilée, 1987.

Derrida, Jacques. *Specters of Marx: The State of the Debt, the Work of Mourning, and the New International*, trans. Peggy Kamuf. New York/London: Routledge, 1994.

Descartes, René. *The Philosophical Writings of Descartes*, trans. John Cottingham, Robert Stoothoff, and Dugald Murdoch. 2 vols. Cambridge, UK: Cambridge University Press, 1985.

Dews, Peter. *Logics of Disintegration: Post-structuralist Thought and the Claims of Critical Theory*. London: Verso, 1987.

Diaspora: A Journal of Transnational Studies.

Eco, Umberto. *Interpretation and Overinterpretation*. With Richard Rorty, Jonathan Culler, Christine Brooke-Rose, ed. Stefan Collini. Cambridge, UK: Cambridge University Press, 1992.

——*The Open Work*, trans. Anna Cancogni. Cambridge, MA: Harvard University Press, 1989.

——*A Theory of Semiotics*. Bloomington: Indiana University Press, 1976.

——"Ur-Fascism," *The New York Review of Books*, vol. 42, no. 11, June 22 1995.

Evan-Zohar, Itamar. *Polysystem Studies*, special issue of *Poetics Today*, vol. 11, nos. 1–2, 1990.

Fanon, Frantz. *Black Skin, White Masks*, trans. Charles Lam Markmann. London: Pluto Press, 1986 [1952].

——*Wretched of the Earth*, trans. Constance Farrington. Harmondsworth: Penguin, 1967.

Felman, Shoshana, and Dori Laub. *Testimony: Crises of Witnessing in Literature, Psychoanalysis, and History*. New York/London: Routledge, 1992.

Foucault, Michel. *The Care of the Self (The History of Sexuality, Volume 3)*, trans. Robert Hurley. New York: Pantheon, 1986.

——*Discipline and Punish: The Birth of the Prison*, trans. Alan Sheridan. New York: Vintage, 1979.

——*The Foucault Reader*, ed. Paul Rabinow. New York: Pantheon, 1984.

——*Michel Foucault: Language, Counter-Memory, Practice*, ed. D. Bouchard, trans. D. Bouchard and S. Simon. Ithaca, NY: Cornell University Press, 1977.

——*Michel Foucault: Politics, Philosophy, Culture. Interviews and Other Writings*, ed. Lawrence D. Kritzman. New York/London: Routledge, 1988.

——*The Order of Things*. New York: Random House, 1970.

——*Power/Knowledge*, ed. Colin Gordon, trans. Colin Gordon *et al*. New York: Pantheon, 1980.

——*Technologies of the Self: A Seminar with Michel Foucault*, eds. Luther H. Martin, Huck Gutman, and Patrick H. Hutton. Amherst: University of Massachusetts Press, 1988.

Freud, Sigmund. *Beyond the Pleasure Principle. The Standard Edition of the Complete Psychological Works of Sigmund Freud*, trans. James Strachey, vol. 18. London: Hogarth, 1955.

——*Civilization and its Discontents*, trans. James Strachey. New York: Norton, 1962.

——"The Uncanny," *The Standard Edition of the Complete Psychological Works of Sigmund Freud*, trans. James Strachey, vol. 17. London: Hogarth, 1955.

Garton Ash, Timothy. "Bosnia in Our Future," *The New York Review of Books*, November 16 1995.

——"Central Europe: the Present Past," *The New York Review of Books*, July 13 1995.

Gilroy, Paul. *The Black Atlantic: Modernity and Double Consciousness*. Cambridge, MA: Harvard University Press, 1993.

Glenny, Misha. *The Fall of Yugoslavia and the Third Balkan War*. London/New York: Penguin, 1992.

Glissant, Edouard. *Caribbean Discourse*, trans. J. Michael Dash. Charlottesville: University Press of Virginia, 1989.

Griffin, Roger. *The Nature of Fascism*. London/New York: Routledge, 1993.

——"Staging the Nation's Rebirth: The Politics and Aesthetics of Performance in the Context of Fascist Studies," in *Fascism and Theatre*, ed. Gunter Berghaus. Providence: Berghahn Books, 1996.

Guillory, John. *Cultural Capital: The Problem of Literary Canon Formation*. Chicago: University of Chicago Press, 1993.

Gunew, Sneja. *Framing Marginalities: Multicultural Literary Studies*. Melbourne Australia: Melbourne University Press, 1994.

Habermas, Jürgen. "Modernity versus Postmodernity," *New German Critique*, 22, 1981.

Habermas, Jürgen. *The Philosophical Discourse of Modernity: Twelve Lectures*, trans. Frederick Lawrence. Cambridge, MA: MIT Press, 1987.

——*The Theory of Communicative Action*, trans. Thomas McCarthy. 2 vols. Boston: Beacon Press, 1984 and 1987.

Halbwachs, Maurice. *On Collective Memory*, ed. and trans. Lewis Coser. Chicago: University of Chicago Press, 1992 [1941].

Hallowell, A. Irving. "Ojibwa Personality and Acculturation," in *Acculturation in the Americas*, ed. Sol Tax. New York: Cooper Square Publishers, 1967.

Haraszti, Miklós. *The Velvet Prison: Artists under State Socialism*, trans. Katalin and Stephen Landesmann. New York: New Republic, 1987.

Harris, Wilson. *The Womb of Space: The Cross-Cultural Imagination*. Westport, CT: Greenwood, 1983.

Hartman, Geoffrey H. *The Fateful Question of Culture*. New York: Columbia University Press, 1997.

——*The Longest Shadow: In the Aftermath of the Holocaust*. Bloomington: Indiana University Press, 1996.

——*Saving the Text: Literature/Derrida/Philosophy*. Baltimore: Johns Hopkins University Press, 1981.

Hayden, Robert and Milica Bakić-Hayden. "Orientalist Variations on the Theme 'Balkans': Symbolic Geography in Recent Yugoslav Cultural Politics," *Slavic Review*, vol. 13, no. 1, 1992.

Heidegger, Martin. "The Origin of the Work of Art," in *Poetry, Language, Thought*, trans. Albert Hofstadter. New York: Harper & Row, 1972.

Heller, Thomas C., David E. Wellbery, and Martin Sosna, eds. *Reconstructing Individualism*. Stanford: Stanford University Press, 1986.

Hinz, Evelyn (ed. and intro.). *Idols of Otherness: The Rhetoric and Reality of Multiculturalism*, special issue of *Mosaic: A Journal for the Interdisciplinary Study of Literature*, vol. 29, no. 3, September 1996.

Hirsch, Marianne. "Family Pictures: *Maus*, Mourning, and Post-Memory," *Discourse*, 15, 1992.

Hirschkop, Ken and David Shepherd (eds.). *Bakhtin and Cultural Theory*. Manchester/New York: Manchester University Press, 1989.

Hobsbawm, Eric, and Terence Ranger. *The Invention of Culture*. Chicago: University of Chicago Press, 1975.

Holquist, Michael. *Dialogism: Bakhtin and his World*. New York/London: Routledge, 1990.

Huizinga, Johan. *Homo Ludens: A Study of the Play Element in Culture*. Boston: Beacon Press, 1955.

Husserl, Edmund. "Philosophy and the Crisis of European Humanity," in *The Crisis of European Sciences and Transcendental Phenomenology: An Introduction to Phenomenological Philosophy*, trans. and intro. David Carr. Evanston, IL: Northwestern University Press, 1970.

Huyssen, Andreas. *After the Great Divide: Modernism, Mass Culture, Postmodernism*. Bloomington: Indiana University Press, 1989.

Irele, Abiola. *The African Experience in Literature and Ideology*. Bloomington: Indiana University Press, 1990.

Jacques, Francis. *Difference and Subjectivity: Dialogue and Personal Identity*, trans. Andrew Rothwell. New Haven: Yale University Press, 1991.

Jameson, Fredric. *Postmodernism, or the Cultural Logic of Late Capitalism*. Durham: Duke University Press, 1991.

JanMohamed, Abdul. "The Economy of Manichean Allegory: The Function of Racial Difference in Colonialist Literature." *Critical Inquiry*, 12, 1985.

——*Manichean Aesthetics: The Politics of Literature in Colonial Africa*. Amherst: University of Massachusetts Press, 1983.

Jolly, Rosemary. "Rehearsals of Liberation: Contemporary Postcolonial Discourse and the New South Africa," *PMLA*, 110, 1995.

Jonas, Hans. *The Imperative of Responsibility: In Search of an Ethics For The Technological Age*. Chicago: University of Chicago Press, 1984.

Judovitz, Dalia. *Subjectivity and Representation in Descartes*. New York: Cambridge University Press, 1988.

Kaprow, Allan. *Essays on Blurring of Art and Life*, ed. Jeff Kelley. Berkeley: University of California Press, 1993.

Kearney, Richard. "Ethics and the Postmodern Imagination," *Thought*, vol. 62, no. 244, 1987.

Khan, Mujeeb R. "Bosnia-Herzegovina and the Crisis of the Post-Cold War International System," *East European Politics and Societies*, vol. 9, no. 3, Fall 1995.

Kristeva, Julia. *Nations without Nationalism*, trans. Leon S. Roudiez. New York: Columbia University Press, 1993.

——*Powers of Horror: An Essay on Abjection*, trans. Leon S. Roudiez. New York: Columbia University Press, 1982.

LaCapra, Dominick. *Representing the Holocaust: History, Theory, Trauma*. Ithaca, NY: Cornell University Press, 1994.

Lacoue-LaBarthe, Philippe. *Heidegger, Art and Politics: The Fiction of the Political*, trans. Chris Turner. Cambridge, MA: Basil Blackwell, 1990.

Langer, Lawrence. *Holocaust Testimonies: The Ruins of Memory*. New Haven: Yale University Press, 1991.

Lazarus, Neil. *Resistance in Postcolonial African Fiction*. New Haven: Yale University Press, 1990.

Levi, Primo. *Survival in Auschwitz*, trans. Stuart Woolf. New York: Collier, 1961.

Lévinas, Emmanuel. *Ethics and Infinity*, trans. Philip Nemo. Pittsburgh: Duquesne University Press, 1985.

——*Otherwise Than Being, or Beyond Essence*, trans. Alphonso Lingis. The Hague: Martinus Nijhoff, 1981.

Levine, Lawrence. "Clio, Canons, and Culture," *The Journal of American History*, vol. 80, no. 3, 1993.

Lewis, Martin W. and Karen E. Wigen. *The Myth of Continents: A Critique of Metageography*. Berkeley and Los Angeles: University of California Press, 1997.

Lionnet, Françoise and R. Scharfman, eds. *Post/Colonial Conditions: Exiles, Migrations, Nomadisms*, double issue of *Yale French Studies*, 82/83, January 1993.

Liszka, Joseph. "Derrida: Philosophy of the Liminal," *Man and World*, 16, 1983.

Lloyd, G. E. R. *Polarity and Analogy: Two Types of Argumentation in Early Greek Thought*. Indianapolis: Hackett Publishing, 1966, 1992.

Longinović, Tomislav Z. *Border Line Culture: The Politics of Identity in Four Twentieth-Century Slavic Novels*. Fayetteville: University of Arkansas Press, 1993.

Lord, Albert Bates. *The Singer of Tales*. Cambridge, MA: Harvard University Press, 1960.

Lowe, Lisa. *Critical Terrains: French and British Orientalism*. Ithaca: Cornell University Press, 1991.

Lungstrum, Janet and Elizabeth Sauer (eds.). *Agonistics: Arenas of Creative Contest*. Albany: SUNY Press, 1997.

Lyotard, Jean-François. *The Differend: Phrases in Dispute*, trans. Georges Van Den Abbeele. Minneapolis: University of Minnesota Press, 1988.

——*La Guerre des Algériens: écrits 1954–1963*. Paris, Galilée, 1989.

——*Heidegger and "the jews."* Minneapolis: University of Minnesota Press, 1990.

——*The Inhuman: Reflections on Time*, trans. Geoffrey Bennington and Rachel Bowlby. Stanford, CA: Stanford University Press, 1991.

——*Lyotard: Political Writings*, trans. Bill Readings. Minneapolis: University of Minnesota Press, 1993.

——*Moralités postmodernes*. Paris: Galilée, 1993.

——*Postmodernism Explained to Children*, trans. Don Barry, Bernadette Maher, Julian Pefanis, Virginia Spate, and Morgan Thomas. Minneapolis: University of Minnesota Press, 1993.

MacIntyre, Alasdair. "The Virtues, the Unity of a Human Life and the Concept of a Tradition," in *After Virtue*. South Bend, IN: University of Notre Dame Press, 1981.

Maines, David R., Noreen M. Sugrue, and Michael A. Katovich. "The Sociological Import of G. H. Mead's Theory of the Past," *American Sociological Review*, 48, April 1983.

Mann, Thomas. *Doctor Faustus: The Life of the German Composer Adrian Leverkühn as Told by a Friend*, trans. H. T. Lowe-Porter. New York: Knopf, 1948.

Martin, B. Edmon. *All We Want is Make us Free: La Amistad and the Reform Abolitionists*. Boston: University Press of America, 1986.

Mauss, Marcel. "A category of the human mind: the notion of person; the notion of self" ["Une catégorie de l'esprit humain: la notion de personne, celle de 'moi'"], trans. W. D. Halls, in *The Category of the Person: anthropology, philosophy, history*, eds. Michael Carrithers, Steven Collins, and Steven Lukes. Cambridge, UK: Cambridge University Press, 1985.

Mead, George Herbert. *The Philosophy of the Present*. Chicago: Open Court Publishing, 1932.

Meyers, Diana Tietjens. *Subjection and Subjectivity: Psychoanalytic Feminism & Moral Philosophy*. New York: Routledge, 1994.

Michaelson, Scott and David E. Johnson (eds.). *Border Theory: The Limits of Cultural Politics*. Minneapolis: University of Minnesota Press, 1997.

Morasso, Mario. *L'imperialismo artistico*. Torino: Fratelli Bocca, 1903.

Mudimbe, V. Y. (ed.). *Nations, Identities, Cultures*. Durham: Duke University Press, 1997.

Mukherjee, Arun. *Towards an Aesthetic of Opposition: Essays on Literature, Criticism, and Cultural Imperialism*. Stratford, Ontario: Williams-Wallace, 1988.

Myrsiades, Kostas and Jerry McGuire (eds.). *Order and Partialities: Theory, Pedagogy, and the "Postcolonial."* Albany: SUNY Press, 1995.

Ogden, C. K. *Opposition: A Linguistic and Psychological Analysis*. Bloomington: Indiana University Press, 1967.

Oliver, Kelly (ed.). *Ethics, Politics, and Difference in Julia Kristeva's Writing*. New York: Routledge, 1993.

Ong, Walter J. *Fight for Life: Contest, Sexuality, and Consciousness*. Ithaca, NY: Cornell University Press, 1981.

Opala, Joseph A. *Ecstatic Renovations: Street Art Celebrating Sierra Leone's 1992 Revolution*. Freetown, Sierra Leone: Ro-Marong Industries, 1994.

Ozick, Cynthia. *The Messiah of Stockholm*. New York: Vintage, 1987.

Pérez-Firmat, Gustavo. *Literature and Liminality: Festive Readings in the Hispanic Tradition*. Durham: Duke University Press, 1986.

Pratt, Mary Louise. *Imperial Eyes: Travel Writing and Transculturation*. New York/London: Routledge, 1992.

Public Culture: Journal of the Society for Transnational Cultural Studies. Durham: Duke University Press.

Rapaport, Herman. *Heidegger and Derrida: Reflections on Time and Language*. Lincoln: University of Nebraska Press, 1989.

Rich, Adrienne. "The Politics of Location," in *Blood, Bread, and Poetry*. London: Virago, 1987.

——"When We Dead Awaken: Writing as Re-Vision," in *On Lies, Secrets, and Silence: Selected Prose, 1966–1978*. New York: W. W. Norton, 1979.

Ricoeur, Paul. *Autour du politique*. Paris: Seuil, 1991.

——"Le Concept de responsabilité: Essai d'analyse sémantique," *Esprit*, 11, November 1994.

——"Ethique et politique," in *Du texte à l'action: essais d'herméneutique II*. Paris: Seuil, 1986.

Rieff, David. *Slaughterhouse: Bosnia and the Failure of the West*. London: Vintage, 1995.

"Roundtable on Central Europe: Second Wheatland Conference on Literature," *Cross Currents*, 9, 1990.

Rowe, John Carlos (ed.). *"Culture" and the Problem of the Disciplines*. New York: Columbia University Press, 1998.

Said, Edward. *Culture and Imperialism*. New York: Knopf, 1993.

——*Orientalism*. New York: Pantheon, 1978.

——"Traveling Theory," in *The World, The Text, and The Critic*. Cambridge, MA: Harvard University Press, 1983.

Saldívar, José David. *Border Matters: Remapping American Cultural Studies*. Berkeley: University of California Press, 1997.

Salvemini, Gaetano. *The Origins of Fascism in Italy*, trans. and intro. Roberto Vivarelli. New York: Harper, 1973.
Santner, Eric. "History Beyond the Pleasure Principle: Some Thoughts on the Representation of Trauma," in *Probing the Limits of Representation: Nazism and the "Final Solution,"* ed. Saul Friedländer. Cambridge, MA: Harvard University Press, 1992.
Scanlon, Thomas. "The Vocabulary of Competition: Agon and Aethlos, Greek Terms for Contest," *Arete*, vol. 1, no. 1, Fall 1983.
Schnapp, Jeffrey and Barbara Spackman (eds.). *Fascism and Culture. Stanford Italian Review*, vol. 8, nos. 1–2.
Schöpflin, George and Nancy Wood (eds.). *In Search of Central Europe*. Totowa, NJ: Barnes & Noble, 1989.
Schwartz, Barry, Yael Zerubavel, and Bernice Barnett. "The Recovery of Masada: A Study in Collective Memory," *The Sociological Quarterly*, vol. 27, no. 2, 1986.
Schwartz, Barry, "The Social Context of Communication: A Study in Collective Memory," *Social Forces*, vol. 61, no. 2, December 1982.
Silber, Laura and Allan Little. *Death of a Nation: The Death of Yugoslavia*. New York: Penguin, 1995.
Smith, Paul. *Discerning the Subject*. Minneapolis: University of Minnesota Press, 1988.
——*Millennial Dreams: Contemporary Culture and Capital in the North*. London: Verso, 1997.
Spackman, Barbara. "The Fascist Rhetoric of Virility," *Stanford Italian Review*, vol. 8, nos. 1–2 (*Fascism and Culture*).
Spariosu, Mihai. *God of Many Names: Play, Poetry, and Power in Hellenic Thought, from Homer to Aristotle*. Durham: Duke University Press, 1991.
——*The Wreath of Wild Olives: Play, Liminality, and the Study of Literature*. Albany: SUNY Press, 1997.
Spivak, Gayatri Chakravorty. *A Critique of Postcolonial Reason: Towards a History of the Vanishing Present*. Cambridge, MA: Harvard University Press, 1999.
——*In Other Worlds: Essays in Cultural Politics*. New York/London: Routledge, 1988.
——*The Postcolonial Critic*. New York/London: Routledge, 1990.
Steiner, George. *Language and Silence*. New York: Atheneum, 1974 [1967].
Sternhell, Zeev with Mario Sznajder and Maia Asheri. *The Birth of Fascist Ideology*, trans. David Maisel. Princeton: Princeton University Press, 1994.
Taylor, Anya. "Coleridge on Persons in Dialogue," *Modern Language Quarterly*, 50, 1989.
Thornton, Robert. "Culture: A Contemporary Definition," in *South African Keywords: The Uses and Abuses of Political Concepts*, ed. E. Boonzaaier and J. Sharp. Cape Town: David Philip, 1981.
Tismaneanu, Vladimir. *Reinventing Politics: Eastern Europe from Stalin to Havel*. New York/Toronto: Free Press, 1992.
Todorov, Tzvetan. *The Conquest of America: The Question of the Other*, trans. Richard Howard. New York: Harper & Row, 1984.
——*Mikhail Bakhtin: The Dialogical Principle*, trans. Wlad Godzich. Minneapolis: University of Minnesota Press, 1984.
——*On Human Diversity: Nationalism, Racism, and Exoticism in French Thought*, trans. Catherine Porter. Cambridge, MA: Harvard University Press, 1993.
Ugresić, Dubravka. *The Culture of Lies: Antipolitical Essays*. University Park: Pennsylvania State University Press, 1998.
Verdery, Katherine. *National Ideology Under Socialism: Identity and Cultural Politics in Ceauşescu's Romania*. Berkeley/Los Angeles: University of California Press, 1991.
Williams, Patrick and Laura Chrisman, eds. and intro. *Colonial Discourse and Post-Colonial Theory: A Reader*. New York: Columbia University Press, 1994.
Williams, Raymond. *Culture and Society, 1780–1950*. London: Chatto and Windus, 1958.
——*Keywords*. London: Fontana, 1976.
Young, James E. *The Texture of Memory: Holocaust Memorials and Meaning*. New Haven: Yale University Press, 1993.
——*Writing and Rewriting the Holocaust*. Bloomington: Indiana University Press, 1988.
Young, Robert. *White Mythologies: Writing History and the West*. London/New York: Routledge, 1990.

Žižek, Slavoj. *The Indivisible Remainder*. London: Verso, 1996.

——*Looking Awry: An Introduction to Lacan Through Popular Culture.* Cambridge, MA: MIT Press, 1991.

——*The Metastases of Enjoyment: Six Essays on Women and Causality*. London: Verso, 1994.

——*The Sublime Object of Ideology*. London: Verso, 1989.

INDEX OF NAMES

INDEX OF TOPICS

CREDITS

"Revisiting the *Amistad* Revolt in Sierra Leone" by Iyunolu Osagie is a revised, restructured, and expanded version of an essay originally published in the *Massachusetts Review*.

"Cultural Hermeneutics and Orientalist Discourse: Loti's Self-Reflexive *Japonisme*" by Rolf Goebel has appeared, in a revised German version, as part of Chapter 4 in *Benjamin heute: Großstadtdiscurs, Postkolonialität und Flanerie zwischen den Kulturen* (München: Iudicium, 2001).

CONTRIBUTORS

Caroline Bayard is Professor of French and Philosophy at McMaster University in Ontario, Canada. Her recent research has focused on postmodern theories in the two Europes and on the resurgence of the Nation-Subject in both Europe and Quebec. Recently, she worked with the Center for Theoretical Study in Prague, in the Czech Republic. She has published several special issues on French theorists (Jean Baudrillard in *Semiotic Inquiry*, 1996; Jean-François Lyotard in *Philosophy Today*, 1992) and a book, *Transatlantiques postmodernités* (Balzac, 1997).

James Berger is Associate Professor of English at Hofstra University. He is author of *After the End: Representations of Post-Apocalypse* (Minnesota, 1999), and is currently working on a book dealing with portrayals of language impairment in modern literature and culture.

Marcel Cornis-Pope is Professor of English and Chair at Virginia Commonwealth University. His publications include *Hermeneutic Desire and Critical Rewriting: Narrative Interpretation in the Wake of Poststructuralism* (1992), *The Unfinished Battles: Romanian Postmodernism before and after 1989* (1996), *Violence and Mediation in Contemporary Culture* (coedited with Ronald Bogue, 1995), and *Narrative Innovation and Cultural Rewriting in the Cold War Era and After* (2001). After seven years as editor of the award-winning journal *The Comparatist*, he is now coediting a major international project, entitled *A History of the Literary Cultures of East Central Europe: Cultural Junctures and Disjunctures in the Nineteenth and Twentieth Centuries*.

Lars Engle, Associate Professor of English at the University of Tulsa, is the author of *Shakespearean Pragmatism: Market of His Time* (Chicago, 1993) and a coeditor of *English Renaissance Drama: A Norton Anthology* (New York, 2002). He began his teaching career in South Africa and writes frequently about contemporary South African literature, often focusing on Nadine Gordimer and J. M. Coetzee.

Eugene Eoyang is Professor of Comparative Literature and of East Asian Languages and Cultures at Indiana University, as well as Chair Professor of English at Lingnan College in Hong Kong. He has published *Selected Poems of Ai Qing* (Indiana, 1982), *The Transparent Eye: Reflections on Translation, Chinese Literature, and Comparative Poetics* (Hawaii, 1993), *Coat of Many Colors: Reflections on Diversity by a Minority of One* (Beacon, 1995), and *Translating Chinese Literature* (Indiana, 1995, coedited with Lin Yao-fu). Many of his translations have appeared in *Sunflower Splendor: Three Thousand Years of Chinese Poetry* (Doubleday, 1975; Indiana, 1990). One of the founders of CLEAR (*Chinese Literature: Essays, Articles, Reviews*), he was President of the American Comparative Literature Association from 1995 to 1997.

Rolf J. Goebel studied German and English Literatures at Kiel University (Germany), Brown University, and the University of Maryland, College Park. He is currently Professor of German at the University of Alabama in Huntsville. His publications include essays on Kafka, Western literary discourse on Japan, and literary theory; a book on Walter Benjamin's urban discourse, postcoloniality, and intercultural "flanerie" has recently appeared from Iudicium Verlag, Munich.

Anthony John Harding teaches at the University of Saskatchewan, Canada. He is author of *The Reception of Myth in English Romanticism* (Missouri, 1995) and of several articles, most recently "Coleridge, Natural History, and the Analogy of Being," in *History of European Ideas*. With Lisa Lowe, he coedited *Milton, the Metaphysicals, and Romanticism* (Cambridge, 1994); and with the late Kathleen Coburn, Volume 5 of *The Notebooks of Samuel Taylor Coleridge* (Princeton), forthcoming in 2002.

Michiel Heyns studied at the University of Stellenbosch in the Republic of South Africa and at Cambridge University; he is now Professor in the Department of English at Stellenbosch. Apart from his interest in postcolonial literature, he has written on the nineteeth-century English novel, notably *Expulsion and the Nineteenth-Century Novel: the Scapegoat in English Realist Fiction* (Oxford, 1994).

Tomislav Z. Longinović is Professor of Slavic and Comparative Literature at the University of Wisconsin-Madison and Director of the Cultural Translation Project. He is the author of *Borderline Culture: The Politics of Identity in Four Slavic Novels*, on works by Bulgakov, Gombrowicz, Kiš, and Kundera. He is also the author of two novels, *Moment of Silence* and *Sama Amerika* (in Serbo-Croatian), and of a translation of Serbian women's songs, *Red Knight*. He is currently a Visiting Professor at Harvard University.

Nikita Nankov is completing a doctorate at Indiana University, Bloomington, in Comparative Literature and Slavic Languages and Literatures. He has published extensively on various topics in the field of comparative literature, and also writes fiction – tales for children and adults.

Iyunolu Osagie is Associate Professor of English at the Pennsylvania State University, where her research is in the area of black diasporic literatures and theories. She has published articles and a book titled, *The Amistad Revolt: Memory, Slavery, and Politics of Identity in the United States and Sierra Leone* (Georgia, 2000).

Herman Rapaport is Chair Professor of English at the University of Southampton. He is the author of *Milton and the Postmodern*, *Heidegger and Derrida: Reflections on Time and Language*, *Between the Sign and the Gaze*, and *Is There Truth in Art?* His most recent book is *The Theory Mess* (Columbia, 2001).

Robert M. Strozier is an Emeritus Professor in the English Department at Wayne State University in Detroit. He is the author of *Epicurus and Hellenistic Philosophy*, of *Saussure, Derrida, and the Metaphysics of Subjectivity*, and of *Foucault, Subjectivity, and Identity*.

Mary Ann Frese Witt is Professor of French and Italian at North Carolina State University, and has published widely in the field of twentieth-century literature, including *Existential Prisons* (Duke, 1985). Her most recent book is *The Search for Modern Tragedy: Aesthetic Fascism in Italy and France* (Cornell, 2001).

EDITORS

John Burt Foster, Jr. is Professor of English and Cultural Studies at George Mason University. Trained in comparative literature at Yale, he has published widely in nineteenth- and twentieth-century narrative and thought. He is the author of *Heirs to Dionysus: A Nietzschean Current in Literary Modernism* and of *Nabokov's Art of Memory and European Modernism*, both from Princeton, and is currently working on Tolstoyan "itineraries" in Western fiction and culture. He recently coedited a forum on Slavic Identities for the *Slavic and East European Journal*, and is also editor of *The Comparatist*, an annual journal of cross-cultural literary study.

Wayne J. Froman is a member of the Department of Philosophy and Religious Studies at George Mason University, where he served as Department Chair from 1989 until 1999. As a Senior Fulbright Research Scholar in 1995–6, he was a Visiting Professor at the Hegel-Archiv, Ruhr Universität/Bochum. He is the author of *Merleau-Ponty: Language and the Act of Speech* (Bucknell), and a contributor to leading journals in the fields of phenomenology, art, and poststructuralism. He was a member of the Executive Committee of the International Association of Philosophy and Literature from 1995 until 2001.